ART FOR LIFE

ART FOR LIFE

Authentic Instruction in Art

TOM ANDERSON
Florida State University

MELODY K. MILBRANDT
Georgia State University

McGraw Hill

Boston   Burr Ridge, IL   Dubuque, IA   Madison, WI   New York   San Francisco   St. Louis
Bangkok   Bogotá   Caracas   Kuala Lumpur   Lisbon   London   Madrid   Mexico City
Milan   Montreal   New Delhi   Santiago   Seoul   Singapore   Sydney   Taipei   Toronto

The McGraw-Hill Companies

Mc Graw Hill Higher Education

ART FOR LIFE: AUTHENTIC INSTRUCTION IN ART
Published by McGraw-Hill, a business unit of The McGraw-Hill Companies, Inc.,
1221 Avenue of the Americas, New York, NY, 10020. Copyright © 2005, by The
McGraw-Hill Companies, Inc. All rights reserved. No part of this publication may
be reproduced or distributed in any form or by any means, or stored in a database
or retrieval system, without the prior written consent of The McGraw-Hill
Companies, Inc., including, but not limited to, in any network or other electronic
storage or transmission, or broadcast for distance learning.

Some ancillaries, including electronic and print components, may not be available
to customers outside the United States.

This book is printed on acid-free paper.

3 4 5 6 7 8 9 0 DOW/DOW 0 9 8 7

ISBN: 978-0-07-250864-2
MHID: 0-07-250864-7

Publisher: *Christopher Freitag*
Sponsoring editor: *Joe Hanson*
Developmental editor: *Jill Gordon*
Marketing manager: *Lisa Berry*
Media producer: *Shannon Gattens*
Project manager: *Diane M. Folliard*
Production supervisor: *Carol A. Bielski*
Senior designer: *Kim Menning*
Supplemental producer: *Kathleen Boylan*
Photo research coordinator: *Alexandra Ambrose*
Associate art editor: *Carin C. Yancey*
Photo researcher: *Robin Sand*
Cover and interior design: *Caroline McGowan*
Typeface: *9.5/12 Palatino*
Compositor: *ProGraphics*
Printer: *R. R. Donnelley/Willard*

Cover and Preface credit: "Reach High and You Will Go Far" © 2002 by Joshua
Sarantitis. All Rights Reserved. Sponsored by The Philadelphia Mural Arts
Program. © 2002 by Joshua Sarantitis. All Rights Reserved.

Library of Congress Cataloging In-Publication Data

Anderson, Tom, 1949-
    Art for life: authentic instruction in art/Tom Anderson, Melody K. Milbrandt.
        p. cm.
    Includes bibliographical references and index.
    ISBN 0-07-250864-7 (softcover : alk. paper)
    1. Art—Study and teaching (Higher) 2. Art and society. I. Milbrandt, Melody
    K. II. Title
N345.A63 2005
707'.1'1—dc22
                                                                    2003061537

www.mhhe.com

To Carrie and Amelia, and for Mary Beth
To my family, especially Aaron, Mira, Lanny and my
Kennedy clan

ABOUT THE AUTHORS

TOM ANDERSON a native of Montana and longtime resident of Florida, is professor and former chair in the Department of Art Education at Florida State University (FSU) in Tallahassee. He also has worked as a public school art teacher in Oregon and as a commercial artist in Chicago. He has written more than seventy articles, reviews, and book chapters and is the author of one other book, *Real Lives: Art Teachers and the Cultures of School*. He was a cofounder, in 1995, and is still a member of the International Advisory Committee of the Children's Guernica Peace Mural Project, which at this writing is responsible for some seventy murals, exhibits, and accompanying peace workshops around the world. His international teaching and service include stints in Italy, Spain, Kuwait, and Japan; talks to international audiences in Taiwan, Korea, Canada, and Australia; and service in the International Baccalaureate Program in Wales, Italy, Canada, and the United States. He has given more than 100 speeches and workshops in the United States, including Hawaii. At FSU, he has directed twenty-five doctoral dissertations thus far and is proud of his former students' accomplishments in art education and arts administration worldwide. Over the course of his career, Dr. Anderson has been particularly interested in the social foundations of art and education, as well as art criticism and aesthetic inquiry, especially in art for life. He is a frequent community muralist and currently is engaged in digital photography as a means of recording his own life and his place in his local community, as well as in the larger social context. He's married to Mary Beth McBride and has two adult daughters, Carrie and Amelia.

MELODY K. MILBRANDT is an associate professor and coordinator of art education at Georgia State University in Atlanta. She taught art in public schools (K–12) for eighteen years before moving to higher education in 1996. Throughout her teaching career she has been active in state and national art education associations, providing approximately fifty workshops and presentations at professional meetings. These presentations have addressed her long-standing interests in creativity, cognitive abilities, and social issues in the art classroom. Her dissertation, *An Authentic Instructional Model for Fifth Grade Art Using Postmodern Content*, was awarded a J. Paul Getty Fellowship in 1995. Since then she has written a number of articles, reviews, and book chapters on a variety of topics related to contemporary issues in art education. Her current teaching and research interests include the role of art criticism and aesthetics in a multicultural setting. Dr. Milbrandt has served on numerous advisory boards for local, state, and national art organizations. She is a past president of the Kansas Art Education Association and was honored as Elementary Art Educator of the Year in both Kansas and Georgia. She is active in the Georgia Art Education Association and received the Southeastern Region Higher Education Award for 2004. She and her husband, Dr. Lanny Milbrandt, have four adult children and five grandchildren. Her studio interest is mixed-media painting.

PREFACE

Art for Life is a textbook designed for elementary and secondary classes in the theory and practice of art education at the undergraduate and graduate levels. It is based on the idea that art and visual culture engage viewers in communicating, reflecting, and responding to the meaning of their lives. A quest for personal and social meaning is therefore at the center of art for life.

Beginning with the premise that art is aesthetic communication about things that count, art for life is a cognitive approach to art education that stresses the construction and intelligent interpretation of art and other aspects of visual culture in their authentic social contexts.

A second premise of art for life is that information resides not only in an artifact or a performance but also in the context of that object or process: the culture and conditions in which it came to be. Art as intelligent communication, then, requires that information be gained not only *from* the work (regarding, for instance, its aesthetic quality and intrinsic nature) but also *about* the work (its functions and place in the world).

A third premise of art for life is that making, interpreting, teaching, and learning about art and visual culture in a meaningful way entails the idea that aesthetic symbolic expression, as cognition, has both affective and intellectual components. Both intellect and emotion are intrinsic to making and "reading" art and visual culture and are equally important in art for life as a reflection of human experience.

The goal is to engage in teaching and learning in art for the sake of life. We address skills, concepts, and ways of approaching art that foster students' understanding of their own lives and the lives of others. It is art education that, in addition to understanding art for its own sake, seeks to understand it as an expression of emotions, values, mores, and institutions.

The strategies we use in art for life are based on themes (rather than on elements and principles of design, media, or historical periods) and are, as appropriate, interdisciplinary. Guided by the principles of authentic instruction and assessment, we explore the rationales and substance of traditional, modern, and postmodern understandings of culture and art, as well as historical models of art education, extracting whatever is useful for our model of comprehensive art education: art for life. We hold that particular current and historical movements and trends in art education are not necessarily mutually exclusive, as they have been considered in the past; we present them here as mutually supportive toward real-life ends. The disciplinary foci of art for life then are making art, aesthetics and aesthetic inquiry, art criticism and critique, art history and other contextual research, visual culture studies, creative self-expression, and new (electronic) technologies.

Art for Life is meant for both preservice and practicing art educators. Its aim is to provide a theoretical base for the study of art, education, and art education as well as to present practical ideas and examples. Part One addresses conceptual foundations, with particular attention to the aims, goals, objectives, and

About the cover: Community mural artist Joshua Sarantitis has been creating public art for more than twelve years and his work can be seen in many major American cities. His approach to making art comes from a tradition of artists who believe the creative process should be shared with the public in locations that are both accessible and socially relevant. He can be reached by email at murals@earthlink.net. This image reflects the philosophy of authentic instruction that centers art for life. As shown here the roots of our discoveries already lie within us. It just remains for all of us to discover ourselves in our own personal and social contexts as the foundation for reaching our full potential.

instructional strategies of art for life in the larger context of authentic instruction and assessment. Authentic instruction is the educational framework of art for life; it involves strategies that foster high-level cognition, deep learning, connections to the world beyond the classroom, and substantial discussion by and support from peers.

Part Two addresses the disciplinary and conceptual foci with particular attention to visual culture, creative self-expression in a social context, aesthetics and aesthetic inquiry, art criticism and critique, art history, making art, and contemporary technologies.

Part Three begins with a description and discussion of thematic instruction, then presents curriculum units for K–12. These units are focused on central tenets of art for life such as personal development in a social context, environmental concerns, and social justice. We present practical lessons and suggested activities as models for learning, *not* as formulas for teachers to replicate. We hope teachers will use this text as a springboard for their own investigation of art for life in their own classrooms.

Art for Life is primarily a collaborative effort between two authors but also includes the theoretical contributions and classroom experience of numerous other art educators at all grade levels, including university colleagues. We value their input and hope that this text will stimulate discussion regarding the goals and mission of art education. Toward that end, we invite you to visit the Art for Life website maintained by McGraw-Hill.

Teachers are often asked to envision the outcomes they want students to achieve. Accordingly, we envision the outcome of art for life as students who think critically about art and artifacts in the visual world and feel deeply about the artwork they create and see. We envision students who care for people and the environment in their art classroom and beyond, in the global community; who develop skills for making art and are able to voice their ideas and concerns visibly and audibly. We envision art students who will someday be leaders because they solve problems with empathy and understanding, hold fast to the values of human rights, respect the sanctity of life, and seek peace as a fundamental good. This is our dream, but it is not ours alone. We invite you to join us in constructing a new tomorrow through the comprehensive model of art education that we call art for life.

http://www.mhhe.com/artforlife1
Visit our website to continue your education about Art for Life and to engage like-minded art educators at all levels.

ACKNOWLEDGMENTS

The authors wish to thank the McGraw-Hill team: publisher, Chris Freitag; sponsoring editor, Joe Hanson, who recognized the potential value of this project and guided it unwaveringly through the course to completion; development editor, Jill Gordon, and project manager, Diane Folliard, for their dedicated commitment, caring attention, and good judgment; as well as marketing manager, Lisa Berry; media producer, Shannon Gattens; production supervisor, Carol Bielski; designer, Kim Menning; photo researcher, Alexandra Ambrose; media supplement producer, Kathleen Boylan; art editor, Cristin Yancey; and freelancers, copy editor, Sue Gamer, proofreader, Judith Gallagher, and indexer, Mary Mortgensen. The entire McGraw-Hill team has truly been superbly professional and a joy to work with.

We also wish to thank the following reviewers for invaluable insights, many of which contribute to the shape and content of this book:

      Terry Barrett—*Ohio State University*

      Minuette Floyd—*University of South Carolina*

      Lynn Galbraith—*University of Arizona*

      Christopher Greenman—*Alabama State University*

      Holle Humphries—*University of Texas Austin*

      Andra Nyman—formerly of the *University of Georgia*

      Peg Speirs—*Kutztown University*

      Mary Wyrick—*Buffalo State College*

Tom Anderson also wants to thank my teachers, who guided me in this book by what they taught me. In particular I want to thank Will Clark, who helped me believe I can make art that counts, Vincent Lanier and June King McFee who gave me a broad and deep introduction to art education and whet my appetite for social engagement through art; Edmund Burke Feldman, for knowing and sharing how to write short sentences with big meanings; and Paul Edmondston who believed in me and encouraged me to follow my heart. I also want to acknowledge my colleagues at Florida State University for continuing to provide a rich intellectual tradition within which my own ideas have formed and been refined. Especially, I want to acknowledge my students, in whose caring presence, meanings have been finally tested, refined, and transformed. Finally, I want to thank my colleague and co-author, Melody Milbrandt, for hanging in there for the eight long years this project has been in the making. As she put it, if nothing else, it shows we're optimists!

Finally, more personally, my deepest gratitude goes to my wife, Mary Beth McBride, who has listened to my ideas, given me wise counsel and centering advice, and sincerely shared my elation and frustration with equal grace. She's my anchor and my compass.

Melody Milbrandt wishes to thank Tom Anderson for his initial invitation to collaborate on this text (he undoubtedly didn't foresee the eight years of effort) along with the art departments of the State University of West Georgia and Georgia State University for their support of her continued research and writing. A special thanks to graduate assistants Mandy Lebowitz and Zenia Zed who, along with numerous other graduate and undergraduate students, contributed and participated in the development and implementation of many of the ideas presented. Thank you also to art teachers and students who provided the wonderful artwork found throughout our book. Thank you to Linda Clay, Kirby Meng, and Elizabeth Willett who took time from their busy schedules to document and share moments of their meaningful classroom practice with us.

I would like to take this opportunity to thank the membership and leadership of the National Art Education Association for the many professional growth experiences and support provided by this organization. The dedication to research, leadership and professional excellence exhibited in this multi-faceted and diverse organization has been a continual source of inspiration and motivation. I would like to acknowledge and thank Elliott Eisner and June King McFee for their early research and writing that conceptually set me on my educational path, along with my art education professors at Wichita State University and Florida State University. Each person holds a special place in my heart for their valuable insights and contributions to both my individual educational experience and the field of art education.

This is also an appropriate place to acknowledge and thank my art education colleague and husband for almost twenty years, Lanny Milbrandt. His belief in the creative process, the value of work done well, and commitment to the indisputable value of art and art education fund his constant and patient support of all of my professional endeavors. I thank him for sharing a professional, as well as a personal life journey, with me.

Finally, in the positive spirit of *Art for Life*, the authors salute and commend our art teacher colleagues and the work they do for students around the world. As a profession we've come a long way, and we believe the best is yet to be.

CONTENTS

INTRODUCTION

ART AS THE SEARCH FOR MEANING

This book is based on the idea that teaching and learning in art should be about something that counts in our lives. Human beings are programmed, biologically and psychologically, to seek and make meaning. Art is decorative or beautiful for its own sake; in addition, one of its primary functions in all cultures around the world has been to tell our human stories, to help us know who we are and how and what we believe. This concept assumes that the aesthetic form at the heart of most artworks is used to effect some kind of communication, and that the artist uses his or her skills in composition and technique to create works that extend beyond themselves to tell us something about the human experience.

The purpose of this book, then, goes beyond understanding art for its own sake. It is, rather, to help future art teachers and their students understand something about themselves and others through art and visual artifacts. Our focus is on art and visual culture less for art's sake than for life's sake, on art that counts in the lives of you and your students as personal and social expression. The book is about forms that arise from a need to say something of significance, about art and visual culture that reflect and contribute to the human story. Authentic, content-based art education recognizes works of art as both windows into and mirrors of our lives. It reflects the stories of individual human beings and the groups we live in, told through art and visual culture.

Art for Life as Social Reconstructionism

Art attains and constructs meanings in the context of its use in particular groups or cultures. People make and receive art because it tells them important things about themselves and others. By extension, art education can and should, at least in part, be a social instrument for improving people's lives. This idea, called social reconstructionism, encourages us to examine competing philosophical systems or narratives, in the conviction that there is no single right way to do things. In this book, we vigorously embrace the notion of cultural and individual plurality in making and receiving meaning through art and visual culture.

To help students view learning not merely as the acquisition of knowledge but also as practices that provide them with a sense of identity, value, and worth, educators must encourage the use of art in its authentic contexts as a vehicle of change in a world where racism, class oppression, sexism, and nationalism must be continually challenged. Students need to be introduced to content and concepts that address how community life can be structured for equality and justice, and we have addressed these themes throughout the book. Students also need to develop an understanding of the richness and strength in diverse cultural traditions. Through understanding differences, they will be better prepared to change prevailing relations of power.

Moreover, we believe teachers need to implement programs that allow discourse on morality and social criticism, giving students points of reference for making choices in a world of competing ideologies, claims, and interests. Such programs build moral courage and connect both the teacher and the students to the most pressing contemporary problems and opportunities.

In Part Three, we present examples of artists who advocate social reconstruction, and curriculum units built around those ideas for K–12 instruction. For example, in Chapter 11 Krzysztof Wodiczko focuses our attention on homelessness and military threats, and in Chapter 13 Fred Wilson's work is used to focus on racism and social inequality. There are also units on developing self-awareness and personal choice through journals (Chapter 10), on environmental consciousness (Chapter 12), on human equality and feminism (Chapter 14), and on developing a "sensibility of peace" (Chapter 15). The point of these units is to explore and understand strategies that make life better through art.

It is important to acknowledge here that social activism is not a new idea in art education. June King McFee, for example, was an early advocate of connecting art instruction to real life. She wrote that equal rights without economic opportunity and meaningful education could compound social problems. She expressed concern for individuals marginalized by society—a concern many minorities, feminists, and others share today. McFee stressed that it is each citizen's responsibility to evaluate the quality of his or her aesthetic contribution to society, subject to the public view. She rejected the tradition of socially irresponsible individualism in art, described the interdependence of major social forces, and questioned the values perpetuated by the mass media when those values accentuate cultural and economic differences as appropriate topics for art education. Many other social reconstructionists, including Laura Chapman and more recently Graeme Chalmers, Paul Duncum, Kerry Freedman, and Kristin Congdon, have addressed similar issues. Here, we join them.

WHO OUR READERS ARE

This book is primarily for future art teachers and for practicing art teachers who want to explore new and long-held ideas about art education. Our purpose is to present a foundation and concepts for art instruction for real-life purposes in and beyond school, as well as to present practical examples and exemplary curricula. We call this approach art for life.

THE STRUCTURE OF THIS TEXT

This book has three parts. Part One, consisting of Chapters 1 and 2, presents the structure and theoretical foundations of art for life, placing our approach in the larger context of art education and society. Part Two, consisting of Chapters 3 through 9, focuses on particular concepts and associated teaching and learning strategies, both disciplinary and interdisciplinary, including visual culture, creative personal expression, aesthetics, art criticism, art history, the making of art, and new technologies. Part Three, consisting of Chapters 10 through 16, is a series of curriculum units. These include real-life motivations and content and can be used by current and future art teachers for K–12 instruction. The key throughout is theme-based authentic instruction that starts with art but extends to other disciplines using students' own drives, interests, and abilities to achieve meaningful, holistic educational experiences centered in art. Visit our website to continue the dialogue about art education for life.

PART 1

THE FOUNDATIONS OF
ART FOR LIFE

Art for Life: Conceptual and Cultural Foundations: The Purpose of Art for Life

Self-Portrait, Debbie Zhuang, Atlantic Community High School, Delray Beach, FL., Genia Howard, art teacher. *When approached with sensitivity the self-portrait can be a vehicle to explore a student's identity and relationship to the world. Assurance and determination appear to be characteristics of this young artist.*

The Cultural Content of Art
for Life

Real-World Issues

The Curricular Structure of Art
for Life

This book, for future art teachers and art teachers in service, is about teaching and learning art for life's sake. Our premise is that art and visual culture are imbued with and communicate personal and social meanings. Therefore, in art for life the focus is on making and examining art and visual artifacts and performances in order to understand these meanings both in school and in real life.

Recent world events have made it apparent that we are all one global community and that no one is outside the relationships, good or bad, which affect this community. Art education for life is about these relationships, about the way we understand ourselves and others at home and elsewhere, all around our small blue planet.

In the past thirty or forty years, it has become increasingly clear to western artists and theorists that art should be engaged in, not isolated from, the everyday concerns of society. This premise—that art is and should be about something beyond itself—is well established outside western culture and western art education. In most cultures around the world, throughout most of history, art has had very specific functions beyond being decorative or beautiful or existing simply for its own sake. As we noted in the Introduction, one of its primary functions has been to help tell our human stories, to help us know who we are and what we believe. This concept assumes that the aesthetic form, which is at the heart of most artworks, is used to effect some kind of communication. It also assumes that artists use skills, composition, and technique to create artworks that extend beyond themselves to tell us something about human experience. Thus the chief purpose of art education for life is to help students understand something about themselves and others through art and thereby to contribute to personal growth, social progress, and a sense of global community.

In art for life, the content of the curriculum and the teaching and learning strategies are focused on things that count in students' lives as personal and social expression. Art for life is the story of individual human beings and the groups we live in, told through art. Art education for life is comprehensive education based on content and on the premises of authentic instruction, which recognizes works of art as both windows into and mirrors of our lives.

Where do these meanings come from? To answer this question, we will first examine content. If, indeed, we are a product of our heritage and our history as much as of our personal choices, then we have to look to heritage and our history as sources. To find out what we now are, it is useful to start by examining what we have been. In that context, we first go back to tradition, considering certain traditional understandings of art in society. We then explore **modernism** as a reaction to **traditionalism**. Next, we examine **postmodernism** for the insights it may give us. Finally, we draw on all three of these historical phenomena to synthesize understandings and content for a contemporary approach to art education—the approach known as art for life.

The Cultural Content of Art for Life

Traditional Art and Understandings

Tradition transmits collective wisdom and thus gives people rules to live by. It is centered on the social group rather than the individual as the source of wisdom and authority. Traditional peoples assume that social control is a necessary and positive aspect of culture. It follows that most art of traditional or indigenous societies is conservative rather than creative; their art is meant primarily to reinforce and transmit core cultural values and beliefs by serving particular social functions. These functions—spiritual, sacramental, idealistic, and so on—reflect and reinforce the values of the society. Art in traditional societies symbolizes goodness, energy, masculinity, femininity, beauty, and other ideals, both in its forms and in its uses. Dancing, singing, poetic speech, rattles, wind instruments, drums, jewelry, masks, painting, headrests, power symbols, ceremonial garments, fabrics, doors, theater, funeral rites, lullabies, gardens, tattooing, and many other forms have all evolved within given cultures as social expressions of belief and self-affirmation. Traditional art helps people clarify and cement their social relationships, history, mores, and values; attract a mate; establish kinship and hierarchy; and so on. These are not merely aesthetic functions. They are solutions to problems—practical functions necessary for the survival of the individual and the group.

If the purpose of art or performance in traditional societies is to carry values and beliefs from one person and one generation to another, then the purpose of the aesthetic element in artworks is to get people to pay attention to that message. Beauty and skillfully elaborated forms are not intended for their own sake. Rather, they are intended to make the object or performance special and worthy of special notice. Then, people will be drawn to it and, through its aesthetic power, will come to believe in the message it carries. The style of such traditional artworks must be consistent, so that the people of the culture can "read" them and understand them over time.

Elaboration, beauty, and replication are the primary qualities valued in traditional art, and the skill to achieve these ends is the primary quality valued in traditional artists. The necessity for consistency over the generations normally selects against creativity as a valued quality of art. It is not the artist's place to invent new forms. In traditional society, if an artist changes a designated form, it is usually because of a mistake or a lack of talent rather than a result of deliberate exploration. In this regard, traditional art is unlike modern art, in which creativity may be the most highly valued quality.

Modern Art and Understandings

Modernism is centered on the individual, not the group. Modernism was a western cultural reaction against traditionalism. Modernism values the idea of individual progress and technological advancement rising from individual rationality. The social agenda is to rise above, escape, or—best of all—to reform traditions, which are seen as inherently repressive. It follows that individual expression in art is highly valued. Unlike traditional art, the best modern art was seen as that which was most creatively self-expressive. The positive emphasis on creativity also made imitation undesirable. Copying was bad because it wasn't creative. The traditionally valued qualities of elaboration and craft were also demoted to secondary status except as they served creativity. Artifacts of communal belief, no matter how skillfully made, were reduced to the level of mere craft, and the artists who continued to convey communal beliefs were reduced to a mere craftspeople because their work lacked the essential quality of modern art—individual creativity.

FIGURE 1.1 Dogon Dancers wearing Sirige and female warrior masks, photographed approximately 1975. *In traditional societies, art objects convey specific meaning and serve specific functions within the community such as clarifying and cementing social relationships and transmitting history, mores, and values.*

FIGURE 1.2 Helen Frankenthaler, *Flood,* 1967. Synthetic polymer on canvas, 10 ft. 4 in. x 11 ft. 8 in. *Modern art celebrates the creative expression of the solitary artist. Aesthetic response was the highest purpose and end goal of modern art.*

Modern art, in striving for creativity, came to represent individual personalities rather than collective sensibility, and it increasingly came to exist for its own sake. In traditional societies, the aesthetic response was an attention-getting device, only the first step in serving an extrinsic social purpose; but in modernism, the aesthetic response was itself the highest purpose and ultimate goal of art. Art was to be judged by the intrinsic qualities of the work itself: the composition, the aesthetic quality, how well the elements and principles of design and style carried the intended expressive message. That is, art was judged by what came to be called significant form, or the lack thereof.

In modernism, artifacts and artworks with functions beyond the aesthetic—that carried group beliefs, told stories, held things, or were sat on or drunk from—were considered less significant, and were often deemed mere craft despite their aesthetic dynamics. In late modernism, in fact, one art critic, Clement Greenberg, argued that the so-called fine arts or high arts were a bastion of good taste, high ideals, and significant aesthetic form, holding out against the rabble and degradation of popular culture.

The core of modern art, then, was the autonomy of the creative individual artist who acts alone to rise above an inherently repressive society. Seeking through aesthetic means to overcome a tasteless, degraded popular culture through the creation of beauty, thus significance, became the very fiber of modern art. In modernism, art and its formal aesthetic qualities stood against cultural degradations.

Contemporary Postmodern Art and Understandings

Current theorists, however, ask whether the modern idea of the "free" individual, rising above and rejecting tradition and escaping from its repression, is desirable or even possible. How good is it, they ask, for individuals to deny, devalue, ignore, or

FIGURE 1.3   Maya Ying Lin, *Civil Rights Memorial*, 1988–89, black granite and water. Southern Poverty Law Center, Montgomery, AL. *Contemporary postmodern artists frequently center the concerns of community. Incised in this memorial are the names of the fallen civil rights figures with the words of Dr. Martin Luther King quoting the Bible: "We are not satisfied and we will not be satisfied until 'justice rolls down like water and righteousness like a mighty stream.'" The intimate black granite and water invite visitors to touch the names of forty men, women, and children slain during the struggle for civil rights and reflect on the sacrifice of individuals who shape history.*

obscure their collective social values, mores, institutions, and practices? How much is lost when individuals fail to acknowledge that they are the bearers of tradition? These theorists argue that tradition is enabling and supporting in as many ways as it is restrictive. It provides patterns that make communication and collective living possible. To a large degree, it determines how one thinks and what one thinks about. From a **postmodern** perspective, any given meaning exists only in a socially constructed web of other meanings. These meanings are constructed in a group context, through dialogue. In this way, the power of the group, not the individual, is again at the center.

The postmodern questioning of both traditional and modern assumptions, structures, and beliefs is a valuable educational tool. However, all education, everywhere, ultimately develops and builds on systems of belief and understanding, rather than tearing them down. Postmodern deconstruction of systems of belief, carried to its logical conclusion, is, then, eventually antieducational. Fortunately, neo-Marxists, feminists, environmentalists, and social **reconstructionists,** among others, have made use of postmodern questioning without abandoning functional philosophical systems such as Marxism or democracy. These philosophers and artists deconstruct primarily modernist ideas, but they also reconstruct other beliefs. Among the most important sources of their reconstructions are the traditions of indigenous societies and pre-Renaissance Europe. Particularly important for art education for life is the fact that many of these thinkers have once again focused on art as an artifact or performance that reflects and facilitates communal culture. Moreover, the community is now increasingly planetary and visual. We address this contemporary visual culture in Chapter 3.

Art for Life: Content from Three Worldviews

How can we foster individual success and global community through art education? We take from both traditionalism and postmodernism the idea of centering art in the community by returning it to the center of students' lives. Art should be taught for the sake of what it can tell us, through aesthetic means, about life. In addition to the traditional idea of art at the center of communal belief, we retain the traditional emphasis on skill, craft, and elaboration of form. From modernism, we take the idea of the artist, and the student, as an independent, creative individual; in fact, we devote an entire chapter to personal creativity. From poststructuralism, we retain the valuable idea of **critique,** especially critiques of art forms and visual artifacts and their philosophical foundations. By extension, we retain the idea of competing philosophical systems, or narratives of belief. Conceptually, this is the content of art for life.

Art for Life's Aim, Goals, and Educational Premises

The educational aim of art for life is to help students prepare for success at school and in life, through teaching and learning centered on art. Several goals follow from this. Students engaged in art for life will:

1. Understand that art and visual culture are visual communication between human beings about things that count.

2. Understand that art has both intrinsic and extrinsic value and meaning; that its forms, meanings, uses, and values are important aesthetically and also instrumentally or functionally, in their social purposes.

3. Personally engage in making art and in studying art and visual culture, both individually and cooperatively, to express themselves as well to find out about meanings, values, and ways of living in the world.

Art for life, as an approach to art education, emphasizes the construction of meaning through depth of learning and through connections rather than through superficial formalized methods. The educational premise is that teaching and learning should:

1. Make real-world connections.

2. Involve the active construction of knowledge, as opposed to the passive reception of knowledge from authorities.

3. Develop intellectual, emotional, skills-based, and expressive knowledge, abilities, and sensibilities.

These educational propositions are interdependent and mutually supporting and reflect a philosophy called **authentic instruction** (described below, and examined in Chapter 2). The following section gives a detailed examination of the academic structure of art for life based on its aim, goals, and premises.

THE CURRICULAR STRUCTURE OF ART FOR LIFE

Art for life is grounded in authentic instruction, which we examine in Chapter 2. Here, it is enough to say that authentic education focuses on teaching and learning and addresses real-world issues and meanings beyond school and thus guides the curricular structure of art for life: **comprehensive art education.** There are many versions of comprehensive art education, but its primary features are that it is discipline-centered, cognitive, thematic, interdisciplinary (as appropriate), and life-centered. (An example of an artist who uses an interdisciplinary life-centered approach to her artwork is Lynne Hull. See *Flowing Water Moon, Hydrogylph,* 1992–95, Color Plate #1.) Comprehensive art education almost always includes four disciplines: art production, aesthetics, art criticism, and art history. To these, in the curriculum of art for life, we add three more foci: the study of visual culture, personal creativity, and new technology. In sum, the components of art for life are:

http://www.mhhe.com/artforlife1
Visit our website to find out more about comprehensive art education.

1. Visual culture studies (including art).

2. Creative self-expression in a social context.

3. Aesthetics and aesthetic inquiry.

4. Art criticism.

5. Art history.

6. Art making.

7. Contemporary technologies.

We devote Chapters 3 through 9—Part Two of this book—to these disciplines and foci, suggesting how they might be used in art for life.

A Word about Creativity, Visual Culture, and New Technology as Foci for Art for Life

We have added the study of visual culture, creativity, and new technology to the traditional four disciplines of comprehensive art education because each of the three is important for understanding art and visual culture in contemporary life. To understand our rationale it is useful to put our decision in a historical context.

Creativity was a primary focus and goal of art education in the mid-twentieth century, before the advent of **discipline-based art education** (DBAE). Advocates of creativity, especially Viktor Lowenfeld, promoted creative and mental growth through art, rather than the study of art for its own sake. Then, in the late twentieth century, in reaction against art education focused on creativity, and especially as a result of the Penn State Conference of 1964, discipline-centered approaches came to the fore. In particular, the academically oriented DBAE model sponsored by the Getty Foundation emerged. However, DBAE too eventually fell out of favor. Whereas creativity as an approach had been criticized as too loosely structured and insufficiently focused on art, DBAE was criticized as overly focused on (high) art, overly academic, Eurocentric, and disconnected from life. Accordingly, DBAE was revised by its advocates and was eventually transformed into comprehensive art education, a model that is more sensitive to the cultural foundations of art and to multiculturalism.

Still, comprehensive art education, focused on the four traditional disciplines, largely fails to address the very important issues of popular **visual culture** or new digital technologies in any systematic way. Also, having originated as a reaction against art education focused on creativity, it mostly ignores the older tradition of the individual creative spirit. This is a serious failing, given the state of contemporary society and the fact that journals of art education address each of these aspects separately from the comprehensive art education paradigm. But approaches to art education based on creativity, visual culture, technology, and comprehensive art education are not necessarily mutually exclusive. In fact, creativity, visual culture, and technology can complement and extend comprehensive art education. (Artwork by Nam June Paik, a pioneer of the use of technology as an artistic medium, continues to evolve. See *Electronic Superhighway*, 1995, Color Plate #2.)

Inclusion of the three additional foci also extends from the cultural premises of art for life. From the discussion of traditionalism, modernism, and postmodernism above, it becomes apparent that a study of visual culture is supported by both traditional and postmodern beliefs; creativity arises from modernism; and newer technology is supported by beliefs from the modern and postmodern periods.

Because these three foci—visual culture, creativity, and technology—have been and continue to be important in life and in art education, we include them as equal partners with studio production, aesthetics, art criticism, and art history. We now present the premises, structure, and strategies of our approach.

Comprehensive Art Education for Life

As we have said, comprehensive art education, the curricular structure of art for life, is a discipline-centered approach. It is cognitive, thematic, and interdisciplinary. Most important, it furthers the purposes of authentic instruction in art for life. It evolved from discipline-based art education (DBAE), which, as described above, focused on the work of art or the artistic performance, using four disciplines—art production, art criticism, aesthetics, and art history—as lenses or ways of understanding the artwork.

To repeat, comprehensive art education for life retains these four art disciplines but adds three foci: visual culture, technology, and creativity. It also changes the emphasis from understanding art itself to understanding life through art. Comprehensive art education for life asks the question: What can art tell us about ourselves and our world? When we seek and develop meanings by asking such a question, our aims and foci determine what we attend to and how. These purposes are very seldom restricted to a single discipline—say, art history or art criticism. Rather, they normally range across disciplines and reflect cross-disciplinary concerns. The protocol for examining meanings, then, is making connections between ideas and the forms in which ideas present themselves, rather than keeping these ideas separate within specific academic disciplines.

Although comprehensive art education for life begins with art and the disciplines of art, it expands beyond artistic concerns to the larger visual culture in seeking contextual information about art-centered questions. Through this comprehensive **interdisciplinary instructional** approach, art for life seeks to understand art and visual culture, to engage in creative expression, and ultimately to achieve the primary purpose of developing real-life skills and meanings through instruction in art.

Instructional Strategies in Art for Life

The heart of art for life is engaging in and understanding life through art. Following from the purposes of authentic instruction (discussed in Chapter 2), the primary instructional strategies of art education for life are

1. Thematic inquiry.

2. Dialogue and cooperative exploration.

3. Critical analysis of art and visual culture in authentic contexts.

4. Historical and other contextual research.

5. Visual research and development of skills in making art.

6. Creative expression.

7. Critical reflection on personal and social meanings understood through the study of art.

These strategies are designed to be interactive and mutually supportive. They can be shown as a diagram.

Centering Thematic Instruction   The central instructional strategy for understanding ourselves and others through art and the visual culture in which it is embedded is the use of themes. This involves attaining meanings by considering ideas and emotions and following them through to their natural conclusions. The guide in this endeavor is students' own logical and emotional connections. Researchers have found that students learn better and more deeply when they take up powerful ideas, with units and lessons organized around key supporting concepts, than when they learn merely facts or techniques.

Because it is centered on powerful ideas, art for life is structured around themes rather than being framed by units of instruction such as elements and principles of design, media, periods of art history, or art disciplines. Art for life is intended to develop meanings through art. Domain-specific learning (for example, studying Van Gogh's compositions or developing artistic skills) is only a step on the path, not the goal. Rather than taking a one-design-fits-all approach, art education for life utilizes disciplinary, domain-specific knowledge and skills to explore human ideas, emotions, and purposes and to solve real problems—problems that are significant beyond the classroom—through art. Thus activities should be developed

CHART 1   Developing meaning through thematic inquiry.

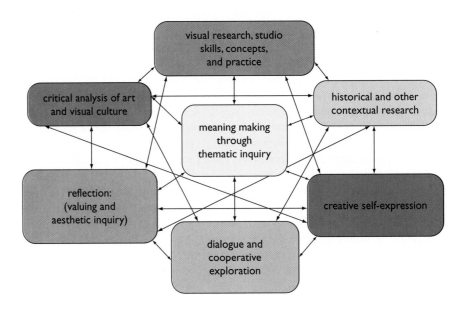

that foster individual solutions to conceptual and design problems in relation to some of the great human themes (Chapter 10 is a good example of this approach).

Themes should be taken first from personal experience and contemporary art and culture because these sources are most accessible and most immediately compelling to students. Then a theme should be allowed to expand naturally or organically to include a cross section of artifacts and performances from many times and cultures as a reflection of students' interests and concerns, since the rituals that support cosmological beliefs in all cultures are so permeated by the arts as to be frequently inseparable from them. Through examining art thematically as a manifestation and reflection of life, students learn about themselves and about others in relation to themselves. Potentially, such learning fosters tolerance and global community, which are ideals of art for life.

The Role of the Art Disciplines and Skills in Thematic Instruction   To some degree, we must understand the vehicle we are driving, or we won't get where we're going. We need to be able to read and interpret the gas gauge so as not run out of gas, and have a feel for the steering wheel so as not to turn too sharply or run off the road. The vehicle we now need to understand is art. It is art, broadly defined in the context of visual culture, that takes us down the road to understanding. In this sense, art and understandings attained through disciplinary study are the vehicle of art for life.

Therefore, the seven components of art for life—studio production, aesthetics, art criticism, art history, visual culture, creativity, and new technologies—and the related skills and understandings are central to the content and strategies of the curriculum. For inquiry, students use the strategies and methods of artists, critics, historians, and aestheticians. They also use time-honored strategies of creativity and the latest technologies, as well as cultural critique, to learn about art and visual culture and to integrate what they learn into their lives. Exploration can and usually should expand to other disciplines beyond art, as themes suggest, but should not begin with them. The heart of art for life is art and its concerns and disciplines.

The focus of art for life is art, not social studies. Skills such as the ability to manipulate color and form, to develop strong compositions, or to manipulate clay on a potter's wheel are critical to students' development of meaning. In order to express themselves through art, students must have physical art skills as well as clear concepts and emotions they want to express. Skill is at the heart of making art and is integral to art for life. Clumsy, unskilled art won't communicate anything, no matter how good the idea behind it may be. The difference between art for life and approaches based on the elements and principles of design or media is that skills become the means to the end rather than the end itself.

In short, a good program of art for life addresses composition, media, tools, the development of concepts and styles, and other skills in the pursuit of meaningful expression. Art for life does not involve projects that look good but mean little or nothing to the students. It avoids activities in which all the students work on the same project and create the same forms, forms based on compositional and design premises that have no inherent value in the students' own social or personal lives. Rather, skills should be developed in conjunction with and for the purpose of exploring themes related to real life. As Richard Anderson (1990) puts it, art is culturally significant meaning, skillfully encoded in an affecting, sensuous medium. The skillful encoding of content in an affective medium is precisely what gives art its expressive quality; the recognition of this fact separates thematic art education from social studies.

We address the seven components of art for life in Chapters 3 through 9—Part Two of this book. The intention of Part Two is to enhance your understanding, as a teacher or future teacher, of the disciplines and foci. These chapters are directed to adults who have the maturity and mental capacities to function in a discipline-specific way. We expect that the adults reading this text will benefit from the insights, rigor, and accuracy of the disciplinary strategies and will then use their understanding to facilitate comprehensive programs in art for their own K–12 students. Part Three consists of examples of how this can be done.

Themes or Topics? The Importance of Personal Engagement and Relationship   It is important to distinguish between topics and themes. Horses, dogs, and airplanes are topics; they may stimulate students to make or study art—but they are not themes, or if they are themes they are trivial themes. True themes arise from our relationships to topics, our personal connections: for example, our love of horses, our fear of dogs, our thrill when we fly in an airplane. When we personalize and humanize a topic through our own connection, it takes on the dimensions of a theme.

This quality of relationship makes **thematic teaching and learning** an ideal vehicle for reaching out to others. Toward that end, the themes should be life-centered, describing our human stories. They should be focused on who we are, where we think we belong, and our sense of community. In an increasingly multicultural world, an effort should be made to focus on ideas and works of nonwestern and indigenous cultures, as well as ethnic and cultural minorities, in addition to the western art and ideas that normally constitute art instruction in North America. Constructing and exploring meanings thematically through art and visual culture can become a channel for students' personal transformation and social reconstruction. Extending the narrative and communicative function of art from students' own cultures to the cultures of others can be an important step toward intercultural understanding. Whatever their ethnicity or cultural allegiance, by reaching out beyond the narrow confines of their own cultural understandings, students may come to see others not as exotic or alien but as people who, although they may express themselves differently, have drives, emotions, and sensibilities much like their own. An excellent example of intercultural art education for life is the International Guernica Children's Peace Mural Project, described in Chapter 15.

http://www.mhhe.com/artforlife1
Visit our website to find out more about the Guernica Children's Peace Mural Project.

Central Themes of Art Education for Life   The three central themes of art for life are (1) a sense of self, (2) a sense of place, and (3) a sense of community. In the introduction to Part Three of this book, we discuss these themes in detail, present a more detailed discussion of theme-centered teaching and learning, and offer a list of starter themes for instruction.

Dialogue and Cooperative Exploration

Two other important instructional strategies for art for life, **dialogue** and cooperative activity, extend the idea of relationship. There are many examples of dialogue and cooperative activities throughout this book. In particular, Chapter 4, on socially embedded creative expression, Chapter 5, on aesthetic inquiry, and Chapter 6, on art criticism, are filled with such examples, as are the instructional units in Part Three. In cooperative ventures such as dialogue, and in cooperative exploration such as brainstorming, a crucial feature is that students have a sense of safety. That is, they need to know that they will be taken seriously and respected, that they will not be made to feel foolish or wrong. These aspects of cooperation and dialogue and others are fully explored both in Chapter 2 and in Chapter 4.

Critical Analysis of Art and Visual Culture

Another important strategy is talking and writing about art and visual culture. This **critical analysis** of art in authentic contexts involves examination of the artwork or visual artifact itself and its uses and meanings. Both form and contextual information are examined. Gathering information about history and context (discussed in more detail below) supplies critical analysis with much of its substance. When students undertake critical inquiry in depth, they find that the world of art has many competing narratives expressed through substance and style. In addition, when students are guided to assimilate knowledge through such activities as writing about art critically or creatively (rather than rote memorization), they create or interpret meaning. This construction and contextual interpretation of meaning is a basic skill in life. For that reason, in critical examination of artworks students need to be aided and given strategies for going below the surface.

These strategies are explored in Chapter 3, on visual culture, and in Chapter 6, on art criticism. Here, it is important to note that art criticism is potentially an important overarching strategy for inquiry that can incorporate historical, contextual, and aesthetic inquiry and research. Initially, students can be motivated to consider performances or artifacts they find interesting for personal reasons. This is a key to extending their interest to achieve authentic (contextually situated) personal meanings from art. As an open-ended activity, art criticism also calls for creativity in developing meanings and seeking connections. It can and should involve historical and **contextual research** in developing relevant information about an artifact or performance. It requires reflection on cultural meanings and values of art. If critiques are given orally, they will involve dialogue and cooperative exploration. Art criticism is truly a central strategy in exploring art for life.

Historical and Other Contextual Research

Art history is the core discipline for contextual research in art for life. All contextual research, including art history, considers the conditions surrounding an artwork or a performance, rather than the qualities of the work or performance itself; the purpose is to understand the circumstances in which a work was created, used, and valued. This is research *about* art and visual culture rather than research that *looks at* the object or performance, which is the focus of art criticism.

As they examine the context of artworks and visual culture, students of art for life should examine forms and meanings of works from around the world. They should consider work from other times and cultures not only for its own sake but also as a means of enhancing their understanding of themselves and their own circumstances. They should attempt to ascertain the values projected into a work by its makers and users, rather than projecting their own values, to determine worth and meaning. This leads to broader and deeper understanding not only of others but also of ourselves. We are cultural creatures who imitate and then integrate ideas and behaviors; therefore, the broader our knowledge and basic values, the better.

Contextual research is the heart of an interdisciplinary focus. It isn't just art history that students should examine for contextual information. To reiterate an important point, art for life starts with art as the means of access to ideas that count, but it potentially includes all disciplines in the search, depending on where authentic inquiry leads. Thematic teaching and learning designed to explore students' own meanings certainly will move beyond the disciplines of art. This interdisciplinary focus will be used most often in contextual research. For an example, look at the activity in Chapter 10 that is centered on developing individual students' research notebooks. Let's say as a theme one student is interested in exploring her own ethnicity. She would have to do research in family history, social studies (the conditions that exist or existed within and around the family; what values the family members hold), geography (where the family comes from), and so on. Another student may find out that his family is from Rome and become interested in all things Roman. In his case, the inquiry could move into architecture or the history of Roman conquests. But it is important for inquiry to remain centered on and keep returning to art and visual culture as the core of interdisciplinary inquiry. Art history or other contextual research serves to supply information relevant to the search for meaning, which is centered on art. Chapter 7 examines strategies for art history as contextual research.

Visual Research and Skills in Making Art

Another strategy for understanding art is making it—not so much as creative expression, but rather as research. In thinking of art and visual culture as vessels of meaning, students will find abundant **themes** and inspiration as well as forms and technical solutions in significant works of past and present artists and designers. All these are there for the taking.

Following from critical analysis, students also can use other artists' forms to further their understanding. The purpose is not simplistic replication of artworks that were made in other times and places for reasons other than the students' own. Instead, the idea is to engage students deeply and meaningfully in the ideas, feelings, and forms of others as stimulus for their own personally significant creative expression. This suggests that in studio activity it is important for teachers not to ask students to mindlessly replicate African masks, Japanese calligraphy, or Jackson Pollock's drip paintings. Rather, through analysis and reflection, the process of production should integrate the sensibility behind the work—the "why"—rather than just replicating the form. Then replicated forms should be used in different ways and in different contexts that reflect the students' own sensibilities.

In visual research, students should strive to understand aesthetic forms as representing the ideas and feelings of others, and ask themselves how similar forms can be incorporated and integrated into their own drives, interests, and need for expression. As Bruner (1960) suggests, the process of education must not only transmit culture but also provide alternative views of the world and strengthen the will to explore them. These ideas are explored in Chapter 8.

Creative Expression

Creativity—the exploratory spirit—is at the heart of making art as the expression of meaning (as we discuss in Chapter 4) and another overarching strategy of instruction in art for life. Again, creativity starts with the impulse to develop meaning. Students' individual drives and concerns are an excellent motivation for making art. These drives lead students to ask questions about form and content that not only can satisfy their creative desires but also give them insights into their larger questions about life (see Chapter 10 for an example). Especially when students are making art in the context of examining artworks worldwide, as described above, their solutions are likely to be personal syntheses reflecting a global sensibility. Some of the greatest artworks reflect a cross-cultural synthesis: for example, Sumi-e was influenced by the Chinese, the young Picasso by Africans, and Mary Cassatt by Ukiyo-e.

Chapter 4 describes how an individual sensibility functioning creatively within a larger social context benefits us all. Creative activity, not usually encouraged at school, is an appropriate counterbalance to unquestioning acceptance of social authority. In art for life, the community spirit should be in balance with individual students' free creative artistic expression. Creativity that contributes to a sense of global community will result from accumulating cultural capital—from one's own and other cultures. Such creativity not only allows for individual accomplishment but also facilitates thinking in global terms. Self-reflection—that is, asking questions about who we are, what we believe, and where we fit in the universe—is a path to creative expression.

Critical Reflection on Personal and Social Meanings and Values Understood through the Study of Art

Thematic inquiry, dialogue and cooperation, aesthetic inquiry, critical analysis, contextual research, visual research, and creative self-expression all encourage students to reflect on the meaning and value of artworks and visual culture, for themselves and for the larger society. This development of personal meanings through guided inquiry in a larger social context is at the heart of authentic instruction and of art for life. Again, for the purposes of broad and deep understanding of art for life, reflecting on the meanings and value of works and performances beyond students' own cultures is a good idea in that it helps them see how forms and meanings are contextual. For example, they might ask why Jeff Koons and Andrew Wyeth, artists who lived at the same time, depicted such different worlds. Students should consider other artists cross-culturally, see how these artists examined life issues, try out their ideas and forms, and personally incorporate whatever fits. Through critically examining and reflecting on artworks interculturally, students may gain access to attitudes, mores, and cultural understandings of themselves as beings in their own culture and in relation to the cultures of others, thus fostering a sense of global community. Aesthetics and aesthetic inquiry can channel the drive to understand how and why we value artworks and expressive visual artifacts. Aesthetics and aesthetic inquiry are discussed in Chapter 5 and are also examined throughout the book, particularly in Chapters 3 through 9.

Having addressed the structure of art for life and the overarching instructional strategies, we now examine instructional objectives, outcomes, and assessment.

Instructional Objectives, Outcomes, and Assessment

The curriculum of art for life includes closed-ended instructional objectives and open-ended instructional outcomes that lead to and complement each other. Closed-ended objectives are designed to teach skills and concepts. Open-ended expressive outcomes are designed to allow students to use the skills and concepts they've gained to express themselves meaningfully. Teaching and learning in art for life require a natural relationship between the skills and concepts achieved through closed-ended objectives and the creative self-expression achieved through open-ended outcomes. One rises from and feeds the other. Together they carry the student forward like a left and a right foot, one facilitating and causing a need to use the other. Neglect of either a meaningful idea or the skills to carry it off will impede progress. In authentic art curricula there is no split between process and product: the two are integrated. That is the strategy of art for life.

Assessment in the art for life curriculum is tied to desired objectives and outcomes, which are in turn tied to life purposes. These life purposes are for the most part social **reconstructionist.** The objectives and accompanying assessment strategies are therefore activist. Still, skills need to be taught and learned, as we discussed earlier, so there is a need for closed-ended as well as open-ended assessment.

Closed-ended instructional objectives, which reflect skills development and knowledge acquisition, can be assessed primarily through examining the product (the artwork, paper, or performance) for accuracy and fulfillment of specified criteria. (Either students are able to mix red and green to make a neutral brown or not; either they're able to describe three qualities of expressionism—exaggerated form, arbitrary and exaggerated color, and still recognizable imagery—or not.) But acquiring skills and developing concepts are not the ends of art for life. They are the means to the end, which is understanding and creating art for human meaning: understanding ourselves through art.

At the heart of art for life are the open-ended outcomes that are more difficult to assess using traditional means. What is being assessed in open-ended activities, really, is not the product but the process itself and the value of the process for the student in understanding life through art. Chapter 2 examines how high levels of cognition, the acquisition of profound knowledge, webbing, connective understanding (thematically constructed), substantial conversation, and real-world connections are all indicators of authentic achievement in and through art for life.

Authentic assessment, ideally, is seamlessly integrated with authentic instruction. The goal of assessment is not to determine a grade, but to recognize art as a means to understand others and ourselves in the context of community—and perhaps even as a **social-reconstructionist** means to change the world for the better in some small way. Exhibitions, demonstrations, journals, portfolios, videos, and written or oral responses are important strategies for authentic assessment. These require students to think, feel, and become engaged with each other and the larger world, and in so doing they also serve as feedback, as assessment.

The educational benefit of open-ended process-centered learning and assessment is that the results lead to personal transformation, an outcome that is highly valued when art is taught for the sake of life. We look at authentic instruction and assessment in Chapter 2, along with practical ideas for assessing art for life. Examples of authentic assessment strategies are incorporated in all the units presented in Part Three.

REAL-WORLD ISSUES

National Standards, Assessments, and Art for Life

No teacher works in a social vacuum. In the real world, art teachers, like other teachers, are held accountable for their programs, usually by some combination of local, state, and national mandates. Art for life is compatible with many of these requirements.

Like art for life, *The National Standards for Art* reflect a shift from a curriculum of static knowledge passed from authorities (teachers and books) to passive recipients (students) to a curriculum of dynamic and challenging intellectual inquiry. As with most attempts to categorize students' behaviors and performance, there is some duplication and overlapping among the desired behaviors and expectations, but the standards really do support authentic instruction in art, or art for life. As American art classrooms are transformed by these standards, the intellectual quality of learning will also be transformed. The standards support a more holistic approach to art education than was previously taken; this holistic approach facilitates authentic instruction in art. Art education for life accords well with the national standards.

http://www.mhhe.com/artforlife1
Visit our website to link to the
National Standards for Art, **the INTASC**
Standards, and the NCATE Standards.

The national standards are student-centered and are commonly understood as minimum competencies that teachers need to help their students attain. They are organized into six "content standards" that articulate broad understandings of what students should know and be able to do to demonstrate competency in the discipline of art. The "achievement standards" describe the levels of competence that students should attain at specific intervals: grades four, eight, and twelve.

Other standards are also in place. For example, Interstate New Teacher Assessment and Support Consortium (INTASC) standards are teacher-centered rather

A CLOSER LOOK   The INTASC Standards

Principle 1:
Knowledge of subject matter: The teacher understands the central concepts, tools of inquiry, and structures of the discipline(s) he or she teaches and can create learning experiences that make these aspects of subject matter meaningful for students.

Principle 2:
Knowledge of human development and learning: The teacher understands how children learn and develop and can provide learning opportunities that support their intellectual, social, and personal development.

Principle 3:
Adapting instruction for individual needs: The teacher understands how students differ in their approaches to learning and creates instructional opportunities that are adapted to diverse learners.

Principle 4:
Multiple instructional strategies: The teacher understands and uses a variety of instructional strategies to encourage students' development of critical thinking, problem solving, and performance skills.

Principle 5:
Classroom motivation and management: The teacher uses an understanding of individual and group motivation and behavior to create a learning environment that encourages positive social interaction, active engagement in learning, and self-motivation.

Principle 6:
Communication skills: The teacher uses knowledge of effective verbal, nonverbal, and media communication techniques to foster active inquiry, collaboration, and supportive interaction in the classroom.

Principle 7:
Instructional planning skills: The teacher plans instruction based upon knowledge of subject matter, students, the community, and curriculum goals.

Principle 8:
Assessment of student learning: The teacher understands and uses formal and informal assessment strategies to evaluate and ensure the continuous intellectual, social, and physical development of the learner.

Principle 9:
Professional commitment and responsibility: The teacher is a reflective practitioner who continually evaluates the effects of his or her choices and actions on others (students, parents, and other professionals in the learning community) and who actively seeks out opportunities to grow professionally.

Principle 10:
Partnerships: The teacher fosters relationships with school colleagues, parents, and agencies in the larger community to support students' learning and well-being.

than student-centered. That is, they suggest what the teacher should accomplish rather than what the students should accomplish. The sidebar gives a closer look at these INTASC standards, which were developed for a consortium of more than thirty states operating under the Council of Chief State School Officers.

Another increasingly influential teacher-centered assessment instrument has been developed by the National Professional Teaching Board. It is based on five "core propositions" developed by the National Council for Accreditation of Teacher Education (NCATE). This instrument serves as the foundation for master teachers to earn National Board Teaching Certification. The five core propositions are: (1) Educators are committed to students and students' learning. (2) Educators know the subjects they teach and how to teach those subjects to students. (3) Educators are responsible for managing and monitoring students' learning. (4) Educators think systematically about their practice and learn from experience. (5) Educators are members of learning communities.

Art for life, embedded in the philosophy of authentic instruction, supports and facilitates the high standards of teachers' performance and students' achievement advocated by these national bodies. The strategies for authentic instruction utilized in art for life are planned to assist both the novice teacher and any other teacher engaged in the process of reflecting and learning about his or her profession. Especially if you are a beginning art teacher, as you engage in teaching for the first time you will have opportunities to try many different lessons and teaching strategies. Some well-planned lessons will go exceedingly well from the beginning, but more often you will learn something about how to improve a lesson every time you teach it. You will learn that what interests one student or one class may not interest another, or something you think will be very easy for students to understand is much more difficult than you had imagined. You will develop skills in leading class discussions, posing questions, and resolving conflicts. From these experiences you will become a reflective diagnostician and practitioner. The master teacher develops teaching as an art with a repertoire of skills that make teaching look easy, but don't be misled. Teaching is hard work. It takes dedication, determination, and a willingness to become a lifelong learner.

We have developed art for life to provide you with a structure that can facilitate your development, in light of national and state initiatives. The connections will become more apparent after you read Chapter 2. But it ultimately is you, the teacher, who will control what goes on in your art class. You set the standards. The key is understanding your own values as a teacher and how those values can be integrated within the framework of state and national standards.

Beyond the Art Room: Aesthetic Practice, Ethical Understanding and Behavior, and Social Reconstructionism

Ultimately, any curriculum you teach has implications for real-world experience. In this case, as always, the key to your success in adopting and implementing the curriculum is understanding your own values as a teacher and how those values can be integrated within the larger social framework. The demands of your students, your administration, your own teaching situation, and your state and national standards will all play a part. To address that issue, we turn to ethical concerns and aesthetics.

It may seem odd at to link aesthetics with ethics, but a number of scholars argue that these concepts come from the same root understandings and impulses. Ethics (the study of goodness) and aesthetics (the study of beauty and art) both have the metaphorical power to shape and reflect our lives. Jean-Luc Godard observed that whether one chooses ethics or aesthetics, the other is always at the other end of the road. And Howard Gardner (1994) suggests that the symbolism involved in making art is based on body consciousness and is a fundamental prerequisite of aesthetic practice. This ability to manipulate affective symbols is the heart and soul of artistic performance, and its recognition and appreciation are the crux of aesthetic perception—which, according to Dissanayake (1988), is the seat of ethical understanding and behavior.

If this is true, then art and design become a conscious and intuitive effort to impose a meaningful ethical order, to offer a bridge among human needs, culture, and the environment. Any concern for the future naturally requires that artists become involved in ethics and social responsibility. In fostering this outcome, aesthetic experiences inspire us by providing energy, passion, and renewal; awakening our imagination; and providing models for us to learn from and strive for. The relationship between the ethical and the aesthetic is that the aesthetic provides a vision and fuel for the ethical, and the ethical provides a reason for the aesthetic.

In this context, art for life has to do with making and critically receiving art that will contribute to improving the world. It involves teaching art with the goal of achieving sustainability of life on this planet through aesthetically framed ethical means, being mindful not only of humans but of all species. Guiding students toward increased social responsibility suggests fostering their creative seeing and thinking so that they can look at the world from multiple perspectives, breaking old routines and destructive habits and patterns of thought. The social reconstructionism of art for life fosters students' ability to look at the world and dare to ask, "What if it were different?" and "How can I make it better?" Ultimately art can and should serve as a bridge of respect and understanding between people and contribute to a global sense of self, of community, and of place. You will find that all the units presented in Part Three of this book adhere to this ideal of ethical development through aesthetic means.

What does it take to make the world a better place? In the context of larger social forces such as local and national standards and frameworks, art teachers and future art teachers need to closely examine their own aesthetic and ethical values and goals. Then tools for teaching and learning that further those values and goals need to be developed and put in place. To help you, Chapter Five, on aesthetics and aesthetic inquiry, examines many of these issues in detail.

CONCLUSION

This chapter began and ends with the idea that art should be taught for the sake of life and should focus on a sense of global community. Art education for life, therefore, draws from traditional, modern, and contemporary concerns of art in society for its content and strategies to understand art in cultural contexts. Two concepts of both postmodernism and traditionalism—the centering of art in the community and the centering of art in students' lives—are at the heart of art education for life. It is also valuable to retain the traditional emphasis on skilled crafts and elaboration of form, and the modernist idea of the student artist as an independent, creative individual. It is valuable as well to retain the postmodernist idea of critique, especially critiques of art forms and their philosophical foundations, and by extension the idea that there are competing philosophical systems or narratives.

Philosophically, art for life is a socially responsible way of thinking involving whole systems rather than fragments. It relies on collaboration and cooperation rather than so-called expert opinion or other authoritarian, top-down approaches to guide educational discourse. Art for life de-emphasizes the egoistic artist as a model for art education and emphasizes the collective and environmental good and social creativity. In seeking to make the world a better place, art for life is also concerned with the effects of our consumer culture as well as the controlling effects of mass media in the larger context of visual culture.

A fundamental premise is that art and visual culture convey something meaningful from one human being to another. The purpose of art education for life is, therefore, to help students understand something about themselves and others through art and move toward the (social reconstructionist) goal of making the world a better place for everyone.

The educational foundations of art for life are informed primarily by the philosophy of authentic educa-

tion. The premises of authentic education are that (1) teaching and learning make real-world connections; (2) it is important to construct knowledge actively rather than receive it passively from authorities; and (3) we need to acquire intellectual, emotional, skills-based, and expressive knowledge, abilities, and sensibilities.

The curricular structure we've developed as the means to accomplish these ends is a version of comprehensive art education, which in addition to the usual disciplines—art production, art criticism, art history, and aesthetics—includes a focus on visual culture, new technologies, and creativity. The instructional strategies to be used in this comprehensive curriculum are, most centrally, that instruction and inquiry are thematic; that inquiry involves dialogue and cooperative exploration; that students should undertake critical analysis of art and visual culture in authentic contexts, through historical and other contextual research and visual research; that they should develop skills in the practice of making art and creative expression; and that they should engage in critical reflection on personal and social meanings understood through the study of art. The primary themes suggested for art for life are a sense of self, a sense of place, and a sense of community. These primary themes encompass and contain all the other themes used as specific guides for instruction throughout the book. These educational strategies are meant to be interactive and mutually reinforcing and to be used within the larger context of comprehensive art education.

Finally, we address real-life issues in structuring and teaching art for life. These include, in particular, national standards and assessment instruments; the relationship of ethics and aesthetics in building a better world; and how you may be able to develop your own values and teaching and learning strategies in the context of national and state mandates. It should be reiterated here that if the goal of art for life is to understand ourselves and others through art and move toward a better world, then art is the means, not the end; and aesthetic activity is not only for its own sake but for the sake of personal growth and social progress.

Chapter 2 explores authentic instruction, the educational theory underlying art for life.

QUESTIONS FOR STUDY AND DISCUSSION

1. Discuss whether you think art should be taught for its own sake or for life's sake, and why. Do you think there's room for both positions, or does one necessarily eliminate the other?

2. On the basis of your reading in this chapter, compare and contrast the functions of art in traditional, modern, and postmodern societies. Which functions do you think are most important? Why? Which ones will you emphasize in teaching art?

3. Do you think finding out about what you think and feel and what others think and feel through aesthetic means can really contribute to global community? How? How can you relate this to personal creative expression in art?

4. Do you think art teachers should concern themselves with the contemporary culture of visual imagery and technology, or should the curriculum be about art, pure and simple?

5. What is comprehensive art education? What are the components of art for life as a model of comprehensive art education? What does disciplinary understanding contribute to interdisciplinary teaching and learning?

6. What do you think it means to teach art for meaning? How could you go about it?

7. This chapter advocates using themes as a focus in art education rather than the traditional focus of elements and principles of design or media. How does that change the structure of teaching and learning in art? What do you think are the strengths and weaknesses of teaching thematically?

8. Describe how and why thematic instruction should begin with and be centered in making and understanding art. How does art reflect people's values, mores, and concerns in its forms and uses? How does understanding the disciplines of art help you, the art teacher, be a better thematic interdisciplinary instructor, according to the text? Do you agree with this?

9. Look at the chart on page 10, describing activities and foci in art for life. Think about and discuss with your group which aspects of art for life may be easier or more difficult to implement with high school students, middle school students, and elementary students. Why?

10. Describe closed-ended instructional objectives and open-ended instructional outcomes and tell what sort of activity each is best at directing.

11. We claim that art for life fits very nicely with many of the goals and objectives of the National Standards for Art. Look at the Standards and see if you agree.

12. What is the value for the student of integrated or cross-disciplinary art lessons? Do you remember any integrated or cross-disciplinary learning experiences during your own education? If so, describe them and discuss them with your classmates.

13. The key to the curriculum you construct for your own classroom is your own values. What ethical, social, personal, or artistic values do you think are crucial in structuring a K–12 art program?

FURTHER READING

Anderson, R. (1990). *Calliope's sisters: A comparative study of philosophies of art.* Englewood Cliffs, NJ: Prentice Hall.

Art Education: Journal of the National Art Education Association 51(3). (1998). (This thematic issue, edited by Mary Ann Stankiewicz, entitled "Community, Art, and Culture," has articles by Therese Marche; Christine Ballengee Morris; John Howell White and Kristin Congdon; Catherine Coleman; Louis Rufer, Betty Lake, Ellen Robinson, and John Hicks; and Steve Elliott and Sue Bartley.)

Art Education: Journal of the National Art Education Association 52(4). (1999). (This thematic issue, edited by Paul Bolin, entitled "Teaching Art as If the World Mattered," has articles by Peggy Albers, Lisa Lefler Brunick, Michelle Wiebe and Zederayko and Kelly Ward, and Elizabeth Manley Delacruz.)

ArtsEdNet *http://www.getty.edu/artsednet/* (This ultimate online source for DBAE includes lesson plans, resources, and more.)

Banks, J., & Banks, C. (2001). *Multicultural education: Issues and perspectives.* New York: Wiley.

Bruner, J. (1960). *The process of education.* Cambridge, MA: Harvard. (For an understanding of discipline-based education, from one of its founders.)

Chalmers, G. (1996). *Celebrating pluralism: Art, education, and cultural diversity.* Los Angeles: Getty Education Institute for the Arts.

Dewey, J. (1963/1938). *Experience and education.* New York: Collier.

Dissanayake, E. (1988). *What is art for?* Seattle: University of Washington.

Efland, A., Freedman, K., & Stuhr, P. (1996). *Postmodern art education: An approach to curriculum.* Reston, VA: National Art Education Association.

Freire, P. (1973). *Education for critical consciousness.* New York: Seabury.

Goldberg, M. (2001) *Arts and learning: An integrated approach to teaching and learning in multicultural and multilingual settings* (2nd ed.). New York: Longman.

Grant, C., & Sleeter, C. (1994). *Making choices for multicultural education: Five approaches to race, class, and gender* (2nd ed.). New York: Merrill.

Journal of Aesthetic Education 21(2). (1987). (The definitive, Getty-sponsored articulation of discipline-based art education. Articles by Ralph Smith (editor); Evan Kern; Arthur Efland; Maurice Sevigny; Gilbert Clark, Dwayne Greer, and Michael Day; Frederick Spratt; Eugene Kleinbauer; Howard Risatti; Donald Crawford; and David Henry Feldman explain what it is and how it works.)

Journal of Social Theory and Art Education, 18. (1998). (This thematic issue, edited by Jan Jagodzinski, focuses on community and art education and includes articles by Deborah Smith-Shank, Rita Irwin, Christine Ballengee Morris, Seymour Simmons III, and Gay Leigh Green.)

Kovalik, S., with Olsen, K. (1997). *ITI: The Model: Integrated Thematic Instruction* (3rd ed.). Kent, WA: Books for Educators. (A great practical source for understanding integrated thematic instruction.)

McFee, J. (1998). *Cultural diversity and the structure and practice of art education.* Reston, VA. National Art Education Association.

McFee, J., & Degge, R. (1980). *Art, culture, and environment: A catalyst for teaching.* Dubuque, IA. Kendall-Hunt.

Neperud, R. W. (Ed.). (1995). *Context, content, and community in art education.* New York: Teachers College Press.

Sarup, M. (1995). *An introductory guide to post-structuralism and postmodernism.* Athens, GA: University of Georgia.

Wasson, R., Stuhr, P. L., & Petrovich-Mwaniki, L. (1990). Teaching art in the multicultural classroom: Six position statements. *Studies in Art Education, 31*(4), 234–246.

Whitehead, A. (1929). *The aims of education and other essays.* New York: Macmillan.

Wilson, B. (1997). *The quiet evolution: Changing the face of arts education.* Los Angeles: Getty Center for Education in the Arts.

More resources on concepts and movements, including traditionalism, modernism, and postmodernism, can be found in the Further Readings list at the end of Chapter 5. Resources for visual culture are listed in Chapter 3. Resources for creative personal expression are listed in Chapter 4. Resources for authentic education are listed in Chapter 2. Additional resources for this chapter can be found at the McGraw-Hill Web Link.

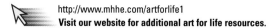

http://www.mhhe.com/artforlife1
Visit our website for additional art for life resources.

2

Authentic Instruction: The Theoretical Foundation for Art for Life

Girl in a Mirror, Lee Cromwell, Druid Hills High School, DeKalb County Schools, Decatur, GA. Betsy Epps, Art Teacher. *A moment of solemn introspection is revealed in this portrait of a young woman, providing a glimpse of her inner identity as well as her outer appearance.*

EDUCATIONAL THEORY: WHY SHOULD WE CARE?

A university colleague, teaching preservice education courses, recently shared a scathing evaluation of his department from an intern teacher. The intern was frustrated because the courses in his undergraduate program had done little to prepare him for the "real world" of teaching. The university had required courses in educational theory, but these seemed to have no application in the classroom, where managing students' behavior, managing paperwork, and raising students' test scores were the teacher's highest priorities. The intern insisted that knowledge of multicultural education, multiple intelligences, constructivist methodologies, written lesson plans, and objectives had been of no value when he entered the real classroom. He was, laudably, interested in knowing how to get immediate results from teaching; but unfortunately he had little interest in long-term goals or the potential effects of his teaching on his students or on society. Within weeks of leaving the ivory tower of the university, he had a new, pragmatic goal: to develop a formula for teaching that would ensure students' success on standardized tests.

This reductive concept of education currently pervades much of our culture. In many places the educational system has become so obsessed with students' achievement on standardized tests that many other educational goals have been ignored. In practice, the goal of education seems to be moving away from developing capabilities of mind and toward developing knowledge, principally of mathematics and reading, that can be measured on a standardized test—this being the only knowledge considered worthwhile. If students do not achieve these narrow educational goals, they are considered unworthy of serious academic consideration. This restricted definition of education closes doors to many students and limits the horizons of countless more. But although we believe that in many regards standardized testing is counterproductive to learning, it is a reality in many school systems today.

The intern's frustration was also a result of another damaging myth about teaching: the public perception that teaching is an easy job rather than a demanding profession. Teaching is hard work, requiring planning and dedication. There is no single formula guaranteeing students' success in every endeavor. In a world of instant coffee and fast food, individual growth can seem exceedingly slow, and efforts at reform in schools rarely last long enough to produce results.

Art teachers face additional myths regarding the value of art and art education. The model of the artist as mentor—or the apprenticeship model—may lead some teachers to question the need for educational theory and pedagogy. While mentoring may work well with small numbers of interested students, most situations in public school require another set of communication and management skills because larger groups of students are involved. Educational theories and pedagogy are embedded in each educational experience, as are aesthetic and artistic preferences. Art teachers should possess strong knowledge of content in the discipline of art, as well

FIGURE 2.1   AIDS Memorial Quilt *A view from the Washington Monument on October 11, 1996, shows the huge AIDS Quilt lying on the ground, stretching from the monument to the U.S. Capitol. The quilt demonstrates the commemorative power of art to inspire and communicate a collective collaborative response to human suffering and need.*

as comprehensive understanding of a variety of pedagogical approaches and strategies. Since art for life assumes that all students will be included, it is necessary for teachers to work with students who have many different learning styles, cultural backgrounds, and cognitive abilities; these students should find their own voices, interests, and styles rather than imitating those of the instructor.

Although educational reform and its variety of proposals are beyond the scope of this text, ideology is important, because belief systems provide the premises about values which guide decisions about practical education. Traditionally, a school may have numerous explicit and tacit value systems that provide direction, emphases, and functions and affect the structure, timing, and support of the programs that are taught. Ideologies regarding the curriculum may marginalize some programs, such as art, because they are not perceived as contributing to the overall achievement of all students. Also, because some educational goals are not clearly articulated, it is important for teachers to develop awareness and understanding of the traditional school culture—in order to function well in the school environment and also to work toward a more ideal learning community.

For these reasons, it is important to establish the ideological foundations for teaching and learning. Success in teaching depends on being clear about your aims and goals; clear aims and goals lead to successful strategies. Our model for comprehensive art education—art for life—is based on authentic instruction, which is described in detail in the rest of this chapter.

AUTHENTIC INSTRUCTION: THE MODEL FOR ART FOR LIFE

What Authentic Instruction Is

The curriculum of art for life is not a simplistic approach. It is complex, because life, art, and teaching are all complex experiences. Any attempt to oversimplify the processes involved denies the richness and infinite possibilities that each process may generate. Emphasizing the connections between art education and life challenges teachers and students to focus on the meaning of all educational activities. Such a focus requires an integrated, thematic, cognitive approach. This focus does not preclude study of the individual disciplines of art; in fact, it relies on knowledge of disciplines. Yet it does shift from the heart of each discipline to art of the borderlands, where disciplines overlap and merge. As teachers of art, we continue to give our students a foundation of art history, art criticism, aesthetics, and studio production. In 1984 a term was coined for this disciplinary focus: discipline-based art education (DBAE). But the strength of the current comprehensive model is due not to focusing on any one discipline individually but to blending and melding disciplines.

Because human beings are predisposed to seek and develop meaning, a natural goal of education is to nurture students' abilities, conceptual tools, and strategies in order to construct meaning and achieve understanding. One purpose of the comprehensive approach to art education is to make learning at school more meaningful, avoiding any fragmentation of subject matter by seeking cross-disciplinary, **integrated learning.** We learn facts, patterns, and configurations best when they are based on what we care about. People learn better and more deeply through powerful ideas—that is, when units and lessons are organized around key concepts—than by learning facts or techniques for their own sake. The goal of art for life is to create meaning and deep learning through a thematic comprehensive approach.

Authentic instruction is the system most compatible with, or most supportive of, comprehensive art for life. Through authentic learning, students may construct profound knowledge and meaning about life from experiences in the disciplines of art. Authentic learning often involves students in creating cross-disciplinary connections, which continue to evolve as they construct understanding from their own psychology and their own communal worlds. Much in the authentic instructional model is what good art teachers are already doing daily in their classrooms. Authentic instruction is conducive to teaching art; it offers a structure to help teachers consider strategies and approaches that best support students' learning. Authentic instruction is presented not as a prescribed method or formula for teaching, but as a guide for thinking about how we teach, what skills and content we want students to learn, and why.

Goals and Characteristics of Authentic Instruction

The terms **authentic instruction** and **authentic assessment** have been used by general educational theorists and by a generation of researchers working in all curriculum areas. Theorists describe authentic instruction as meaningful learning that connects to the real world beyond the classroom, and authentic assessment as evaluating students' learning in ways that respect the qualities of the specific learning experience, rather than through standardized indicators. Research suggests that authentic instruction and assessment improve learning in all social and economic groups, in various course structures, and with various contents. These qualities make authentic instruction a natural model for comprehensive art for life. In addition, the goals and characteristics of authentic instruction conform to those set by the **National Standards for Art Education,** the Interstate New Teacher Assessment and Support Consortium (INTASC), and the National Board for Professional Teaching Standards (NBPTS).

Research by Newmann and Wehlage (1993) delineating the operational goals and characteristics of authentic instruction is particularly useful in constructing an art for life curriculum. The goal of authentic instruction is that students participate in the construction of knowledge through disciplined inquiry and connect that knowledge to the world beyond school in order to deepen learning.

The three components of this goal—real-world learning and connections, **construction of knowledge,** and learning in depth—serve as basic educational premises and are supported by specific characteristics of teaching. These characteristics include (1) involving students in higher levels of cognition or thinking, (2) leading students in **substantial conversation** about a topic, (3) promoting social support for peers' achievement, and (4) developing themes for teaching that support integrated learning beyond the art classroom. It is important to remember that in the art classroom all the characteristics of authentic instruction overlap. For example, higher-level thinking is a characteristic we would expect to flourish during substantial conversation and in the construction of deeper meanings beyond the classroom. These characteristics are highly integrated in the art classroom, but they are examined individually in this chapter so that you can consider how teachers might best construct lessons that incorporate these student behaviors as indicators of achievement. As you read about each characteristic and its potential application to art for life, you are encouraged to discuss and consider other activities that increase students' performance for each indicator of authentic instruction.

BUILDING AUTHENTIC TEACHING AND LEARNING IN ART

Real-World Connections and the Construction of Community

The signature of authentic instruction and art for life is a continual search for real-world connections for learning. A key to students' motivation and engagement is the need for real-world, personally authentic problems. (An example of a

Kirby Meng, of Hickory Flats Elementary School in Henry County, Georgia, worked as a graphic designer for three years before beginning her teaching career, so she understands the importance of visual culture and communication. (See Color Plate 4, students painting a billboard.) She wrote the following description of authentic instruction.

"As an art teacher, I see the importance of students' constructing knowledge for themselves. From my viewpoint the teacher provides the environment and the content to be studied, but the more the content is presented in a real-world context, the better. I like to encourage students to explain what they see, hear, or are experiencing instead of explaining it to them. The more the students try to explain, the more they need to explore and seek out information; the more information they find, the more fully they can explain the topic.

"A lesson that I implemented with real-world connections for fifth-grade students is for students to create a personal logotype or trademark. This activity appeals to the students' interest in themselves at this age as well as to an interest in the visual environment. As I taught the lesson, we discussed the progression of the trademark from before Christ to the present time. Students were impressed that the purpose of visual communication in trademarks has not really changed in thousands of years.

"Following our discussion I asked students to come up to the chalkboard and draw a trademark symbol. They drew numerous trademark symbols for a great variety of products. After discussion about the use of lettering or type in logos they could easily distinguish between a logotype and a trademark.

"From the discussion about logos and trademarks it was a natural progression for students to create a symbol for themselves. They generated ten to twelve thumbnail sketches. These ideas were then adjusted, combined, and manipulated to create the final logo that could stand for each student.

"After our logo lesson we extended our discussion to include a study of advertising in general. This lesson culminated in students' touring an advertising agency. We timed our visit as a part of our Youth Art Month celebration, and the students painted a billboard at Lamar Advertising in Macon, Georgia. Equipped with sketches of their personal symbols, students enlarged and then painted these symbols directly on the billboard. While part of the group was involved in the painting process, other students toured the advertising facility. The artists at Lamar demonstrated design techniques and color mixing with computer graphics used in the planning phase of the billboard production.

"Looking back on this experience, we can see that standards of authentic instruction were addressed in many ways. Students used higher-order thinking to manipulate and synthesize their ideas in creating a symbol to represent themselves. They constructed deeper knowledge about the subject of logos and trademarks through class discussions and firsthand experience with the employees of Lamar Advertising who explained the various aspects of creating a billboard. This lesson connected the art class to the world by using an advertising form which students recognized as a part of their daily lives.

"There was a great deal of vigorous discussion throughout this lesson. Students talked about the logos that they see around them and the ones that they wear. They asked questions of the professionals at Lamar Advertising. Every student was engaged in the learning process through this lesson.

"In my opinion, authentic instruction is important in all classrooms, but especially in the art classroom. If a teacher can make art interesting and relevant to students, they will be anxious to learn about it even though it may not be their strength. Authentic instruction in the art room can bring interest and success to students who do not have a natural desire to learn about art and can increase the success of those already interested."

real-world connection is illustrated in Color Plate 3, *Banana Kelly Double Dutch*, 1981–82, a collaborative sculpture by Ahearn and Torres.) Real-world problems are by their very nature not only personally engaging but also socially defined because they reach out into the larger society. In this context, an art class can be a place where students work cooperatively to understand (and reframe) values and practical real-world issues. Such understanding frames the idea of community and the examination, construction, and reconstruction of community through art.

For example, in an elementary school, students focused on their personal connections to visual culture and mass media; discussed a number of logos found in popular advertising; and then developed personal logos that were displayed on a billboard. Understanding the artistic process as a vehicle for mass communication can open students' eyes to the impact of the visual arts on popular culture and daily life.

Another aspect of real-world pedagogy in art for life is understanding **social acculturation.** In *Pedagogy of the Oppressed* (1970), Paulo Freire discusses teaching reading and writing to poor people in Brazil. Although few art educators consider their students oppressed in the traditional sense of the word, we might consider oppression as it relates to acculturation. For example, many students feel the oppression of being different—of being of a different status, ethnic group, or religion. Meaningful dialogue, substantial conversation, and other substantive cooperation are the means for overcoming isolation, repression, and hierarchical attitudes.

If students relate only to peers of the same economic, social, neighborhood, or family group, their worlds become confined or closed in by walls of words. Attitudes may be formed early in life on the basis of class, wealth, and even birth order within a family. But as students encounter art for life, a learning environment characterized by cooperative authentic instruction, they may find their assumptions about class and status shaken as they learn of alternative opinions and unfamiliar cultures.

Ideally, education not only represents the acquisition of new information and skills, but also prepares students for growth and cultural change through discussions that encourage multiple perspectives and expand young people's sensibilities. For students encountering alternative views of the world, learning may become a process of reculturation. In a constructive classroom atmosphere and dialogue, a culture of critical thinking may develop. Issues of isolation, community values, and cultural understandings can be addressed through education in the visual arts. This can be accomplished when we see visual artworks as artifacts of culture and explore their meanings in a cultural context.

Collaboration may be one of the most effective tools in this difficult process of understanding, constructing, and restructuring community. As people's ideas change and grow, the most powerful force driving them is often their influence on one another. Books and teachers may offer the fuel for discussion, yet learning is actually manifested in relations with others. Beginning with examinations of aesthetic artifacts as a center of instruction and inquiry, students can start to explore broader cultural and intercultural understanding than would be possible if they remained isolated in their own social groups. Such exploration can start simply as a search for markers of hierarchy—beads, feathers, crowns, generals' caps, or sports shoes endorsed by celebrities. It can then progress to critical analysis of such objects, then to a discussion of these artifacts' deep social meanings, and then to construction of hierarchical or antihierarchical artworks set in particular social contexts.

Inquiry or knowledge in any discipline is socially constructed and interpreted through language and symbols by individuals who form groups and communities. Therefore, collaboration can bridge the gap between critical thought and life experience. In the example above, students' values and beliefs about art and visual culture and their roles in society are compared, and the social implications are examined. The teacher's job in promoting this cooperative model of learning is to design tasks that encourage students to discover and take advantage of group heterogeneity so as to build consensus. Asking groups to investigate even generic questions leads them to explore many important disciplinary topics.

Perhaps the most important task in this process is to unearth presuppositions and biases and to resolve conflicts that result from them. Being required to arrive at a position that the whole group can live with can hurl students headlong into the knottiest and most sophisticated issues of almost any discipline. It can therefore lead them to a firmer and more sophisticated grasp not only of the subject matter but also of themselves. Questions of philosophy, morality, and ethics arise. Such discussions connect students to authentic issues beyond the classroom, motivate them, and enhance their achievement in school and in life.

Here is one more point related to collaboration and the construction of community. When asked where in school they feel most important, students frequently mention extracurricular activities in which the support of their peers is crucial—in other words, they feel best in activities they personally choose. Even though they actually may work harder mentally and physically in these optional situations, students feel more positive about their accomplishments because they help each other, and because they have more fun here than in the traditional teacher-directed classroom. Group activities and cooperative interaction are critical in strengthening socialization skills, which act as a natural motivation for learning.

Construction of Knowledge

A basic tenet of authentic instruction is learning as an active construction of meaning rather than a passive acceptance and memorization of others' meanings, based on their authority. The idea that knowledge is constructed rather than given from on high suggests that teaching and learning are centered on community. Constructing knowledge implies that students will engage in higher levels of thinking as they analyze, synthesize, and evaluate information to create both personal and public meanings. Such high-level cognition engages not only the intellect but also the emotions and can take place through both making art and receiving it.

High-level thinking and the construction of knowledge do not always come naturally to students. These processes need to be facilitated in art for life. For example, Karen Hamblen (1984) describes aiding students' thinking in art criticism, from low levels of cognition as they describe the visual objects and elements in a work of art to mid-level cognition as they notice relationships within the composition to the highest levels, which involve interpretation, synthesis, and judgments about the work. Benjamin Bloom suggests that the lowest levels of cognitive functioning have to do with naming, describing, and memorizing, whereas the highest levels involve synthesis of knowledge, and evaluation. The construction of meaning and value in critically making and receiving art is an act that involves both synthesis and judgment, which is cognition at its highest level: the construction of knowledge.

Likewise, making art is constructing knowledge. Howard Gardner (1991) tells us that the artist shapes form and gives voice to perceptions, ideas, and feelings through manipulating symbol systems for meaning. In this context students should be encouraged to develop receptiveness for exploring visual culture, their own art, and the art of others. When art is seen as symbolic communication about things that count, students explore and come to understand not only their personal ideas and feelings but also the ideas and feelings of others. Making art can become social as well as personal development. When an expectation is established that students will demonstrate high levels of cognition with a focus on making art for life, personal reflection also becomes a respected and important activity.

One of the most common problems in the development of authentic instruction is the failure of teachers to set high expectations for their students. If expectations are too low, only low levels of cognition result. Students tend to learn as little or as much as their teachers expect; therefore, high expectations lead to high performance. Art teachers should engage students in learning that requires them to construct meaning beyond the mere acquisition of knowledge or the simple application of a concept. Fortunately, the National Standards for Art Education provide sophisticated standards: students are required to achieve complex levels of cognition, and as teachers develop appropriate levels of expectation, it is useful to consult these standards in creating cognitive activities in art.

The ability to understand and use interdisciplinary strategies is also an important factor in high levels of cognition. Since life rarely presents itself in the fragmented, disconnected, disciplinary school-day mode, it is important for students to understand how to identify and solve problems in various ways through the use of connecting topics or themes. Cross-disciplinary holistic objectives and themes can help students develop and assess their own higher levels of cognition. Research journals in which students develop themes, record questions, develop and document a knowledge base, make personal connections to art experiences, and interpret meaning are an important tool for developing connective, interdisciplinary

http://www.mhhe.com/artforlife1
Visit our website to link to the National Standards for Art Education.

FIGURE 2.2 *Collaborative Collage, Girl Perfect Exhibit.* Boys and Girls Club of Metro Atlanta, Youth Art Connection, Tracye Marino and Cathy Byrd, exhibit curators. *These young artists created a collaborative collage comparing popular culture's representations of women and girls and the implicit messages conveyed with their own self-images.*

thinking. These journals, described in Chapter 10, are also an excellent means of assessment: they can be evaluated by both the teacher and the student for organization and clarity of meaning in terms of stated aims and goals.

Substantial Conversation and the Construction of Knowledge
Substantial conversation is a critical component in high-level thinking and the construction of knowledge. In art for life, it consists not only of verbal conversation but also of visual conversation. The power of observation, crucial to artistic expression, is immeasurably enhanced by shared experience and dialogue about the nature of observation. If silence surrounds the making of art, the visual information many young artists may routinely gather will be only low-level understanding and stereotypes. Their ability to question or construct meaning beyond stereotypical responses may be limited. In constructing knowledge in art, as elsewhere, high levels of substantial conversation characterized by considerable interaction about the topic, evident sharing of ideas, and an improved collective understanding are essential. A simple example of this visual and verbal dialogue in constructing visual information in drawing is McFee's (1961) classic admonition to look at a table or a door and notice that, visually, it is not really rectangular from most points of view.

Substantial conversation may be directed to the art of others, allowing multiple ideas and viewpoints to emerge that provide alternative ways of looking at an image or situation. General guidelines for such discussion might include having only one participant speak at once, having elaboration of ideas by each participant build on ideas or questions of classmates or the teacher for a sustained period, and requiring participants to tolerate diverse viewpoints. If students are timid about speaking up or if one or two individuals tend to dominate the discussion, the teacher may have to devise guidelines to maintain a more balanced input. Obviously, the support of peers is crucial to a productive sustained conversation.

Newmann, Secada, and Wehlage (1993) suggest a number of criteria for assessing such conversation. These include (1) talk about subject matter that uses higher-level thinking to make distinctions, form hypotheses, and raise questions; (2) authentic sharing of ideas that is not scripted or totally controlled by the teacher; and (3) discussion that builds on the participants' thoughts to promote an improved

A CLOSER LOOK   Constructivism

In constructivist learning theory the emphasis is on the learner's active participation in the environment. Constructivist theorists do not suggest that there is no real world to know; they argue only that we cannot truly know the real world completely in all its aspects. As a result, they hold, we perceive and represent the world partially, through signs and symbols that we construct. In other words, constructivists consider knowledge to be constructed rather than preexistent or given by an expert or authority. Based on this understanding, however, some critics of constructivist teaching suggest that it is overly permissive and tends to lack rigorous content.

For many teachers, a constructivist approach involves balancing the increased demands of accountability and high performance standards with students' interests and needs. Any art class offers many opportunities for individual decision making, but constructing art lessons based on students' input requires additional collaboration between student and teacher. Linda Clay, an art teacher at the Taylor Road Middle School in Fulton County, Georgia, who is NPBT certified, describes her experience as follows.

"I began this unit by surveying eighth-grade students to determine what they liked and disliked about the art classes they had taken in the past. Then I invited students to assist me in developing a curriculum that they thought they would enjoy, with the understanding that we would still cover the state and district standards. Students were surprised to learn how much I'm expected to teach, and I was surprised by the students' range of interests and enthusiasm. As a starting point the students suggested a variety of media, particularly video and digital photography, as areas they wanted to learn more about. They also suggested specific projects. I developed a series of alternative assignments based on their suggestions.

"Students began the unit on photography by watching a video on the history of photography. The students had not chosen to view this video, but I saw it as a means of providing all students with a knowledge base from which they could make decisions about photographic direction and imagery they wished to investigate.

"Students were given a packet of assignments and support materials, which outlined a variety of photographic projects. They were asked to choose one theme to pursue. They discussed their interests so that they could form small groups of students interested in the same theme. Groups ranged in size from two to six students. The assignment packets provided detailed written instructions regarding the technical aspects of each assignment, and within each group the members worked together to help one another fulfill their specific requirements.

"During the next phase of the lesson, students began shooting their own photos using digital cameras.

"Once the students had finished shooting their pictures, they worked with their groups in the computer lab to create digital collages from the photos. I provided general instructions to the entire class in the initial lab presentation. From that point detailed written instructions allowed students to work independently in their groups. Students were encouraged to collaborate and became in a sense "peer coaches" throughout the project.

"The students seemed to have more positive relationships within the class as they worked together on the assignment. They used time more efficiently because they helped each other solve problems when I was not immediately available for technical advice. I believe this constructivist approach in middle school transferred more responsibility for learning to the students and promoted positive peer relationships and attitudes about the nature of learning in the art classroom."

collective understanding of a theme or topic. Assessment and evaluation of these conversations should be based not only on students' participation but also on the their adherence to discussion procedures and protocols, and on their cooperation.

Social Support for Students' Achievement   Closely allied with substantial conversation is social support for students' achievement. Ideally, achievement is cooperative rather than competitive, and support comes from teachers, peers, home, and the community.

With regard to support from peers, researchers have found that cooperative strategies among peers accelerate learning, improve retention of material, enhance achievement, and result in positive attitudes toward learning.

Teachers' support of students' perceived issues and needs is also very important. For example, a middle school teacher invited her eighth-grade students to assist her in developing an enjoyable curriculum that would still cover the state and district standards she needed to teach. Her students responded by suggesting media such as video and digital photography as a starting point. They also suggested projects they thought they would enjoy, and the teacher developed a series of alternative assignments based on their suggestions. The students were assigned to small groups to help one another deal with problems they encountered in a technological assignment and meet the criteria for the assignment. This constructivist approach gave students more responsibility for their own learning, promoted more positive peer relationships, and fostered more positive attitudes about learning in the art class.

Underlying social support for students' achievement is a message that the teacher cares. Before students care what you know, they need to know that you care. The same principle applies between students. A caring attitude is essential in how people relate to one another and is also a basic motivation for learning. Most students—even poor achievers—would like to get good grades, although they conceal this desire with excuses like "Work is boring, and nobody cares what I do (or think or feel)." In a classroom where a caring attitude prevails, the students as well as the teacher will make it clear that all opinions and all expressive drives are important and valid. In such a classroom, each student's self-concept is enhanced, and the quality of ideas exchanged and of the work itself improves dramatically.

Social Support in Developing Skills and Concepts   Although students are the ultimate judge of what is important to them, they are often given tasks that do not immediately appear to satisfy their needs or drives. Such tasks often involve developing skills and concepts related to making and understanding art: mixing colors, drawing basic contours, practicing and integrating basic art criticism, and so on. Today's culture stresses instant gratification, and students may have little or no tolerance for delaying gratification. In addition, even if they are working on projects they have chosen, many students have no strong support from their homes or their peers to bolster their sense of self-worth. As a result, they lack the perseverance to keep working when they encounter even the normal problems and setbacks of studio art process or the inevitable dead ends of research. Over time, such problems become self-perpetuating, lead to more problems, and make the students feel frustrated and powerless— a feeling often expressed as "I don't care about this and nobody else does either."

In teaching closed-ended skills and concepts, then, it is important to motivate the students by helping them understand how apparently unconnected skills and concepts may, over the long term, enhance their artistic expression. In student-directed projects and activities it sometimes requires a whole community of support to keep a student going—support from the teacher, from fellow students, and from home. This requires a sense of shared goals, mutual trust, communal knowledge, and understanding of the values of art for life.

The Value of Social Collaboration   John Dewey (1899) described collective inquiry as a mode of activity that is socially conditioned and has cultural consequences. Researchers have found that these consequences include tolerance for opinions other than one's own, and possibly even cross-cultural acceptance—a crucial factor in our ever-smaller world—as students discuss and collaborate on personally meaningful projects. Increasingly, collaborative strategies are being considered and applied in art education: in aesthetic inquiry, criticism, historical research, and studio art. Much of the shift to more collaborative models is a result of feminist pedagogy (discussed in Chapter 6), which emphasises collaboration, cooperation, and interaction rather than competition, isolation, or hierarchy. Examples of community-centered cooperative strategies are described in Part Three of this book.

Acquiring a Depth of Knowledge

The third major quality of authentic instruction is the acquisition of a depth of knowledge. Here, the operational component is at least as much about *how* knowledge is acquired as about the knowledge itself. Achieving high-level cognition

Elizabeth Willett of Fort Worth, Texas, is a teacher who has successfully used theme-based instruction. Willett used a Getty-Annenburg grant to develop themes for her entire elementary school. Art images were the primary point of contact with these themes, which were first introduced in Willett's art classes and then became a focus of instruction throughout the school.

For example, in one theme-centered project, fourth-graders went to the Amon Carter Art Museum, looked at five paintings of which the school had prints, and then came back and worked from "art links" (conceptual and aesthetic cueing devices) on the back of each print to develop a piece of narrative writing, based on themes set by the classroom teachers. The school committee framed the project so that it conformed to the Texas Assessment of Academic Achievement Skills (TAAS) for the fourth grade under the category "expressive narrative." To meet the requirements, each story had a general introduction, transitional words, an introduction and description of a character using much detail, the presentation of a problem, an explication of events, a resolution, and a conclusion.

Another example started with a general interest in Japanese art and culture and became focused on the story of Sadako, a Japanese girl caught in the bombing of Hiroshima, who wanted to fold a thousand cranes for long life. Sadako had made only about 600 cranes when she died of radiation poisoning, but she inspired many people worldwide, including Willett. She and her students, who felt a natural empathy for Sadako and for all victims of war, helped organize and marched in a Japanese celebration and parade (with international attendees) and developed a Japanese peace garden outside the art room.

"I love to teach art as an integrated subject," said Willett, "but I don't want to give up the qualities that art has. I want to be seen as an academic teacher. I don't want to be a frill. I want to be an essential part: someone who's included in the planning, someone who has input in what's going on in the school."

You can read more about Elizabeth Willett in *Real Lives: Art Teachers and the Cultures of School* (Anderson 2000).

(discussed earlier) is one aspect of acquiring deeper knowledge. We now discuss other aspects that also are important in art for life. Particularly important, as we suggested in Chapter 1, is an integrated, comprehensive approach to understanding art and visual culture. Thus we will also examine two important structural strategies: thematics and **webbing.**

In authentic instruction, students are expected to construct a depth of knowledge through disciplined inquiry. Thus rather than rejecting discipline-centered inquiry, art for life extends it beyond the limited scope of a single discipline. This extension entails developing understandings unique to particular inquiries—for example, art history or aesthetics—but also centering instruction in themes rather than in disciplinary strategies, media, or composition. In art for life, the goal is to find and use information and meanings and follow them wherever they may lead, including across disciplines if necessary. Instructional themes and themes developed by students are the primary strategies for involving students in making connections among information, strategies, and meanings found in separate disciplines.

Thematic Instruction   Using themes as a focus of teaching and learning is an important strategy in art for life. Themes give students an intellectual framework for connecting otherwise unrelated bits of information and modes of inquiry so as to find more relevance and meaning. Themes allow the structure of teaching and learning to be authentic—to include real-world content and processes. Themes are crucial to constructing meaning in making and receiving art.

A theme is a structure that holds subject matter and approaches together within a discipline and across disciplines. For example, suppose that a student is interested in ecological balance. That's the theme. The subject matter may be water. The disciplinary strategies for approaching water as an aspect of ecology may be many and varied. Water can be studied for its properties (chemistry), its critical role in life (biology), and how it moves and the diamond shapes made on its surface (physics). These disciplinary approaches to the subject of water may be informed by reading; by direct sensory perception; by drawing, photographing, and painting water (studio art); and by historical examinations of artists who worked with water in different ways and for different purposes, such as Bernini, Monet, and Ukeles. Aesthetic inquiry and art criticism may be useful in determining what ecological issues, if any, were addressed by the artists in question. Then historical inquiry may be used to examine the social attitudes the artists had toward water and their ecological awareness in that context. Developing thematic meanings also has a reflective component—for instance, thinking about the value of conserving and preserving water, what water means to our culture and to people in other circumstances and cultures (social sciences, philosophy), and the value of artistic activity in the pursuit of ecological balance. This component might arise from or lead into critiques of environmentally activist artworks such as Andy Goldsworthy's. In turn, those critiques can lead to new meanings derived from making and receiving art in authentic contexts. This sort of inquiry cuts across disciplines and uses varied strategies but is held together by the meaning-making purposes of the operational theme.

http://www.mhhe.com/artforlife1
Visit our website to link to resources and curricula related to Andy Goldsworthy.

The most useful themes in art for life center on fundamental human concerns: love, death, war, fear, status, work, community, and so on. Although the themes are limited, their use is unlimited because they can be drawn from a broad range of personal and social contexts. (A comprehensive list of themes is presented in the Introduction to Part Three). With regard to community, the themes selected should have both a personal and a larger social or contextual aspect. Through investigating meaningful themes, students can weigh and synthesize new information in relation to their own personal experience and so can create or construct new knowledge. The teacher should stimulate students' connection of their own personal expression to that of other students, artists, artworks, and philosophies; this will give them a sense of their place in the larger world and of the many possibilities for choosing and making meanings in that world. Each teaching and learning activity should be centered on some big idea or theme, whether it is teacher or student generated.

Teachers can trace and expand the exploration of themes by developing and maintaining an ongoing chart of themes related to the artists or cultures that are studied. This allows students to explore artists' styles and techniques and consider the intentions, aesthetic issues, ideas, and emotions underlying artworks. Ultimately, the students can even consider the sensibility of an era. After several lessons students may begin to compare and contrast themes or topics across eras and cultures. Issues or questions in aesthetics also can be recorded on a large ongoing chart of ideas or themes that students may revisit, relate to, and build on throughout the year. Eventually, the students will understand that artists not only express their own viewpoint, identity, and experience, but also those of their culture. Some themes are specific to a given culture, but many themes may be investigated from multiple cultural viewpoints. Understanding this connection is useful for students as they consider their own views and experience in the world in relation to their artwork.

An outcome of a deepening understanding of themes in art is that students may select an emerging theme to explore further in their own work. In constructing and exploring meanings, students need to sense that they themselves are developing their own ideas, their own themes, and their own direction. Research notebooks, described in Chapter 10, are excellent for that purpose. When students address themes in this way, their understanding increases: they connect their personal experience with larger universal themes found not only in art but in daily life. As a result, their confidence in their own ability to make and understand real-world meanings grows exponentially. Rather than a studio process with a focus on technique and formal qualities of design, the emphasis shifts to real-world content, initiated or agreed to by the student.

Webbing and Charting Connections   Charting connections is a way to facilitate depth of knowledge; it involves generating a web of associations. Webbing is a form of verbal and visual brainstorming that encourages participants to construct thematic bridges among fragmented bits of knowledge and find relationships between ideas. Teachers often use it as an instructional strategy within group discussion, with the teacher or a student introducing a theme for exploration. After the theme is introduced, students may brainstorm to develop a list of questions—things they want to know about the topic—based on the information they already have. This may be done individually or in small groups. As students compile their lists, subthemes or topics begin to emerge, and connections begin to be made, leading back again to larger themes, in addition to the original one. At this point the teacher may guide students in creating a visual web, or chart, that further identifies subthemes and typically generates other relationships and questions. Drawing connecting lines between ideas and concepts helps students understand their complexity and interrelationships.

For example, the web shown here was generated by students in a art education methods class involved in planning a high school art unit. One student was particularly interested in the art of the Holocaust, and it became the starting point for this brainstorming web. The instructor guided students to expand the central theme. Although the ideas generated tended to revolve around World War II and the Holocaust, a larger theme, "conflict," emerged. As the group continued to discuss war and conflict, the controlling effects of propaganda and the media became important issues to explore in making and talking about art.

This webbing strategy is closely allied to brainstorming, another guided method for generating solutions or ideas (discussed in Chapter 4). Prolonged conversations are also likely to emerge from webbing; they can be framed as aesthetic inquiry and art criticism (discussed in Chapters 5 and 6) or as historical inquiry (described in Chapter 7) and can frequently result in or be generated from studio production (as described in Chapter 8).

FIGURE 2.3   *Constructing a web of associations may help students brainstorm ideas and visualize the multiple connections of events, people, places, and concepts.* Web construction by Mandy Lebowitz, Georgia State University, 2003.

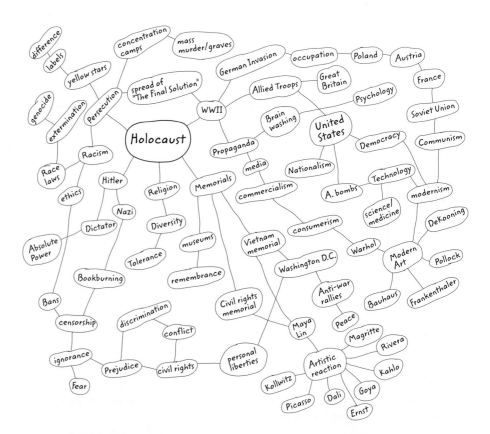

ASSESSMENT OF AUTHENTIC INSTRUCTION

Authentic assessment should be seamlessly integrated with authentic instruction. In fact, teachers often need to consider outcomes or standards early in planning in order to determine what levels of thinking and what conceptual understanding they want students to achieve in each lesson. In an authentic context, the purposes and strategies of assessment and the process of teaching and learning are linked. Establishing goals for students can help teachers develop expectations and benchmarks. In authentic assessment, evaluation is intentionally intertwined with learning, so that they are difficult to separate. The purpose and method of assessment should be readily apparent from the beginning of the lesson, yet allow for unexpected or new avenues of inquiry.

Another aspect of authentic assessment is that students play a role in developing and applying it. If students are going to play an active role in deciding on topics or media for research and on the qualities of their products, they should also be involved in setting criteria for achievement that reflect an understanding of those qualities. Students should take on a substantial portion of the task of gauging their own accomplishments, just as they are in large part responsible for their learning.

As a component of authentic assessment, evaluation in art for life should be ongoing, nonstandardized, and based on performance. It is important to understand that meaningful evaluation is not quick or simple. Ongoing assessments promote students' analysis and direction of their own learning and thus become a part of the learning process rather than something done at the conclusion of the process. To repeat, teaching, learning, and assessment are intertwined. The three major aspects of authentic learning—real-world value and meaning beyond the instructional context, the construction of knowledge using higher-level thinking, and the acquisition of a deeper knowledge—should be evident in all activities.

In art education for life, the most important outcome of assessment is not a grade, but a means of understanding ourselves and others as a community, and maybe even a means of changing the world for the better, even if only in a small way. That is the ideal, but of course art instruction takes place largely within public K–12 education and the strictures of that setting. Standardized outcomes and testing, therefore, often determine instruction. Some aspects of knowledge certainly can be ascertained through standardized tests, but a huge part of what makes us human cannot. How can you measure the truth of principles or ideals? How can you measure the beauty of a sculpture or the meaning of Picasso's *Guernica?* Certain profound human experiences cannot be measured easily, if at all. The arts deal with qualitative issues of value and truth, so much of the assessment of artistic activity must necessarily be qualitative. As you continue through this text, you will find examples of authentic outcomes and assessment that work very well in the K–12 context. These outcomes may be evaluated through indicators such as exhibitions, demonstrations, journals, portfolios, videos, and written or oral responses.

Such assessments require students to think, feel, and engage with each other in ways that reflect the real world and are more authentic than standardized replication of content or standardized testing. In authentic assessment, the overriding purpose is to create pride in and responsibility for one's own learning, as well as to document students' progress. For this reason, authentic assessment is often time-consuming and complex. Nevertheless, it is necessary: it connects evaluation directly to students' learning and provides a more revealing profile of progress for the student as well as for the teacher, which is, after all, the fundamental purpose of educational evaluation.

This suggests that a fundamental aspect of authentic assessment is the student's own reflection. Self-reflection is a key not only to assessment but also to the individual's processing of experience. It is a life skill. In art for life, it is a strategy for both learning and evaluation that helps students develop meanings, relevance, and coherence. It shifts responsibility from the teacher alone to the student and the teacher, with regard to developing and understanding meanings. Self-evaluation is empowering: it helps students to become self-regulated learners. Self-reflection, similarly, provides motivation and transformational learning in an environment where personal interests, values, and goals are respected and accommodated.

FIGURE 2.4 *Example of rubric for portfolio assessment with benchmark criteria and qualitative descriptions.*

Portfolio Rubric

	Excellent	Good	Adequate	Poor

Historical/Contextual Research
   Connections to
   other disciplines or events				

Growth in Artistic Skill
   Composition
   Technique
   Variety of techniques				

Reflective Thinking
   Critiques - self and others
   Interpretations
   Artist statements				

Problem Solving and Creativity				

Excellent: Elaborate, extensive written entries
     Generates questions as well as investigates contextual meanings
     Consistent evidence of project planning, growth in a variety of artistic skills and
     media, and innovative efforts
     Daily entries

Good: Well-developed, thoughtful entries
     Investigates historical and contextual information
     Evidence of significant artistic growth and synthesis of ideas
     Evidence of entries approximately every other day

Adequate: Entries cover basic project information
     Evidence of some research
     Little evidence of cross-disciplinary or event connections
     Some growth in artistic skill, craftsmanship, and creative approach
     Several entries per week

Poor: Little to no historical/conceptual research
     Low conceptual and artistic skill development
     Fewer than three entries per week

EXAMPLES OF AUTHENTIC LEARNING IN ART AS REAL-WORLD PRACTICE

Two examples of authentic art education are the Children's Guernica Peace Mural Movement and the Mandala Peace Project (described in Chapter 15). Both address real-world issues of war and peace, and both are particularly relevant now, in a time of international crises and terrorism, when all people on our small globe need to understand each other. Surely, lifeboat Earth depends on all of us to row together. Both projects also reflect the admonition to think globally but act locally—a good concept for socially activist art.

Another example is in addressing local concerns. In one instance, a teacher collected editorials from a favorite newspaper for several months. The students discussed these commentaries and the issues involved. After several weeks of discussion, they decided to respond to one issue by creating a public artwork. This involved a number of logistical problems, such as obtaining space and permission for this project, which were largely handled by the students themselves. As a final step, the students wrote a letter to the editor of the newspaper directing public attention to their artwork and their point of view.

The model lessons in Part Three center on artists like Krzysztof Wodiczko, Ciel Bergman and Nancy Merrill, and Fred Wilson, who use art as a means of social activism. These lessons offer students models of artists who are sensitive to the social and ecological environment and offer their artwork as means of reconstructing society in a more humane way. Wodiczko, in particular, has taken up issues, such as helping the homeless through his art, that have come to be known in educational terms as community service or service learning. Such service and the relationships established through it are a linchpin of community. As Bob Dylan put it, "You've got to serve somebody." These service lessons are important opportunities for students to recognize and respond to needs in the world around them.

Another example of service learning based on art is the Empty Bowls Project, begun in 1990 by the Imagine/Render Group of Oxford, Michigan, a nonprofit organization dedicated to positive and lasting social change through the arts, education, and projects that build community. The point was to engage students in a cooperative effort against hunger. The students created ceramic bowls and sponsored a soup supper and bowl auction to raise money for a homeless shelter or a soup kitchen.

http://www.mhhe.com/artforlife1 **Connect to the Empty Bowls Project and other socially conscious art through our website.**

Other service based on art might involve art students in renovating their school: cleaning and landscaping the grounds, painting murals on unsightly walls, and initiating recycling programs. Students could help redesign the functional aspects of a school in which space is poorly utilized or traffic flow presents a problem.

All these projects communicate to students that artistic thought is not limited to objects that are hung on a wall or displayed in a museum; rather, art is a part of daily life. Programs that extend these activities into the community direct public attention to environmental or social needs and show students that their artistic knowledge has the capacity to initiate and contribute to change in the public arena.

In these projects, as in all authentic art education, real-world value is increased as the students assume responsibility for understanding and developing meanings in various ways: through conversation, through interactive social support and research, through facilitating their own activities, and through presenting their own products, all impelled by the chosen theme. These types of experience are much more student-centered and community-centered than traditional teacher-centered practices. Students' work and students' responsibility for their work are brought into the world rather than being restricted to the school. Also, the real-world connections will be fairly obvious in these projects. One criterion will be the quality of the artwork produced, but in such projects, unlike traditional projects, evaluation should also consider the degree of responsibility each student takes for connecting classroom learning to his or her own life and to the world at large.

CONCLUSION

We began this chapter by asserting that it is important to understand the educational theory that underlies curricula and teaching and learning models in art and elsewhere. The chapter has focused on authentic instruction and assessment as the foundation of art for life. In particular, it has addressed the goal of authentic instruction: that students participate in the construction of knowledge through disciplined inquiry and connect that knowledge to the world beyond school for deeper learning. The three components of this goal are real-world learning and connections, active construction (rather than passive reception) of knowledge, and learning in depth. These three components serve as educational propositions and are supported by specific characteristics of teaching: (1) involving students in higher levels of cognition or thinking, (2) leading students in substantial conversation about a topic, (3) promoting social support for students' achievement, and (4) developing themes for teaching that support integrated learning beyond the art classroom.

Regarding authentic assessment, the chapter has suggested that it must be contained within and serve the purposes of authentic instruction—purposes that are neither simple nor standardized. Qualitative assessment strategies were suggested that are compatible with the qualitative purposes and methods of authentic instruction. It bears repeating that accountability in education is an important issue that teachers cannot ignore. If something is worth

teaching, worth including in the curriculum, then it deserves to be assessed. But standardized curricula and assessment are exceedingly limited in helping students find their way in life and know what their lives mean and are worth. In authentic instruction, art students may demonstrate more than the required standardized minimal knowledge and comprehension of art and visual culture. Through authentic instruction and assessment, students may engage in educational experiences that allow for construction of meaning and the potential transformation of their lives. Such experiences are empowering to both students and teachers who seek a voice in the educational system.

Finally, the chapter presented examples of real-world curricula and projects in art education. These projects connect students to each other and to their communities not only through personal expression but also through community service.

This chapter completes Part One, on theoretical foundations and general instructional strategies of art education for life. In Part Two, we examine specific teaching and learning strategies and particular aspects of the larger model of art for life. These include visual culture, personal expression, comprehensive educational strategies for aesthetics, art criticism, art history, studio art, and finally newer technologies. In Chapter 3 we take up the emerging field of visual culture and art education in visual culture, a topic and strategy of central importance to art for life.

QUESTIONS FOR STUDY AND DISCUSSION

1. Why does the text say it is important to study educational theory? Do you agree?

2. What is the goal of authentic instruction?

3. What are the three major premises of authentic instruction in support of that goal?

4. What sorts of activities are suggested in this chapter that address real-world issues through art? Can you think of others? Do you agree with the premise that art should be taught for (real-world) purposes beyond aesthetic appreciation? Why or why not?

5. What is meant by higher-level cognition or thinking? How is it different from lower-level thinking? What activities could students engage in to involve them in higher-level thinking in the art classroom?

6. Write two questions for students that require factual recall and two questions that require higher-level thinking. What is the purpose and merit of each kind of question?

7. What do you think is meant by depth of knowledge? How does substantial conversation—that is, serious topical conversation—engage students in more authentic learning?

8. Describe how thematic instruction is central to authentic teaching and learning and art for life. How does a thematic approach to art education encourage interdisciplinary teaching and learning?

9. Describe an instance when a positive learning environment or the support of your peers made a difference in your learning or achievement.

10. If a cooperative, collaborative atmosphere is encouraged, does competition have any place in the art classroom? Explain your personal feelings about competition. Is it important? Is it avoidable? Why or why not?

11. Do you feel that art can really benefit students in the world beyond the classroom? If so, how?

12. Why are self-reflection and evaluation important aspects of authentic assessment? Can you think of instances when self-reflection was built into your own educational experiences? Describe them and tell how they made the learning experience different.

13. What indicators of success are important in authentic assessment? Can you think of examples from your own experience?

FURTHER READING

Anderson, T. (2000). *Real lives: Art teachers and the cultures of school*. Portsmouth, NH: Heinemann.

Dewey, J. (1899). *The school and society*. Chicago, IL: University of Chicago Press.

Efland, A. D., Freedman, K., & Stuhr, P. (1996). *Postmodern art education: An approach to curriculum*. Reston, VA: National Art Education Association.

Freire, P. (1970). *Pedagogy of the oppressed*. New York: Herder & Herder.

Gardner, H. (1991). *The unschooled mind: How children think and how schools should teach*. New York: Basic Books.

Giroux, H. A. (1988). *Teachers as intellectuals: Toward a critical pedagogy of learning*. Boston, MA: Bergin and Garvey.

Hamblen, K. (1984). An art criticism questioning strategy within the framework of Bloom's taxonomy. *Studies in Art Education, 26*(1), 41–50.

McFee, J. (1961). *Preparation for art*. San Francisco: Wadsworth.

Milbrandt, M. (2002). Elementary instruction through postmodern art. In Y. Gaudelius & P. Speirs (eds.), *Contemporary issues in art education* (97–106). Upper Saddle River, NJ: Prentice Hall.

Neperud, R. W. (Ed.) (1995). *Context, content, and community in art education: Beyond postmodernism*. New York: Teachers College Press.

Newmann, F. M., & Wehlage, G. G. (1993). Five standards of authentic instruction. *Educational Leadership, 50*(7), 8–12.

Newmann, F. M., Secada, W. G., & Wehlage, G. G. (1995). *A guide to authentic instruction and assessment: Vision, standards, and scoring*. Madison: Wisconsin Center for Education Research.

Noddings, N. (1992). *The challenge to care in schools: An alternative approach to education*. New York: Teachers College Press.

Perkins, D. (1999). The many faces of constructivism. *Educational Leadership, 57*(3), 6–11.

Project Zero Website: http://www.pzweb.harvard.edu/Default.htm

Slattery, P. (1995). *Curriculum development in the postmodern era*. New York: Garland.

Whitehead, A. (1929). *The aims of education and other essays*. New York: Macmillan.

PART 2

TEACHING AND LEARNING STRATEGIES FOR ART FOR LIFE

Art Education and
Visual Culture

Coffee Break, Joseph Fullerton. Druid Hills High School, DeKalb County Schools, Decatur, GA. Betsy Epps, Art Teacher. *Joseph selected donuts as a popular culture icon to communicate a visual message about contemporary culture.*

INTRODUCTION TO VISUAL CULTURE

"We have become the organic self within a cocoon of artifact."

Susan Josephson

Most of us now live most of our lives in a constructed environment rather than in nature. We seldom see the moon, experience the rain without protection, or meet other animals in their natural habitats. We live in a constructed, climate-controlled world, kept consistently and artificially pleasant, in artificial light that greatly extends our days. Our very sense of space is mediated by our constructed milieu: eight feet high at home, ten or more at work, and almost always squared off except in the case of the car—the cocoon that protects us in the outside world when we move from place to place. Our waking, sleeping, breathing, growing, living, and dying are overwhelmingly constructed. We are cut off from nature, and our own constructions become our world.

Constant and ubiquitous in this constructed world are the electronic phenomena and vicarious experiences brought to us, especially on television and on the Internet. Ninety-eight percent of American households have televison, and the television set is on an average of 7½ hours a day. And when we're not watching television, we're at our computers. Increasingly, television and the Internet tell us what's real beyond our immediate environment. The electronically generated reality they present becomes undifferentiated from our own personal experiences, memories, and sensibility. We may know more about Ellen DeGeneres or Vanna White than about our next-door neighbor. If we watch the Discovery Channel, we may be more familiar with Ayers Rock than with the other side of our own town. Besides affecting our sense of relationship with people and places, these electronic media also affect our sense of time and history. Snippets, cutaways, sound bites, and instant replays are intended to keep us from being bored and are often more appealing and entertaining than real time, but they impair our capacity for sustained concentration.

Language and its linear, logical structures are becoming peripheral because there are so many entertaining visual images with weblike, divergent connections. The news comes to us as a news show—a packaged, predictable format consisting of theatrical fragments presented by perfectly coiffed talking heads as 30-second audio and image bites. The apparent order and control imposed on the chaotic content—murders, political upheaval, scandals, sports, the weather—are only superficial and are predetermined by commercial demands. Elections are won on looks and sound bites. As Marshall McLuhan predicted long ago, now the medium is truly the message.

That medium is mainly visual. Music videos on MTV often rely on slick, suggestive images to make up for a lack of musical talent. There are "visual learning" sections in bookstores; we find rows and rows of books in the computer sections with titles like *Visual Basics for Dummies,* full of instructions and advice on techniques for visual communications, for selling yourself through web pages, for advertising, and for business presentations.

VISUAL CULTURE EDUCATION

This increasingly visual world, constructed by human beings, is the focus of visual culture studies. To succeed in contemporary culture, people must be able to "read" this constructed environment, interpret it, and use the visual signs they find in it. In art for life, then, in addition to teaching the traditional high arts and fine arts, it is important to include the broader category of visual culture.

Visual culture consists of visual artifacts and performances of all kinds, as well as new and emerging technologies, inside and outside the art museum, and the beliefs, values and attitudes imbued in those artifacts and in the way they are made, presented, and used. It is a socially based approach in which making and viewing are as important as the artifacts and performances themselves: the social and ritual meanings of visual forms depend on people's embeddedness in culture for their understanding. Visual culture studies primarily take the consumer's viewpoint rather than that of a producer such as an artist, an architect, a designer, or a cinematographer. The primary purpose is to understand artworks and other visual artifacts, performances, and environments in their authentic contexts rather than to create, attain, or understand the heightened aesthetic experience that is at the center of education based on the fine arts. Many commentators have likened visual culture studies to visual anthropology. Much as anthropologists set out to understand societies (their own and others) through understanding art forms, scholars who study visual culture seek to understand contemporary society through its visual artifacts.

Visual culture studies are usually interdisciplinary. In colleges and universities this interdisciplinary program usually resides in cultural studies, art history, graphic design, and communications. It is a wide-ranging field that may encompass traditional art history and traditional graphic design at one end of the spectrum, and popular culture, television and cinema, digital technology, and mass media at the other. In terms of cognitive psychology, it ranges from traditional concerns with how and what we perceive to postmodern critique.

FIGURE 3.1 Margaret Bourke-White, *At the Time of the Louisville Flood.* Black-and-white photograph, 1937. *Visual culture studies are concerned with how we see and define ourselves, who has power, who doesn't, and why.*

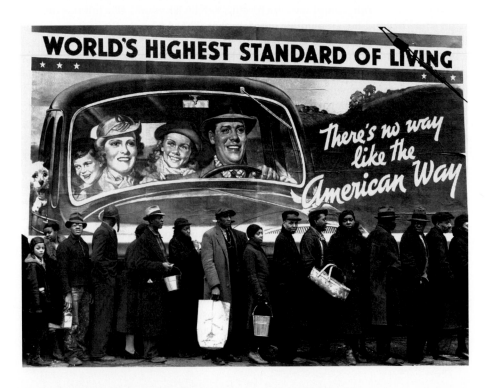

Scholars interested in contemporary popular media and culture often apply postmodern critique. Usually, these scholars have a reconstructionist goal. That is, they examine images and performances to understand the social foundations and ramifications of visual culture and frequently to suggest solutions to the problems they find. They consider images, performances, and aspects of the constructed environment in order to reveal intentions, meanings, implications, and philosophical premises; who has a stake in a given expression, and why; and what impact all this has on individuals and society. Their concerns are frequently with gender and social categories (how we see ourselves and others as men, women, gays, lesbians, people of color, people with mental and physical challenges, and so on) and with who has power and who doesn't and how power and powerlessness are portrayed. Because so many of the visual images we are exposed to are commercial, an important aspect of this study is advertising—its philosophy, goals, purposes, and strategies.

In visual culture studies, then, imagery is examined not for the sake of appreciation, but for the sake of understanding and being able to take intelligent action in the world. Because that also is the perspective of art for life, we have included **visual culture art education** as a component of this book. We agree with Walter Benjamin that it is important to have a visually as well as verbally literate population.

Some Roots of Visual Culture in Art Education: A Historical Perspective

As described above, visual literacy has many aspects, but here we will examine only those that concern art for life. First is the act of seeing itself: how we see (and therefore what we see), a subject rooted in cognitive psychology. Second is visual culture in contemporary society: what visual artifacts do and mean in society, a subjected rooted in sociology and anthropology.

Psychological Roots: How and What We See

Art education has been indebted to a number of researchers in cognitive psychology who have considered how and what we see. Historically, these include Jean Piaget and Rudolf Arnheim, who, among others, are credited with making the case that seeing is a cognitively constructed activity.

Rudolf Arnheim and Basic Seeing   In a cognitive psychology, sensory input is much more than mere reception. Seeing, hearing, smelling, touching, and tasting are the basis of thinking. For example, the human eye, our window on the world, has more than 200 million receptors. To people who were formerly blind but can suddenly see, vision is chaotic, indecipherable, and overwhelming; this suggests that seeing requires an ordering process to make sense: a connection between eye and brain. Aldous Huxley called the brain a reduction valve, saying that if we really saw everything received by the eyes we would instantly go crazy. According to Rudolf Arnheim, the sensory system that is the primary source of our cognitive life requires not only ordering but invention, imagination, pattern making, and so on.

Arnheim's work focused on pattern recognition, perceptual principles, and rules of shape and color. Beginning with his and other cognitive psychologists' basic research, many art educators have examined how and what we see. June McFee, for example, explored how our concepts (word structures) inform our percepts (visual structures) and vice versa. She pointed out that a round table may be seen as oval, depending on our angle of viewing, and that red literally changes color when it's in more or less light. She also noted how word structures—concepts—alter what we see. For example, if a round table is visually oval we may continue to see it as round because of the (verbal) conceptual constancy provided by the word *round*. McFee and Degge, in their classic text *Art, Culture, and Environment*, provide an entire chapter of drawing exercises to help us overcome conceptual constancy. The conceptual idea of what something "really" looks like in naturalistic or realistic art is, arguably, a false idea, since what we see is so strongly influenced by what we know culturally. Is Japanese *sumi-e* or English landscape painting, for example, more natural? That depends on who is seeing it.

Arnheim also made the case that thinking takes place only in a medium. He described thinking in a medium as involving grasping and selecting essential qualities of the medium that apply to a particular expression; then working with, simplifying, altering, and applying them; then presenting them as meaning; then going through the refining, shaping, and articulating process again until the form meets the expressive need. The essential point is that our minds must work with some material—language, paint, or musical tones—until that medium contains the intended quality of expression. This idea has also been important for art educators who are interested in the expressive qualities of art and visual culture.

According to Arnheim, making pictures, imaging, and reconstructing received images for meaning are crucial tools in making sense of the environment. The initial purpose of making sense is, of course, survival. Is that a mean dog or a friendly dog approaching? Is that truck on a collision course with me or not? Essentialist aestheticians and art educators argue that, in the realm of art, we have moved beyond mere survival to perception for the purpose of pure, heightened appreciation. No doubt that is true of purely aesthetic contemplation, but from a contextualist position, when we are dealing with art and aesthetic visual images, in addition to purely aesthetic concerns we want to know the meaning of the work and its practical effects on us and on our world.

Therefore, it is contextualism that most informs visual culture in art education. For contextualists and visual culture art educators, a basic issue is seeing and recognizing the physical and expressive psychological aspects of form, for purposes having to do with life beyond the form itself. They want to know how a visual artifact can inform them about the larger world. They have applied the notion, from Arnheim and others, that seeing is an act of intelligence, that patterns have meanings beyond themselves and can have an impact on the world.

Piaget on the Development of Seeing   Another psychologist who strongly influenced art educators' notions of how and what we see was Jean Piaget. Working with Alfred Binet on Binet's classic intelligence test, Piaget looked at children's incorrect responses and became convinced that older children were qualitatively different from younger children—they saw things differently. He believed that older children had cognitive systems and logical patterns that younger children simply did not have. The question he asked himself, and then spent the next six decades trying to answer, was how and when these systems develop.

Piaget was interested in the growth of intelligence, and he used his own three children as subjects as he tried to work out his theories. He argued that cognitive growth in children is active, not passive, and that it consists of two kinds of activities: assimilation and accommodation. **Assimilation** involves what one takes in from the world through the senses; **accommodation** involves comparisons between new input and what is already stored in the brain as schemata, patterns, and representations. If an existing schema can accommodate new information, there will be no change in it; the same is true of a classification system or a pattern. If new information doesn't fit into an existing schema, however, the person must alter the schema or create a new one. For example, suppose that all the artworks a four-year-old has seen so far have been paintings, but now she encounters a sculpture and is told that it is an artwork. She has to alter her idea of what an artwork is to accommodate three-dimensional sculpture as well as two-dimensional painting.

Piaget theorized that intellectual growth through assimilation and accommodation takes place in four universal or nearly universal developmental stages: (1) sensory-motor, (2) preoperational, (3) concrete operations, and (4) formal operations.

FIGURE 3.2   Mount Rushmore.
Each of us has a different reading not only of the ordinary world but of icons such as Mount Rushmore. What meaning do you think these people have constructed of this famous sculpture? How do they alter that meaning through their own presentation in front of it? Does it match your own values and understandings in relation to Mount Rushmore?

Piaget's Influence on Art Education   Piaget's theory had a tremendous impact on art education. His developmental stages dominated learning theory in art in the mid-twentieth century and are still well represented in the literature today. Viktor Lowenfeld, the leading American art educator in the mid-twentieth century, used Piaget's universal stages as the basis for his own creative and artistic stages of development. In *Creative and Mental Growth,* Lowenfeld linked the idea of (visually framed) intelligence in Piaget's stages to creativity, arguing that they are closely interdependent and that the creative process in visual art is transferable and contributes to children's general creativity. Lowenfeld's stages of development are (1) scribbling, usually between ages two and four; (2) preschematic, ages four to seven; (3) schematic, ages seven to nine; (4) dawning realism, ages nine through eleven; (5) pseudorealistic, ages eleven to thirteen; and (6) as a culmination, the period of decision.

Although in some ways Piaget's ideas have been superseded, his contribution has been valuable in alerting teachers to the idea of development itself, helping them to understand that children in their mental operations are not simply miniature adults. Nor is a child's mind like an open book with blank pages to be filled. Rather, children are different *in kind* as regards their learning operations—that is, in the way they learn as well as in what they have the capacity to learn.

The Role of Culture in the Construction of Seeing   Piaget and Lowenfeld, among others, held that seeing is thinking, that there are ways of seeing and stages of seeing-as-thinking affected by our human development. Trying to understand the qualities and patterns of human development in meaningful sight has become a mainstay of research in art education. But developmental theory has evolved considerably in the past several decades. Most fundamentally, we now understand that children do not develop in contextless universal stages as Piaget claimed. Rather, they develop in specific contexts, which influence when and how they develop. In other words, the environment children grow up in affects their development. That environment consists most significantly of human culture, framing everything from attitudes to schoolrooms.

http://www.mhhe.com/artforlife1
Learn more about developmental theory on our website.

Intersubjectivity and Human Development   Anna Kindler has found in her research that children's visual thinking begins with exploration of media. When children begin to draw, they attach nonvisual as well as visual meanings to the act. They also use gesture, imitative noises, and language in a holistic quest for meaning. This implies that even at the earliest stages children make meaning through their work. This establishes the making of marks as communication: in terms of visual culture perspective, as something to be read and understood. It becomes an aspect of dialogue that changes both the maker and the receiver.

Human development, then, is intersubjective. Human understanding is achieved through the senses in a social context. Whereas Piaget envisioned the infant's world as a buzzing and booming world of interesting but meaningless colors and forms, Jerome Bruner holds that the infant is already engaged in directed, sustained making of meanings. Children want to make sense of things even before they can speak. And it is in attempts to communicate with others—through cultural activity such as making art—that meanings are formed and refined.

Attempts to communicate through visual symbols bring a child's mind to focus and frame the child's ways of seeing and thinking: what he or she ends up calling reality. As they develop, children rely on the knowledge of others, who give them the feedback they need to understand themselves and the world around them. According to Bruner, through intersubjective interaction, a child gradually comes not only to find his or her own feet and to build an inner sense of self-identity, but to understand others, what they are up to, what can be done in the world, and how it operates. Whereas Piaget took an inside-out (biological) view of development, Bruner took an outside-in (cultural) view, arguing that a child's development is framed by established systems of shared meaning, beliefs, values, and understandings.

Langer and the Objectification of Subjectivity   Another important contribution to understanding visual communication was made by Suzanne Langer. Langer described art as the creation of perceptible symbolic forms expressing human feeling in a way unreachable by discursive (verbal) language. **Artistic symbols,** she argued, are "presentational" rather than logical or "discursive," that is, they present the subjective, affective, feelingful nature of life. Franz Marc's *Blue Horses* or one of Cindy Sherman's film stills, for example, can objectify subjective reality, feelings, and affects by giving them concrete form, making them conceivable and understandable emotionally as well as intellectually. The forms and composition carry the content of the work in a subjective, expressive way that makes them a source of belief, reason, even spiritual inspiration, and insight into our own and others' lives.

Langer argued that the dynamic patterns of human feeling find their best expression in the arts, and that the arts we live with do much to reflect and actually form our emotive experience. This is very important for visual culture in art education, and especially for becoming aware of the manipulations of commercial interests, as we shall see.

FIGURE 3.3   Cindy Sherman. Untitled Film Still #21, black-and-white photograph. *Sherman photographs herself in an immense variety of costumes and poses, usually depicting a media image of a feminine stereotype rather than a real person.*

Howard Gardner on Biocultural Development Extending ideas formulated by Langer and by Nelson Goodman, the cognitive psychologist Howard Gardner (1994) argues that visual communication, including art, is actually a language that relies on an understanding between makers and receivers about the symbols used, how these symbols relate to one another, and referents in the world. Gardner says that for preverbal infants, communication and perception center on what he calls modes and vectors, or body-centered, active ways of understanding. A mode is an affective state, a stance toward the world, rising from and understood from our body sense, our sense of ourselves as an organism: living, breathing, eating, coughing, defecating, feeling. Modes such as being open or closed, or feeling restricted, cut off, passive, retentive, or shut down all rise from our sense of our own bodies. A vector is, essentially, how the mode is carried. It gives form to and modifies the mode. Vectors give modes boundedness, directionality, spatial configuration, speed, density, force, and so on. Pursed lips, slouching, bouncing, and a furrowed brow are examples of vectors.

Infants' modal-vectoral activity tends to be characterized by analogy or mimicry. That is, infants copy. This is significant for human and particularly artistic development because it is the essence of engaging in the quality of something: for example sadness, depth, or blueness. Although mode and vector functioning is at first presymbolic, it leads to symbolic activity, particularly the kind of symbolic activity that centers expressive visual communication. Sensitivity to general qualitative properties is essential to artistic expression.

FIGURE 3.4 Young Child Making Marks, photograph, 2003. *A child in the presymbolic stage enjoys the kinesthetic exploration necessary for later symbolic expression.*

As children develop, they continue to feel and respond to direct experience and as an integral part of symbolic expression. The transition to symbolic activity happens as a result of a child's assimilating in his or her own body, through imitation, the physical behaviors of another. In the process, the child gradually comes to understand him- or herself as a subject, independent of and separate from the world of objects, events, and other people. As children's sense of self grows through imitation, their sense of "the other" grows also—through consciousness of the other as similar to themselves. Eventually, children understand aspects of the other in the abstract: a voice, a face, shoes come to stand for mother, father, or sister. This new understanding, or skill, can then be extended to stuffed animals, a favorite blanket, and so on. The feelings of relationship gained through modal-vectoral imitation develop into the first symbolic steps in communicative empathy.

Symbolic behavior and symbolic understanding, based on consciousness of the body, are prerequisites of artistic understanding. In expressive visual communication, symbols carry the message, and we learn their affective quality at the bodily level. We reach the symbolic level when we separate ourselves from others and from the world and recognize that a symbol is not the thing itself: a picture of a dog is not a dog. The essential aesthetic element is the affective qualities that are symbolized. It is not just a dog; it's a friendly dog, a nice dog, a dog we may want to pat. We know such things because they are modally-vectorally part of the picture.

This ability to manipulate affective symbols is the heart and soul of artistic performance. The recognition and appreciation of that ability are the crux of aesthetic perception and qualitative understanding of visual communication.

Gardner's research is important for contemporary visual culture art education because his findings support the early and profound influence of culture on human development. According to Gardner, we don't evolve naturally on our own beyond a certain point, and this point is reached when we are very young. In fact, he claims that there are only two major developmental stages; presymbolic and symbolic. After we reach the symbolic stage at about age seven, growth in expressive visual communication is cultural. It requires exposure to pictures, training in perception and making, education in affective response to images, and guidance as to how these activities connect with cultural codes. Gardner found that tutelage in these areas enhances children's discrimination, the way they make images, and their ability to pay attention to sensory and qualitative aspects of art. As regards visual culture art education, this is important, because children need to be taught to make discriminations about what they are seeing in the media and in popular culture. That doesn't come naturally; it must be taught.

The Social Nature of Symbolic Visual Communication   Symbolic communication involves designating one thing—a symbol or signifier—to stand for another, which is signified. What does this entail? First, it requires object permanence (a recognition that the world consists of objects that endure) and modal-vectoral sensitivity to the world of objects. This foundation allows both denotative (direct) and connotative (subliminal, implied) aspects of a symbol to be understood. It also entails understanding the relationships between symbols, or what might be called the symbol code, which is culturally constructed.

Within the code, symbols have referents not only in the material world but also among other symbols, which are designated by the culture as standing for feelings or concepts often related to signified objects. Because they naturally integrate affect—feelings—artistic symbols are also frequently presentational rather than discursive. That is, they don't so much direct us to action as invite us to contemplation. All this implies that during the stage of symbolic development, knowledge of the code and tradition is a necessary acquisition.

A cultural symbolic code has formal aspects (style, composition) and referential aspects (thematic content). The way style carries content is the expressive stuff of art.

In essence, seeing is based on biology and framed by culture. We all have similar sensory equipment, but at an early age the ways we use it to construct meaning become increasingly social. We have an innate desire to communicate; our communication begins with imitation of others' communications, but as we learn to use the system we become increasingly individuated. It follows from the nature of visual communication and our biological modal-vectoral nature that education in visual thinking should ideally proceed from the general to the specific, from mere recognition of symbols and patterns to specific and particular solutions of expression, meaning, and understanding in art and visual culture.

Visual Communication and Constructed Reality   Clearly, social reality is constructed by the people who are engaged in it, rather than being simply given from on high. Years ago, John Berger held what we see is determined by what we believe, and, even more profoundly, that vision is reciprocal. That is, if we see we can also be seen. Seeing is reflexive. It makes us who we are.

The images we make are an extension of our reflexivity. Every image, photograph, painting, or advertisement embodies a way of seeing. There is no such a thing as a neutral image. Every image embodies the point of view and values of its maker. Further, every image maker is part of a culture and is influenced by it. Deliberately or not, the maker's values, mores, and cultural sensibility will be reflected in the image. Art and design are cultural artifacts and performance; they are visual culture, and they reflect their society.

Anthropological Roots

Two theorists who have contributed greatly to socially based ideas in art education are Richard Anderson and Ellen Dissanayake. Anderson, in *Calliope's Sisters*, examined aesthetic sensibility and rationales and uses for art in ten cultures; he found that although the impulse to make art is universal, the forms it takes are local and cultural. Anderson defined art as "culturally significant meaning encoded in an affecting sensuous medium." Based on this definition, he claimed a meaningful system of symbolic communication is developed and understood in a group context.

Symbolic meanings, as Saussure first noted, are not natural or given but assigned through social agreement.

Dissanayake (1988) takes an etiological approach to visual culture. She asks why art is found everywhere, in all cultures. Her answer is that art is more than just nice; it is necessary. It is a human strategy for survival. She argues that we are a successful species because we cooperate in groups; we therefore must share mores, values, and ways of doing things. We bond with each other, and we form and reinforce values through ritual behavior (ceremonies, festivals, initiations, religious services, and the like), and that is where art comes in. Art (masks, dances, posters, stained-glass windows, advertisements) causes us to pay attention to the values and mores that are promoted through rituals. Dissanayake has stated that the social purpose of art is mutuality, a passage from feeling into shared meaning.

Contextualist Roots

Following from the concerns of Anderson, Dissanayake, and other social scientists, contextualist art education has focused primarily on the meaning of artworks and visual artifacts, rather than on aesthetic experience or understanding for its own sake. Some contextualist educators have been content to describe this phenomenon. Others have moved a step further, into **social reconstructionism.** That is, they have examined visual culture as reflecting social reality and have used their critiques to suggest what's wrong in society and how wrongs can and should be righted.

One of the first and most influential contemporary reconstructionists was June King McFee. McFee, whose husband was an anthropologist, adopted the anthropological method now common among visual culture art educators; she advocated an art curriculum that would seek communicative significance and social meaning. Many of her students—including Kristin Congdon, Doug Blandy, and Graham Chalmers—have carried on that idea in that they take pluralistic and multicultural approaches to art education, arts administration, and art therapy.

Another art educator who engaged the anthropological method was Edmund Burke Feldman. In *Becoming Human through Art,* Feldman explored anthropological, social, cultural, and historical dimensions of art as a foundation for teaching and learning. Another art educator who should be mentioned is Laura Chapman, who is still active today and has produced an enormous body of work for preservice art educators and for K–12 art students. Almost all her work addresses the role of art in contemporary society. Many other current art educators are also exploring social approaches to visual communication; they include Brent Wilson, Patricia Stuhr, Don Krug, and Terry Barrett, among others. Within this contextualist and socially reconstructionist movement a number of art educators are focused on visual culture. Notable among them are Doug Boughton, Kerry Freedman, Kevin Tavin, and Paul Duncum, whose work is discussed below.

http://www.mhhe.com/artforlife1
To learn more about these art educators visit our website.

CONTEMPORARY TRENDS: VCAE

Core Concerns

The point of **"visual culture art education" (VCAE)** is to grasp the meanings of expressive visual artifacts and performances in order to achieve personal and social success in the arena of life. As Duncum points out (Duncum & Bracey, 2001), the social categories that separate art from other objects or activities have collapsed, so that art is no longer a special, privileged domain but simply a way of communication—as common as talking or writing and just as much a part of the fabric of everyday life. Visual culture includes all visual artifacts and performances, from traditional high art to theme parks and shopping malls, and also the popular arts. The literature about VCAE emphasizes the media and consumer culture.

FIGURE 3.5 Rene Magritte, *The Treason of Images*, 1929. Oil on canvas, 21½ x 28½ in. *How a visual image is labeled may totally change the meaning assigned by the viewer. The words say, "This is not a pipe." Ask yourself, if it's not a pipe, what is it?*

VCAE focuses on the artifact in its context—the culture where it is made and used. The object or performance is thought of as representing its society. Thus visual culture deals in the social, economic, and political embeddedness of artifacts and performances. Artworks are said to reflect and constitute social mores and values confirming or challenging the social and political order. Duncum is particularly interested in second-order symbolization, which reflects not just information but values and beliefs; that is, he is concerned with semiotics, or the meaning of signs. Examples of semiotics might be what the clerestory constructed for the roller coaster in the Mall of America represents or signifies, or trying to determine what values are embedded in the latest ad for the Gap.

The Viewpoint of VCAE In VCAE, aesthetic experience informs our response to visual culture, helping us to understand its seductiveness and immediacy, which do not always have positive effects. But the point of inquiry is not to attain heightened aesthetic response; rather, it is to determine meaning by examining all forms of visual culture. The purpose of understanding is to achieve a perspective that helps us live more successfully—ideally, more democratically. In VCAE, meaning lies not only in the qualities of the visual object itself, and not only in the observer's response, but also in the relationship of the object and viewer in their authentic social context. The term for this is *textuality*. Textuality combines the ability of a symbolized performance or object to convey meaning and the capacity of the observer to receive and understand it in a shared context. The (social) conditions in which meanings occur are therefore of as much concern as the conditions of the object and receiver.

Many modernists argued that a visual image should be able to speak for itself, that if it had to be explained it was a failure. In contrast, most contemporary artists and scholars hold that visual and verbal communication are increasingly interdependent, that how we label a visual image verbally makes all the difference in the world. Meanings are embedded in culture and determined by culture. The neo-Nazi's swastika is very different from the Hindu's swastika in meaning and social significance, even though the two look alike. A premise of VCAE is that whereas forms themselves may be universal, their meanings are culturally determined and locally specific.

Another premise, even more basic, is that we see what we know and know what we see. There is an old adage: be careful what you seek, because that's what you'll find. This suggests that seeing is not natural or neutral but is literally determined by our concepts, precepts, and purposes. If we are looking for seashells at the beach, we may not see clouds. Conceptually, if we're looking for literal meaning—for example, in Serrano's *Piss Christ* or in an ad for a Dell computer—we may miss the implied meanings.

The point is that seeing is cultural, and that much of what we see is implied, beneath the surface, invisible to those who don't know the cultural code. VCAE is based on this concept. It continues the contextualist tradition in art education, examining the contexts of visual artifacts and performances—production, reception, functions—as well as the technique and composition.

Critique: The Primary Method of VCAE   Visual culture is a human construction: People make it, and at its heart are people's values, mores, and sensibilities. To unearth these meanings from visual artifacts and performances, the postmodern strategy of critique is the primary teaching and learning tool for visual culture art education. Critique may take both verbal and visual forms. The point is to make what is hidden and invisible in a work visible, that is, to understand how aesthetic images and performances convey meanings as well as to understand the meanings conveyed. Making art and visually critiquing artifacts and performances go hand in hand in this.

Critical understanding for the purpose of empowerment is the primary goal of VCAE. Empowerment means that students explore their own meanings rather than passively accepting meanings from a book or a teacher. The starting point is students' own cultural experience. Visual and verbal critique should, therefore, come from an examination of questions relevant to the students' own lives in and beyond school. This critical pedagogy is a component of VCAE and more broadly of art for life.

Because VCAE examines images in their social, political, and historical contexts, it is also inherently cross-cultural. VCAE considers how different societies

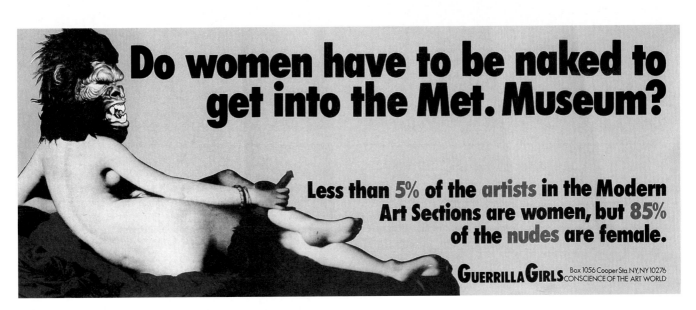

FIGURE 3.6 The Guerrilla Girls, *Do Women Have to Be Naked to Get into the Met. Museum?* 1989. Poster, 11 x 28 in (27.9 x 71.1 cm). Private collection. *The Guerrilla Girls were named both for the gorilla masks they wear to disguise their identities and for the guerrilla warfare-like tactics used in their public relations battle for equal representation of women artists in the art establishment.*

A CLOSER LOOK

The Ethnographic Gaze—An Example of Performance Art as Critique

In the 1990s, the performance artists Coco Fusco and Guillermo Goméz-Peña created a satirical commentary on western concepts of the exotic primitive, the so-called "Other," by displaying themselves as newly discovered noble

FIGURE 3.7 Guillermo Goméz-Peña and Coco Fusco; *Ritual Offering,* installation. *The two artists portray fictional indigenous people from an imaginary island in the Gulf of Mexico, displayed in cages satirically reminiscent of traveling carnival displays early in the twentieth century. In this performance the artists present a ritual welcoming Columbus to their homeland.*

savages. They dressed in feathers, grass skirt and breechcloth, chest plates, beaded necklaces, and dark glasses, and put themselves in a golden cage, presenting themselves as Amerindians from an island in the Gulf of Mexico that had somehow been overlooked by Europeans for 500 years. They called their homeland Guatinau and themselves Guatinauis.

In the cage, they performed tasks such as sawing voodoo dolls in half, lifting weights while watching TV, and working on a laptop computer. A donation box, placed near a description of their habitat, announced that Fusco would dance to rap music for a small fee and Goméz-Peña would tell authentic Amerindian stories (he did, but in a nonsensical language). "Zoo guards" were on hand to speak to the visitors on behalf of the primitives, who couldn't understand them, and to take Fusco and Goméz-Peña to the toilet on leashes. In addition, a peek at authentic Guatinaui male genitals could be had for $5.

In this "reverse ethnography," the performers observed the observers observing them. Their performance was intended to be about making a fetish of so-called primitive peoples and "decontextualizing" and destroying indigenous culture by removing its authenticity and imposing Euro-American culture and the Euro-American "gaze." It was intended to convey the distancing and objectification that make possible genocide, slavery, and the seizure of lands in the name of a king, or Jesus, or national security.

Unexpectedly, many viewers thought that Goméz-Peña and Fusco were really Gautinauis. Also unexpectedly, many intellectuals and artists thought that the performers were misinforming the public. Being taken literally by a public that seemed unable to appreciate subtlety suggested to Fusco the "colonial unconsciousness" of American society. Although now people are generally not displayed against their will, Fusco concluded, to her dismay, that a desire persists to look at "otherness"—freaks and savages—from a safe distance. Racism, elitism, and cultural ethnocentrism were all on display to the performers just outside the bars of their cage.

create identity through visual culture and how they respond to the increasingly universal corporate imagery. Thus aesthetics becomes a social issue. It broadens aesthetic examination beyond high art to T-shirts, corporate logos, media campaigns, shopping malls, theme parks, television, and so on.

A frequent result of critiques of visual culture is social reconstruction. That is, the critiques examine a given concept that represents social power; deconstruct the assumptions, values, and mores at the heart of these privileged constructions in order to find contradictions, disjunctions, and dysfunctions; and thereby move them out of their positions of power. Then other values, mores, and institutions are moved from the periphery to the center. For example, the Guerrilla Girls, feminist critics of what they see as the patriarchy of the art museum establishment, use ver-

A Pedagogical Framework for VCAE

In a National Art Education Association Advisory (spring 2002), Doug Boughton outlined a pedagogical position for VCAE agreed to at a conference on that topic.

1. Focus on curriculum content that is conceptually based, interdisciplinary, and socially relevant through creating and responding to images, artifacts, and performances.

2. Encourage students to take responsibility for their learning under the guidance of a teacher who initiates experiences with a full range of visual culture.

3. Expand awareness and use of newer visual media and alternative sites of teaching and learning.

4. Engage the perspectives of artists who create a variety of forms of visual culture to broaden students' imaginations and inform critiques.

5. Encourage learners to reflect on the relationship of visual culture to the construction of identity, the richness of global cultures, and the integrity of natural and human-made environments.

6. Assess student work using long-term reflective methods and criteria developed and refined by ongoing debate among stakeholders (including students, teachers, and community members) to determine the nature of knowledge acquisition and application.

bal and visual critiques to undermine male-dominated institutions and advocate feminist values and institutions in art. Another example is the conceptual artist Barbara Kruger (discussed in Chapter 9), who challenges male dominance and the strategies and assumptions of corporate America. Still another example of social-reconstructionist critique is that of the artists Guillermo Goméz-Peña and Coco Fusco in their installation and performance piece *Two Undiscovered Amerindians*, described in the sidebar.

In Chapter 5 we describe strategies for aesthetic inquiry; in Chapter 6 we describe three methods for deriving meaning from works of art and expressive visual artifacts and performances. These strategies are compatible with VCAE and have been designed for use with visual culture as well as works of art. This chapter contains a critique for understanding meanings in advertising (in an sample curriculum unit), following the discussion below of the content of VCAE. In the sidebar, we present a potential pedagogical framework for VCAE in general.

The Content of VCAE

The content of VCAE is the broad range of visual culture we are all exposed to every day. Since the traditional fine arts play only a small role in our lives today, the focus is primarily on the popular arts and popular culture. Carried increasingly by newer media, popular art, design art (including the built environment), and advertising art surround us and exert ever more influence over our values and decisions. The majority of created imagery is made for commercial purposes and broadcast on commercial mass media. Therefore, it is increasingly to the mass media and the popular arts that we need to look for the causes of our values and decisions. The central questions are not what these forms have in common that make them art, but what social and cultural functions they have. We should care not about whether they are beautiful but about what they do.

When we attend to this vast array of human-made visual environments, artifacts, and performances, we focus, at the very

If only calories didn't count...

Victoria Thins

SURGEON GENERAL'S WARNING: Smoking Causes Lung Cancer, Heart Disease, Emphysema, And May Complicate Pregnancy.

FIGURE 3.8 *Simulated Cigarette Ad.* Georgia State University, 2003. *In a student rendition of a contemporary cigarette ad, the model holds up one hand rejecting food and possible weight gain, while holding a cigarette in the other hand as her preferred alternative to eating, regardless of the potential health hazards of smoking.*

Smoking kills more Americans each year than alcohol, cocaine, crack, heroin, homicide, suicide, car accidents, fires, and AIDS <u>combined</u>.

FIGURE 3.9   Melissa Antonow, *Come to Where the Cancer Is*, 1989. Subway car poster ad. *As the winner of a student poster contest, Melissa's artwork was replicated and hung in the New York subway system, until objections from a cigarette company forced its removal. Her work presents a visual critique of the original cigarette ad's message.*

least, on the popular arts, including television, movies, and video games; the design arts, including everything from coffee cups to the Mall of America; advertising and other commercial arts; and as much fine art as we actually see in everyday life.

Understanding the visual environment is important because children and young people are formed by their culture, and at the beginning of the twenty-first century, our culture is overwhelmingly constructed and overwhelmingly visual. This constructed environment projects and construes meanings, intentional and unintentional, sincere and manipulative, that constantly communicate something to somebody. Living successfully in this environment requires that we understand what is being communicated. The messages we receive through the media need to be understood in terms of their intent and of who benefits from them, and how.

We also need to understand what we mean by "reality." We work at computers; get money from ATMs; and find entertainment, enlightenment, and solace at the movies, on television, in digital games, or on the Internet. We record our lives and programs on the media with digital or video cameras and replay them over and over for ourselves and others until some images become part of our collective psyche: the planes hitting the World Trade Towers, the boxcars full of people in *Schindler's List*, Homer Simpson's selfish ineptitude. Which of these images are "real"? How can we tell? These questions are important because television and computers are a huge part of our everyday experience. According to Susan Josephson (1996), television has become our primary sensory input and cultural guide, and computers, connected on the Internet, have become our externalized mind.

It is sometimes argued that commercial interests—interests which see children primarily as consumers—have the greatest influence and pedagogical power over youngsters and actually construct the truth. Consequently, some people ask whether education should continue to transmit culture as it has done traditionally, or whether it should it defend children against culture.

The postmodern shift from primarily spoken and written communication to predominantly visual communication, along with the increasing commercialization of visual images, gives art education an opportunity to counteract potentially manipulative media influences in society as framed by the popular arts, the built environment, and advertising. This is a primary impetus for VCAE. The concern in examining a visual object or performance is not a status designation so much as an empirical description of what it does, why, and how. Art has the power to stimulate, reflect, and reinforce mental and emotional attitudes, or states of consciousness and this power is the focus of the examination.

As we consider the content of VCAE, we will look briefly at fine art, and then at popular art, design and environmental arts, and advertising.

Fine Arts   VCAE takes the view that fine art is not the most important art form in postmodern society. Since by and large it takes an aesthetic and disinterested stance, it speaks to a limited community. Fine art is not the force driving contemporary culture. It may critique society. However, although the fine arts can usefully be studied for their perspective on contemporary society, that shouldn't be the focus of VCAE. Fine art simply isn't as large a factor in most people's lives as the popular arts and their everyday built environment, and so should be less of a factor in VCAE.

Popular Arts   With the growth of science and logic in western culture there has been a corresponding decline in narrative and myth. But we need myths and

FIGURE 3.10   Jeff Koons, *Michael Jackson and Bubbles*, 1988. Ceramic, 42 x 70½ x 32½. *Koons mimics popular culture kitsch as he reverses the visual situation of popular art mimicking fine art.*

stories to make sense of our lives, to give them meaning beyond the facts, to help us recognize the nature and value of our experience. According to Josephson, this role increasingly is being assumed not by religion or traditional philosophy but by popular arts and culture. The popular arts provide vicarious experiences and narratives. In fact, the power of popular art is its narrative function. It tells us who we are and who we might be. A form such as soap opera shows us possible life experiences; creates myths (such as a Caribbean island as heaven); and thus gives us values, goals, and desires. Popular art also gives us gods in the form of Ted Turner, Shaquille O'Neal, and Jennifer Lopez, and gives us strategies for reaching them and being like them.

Movies give us vicarious experiences and video then lets us live any such experience over and over until it is set in our psyche and affects our understanding and ways of being. (Do you remember Melanie Griffith's character in *Something Wild* or Orlando Bloom's in *Lord of the Rings?* How many times have you seen them do exactly the same things? How real are these characters in your memory? Have their actions become part of your own psyche?) The popular arts not only reinforce but create cultural values.

Design Arts and the Built Environment   The design arts have replaced unique handmade works with manufactured items and habitats (clothes, cars, furniture, houses) for which psychological cues are provided so that they will seem useful, attractive, and desirable. The point is to sell these objects to consumers. The design arts package messages and functions that are married to industry.

Contemporary design has a narrative function related to market pressures. It tries to assuage consumers' fears and provide what they lack by offering hope and security in the form of products. It represents values, not just aesthetics. Sensual female forms, football heroes, cartoon heroes and antiheroes such as Sponge Bob, and all the values they represent become part of products from lampshades to automobiles. A product is not just a phone or a CD player or a coffee mug but an object of desire because of the values built into it. Contemporary design, beyond the necessary functional aspects, almost always incorporates psychological values into products and packaging.

FIGURE 3.11 Barbara Kruger, *Buy Me: I'll Change Your Life. The ambiguity of this image raises questions about manipulation in advertising and who controls the marketplace.*

In the current economic system, such implicit or built-in values are frequently manipulative, but they need not be. Victor Papanek argued that design can and should be ecologically conscious so as to make our lives better. For example, a chair made of corrugated cardboard, or low-cost foods that come in their own containers made from recycled material, represent a systematic approach in which there is no waste and no trash, and products are affordable for poor and underprivileged people, who are normally left out of consideration.

Advertising The function of advertising is to create a desire for a product or a desire to further some cause—not to create an actual artifact. Advertising is the most ubiquitous art form in contemporary culture, and arguably, of all the arts, it has the most profound effect on our values, mores, and sensibilities. It's everywhere: on the Internet, on television, in print, on billboards, on walls, on windows, even on clothing.

Advertising works on us psychologically to make us identify with a product, to integrate its qualities into our psyche. That is not a simple matter of determining what people need and offering products to meet those needs ("Here's a good soap that will clean your hands"). Rather, the advertiser does research to determine the drives, desires, and especially the insecurities and fears of particular demographic groups, then designs a campaign to create a need for a product.

In creating needs or desires and promising to fulfill them, contemporary advertising uses emotional close-ups, testimonials, quick cuts, and dramatic situations and environments to give the viewer a vicarious experience and the sense that a happy ending will be achieved by buying and consuming. Advertisements show products filling psychological as well as physical needs. Instead of focusing on natural physical thirst, for example, an ad might suggest an imaginary inadequacy or fault that can be cured by Gatorade. The stamina of a professional athlete is implied to be a quality of the drink, a quality most us lack and should want to have. The ad creates discontent and offers a means to resolve it. Contemporary ads also frequently pander to fantasies (of power, beauty, social acceptance, and so on) and sentimentality.

In packaging, symbols, images, and brand names take the place of firsthand experience. We seldom see the cat food or underwear that is inside the package; we have to rely on advertising and packaging as the source of information.

Advertising fosters a world of impressions and images rather than substance in everything from the sale of cigarettes to the sale of politicians. The theme underlying most advertising art is the enhancement of personal identity, and that is the goal of brand recognition. Ads for Tommy Hillfiger, FUBU, and Eddie Bauer are about belonging to a group as much as or more than about warmth or protection or any other functional concern. Wearing a logo is a way of claiming identity, making the wearer a media object, a media image.

Advertising offers us solutions for what are supposed to be our problems. We attain social acceptance by using deodorant, power by wearing basketball shoes or buying stocks, wisdom by having a faster modem and more gigabytes. Ultimately, we are offered transcendence through consumption. As Josephson puts it, the gods no longer live on Mount Olympus; they live on television. Contemporary idolatry is not directed to Zeus or even Abraham Lincoln but to Johny Depp and the Hard Rock Café and the lifestyle and values they represent.

Traditional literacy is declining. Visual modes are ascending. People surf the Net and watch television rather than read books. As a result, webbing and divergence are superseding logic and linearity. This emotive, nonlinear connective tissue is the heartthrob of advertising.

Contemporary advertising reinforces a general state of suspended desire and cynical self-interest. It focuses us on ourselves. What do I want to buy? Can I afford it? How does the ad suggest that I can get it?

But VCAE asks different questions about advertising. What interests are behind the advertiser's presentation? How does this ad serve the advertiser? Who is served when I buy this product, and how? Such questions, in conjunction with some skillful instructional guidance, can bring students quickly to realize the frequently manipulative purposes of advertising. In this regard, VCAE reinforces the purposes of art for life.

EXAMPLE: ADDRESSING ENVIRONMENTAL ADVERTISING

This is a sample unit of instruction that examines advertising imagery, particularly outdoor advertising. The goal is to help students develop their own awareness of advertising. The plan is first to "decode" the aesthetic environment and then present a structure that helps the students to do the same. The examination begins with the object, returns to the object for validation, and ends with an understanding of personal experience, values, and social attitudes. It focuses on making the unconscious conscious. Through critical attention to what exists, students are empowered to act on the world intelligently, rather than being pawns acted on by other forces.

Content Base: The Purposes and Aesthetics of Environmental Advertising

The first question is why the built environment looks as it does. In terms of aesthetics, for example, an obvious first question is why Wilshire Boulevard (Tennessee Street, Biscayne Boulevard, Peachtree Street . . .) is so ugly. Why is it filled with such jumbles of signs that have no integrative aspects and no subtlety? Obviously some philosophy other than traditional aesthetics is at work. (See Color Plate 5: *Las Vegas at Night*.)

The signs on Wilshire Boulevard, like other forms of human communication, must be seen as having a goal. That goal is not to create beauty but to sell things. In other words, the purpose of the signs is commercial. The aesthetics will follow from that purpose: form follows function. To put it still another way, financial gain is premise, so the philosophy of billboards is pecuniary, not aesthetic. The truth of pecuniary philosophy is that if something sells, it's beautiful. If it doesn't sell, it isn't beautiful. Images and combinations of images that contribute to making money are "true" in this pecuniary sense whether or not they are true according to traditional standards. To validate the truth of pecuniary statements and symbols, pecuniary philosophy must develop its own universe, consistent with its goals. Thus pecuniary symbolism meets all the requirements of symbolic communication in general. It is communication with a goal, transmitting a substratum of emotion, and with a meaning agreed on by a cultural group.

The problem is that a pecuniary symbol is a form of propaganda. It has a concealed manipulative purpose. It is not meant for mutual communication. It is meant to serve the advertiser's interests by manipulating the viewer's understandings and behavior.

This does not imply quite as much freedom as we might suppose for advertisers to say whatever they want in the pursuit of sales. If pecuniary philosophy is too obviously out of line with the value systems of other institutions in the culture, it will create conflict in a potential consumer. This conflict will lead to mistrust and probably to a loss of sales. In effect, by blatantly going too far, advertising would be counterproductive. Therefore, methods of circumventing traditional values and standards had to be devised.

According to Gowans, the Romans first made widespread use of outdoor ads and were the first to develop logos: standardized, nonverbal symbols for the purpose of commercial identification. A good example, still used today, is the pawnbrokers' sign, consisting of three balls. The reason for the development of logos was that very few people could read.

In the 1870s machines were introduced that could crank out standardized ads by the thousands. With this change came the repetitive symbol. This standardized symbol is more specialized than something like the pawnbrokers' sign: it represents only one individual seller. Examples in use today include the chevron used by a gasoline company and the swoop used by a shoe company.

Along with standardized ads came the need to display them. Advertising agencies were formed in the 1870s for the prime purpose of constructing billing platforms, or billboards, which they then rented to companies that wanted to advertise. This was the beginning of the modern system.

P. T. Barnum is credited with being the first to use the standardized symbol and the repetitive technique. By the 1890s the use of repetitive, standardized symbols in a billboard format had reached a point of excess. One could not go anywhere, including the deserts of Nevada and the Sudan, without seeing a billboard for Pears Soap. At this time, citizens groups formed in protest, and a great number of billboards came down.

However, this wasn't a serious setback for the billboard industry. The industry had already recognized that the repetitive symbol on billboards was becoming less and less effective because of the increasing sophistication of the consuming public and because everyone in the mercantile trades was using the technique. Individual symbols were simply getting lost in the clash and clamor. Work had already begun on new techniques.

One new technique was the association of ideas. For advertising the most effective form of idea association was soon found to be irrational association. The basic method of creating an irrational association to sell a product is to show a picture or create a word picture that arouses emotions in the viewer, and then transfer those emotions to the merchandiser's product or service by referring directly to the product.

A more recent development in advertising is an extension of idea association: the psychological hard sell. This is usually based on shame or envy but can also be based on any other exploitable human emotion: love, hate, pride, sexual desire, fear of death, family or religious loyalty, and so on. The hard sell appeals to self-interests and motives such as wanting to be healthy, to hoard, to possess, to wear smart clothes, to get something for nothing, to be more like the privileged and successful classes. The hard sell suggests not that a product can make your life good but that your life will be miserable without it. The consumer's motivation to buy is not primarily economic but social. People are not buying Fords, field glasses, and football tickets so much as social security.

The technology that was responsible for the proliferation of outdoor advertising now manifests itself in more powerful advertising media such as television, the Internet, radio, magazines, and newspapers. Advances in technology also allow advertisers to apply sophisticated marketing, focusing on so-called target groups of consumers. Advertisements are directed toward a particular group who will be watching a given television program, reading a certain magazine, or reading a certain section of a newspaper. Advertisements are carefully crafted so that their style and content will appeal to white females aged fifteen to twenty-one, yuppie moms, or black middle-class males who earn over $40,000 a year. While these more efficient media have not eliminated outdoor ads, they have relegated billboards to a supporting role. Billboards now serve mostly to jog the viewer's memory and keep, say, Coca-Cola or Bud Light fresh in the consumer's consciousness.

Psychologically, contemporary advertisers do not see people as self-directed or as having needs other than the material. People are simply containers to be filled with ideas of laxatives, beer, and underwear by a strategy of "need arousal." Convincing the consumer of the availability of the goal object and its value relative to the difficulty of attaining it are supporting strategies. Ownership is the be-all and end-all. The nonmaterialistic aspects of life, such as spiritual and emotional motivations, are appropriated for the buying process.

Manipulative practices include "embedding," in which (as the term implies) emotion-laden words or symbols are embedded in an ad. The perceiver will not be consciously aware of these words or symbols, but they are thought to affect the perceiver subconsciously. Clinical testing found subliminal cues effective in promoting buying. The object of embedding is to arouse emotions subliminally, avoiding the conscious decision-making process; the emotions that are aroused will attach themselves to the product in question when it comes time to buy. Multidimensional printing techniques allow advertising artists to plant even taboo emotional words and symbols dozens of times in a single layout.

Symbols are fairly poor at specific communication but are very effective in communicating a substratum of emotion. For the advertiser's purposes this is an advantage, not a drawback. The idea is only to arouse emotions, not to deliver a message in this mode. Often, the more unspecified the emotions aroused, the better, because it is easier, on the conscious level, for an advertiser to direct such emotions to its product.

Any aesthetic element in an ad that does not contribute to the goal of selling goods and services is dysfunctional. The first task is to attract viewers' attention. Entire scholarly volumes are devoted to understanding how to get the consumers' attention and to understanding their processing strategies. Next, the visual elements must communicate something specific to the potential consumers. This naturally precludes all decoration for its own sake. Since clarity of communication (of intentionally fuzzy concepts) is a prime concern, simplicity is essential in ad design. A good ad is direct, with a minimum of clutter and confusion. In billboard advertising, for example, it is generally accepted that large, simple shapes are the ideal and that more than seven words are too many. Advertisers want the consumer to be able to "read" a board in six seconds or less (which is the time they have estimated, from their research, that it takes for a motorist to get from the point where the board is first seen to the point where it is passed).

In all these processes the advertiser does *not* want the viewer to step back for an objective, critical look. A billboard is not trying to bring the consumer to any kind of heightened awareness. Rather, it is attempting to play on the emotional or intuitive self to make the perceiver one with the collective image of the culture as held up by the ad. For example, the industry contends that shape has sexual connotations. Round and almond shapes are feminine; angular and squarish shapes are masculine. Through the exclusive use of either masculine or feminine shapes, advertisers try to promote products as masculine or feminine.

The aesthetic elements should also contribute to the conceptual vagueness of an ad. This allows the greatest possible number of people to project themselves into the situation shown and thus relate to the product. When an object, place, or event is ambiguous or unstructured, the viewer's inner or behavioral determinants have a greater influence on the precepts that emerge. Ambiguity is particularly important in outdoor advertising, which—unlike other forms—is not directed at a specific audience.

Color in advertising is also used primarily for its psychological, manipulative effects. For example, advertisers have found that children tend to prefer yellow, while middle-aged and older people almost always prefer blue. Violet tends to be a very noncommercial color, as opposed to the primary colors, which are very commercial. The simple colors sell.

Advertising and the Environment

Two types of signs are on-premise and off-premise. On-premise signs are those of shops, distributors, of products or services. Off-premise signs are spaces rented by merchants to promote a product or service. Other common forms are transit advertising and point-of-purchase displays. Billboards are far and away the dominant environmental advertising medium. The typical billboard is 12 feet high by 25 feet wide. Since the point of advertising is to get attention and communicate a message, every ad is in competition with every other ad and with stoplights, street signs, buildings, and so on. Therefore, the typical style is characterized by big, bright, simple forms placed so as to dominate the surroundings. This style creates the environmental clash and clamor we all see.

If clusters of symbols reflect the philosophy of civilization, American streets, with their commercial signs, reflect materialism. These commercial images present jingles and contrived circumstances that have little to do with traditional notions of substantive content, truth, or value. Do they also suggest Americans' willingness to take much of what they buy and how they live at a superficial level?

Another question is, What is the most desirable use of public space? Who has a right to public space, and how should that space appear? Private property is almost sacrosanct in our culture. Is that always a good thing? Do economic institutions take unfair advantage of our desire to protect private property? These questions can serve to develop a curriculum that examines advertising images not only as formal constructions but as carriers of mores, values, and social assumptions. The crucial point is that in commercial images we are dealing primarily not with aesthetic issues but with economic issues. Aesthetic factors either support the pecuniary agenda or are eliminated.

Asking Questions about Environmental Ads

The main strategy for examining environmental advertising is the critique. Questions to be discussed in relation to critiques of advertising imagery might be based on the following: (1) The response to that imagery. (What does it do to you emotionally and intellectually? Why?) (2) A descriptive analysis of what qualities in the image condition the response, including forms, thematic content, formal relationships, and formal characterizations. (3) Interpretation of images. (4) Contextual investigation. (Who is promoting this image? In what context? For what purposes?) (5) Evaluation using not only formal but also societal criteria.

Issues to be addressed, many of which would rise out of critiques, might include the cultural and economic presuppositions of advertising; the history of advertising; and its philosophy, psychology, and ethics, including techniques for making a sale. The aesthetics of environmental advertising could be examined in relation to symbols as such (their nature and forms), repetitive symbols, standardization, technology, association of ideas, emotional arousal through formal qualities, compositional features, style, embedding, and the meaning of advertising for individuals and society. The examination might also include the effects of outdoor advertising on the natural environment, and the built environment as a reflection of values, mores, and beliefs.

Studio activities might include redesigning a "strip" to reflect a nonpecuniary philosophy or at least more honest merchandising, or redesigning an advertisement to convey honest claims, forms, and values. Also, once students understand that this unit involves "sleuthing," they will certainly generate their own activities. (An example of a student critique of advertising media may be found in the satiric art of Eric Barkin, *Nixon Meets Chairman Mao*, in Color Plate 6.)

CONCLUSION

This chapter has focused on visual culture art education (VCAE) as art for life. We first described the broad context of visual culture studies and then examined the roots of VCAE: cognitive psychology, anthropology and sociology, philosophy, and contextualist art education. Then we addressed the premises and content of VCAE, focusing particularly on the popular and design arts and advertising in the mass media. Finally a sample unit centered on environmental advertising was given.

Paolo Freire says that perhaps the greatest tragedy of contemporary society is people's domination by the myths and manipulation of ideological and commercial advertising. If the calculated manipulation of cultural symbols by ideological and commercial forces goes unchecked, it may weaken the associative structure of society. The disassociation of symbols from shared traditional meanings would be cultural schizophrenia. Likewise, Sontag analyzes fascist art as tending to control a populace through emotional manipulation and through self-conscious repudiation of the intellect, with the goal of affecting behavior. This sounds alarmingly like advertising art.

It is vital for students to be given the tools and the sensibility needed to make informed choices in life and in society. If the role of art education is to help students develop the critical ability to go beyond accepting the prescriptions and recipes of established institutional powers, then an understanding of visual culture is crucial. VCAE is capable of addressing major contemporary themes through its strategy of critique and so may be crucial not only for students as individuals but for society as a whole.

In Chapter 4 we will examine creative expression in the arts, again in a social context.

QUESTIONS FOR STUDY AND DISCUSSION

1. It is argued in this chapter that we live primarily in a constructed rather than a natural world. Describe how this takes place. Do you agree?

2. It is also argued that information we receive, and thus learning in general, is increasingly visual rather than verbal. Do you agree? Can you give examples or counterexamples?

3. What is perceptual constancy? As a group activity, using cameras, pencil and paper, or other appropriate tools, construct at least three examples of constancy of shape (or form) or color.

4. In small groups, discuss how and when you learned to draw various objects and configurations (a house, people, flowers, and so on). Did you learn from looking, or from another child, or from an adult? How did your drawings evolve? What or who influenced you? After your discussion, describe what effect culture and biology have had on your own development.

5. What does it mean to say that seeing is constructed rather than given? Describe how cognitive psychologists say this happens. Do you agree?

6. What did Langer mean when she described art as objectifying subjective human experience?

7. How do you think visual expression and verbal language are alike or different as communication? Do you think each has strengths the other doesn't have? Explain.

8. What is the point of VCAE? Given its goals, do you think it is right to de-emphasize the fine arts? Why or why not?

9. Apart from the fine arts, there are three areas of content in VCAE. What are they? Which is most important, in your mind?

10. In your group, critique a billboard or ad of your choice using the sample questions provided. Pay special attention to the social messages of the image. You may want to base your critique on the critical analysis model provided in Chapter 6. (See page 62.)

11. In your group, develop a critical performance piece something like Coco Fusco and Guillermo Goméz-Peña's, focused on a problem that you agree needs to be addressed by society.

FURTHER READING

Adbusters: *http://www.adbusters.org/home/*

Bowers, C. (1974). *Cultural literacy for freedom*. Eugene, OR: Elan.

Dissanayake, E. (1988). *What is art for?* Seattle, WA: University of Washington Press.

Duncum, P,. & Bracey, T. (2001). *On knowing*. Christchurch, New Zealand: University of Canterbury Press.

Evans, J., & Hall, S. (1999). *Visual culture: The reader*. London: Sage. (The most comprehensive and scholarly source of visual culture on this list.)

Gardner, H. (1994). *The arts and human development*. New York: HarperCollins.

Josephson, S. (1996). *From idolatry to advertising: Visual art and contemporary culture*. Armonk, NY: M. E. Sharpe. (An excellent overview of visual culture focused on the popular arts, design, and advertising in particular.)

Journal of Multicultural and Cross-Cultural Research in Art Education, 18. (2000). (Volume 18 is a thematic issue devoted to VCAE, with articles by Kevin Tavin, Brent Wilson, Paul Duncum, and Kerry Freedman. An excellent resource.)

Mirzoeff, N. (1999). *An introduction to visual culture*. London: Routledge. (A good overview, particularly strong in analyzing photographic images as culture.)

4

Individual Expression and Creativity

Zebras and Tigers, Havy Nguyen, Deerfield Beach High School, Deerfield Beach, FL., Nancy Leslie, art teacher. *This student's imaginative eye visualized a creative metamorphosis of zebras and tigers to create this painting, which references the relationship of these animals in nature. Nguyen worked with the theme of metamorphosis throughout her senior year in the International Baccalaureate Program.*

In this chapter we examine individual expression and **creativity** in art, suggesting that making art is both personal and social, and that the creativity of artists and student artists therefore has both a personal and a social aspect. Creativity involves making connections not only between form and meaning but also between art and society. We describe and discuss the traits of creative individuals as well as the social role of creativity. Because a function of metaphor is to connect concepts, ideas, and feelings across disciplinary and other boundaries, we suggest that metaphor is an important creative trait, and we describe strategies for its use in art for life. Finally, we describe how to encourage creativity at school and in the world outside school.

INDIVIDUAL AND SOCIAL CREATIVITY

Individual Expression and Creativity in Art

Human beings are naturally inquisitive and naturally inclined to manipulate and alter their world; for this reason, we believe that fostering creativity should be an integral part of art for life. Art has long been seen as the place for creativity in general education, the place where divergence and open-ended solutions are not only tolerated but encouraged. Yet as Efland's analysis of school art indicates, creativity in school is typically more apparent and superficial than real or profound; there is only an impression of creativity in what is actually a structured, somewhat noncreative environment. Although some school art programs do encourage students' critical and creative thinking, many appear to be characteristically "school-oriented"; that is, students follow the rules, find the one right answer, and apply lower-level cognitive processes. Goodlad argues that such programs generally do not allow for the individual expression and artistic creativity promised by the rhetoric in the field. Peter London (1989) considers a current widely used paradigm—discipline-based art education (DBAE)—unsatisfying because it pays little or no attention to creativity but rather focuses on art criticism, art history, aesthetics, and studio art. Thus we may infer from the literature that creative thinking, like authentic instruction, is not automatically addressed in art education, in spite of descriptions to the contrary.

Yet when most people think of an artist, they think first of creativity: being an artist is synonymous with being creative. Creativity, in our contemporary concept of art, is the one essential quality of the artist, rather than skill in manipulation of materials or in composition. When parents, administrators, or teachers other than art teachers think of the school art program they also think mainly of creativity and personal expression. In North American culture, creativity is thought of as part of artistic activity and, by extension, as a central component of art in school—whether or not that is true. However, while creativity is given lip service by the literature, it is not fostered or well understood in school art programs.

It can be argued that creativity occurs naturally while students are involved in studio art, so the fear that creativity is squelched in comprehensive art education is unwarranted. For example, the synthesizing, interpretative thinking that characterizes art criticism is creative—students create their own meanings in a work of art. It can also be argued that creativity is inherent in aesthetic inquiry because such inquiry is open-ended. But is creativity really a constant component of these processes? We think the answer depends on the nature of the studio project or art criticism, and how the students approach it or are directed to approach it. We believe in creative thinking in making art and talking about art, but we don't think it happens automatically. We believe creativity is an important (or, in most cases, potentially important) quality to be achieved in art education. In this chapter, we will describe creativity and discuss how it can be developed.

The Social Nature of Creativity

To begin, we need to understand that creativity does not happen only inside an individual's head. It happens, as Csikszentmihalyi (1996) says, in the interaction between a person's thoughts and a sociocultural context. This is an important idea. It means that creativity is defined socially. Creativity is a new or unique way of seeing, understanding, or doing something, though we must ask, new and unique in relation to what? The answer is new and unique in relation to what already exists, the way things have been seen or understood or done until now. Creativity, then, is an individual's reaction to, extension of, or reinterpretation of social constructs. Creativity, in this sense, is a challenge to the usual modus operandi. It is a social act. It comes as a response to what is; and if such a response is truly creative, it can be introduced to the social system—the way we see and do things—as a new way of seeing, doing, or believing.

With regard to art for life, this implies that students need to be deeply engaged in existing art and in the ways that people approach and use art in the real world. By extension, it is important to offer students varied content and strategies, because creativity is fostered by cross-cultural, intercultural, cross-generational, multifaceted material. The more viewpoints one has, the more creative one can be.

The comprehensive model of art education focused on art for life is an excellent means of fostering creativity. Art history, art criticism, aesthetic inquiry, and making art (both as visual study and as creative expression) are valuable for the varied content they provide and for the strategies and skills involved in seeking information in each discipline. As Csikszentmihalyi notes, a person cannot be creative in a domain to which he or she is not exposed.

According to Csikszentmihalyi, a domain, such as art, is a system with a certain set of socially determined symbolic rules and procedures. These are formulated and nested within the larger set of societal rules and procedures—which we call culture. In any domain there are gatekeepers who decide whether, given the rules and procedures, any particular act or thought is creative. In art, the gatekeepers are, for instance, curators, arts administrators, critics, historians, aestheticians, and—most important for our purposes—art teachers. Another component of creativity is the individual who acts within a domain and is judged by the gatekeepers to have acted creatively or not.

For our purposes, the domain is art; the gatekeepers are primarily art teachers and secondarily students' peers; and the individual is the student. In this social context, creativity occurs when an individual student (or group of students), using the symbols and procedures established in the domain of art, has a new idea, or sees a new pattern that is acknowledged by the significant others in the environment as being novel or creative. Clearly, this situation demands that students understand the domain—the rules and procedures—in order to bend and alter it in creative ways. A creative act in art history, for example, could be a reassessment, a creative reconstruction of the way something has been understood in the past. In art criticism it might be a new analytical perspective or a unique analytical strategy; a creative act in aesthetics could be a reevaluation of an artwork based on traditional criteria. In the studio, a creative act might be developing a unique visual form or altering the meaning of a well-worn form by applying a new understanding from art history, art criticism, or aesthetics.

CREATIVE TRAITS AND ART INSTRUCTION: A SOCIAL PERSPECTIVE

Personal Traits of Creative Individuals

Advocates of creativity generally point out that imagination is universal to humankind; thus everyone is creative to some degree. Ultimately, in his or her interaction with a given domain and field (which consists of people who work within a domain), it is the individual who is or is not creative. It is, therefore, useful to look at the qualities of creative people.

Guilford identified certain characteristics of creative people. First, they are fluent in their thinking and skilled in communication. They can make many connections among words or ideas and can produce many meaningful phrases and sentences, ideas, and solutions to problems. Second, they are flexible in their thinking. They can roam freely amid their thoughts to produce a great variety of ideas, and they can adapt thoughts skillfully to new situations. Third, they are original in their thinking and frequently unique in their responses. They often come up with remote associations or relationships, rejecting obvious or conventional solutions. Fourth, they can generally elaborate on a simple foundation to create a complex structure, extending what is given and adding details. Fifth, they can improvise. They frequently give up an old interpretation of a familiar object in order to use it or its parts in new ways.

Also, creative people typically have certain personal qualities. They are self-disciplined: they can concentrate for long periods of time on a project or idea. They have no false pride: they can change their minds when it's apparent that an idea is wrong. They do not depend on external rewards: they have confidence in their ability to succeed, and they can pursue a project for its own sake. They are constructively discontented: they want to change something, enjoy a challenge, seek to have their views heard. They have a holistic sensory viewpoint: they have "connective vision" and frequently are visual learners. They can control their habits: they are not bound by conformity or habitual thinking.

A class full of students with all or most of these traits may be an art teacher's worst nightmare. Highly creative people may not be the easiest students to manage or motivate in a traditional classroom setting. They will be the kids who are always rocking the boat. For that reason, creativity is not to be pursued lightly. An art teacher who is concerned primarily with district, state, and national standards may prefer simply to produce technically skillful portfolios—safe, formulaic, so-called school art.

Is Creativity Worth It?

Creativity is a messy, open-ended business. But, then, so is life—and art for life should be a model for life. Therefore, we believe in creativity. We believe that a good program not only teaches skills and content but also specifies open-ended expressive outcomes designed to encourage students to use skills and content to express themselves in art. For the sake of educational accountability, many school districts properly insist on the development of predetermined skills and content. That's a start. But we think it's critically important to go further, to encourage students to use content and skills they've developed to communicate something meaningful, to express something they think or feel about themselves in their world. Expressive outcomes are a holistic strategy for teaching and learning that utilizes all three of Bloom's developmental categories. That is, students use psychomotor skills to grow in the affective and cognitive realms.

Using expressive outcomes in tandem with closed-ended instructional objectives is not merely formulaic school art. It is more like patterns in life. Skills are developed because of a perceived need—an impulse to create something, to express oneself, to communicate something real about one's perceptions, values, understanding, or intuition. Expressive outcomes are on a higher level and are therefore of more educational value than mere acquisition of skills and content. Art education should center creativity and metacognition so that students will develop higher-level thinking and the deeper learning that result from authentic instruction.

Csikszentmihalyi's Ten Paradoxical Qualities

Csikszentmihalyi (1996) describes ten socially defined paradoxical qualities that may be useful to consider with regard to developing a classroom climate that will enhance creativity. First, he says, creative individuals have a great deal of energy, frequently working long hours with great concentration—but just as often they are quiet and at rest. In art education, therefore, creativity should not be regulated by the clock or the calendar. Creative students will have periods of laser-sharp focus as well as periods of idleness, and the teacher should recognize the latter as time to recharge the batteries. Block scheduling would be ideal for enhancing creativity in students, but when this is not possible, it's still important for teachers to understand that seemingly doing nothing is in fact an important part of the creative process, a time of reflection. A student who isn't "working" in the conventional sense may be working in some other sense. The instructor should exercise good judgment in guiding individual students. Some students may occasionally break away from the routine, although prolonged disengagement may be a sign of depression or some other dysfunction rather than creativity.

In seeking creative artistic solutions, students should be encouraged to let problems incubate for several days. In the meantime, while the subconscious mind and the conscious mind put one project in order, a variety of ideas may be sketched or planned, and another project may be worked on. This requires the teacher to introduce creative problems well in advance, to allow enough time for solutions to germinate.

The second paradoxical quality of creative people is that they tend to be both smart and naive. Their thinking is both convergent and divergent. Studies suggest that an IQ of 120 or so is necessary for true creativity, but that a very high IQ may be a detriment—students with very high IQs may become complacent because they know how to play the game. In schools, convergent thinking is generally valued and measured (for example, by IQ tests), but creative people don't restrict themselves to agreed-on ways of thinking or agreed-on solutions. They may tackle a problem or idea that seems absurd from a logical, linear perspective, but they say to themselves, naively, "Why not?" A high IQ is less important for creativity than an intuitive naïveté that allows for entertaining new possibilities, nonlinear divergent thinking, and shifts from one perspective to another, so that problem solving is enhanced. In the art room, this naïveté selects against "correct" answers or solutions given from on high by the teacher. It also suggests that interdisciplinary study and research (outlined in the research notebooks described in Chapter 10) is an excellent strategy for fostering creativity and that nonthreatening open-ended activities should be encouraged in art education.

According to Csikszentmihalyi, the third paradoxical trait of creative people is a combination of playfulness and discipline. Playfulness—the ability to take lightly that which is given—is crucial to creativity, though it must be accompanied by perseverance and, often, plain dogged hard work. The art room needs an atmosphere of open-ended playfulness with regard to problems: the focus should be on generating visual and conceptual questions rather than answers. A playful spirit includes willingness to engage in brainstorming without necessarily knowing where it will lead but trusting that it will be somehow valuable. Once a problem is defined, judgment should be suspended so that the students can generate many possible creative solutions. Problems and ideas should be reframed or approached from new perspectives—students should be encouraged to take multiple viewpoints, literally and figuratively.

An idea that something might be different cannot develop very far without perseverance and endurance—the willingness and ability to spend long hours seeing the idea through to completion. Entertaining new ideas incurs a risk of failure; students need to be persistent in seeking the best possible solution. An idea for a sculpture, for example, doesn't become an actual sculpture until the artist spends long hours making it. Both playfulness in the generation of ideas and a dedicated work ethic must be fostered in the art room to enhance student creativity. In terms of time spent, the old formula—1 percent inspiration, 99 percent perspiration—applies.

This suggests a fourth paradoxical trait. Creative people alternate between fantasy and imagination on one hand and a strong sense of reality on the other. They are original without leaving the realm of reality. They are not bizarre or disconnected. As Salvador Dalí put it: "The difference between a crazy person and me is that I'm not crazy." They are by definition creative, not crazy, because they come up with concepts that can be tested and that make sense in the real world. Creative people can envision multiple reasonable realities.

Association of ideas is a component of synthetic thinking and thus of the creative process. Sometimes creativity is seen as remote or forced associations. Mednick suggests that the more remote or unlike the ideas that are pulled together, the more unusual the response. Remote associations are often useful in developing a form to fit a function. For example, in devising flying machines Leonardo da Vinci used a direct visual analogy—the wings of birds. Other examples of remote associations are the dreamlike images of the surrealists, who depicted images from the subconscious, often placing ordinary objects in unreal combinations. These examples suggest there is some truth to the adage that nothing is new under the sun. Most ideas are combinations or modifications of other ideas, so the ability to develop ideas and search out hidden potential alternative ideas is important.

In the art classroom, dreams and fantasies should be encouraged and welcomed, as students learn to recognize and accept the subconscious as a part of the creative self. Teachers can foster creativity by broadening the base of inquiry, giving students more information, and showing students more ways in which things can be done. Once again, therefore, intercultural content and deep exploration are valuable. And students' own standards for success should involve reflection on the process as well as evaluation of the product.

Fifth, creative people seem to be simultaneously both extroverted and introverted. They can tolerate being alone to explore and master the symbolic content of art, yet they also interact with others in order to know what else is going on and what additional ideas are available, to be stimulated, and to test their own ideas. In the art room, students should engage in cooperative activity and also be allowed space and time to reflect, dream, and work on their own.

Sixth, Csikszentmihalyi suggests that creative people are both humble and proud: they take pride in their accomplishments but realize that their own contribution to the whole is really quite small—that they stand on the shoulders of giants. They can also be described as both ambitious and selfless, or as both competitive and cooperative. They may be proud of initiating an idea or activity but also willing to subordinate their self-interest and work with others for the good of the

FIGURE 4.1 Herbert Bayer. *Lonely Metropolitan.* 1932. Gelatin silver print. 13⅜ x 10½". *The placement of dissimilar objects together in an unusual combination creates startling new associations and mysterious meanings in this image.*

project. The project becomes larger than any person. In art education, students therefore need to recognize the worth but also the place of their own contributions and be willing to work cooperatively with one another to achieve ends they might not be able to achieve individually. A good example is a collaborative mural, in which the whole is larger than the sum of the parts.

The seventh paradoxical quality discussed by Csikszentmihalyi is that creative people are not restricted by gender designations and roles. They can function in both masculine and feminine modes. Researchers have found that creative girls are tougher and more aggressive than other girls, and creative boys are more sensitive and less aggressive than other boys. In the art room, an atmosphere that is safe for more assertive girls and more sensitive boys promotes creativity.

Eighth, while creative people are considered independent, even rebellious, they must also be cooperative in the sense that they must understand and internalize the rules of a domain. They must be traditional and conservative and at the same time must want to bend the rules. Many postmodern artists, for example, rely on traditional forms such as folk art and indigenous arts. In the art room, the content of art must be studied and integrated before creative expression can develop. At the same time, students must be encouraged to take risks with the rules of the domain.

A ninth paradoxical quality is that creative people are both very passionate and very objective about their work, attached and at the same time detached. Passion drives their creativity; objectivity makes their work realistic and credible. Thus students must be encouraged to follow their hearts as they make and critique art, yet they must also undertake objective, formative analyses of whether what they're doing is working and how it might work better, physically or conceptually. In K–12 art education this requires sensitive input from the teacher, who serves as a gatekeeper to the domain.

Tenth, Csikszentmihalyi suggests that the openness and sensitivity of creative people expose them to both joy and pain. They are sensitive not only to poorly conceived and poorly executed projects but also to criticism of their work. This trait probably explains the image of artists, such as Van Gogh, as thin-skinned and "misunderstood." At the same time, creative people derive great satisfaction, even joy, from an idea that succeeds and from the process of working. All artists know the feeling of being lost in the process of making art, of being in harmony with the process—a feeling that might be called bliss. In the art class, this trait implies that students should be given time to do research undisturbed, and that criticism should be gentle and constructive.

Generally, as students develop creative thinking, they need to understand that in problem solving, creative thinking is applied continuously along with critical thinking. As criteria or standards for problem solving are established, critical thinking is applied to select the best solutions from all the ideas generated. Thinking must be taught as a holistic skill in order to increase students' ability to generate ideas and alternatives as well as analyze and evaluate solutions in terms of established criteria.

CREATIVITY AS COGNITION: THE CRUCIAL ROLE OF METAPHOR

Metaphor as the Core of Creativity

A crucial part of creative thinking and self-expression is the ability to use metaphor. It recently has become quite clear that metaphor, in fact, is crucial to our ability to think at all.

Metaphor is a symbolic transformation that occurs when one thing (a visual image, a figure of speech, a musical configuration, or the like) in its entirety denotes another thing in its entirety: for example, the sun as life, a circle as wholeness, or

Copland's musical composition as an Appalachian spring. This transformation need not be verbal or linguistic. Visualization is a form of thought, and visual metaphors function as nonverbal, symbolic, conceptual information about the world. Visual metaphors give form to something that may otherwise be unknowable, objectifying feeling and imagination. This is an essential human thought process.

Visual metaphor communicates on many levels, compressing and intensifying information. This concentration of meaning allows for enlarged understanding. Visual metaphor, much more than linear description, is able to carry huge amounts of information simultaneously. Visual metaphor tells us about not only the intellectual but also the emotional aspects of our lives. Visual arts and artifacts, when recognized as visual metaphors, are global, holistic records of experience—perceptions and feelings. They are records of life that link vision, emotion, and imagination.

Metaphor is also crucial to our sense of balance as a society. As Woodman observes, to lose our sense of parallelism or similarity between things, or our sense of the connection between different realms of experience, is a sort of cultural blindness and deafness. She notes that the word *metaphor,* from the Greek, means to cross over, to transfer to one thing the sense of another; and she argues that the underlying power of metaphor is the belief that all things in life are connected.

Creativity involves precisely this ability to make connections across conceptual boundaries such as those between disciplines and mediums, especially in art. In the broadest sense, all art is metaphorical because it stands for the artist's thoughts and emotions. It represents the human heart and mind in visual form. The abstract artist Mark Rothko, for example, said that his color-field paintings represented the whole of his experience. Just as we are more than our external selves, artworks are more than their surfaces. They stand for and reflect realities within and beyond themselves.

Cultural Metaphor

If we look closely and feel a work deeply enough (and do some research), we can see cultural myths within and as an extension of an artist's personal expression. An artwork is specific not only to the artist but to his or her worldview—democratic, capitalist, Marxist, Christian, Buddhist, animist, anarchist, and so on. A worldview is shaped within a culture, so artworks are not universal across cultures, places, or time. Rather, they are specific to societies and cultures. A swastika means one thing in Germany and something totally different in India. These meanings do not reside in the form itself; they are culturally constructed. In this sense, artworks are *cultural* visual metaphors whose meaning depends on creative human connections.

Closely related to metaphor is analogy, which we explore in the "synectics" sidebar.

Metaphor as Creative Activity in Students' Art

The artist Anne Truitt says that marks on paper are as meaningless as chicken tracks until someone makes a vital connection and attaches meaning to them. Students should constantly be reminded that the forms they study have meaning, and that the forms they make should represent something beyond form itself. They should also be encouraged to look below the surface and beyond obvious forms and obvious themes to find the metaphor at the heart of the work. Creativity lies in connections beneath surfaces and beyond forms.

Osborn developed strategies to help students make sophisticated metaphoric statements in art. Eberle developed techniques for adapting these strategies, called SCAMPER: substituting, combining, altering, multiplying, eliminating, reversing. When we ask ourselves how each process may affect a project, new solutions may appear. For example, students could be asked what would happen to their work if they substituted a rectangle for a circle, or yellow for blue, or a woman

William J. J. Gordon (1961) coined the term "synectics" and defined it as "the joining together of different and apparently irrelevant elements." Synectic methods are conscious approaches to constructing analogies—direct, personal, fantastic, or symbolic—in order to solve problems or generate ideas.

A problem solver who uses direct analogy considers how similar or related problems have been or may be solved. Gordon and Poze speculated that early humans used direct analogies with nature to solve problems that arose in hunting and gathering. For example, the problem of how to catch large quantities of fish may have been solved when cave people noticed a spiderweb, saw its potential, and made a fishnet. A contemporary example is Pringles potato chips. The problem was how to package potato chips compactly, without breaking them, in order to lower shipping costs. The analogy in this case was wet leaves, which pack together snugly without breaking, and it led to a new method of processing and packaging.

Problem solvers who use personal analogy find new perspectives by imagining themselves as objects. For instance, they might imagine how would it feel to be a grocery bag in order to solve a problem involving recycling; or they might imagine being a checkbook in order to avoid loss or theft. This strategy was used by Albert Einstein when he imagined himself traveling on a beam of light, an image that contributed to his theory of relativity.

Problem solvers who use fantastic analogy think of the most nearly perfect, most ideal, or most far-fetched solution or product possible. Fantastic analogies have led to many everyday products. How can we make an oven that will clean itself? How can we make a fabric that needs no ironing? How can we travel to the moon and beyond? Imagining an ideal and then working backward to determine the necessary steps toward achieving it is an effective problem-solving strategy.

The fourth approach in synectics is called symbolic analogy. It involves looking at situations and creating appropriate descriptive oxymorons or two-word phrases that read like book titles. For example, imagine you have a littering problem around your school, even though there are plenty of trash barrels available. Titles might include "Sight (or Site) Blindness" or "Irresponsible Responsibility." Such titles often encapsulate a conflict that has led to the problem.

Davis (1999) provides numerous examples of exercises for synectics: How can softness be heard? How is life like a flashlight battery? Which is stronger, a brick wall or a young tree? Why? What could have given a cave dweller the idea of a spear? What connection could have been made? What would it be like to be inside a lemon? When you are happy, you are like a _____. When you are busy, you are like a _____. How is vandalizing like sticking a finger into a light socket?

Analogical thinking, like metaphorical thinking, can strengthen creative thinking.

for a man. What would happen if they combined the circle and the rectangle, or the woman and the man? What would happen if they made the woman taller than the man, or if they multiplied her to make ten identical women in the composition, or if they eliminated her altogether? What would happen if the man's and the woman's roles were reversed? How would each alteration affect the meaning of the piece?

These creative strategies also work very well with art criticism and other forms of critical inquiry. For example, a teacher could ask what would happen if the ocean in an image were eliminated and a desert were substituted for it? How would that affect the meaning? In art for life, students need to be reminded that every image stands for something beyond itself, and the substitution of one image or strategy for another changes not only the image itself but the relationship of the image to the work as a whole and its place in the larger context of social meanings.

Metaphor and Creative Interpretation

When we think of artworks as visual metaphors, interpretation is not a search for scientific truth or the one right answer. Rather, visual metaphor, like philosophy and religion, has to do with values and emotions. It deals with love, soul, and

A CLOSER LOOK   Metamorphic Problem Solving (MPS)

Metamorphic problem solving is helpful in observing and reflecting on many facets of a problem. Listing elements and attributes of a problem and possible criteria for solutions is a means of analyzing discrete characteristics of a problematic situation. As the attributes of the situation are analyzed, specific elements and potential solutions may be more easily identified.

Think of the Greek word *morphe*, "form," and the English *metamorphosis*, meaning a transformation. Then follow these steps:

1. Identify a problem or object.

2. List (at least) five elements of your problem or object across the top row of the matrix shown here (an element is a generalization or an abstract concept).

3. List attributes of each element below it (an attribute is specific).

4. Establish criteria and apply them to determine the relative utility or value of each solution.

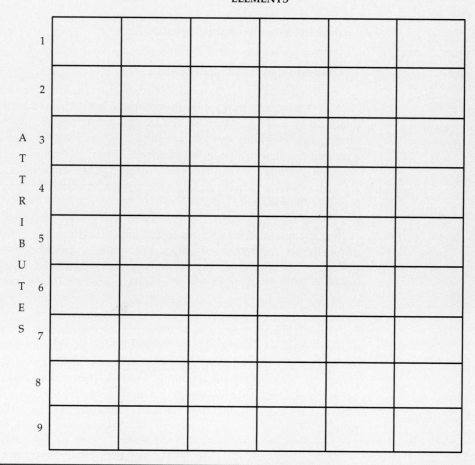

ELEMENTS

spirit. In such a context, an interpretation is right when it feels right in the fiber of our being. It is intuitive, and it varies from one person to another. Thus there can be many "correct" interpretations of an image. The connections students make to their own lives can result in as many correct interpretations as there are students in a class. Creative interpretation depends on open, connective, often divergent inquiry.

DEVELOPING A CREATIVE ENVIRONMENT AT SCHOOL

Overcoming Blocks to Creativity

There are numerous blocks to students' creative self-expression in art. Most blocks are encountered daily in the art room but go unrecognized by many art teachers. The structure of a program can impede creativity, or the students themselves can be the impediment. The following list, from *The Universal Traveler* (Koberg & Bagnall, 1974), notes the emotional risks and fears associated with being creative:

Fear of making mistakes.

Fear of being seen as a fool.

Fear of being criticized.

Fear of being misused.

Fear of being alone (a person with an idea is a minority of one).

Fear of disturbing traditions by making changes.

Fear of breaking taboos.

Fear of losing the security of habit.

Fear of losing the love of the group.

Fear of truly being an individual.

As this list suggests, most blocks to creativity are social, since creative thinking often does require pushing or breaking societal boundaries or norms. And while the rhetoric may indicate otherwise, the art classroom does not always provide a nurturing, psychologically safe environment for students to develop constructive creative thinking that challenges social norms. The art classroom is, after all, still a part of school. But there are strategies for overcoming self-imposed or other blocks. The art teacher needs to recognize the social context of creativity and create a safe, fostering environment.

The art teacher's role is first of all to foster creativity. This involves fostering the skills and content of the domain of art, using the strategies of artists, critics, aestheticians, art historians, and others. The symbolic knowledge of any domain, in this case art, is not a given; it is not biological. It is learned and passed on from one person to another and from one generation to another. To be creative in the domain of art one must first know the rules—the conventions. Students must acquire and internalize the system in order to be able to manipulate it.

Second, the teacher's role is to encourage the creative process and honestly evaluate the product—the painting, evaluation, or reassessment—as genuinely creative or simply conventional. This demands an atmosphere in which the student learns the rules and then is encouraged to take chances by breaking them. During open-ended activities an overly judgmental or reactive teacher will stifle creativity. The students must feel that they can take chances without incurring disapproval or ridicule if the result is a dead end or failure. For every successful innovation, there must necessarily be many failures.

Accordingly, students should be engaged in their own substantive problems, meanings, and processes. They will then be engaged in each process for its own sake, thinking less about success and failure, less about getting it right, and more of exploring, following a problem through. Art is, as a result, immediately connected to the student's real-life concerns and by extension to the larger social domain. A good example of potentially creative inquiry initiated by students is developing research journals, as described in Chapter 10. By contrast, activities directed by the teacher, particularly activities based solely on elements and principles, stifle creativity.

When people become absorbed in an aesthetic moment, their experience is similar to that of the artist during intensely creative work. In both cases, individuals lose track of time and are totally absorbed in the sensations, interactions, and feelings of the moment. This experience must be fostered and extended in the pursuit of creativity. Whereas the typical approach to art education is to expose students to a broad range of media, activities, and skills, creative art education requires working on a given problem in depth. The commitment to deeper learning entails allowing the student enough time to solve the problem. Fostering creativity requires a depth approach to art education rather than the traditional breadth approach. Students should have time to explore and solve the problems they choose.

Another social aspect of creativity at school is the opinions of the art teacher and of the students' peers. Students must feel that it is safe to take chances. But chance, intuition, and open-ended self-expression are somewhat frightening to many students, especially in a rule-governed, closed-ended system. This may explain why students in many secondary schools today are seldom absorbed in aesthetic or creative experiences. Low-achieving students avoid unpleasant experiences by disengaging and by passively waiting for better, less threatening situations in the future; they can thus avoid commitment to engaging in aesthetics or intense creativity. High-achieving students who worry about getting good grades, fitting in with the right group, and getting into the right college may also avoid the risks of pursuing undetermined outcomes. They too may postpone investing in the real world today, in the hope of finding something better tomorrow. Such students may awaken as adults to find that life has passed them by and that they can recall few moments of joy or even satisfaction.

FIGURE 4.2 Jerry Uelsmann, *Untitled*, 1998. *Uelsmann's breathtaking photography combines real images in unrealistic situations, conveying a sense of otherworldliness, fantasy, and surrealism.*

One approach to increasing students' involvement in the moment is to teach skills of observation as well as research in all the disciplines of art and to teach technical and compositional skills as a means of becoming deeply engaged in the world around them. Helping students focus closely on the surrounding world through various "lenses"—the various disciplines—may be a first step toward heightened perception and appreciation. This is aesthetic perception. If students can be helped to see appreciatively with heart and mind as well as eyes, they can acquire a rich store of imagery and understanding and develop attitudes that lead them to invent, create, and respond to art. They will also make connections with real-world issues and devise means to deal with these issues creatively. This is the social aspect of creativity.

Cooperative Problem Solving and Individual Research

Brainstorming   One good strategy for creative problem solving is brainstorming. Osborn gives four basic guidelines for the **brainstorming** process. First, negative criticism is ruled out, particularly because deferring judgment is important. Toleration of ambiguity is important in brainstorming. Second, freewheeling with regard to ideas is welcomed. The wilder the idea, the better. Third, quantity is sought, on the premise that the greater the number of ideas, the greater the chance of a workable solution. Fourth, combinations of and improvements in ideas are sought. Participants are encouraged to piggyback or build on one another's ideas.

For creative people, problem solving is often a generative process. That is, they generate many alternative solutions, select the best, and then either intuitively or consciously seek another problem to solve. That is why it is so important to defer judgment. Only after the generation of many ideas should criteria be established for determining the best solutions. Regardless of the feasibility of the solutions offered, the generation of ideas in itself may suggest new avenues for exploration.

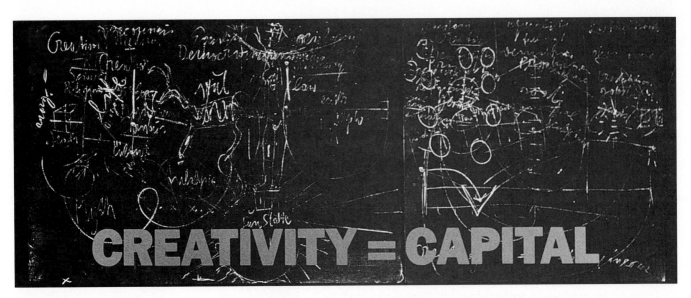

FIGURE 4.3   Joseph Beuys. *Creativity=Capital*, 1983. *Beuys took an anthropological view of art, seeing any kind of action in life that could potentially transform the fabric of society as art.*

Research Journals   A fine strategy for connecting students' personal expression to real-world concerns is the **research journal.** The criteria for a creative research journal may be developed by teachers and students together, but students should start with their own reflections—their own sense of what is interesting and important—and then proceed to critical inquiry and historical, contextual, and visual research. (See the chart in Chapter 1.) Personal reflection is important, as is regular feedback from the teacher.

Howard Gardner and his colleagues at Harvard's Project Zero have provided a model for process portfolios, which are what we call research journals. Gardner suggests that the portfolio should contain not only the students' finished artworks but also original sketches, interim drafts, critiques by the students themselves and others, and other artwork that is relevant to the students' work. Students are sometimes asked to present an assessment of the entire folder, or to select work they consider pivotal in their development. The portfolio assessment is focused on the process of learning rather than on the artwork itself.

General criteria for evaluating portfolios might include these: (1) conceptualizing and carrying out a project; (2) use of historical and critical materials that are related to or help explicate the student's own work; (3) regular, relevant, precise entries; (4) thinking directly in an artistic medium; (5) signs of development and linkage from one work or set of works to another; (6) students' sensitivity to their own development; and (7) expression of personal meanings that are given some universal form. Judging these components is not easy, according to Gardner, but even the attempt to monitor the development of a student's work over a period of time has proved worthwhile.

Another type of journal, or set of journal entries, is one kept by a team of four or five students. Periodically, the teacher could assign a theme for the class to consider. A team leader might be selected to write a response first; then each team member in turn would be given an opportunity to write. The position of leader should be rotated so that each participant has an opportunity to write first. After the team leader makes the first entry in the journal, other members are asked to comment on at least one previous entry. Such an activity may help students develop tolerance for a variety of opinions. It also gives students who are less inclined to speak out in a group a chance to voice and defend an opinion. The teacher then reads the entries and adds his or her own entry. Then, individual or collaborative studio projects may be assigned as a response to the themes examined.

The teaching portfolio or research journal that we recommend is formative. It is a tool, and the process of learning is encouraged and valued above the final product. Therefore, students' responses may reflect the indecision and searching that indicate growth. Evaluation of portfolios is qualitative; thus the teacher's comments should be thoughtful and sensitive. Students need to be informed that their own investment, learning, and self-evaluation are of paramount importance. However, students may also need to be reminded that their journal entries and assignments are somewhat public, because the teacher will read them.

If censorship becomes an issue, teachers may wish to encourage students to create a second journal or diary for their more personal thoughts and drawings. Students should also be allowed to seal pages that the teacher is not to see. Issues of freedom of expression and censorship should be discussed with the students. Art teachers have a legal obligation to uphold the rules of their schools, but they also have a professional obligation to help each student find his or her own artistic voice and thereby relate to the world.

For further discussion of research journals, see Chapter 10.*

CONCLUSION

In this chapter we have examined individual expression and creativity in art, suggesting that making art is both personal and public and that the creativity of artists and student artists has a personal and a social aspect. This is because the core of creativity is making connections between form and meaning, and between art and society. We described and discussed traits of creative individuals and the social role of creativity. Because of its intrinsic function of connecting concepts, ideas, and feelings across disciplinary and other boundaries, we have suggested that metaphorical thinking is a core creative trait and described strategies for enhancing its use in an art for life context. Finally, we have described aspects of establishing a creativity-friendly environment at school and strategies to encourage creativity in a real-world context.

The next chapter focuses on aesthetics both as philosophical foundations for art for life and as inquiry strategies for teaching and learning.

QUESTIONS FOR STUDY AND DISCUSSION

1. Describe the course you took that you feel most enhanced your own creative thinking. What was the most memorable aspect of that experience?

2. Explain how creativity can be social as well as personal.

3. The text offers a list of abilities in creative thinking and a list of creative people's personality traits. Identify three to five of the traits that you think describe you, rate your own creative thinking, and explain your reasoning.

4. What is a metaphor and how does it affect our ability to think and create?

5. What does the acronym SCAMPER stand for? How might this concept be used in an art lesson?

6. What do you consider three of the worst blocks to creativity in the art classroom? Why?

7. Why does true creativity require a depth approach rather than a breadth approach in the art classroom?

8. How do you think teachers can foster a more creative atmosphere in the art classroom?

9. How is keeping a research journal a valuable way to develop creative thinking?

10. Do you think creativity has survival value for humankind? Explain.

---

*Thanks to Lanny Milbrandt for the compilation of many of the ideas presented here in his course, "Stimulating Creative Behavior," Wichita State University, 1982.

FURTHER READING

Amabile, T. M. (1996). *Creativity in context*. Boulder, CO: Westview.

Anderson, T. (1989). Interpreting works of art as social metaphors. *Visual Arts Research 15*(2), 42–51.

Arnheim, R. (1969). *Visual thinking*. Berkeley: University of California Press.

Csikszentmihalyi, M. (1996). *Creativity*. New York: HarperCollins.

Davis, G. A. (1999). *Creativity is forever*. (4th ed.). Dubuque, IA.: Kendall/Hunt.

Gardner, H. (1982). *Art, mind, and brain*. New York: Basic Books.

Gordon, W. (1961). *Synectics*. New York: Harper & Row.

Gordon, W. J. & Poze, T. (1980). *The new art of the possible*. Cambridge, MA: Porpoise Books.

Green, M. (1995). *Releasing the imagination: Essays on education, the arts, and social change*. San Francisco, CA: Jossey-Bass.

Koberg, D., & Bagnall, J. (1974). *The universal traveler*. Los Altos, CA: William Kaufman.

London, P. (1989). *No more second-hand art: Awakening the artist within*. Boston: Shambhala.

Lowenfeld, V. (1947). *Creative and mental growth*. New York: Macmillan.

Roukes, N. (1982). *Art synectics*. Calgary, Alberta, Canada: Juniro Arts.

Szekely, G. (1988). *Encouraging creativity in art lessons*. New York: Teachers College Press.

Von Oech, R. (1986). *A kick in the seat of the pants*. New York: Warner.

Aesthetics

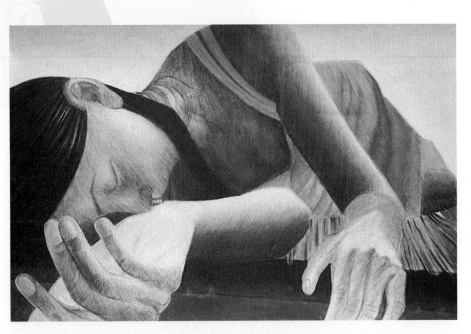

Girl Reclining, Lin Hsieh, Chamblee High, DeKalb County Schools, Atlanta, GA. Kymberly Landers, Art Teacher. *The graceful lines of this resting figure express a serene and peaceful mood. Metacriticism, as aesthetic inquiry, addresses how we talk about such images.*

In Part One we suggested that art for life should be thematic and interdisciplinary and that future art teachers can benefit from understanding the disciplines and foci of art for life in order to implement their own comprehensive interdisciplinary programs. Here, in Chapter 5, we explore aesthetics. It is through **aesthetic inquiry** that we establish the identity and value of art. We will address **aesthetics** first as a philosophical discipline for teachers and then as content and strategies of inquiry for students.

WHAT IS AESTHETICS?

Most cultures have some philosophy of art and beauty. Some of these philosophies—for example, in India, in European and American culture, and among the Yoruba people of West Africa—are highly articulated and defined by experts. Others are simply implicit in how people make, see, and value things, as in American folk art and among the Shuor people of South America. In this chapter, we are dealing with the discipline of aesthetics that is a branch of western philosophy. Categorically, western philosophical aesthetics addresses the nature of art, beauty, aesthetic experience, and talk about art and visual culture. Less intrinsically it also addresses these aspects of other cultures. Aesthetics is a sophisticated, philosophically grounded, explicit, systematic examination of these issues.

Systematically, aesthetics consists of asking questions and then developing arguments or theories to answer them. Its content is these questions and answers, presented as theories. In aesthetics there are no ultimate answers; there are only stronger and weaker arguments. There is no ultimate truth; there are only constructed meanings. This will become apparent in a brief examination of some primary issues in the history of aesthetics.

WHAT ARE THE PRIMARY CONCERNS OF AESTHETICS?

Traditionally, aesthetics addresses questions of beauty, the nature of the **aesthetic response,** how we define and value art, and how we talk about art. These are not the only possibilities for aesthetic inquiry, but they do provide a good start, and we will look at each topic in some detail.

Beauty

Possibly the earliest aesthetic issue, going back to the ancient Greeks, is the nature of beauty. How can beauty be defined so that it can be recognized and its qualities agreed upon by everyone? At least since the time of Socrates, philosophers have been debating what is beautiful and what is not, why, and how we are to decide. Recently, some theorists have argued that beauty is defined and agreed on by groups of people who make different decisions at different times and places. According to this argument, beauty would change from time to time and place to place. Today, thousands of years after this issue first arose, it is still impossible to define beauty. Is a Lexus SUV or a Honda Prius more beautiful? Long straight hair or curly short hair? A painting by Jackson Pollock or an Iroquois false face mask? Beauty, simply put, is in the eye of the beholder and is based on the beholder's values and experience in the world.

Aesthetic Response

Although it is nearly impossible to define beauty exactly, a second primary issue in aesthetics, the nature of aesthetic experience, is rooted firmly in notions of beauty. We have all had a heightened emotional response to a sunset, a ride in a fast car, or the sound of an aria bouncing off stone walls in a darkened Italian city. Western philosophers have typically linked this response to the beauty inherent in those objects and events. This heightened reaction to beautiful or special things is called the aesthetic response. Traditional aestheticians describe it as functionally disinterested: that is, we are interested in having this feeling for its own sake rather than for any extrinsic purpose. The aesthetic response is also described as holistic: it is perceived as a whole, unified experience which is given unity by a driving, pervasive emotion. But contemporary aestheticians are not so sure that a totally disinterested response exists or can exist in human beings, because perception—what we see—has to do with how we see and why we are looking.

Defining and Valuing Art: Theories

The nature of aesthetic experience is a convenient springboard for a third issue, which is probably the most important issue for art education: how we define and value art and, more recently, visual culture. Notions of aesthetic response were important to the eighteenth-century philosophers who developed the foundations of modern aesthetic theory.

In the late Middle Ages and early Renaissance, the nature and functions of western art began to change fundamentally. Before that time, most art in western culture, like most art everywhere, was functional. It was skillfully made to be beautiful and special, to call attention to itself, not for its own sake but so that it could point to or serve some extrinsic function. Church murals created the necessary awe and gave appropriate visual instructions on how to live well or how to get to heaven; the carved dragons on the prows of Viking ships were designed to contain the spirit of the dragon so as to keep mariners safe at sea; and so on. Then, in Italy and elsewhere, there arose a new philosophy of humanism, which gave people more sense of themselves as individuals. Individual artists increasingly began to use art for self-expression rather than for practical and social functions. Eventually, the idea of art as personal expression became predominant. This idea focused not on the extrinsic functions of art but on its capacity to evoke an aesthetic response through its expressive power.

The German philosopher Baumgarten coined the term "aesthetics" about 1750 to mean "the science of perception." Artworks, in Baumgarten's aesthetics, were characterized by their capacity to elicit an aesthetic response from the viewer. If art was fundamentally aesthetic (existing for its own sake and detached from any social or practical functions), its value could be determined only aesthetically. The philosophers of the British empirical tradition, most notably Hume, took it upon themselves to develop a way to judge art within this aesthetic context. What they came up with is called the "faculty of taste."

The faculty of taste was thought of as sort of a sixth sense—an interior sense—that made forms, colors, and composition of works of art and natural phenomena aesthetically meaningful. The German philosopher Kant synthesized this Enlightenment view and in doing so became the acknowledged father of modern aesthetics. The nature of art, as defined by aesthetics, until fairly recent times revolved around the idea that artworks were aesthetic objects designed to arouse a disinterested aesthetic response in the viewer. Artworks were to be judged, therefore, primarily on their compositional qualities and whether those qualities were thought by one having a certain faculty of taste to present sufficient unity or wholeness to be aesthetically appealing. This set of ideas has become the foundation for the aesthetic theory of formalism (which is discussed below and also in Chapter 8). But formalism is only one way to understand and value art. There are other theories as well.

Since the eighteenth century the discussion of how art is defined and valued has expanded considerably. Discussion, theory, and debate tend to be focused on questions about (1) the work of art itself (its physical, compositional, and technical qualities); (2) the artist, particularly the artist's intentions in making the work; (3) the viewer, particularly his or her sensory experience and emotional and intellectual states; and (4) the context in which the work is made, seen, and used. Aesthetic theories tend to be based on which of these issues aestheticians focus on and how. Among the dominant aesthetic theories are mimesis, formalism, expressionism, and pragmatism.

Probably the most widely held and perhaps the oldest clearly defined aesthetic theory in western culture is mimesis. Although very few serious philosophers still advocate **mimetic theory,** many artists work in a realistic or naturalistic mode, and most North Americans unconsciously judge art according to how well an artist can imitate the real world. "I don't know much about art, but that doesn't look like a palm tree to me" is an uninformed mimetic judgment. The aim of mimesis is objective accuracy. Many contemporary theorists see this goal as unworthy of serious artistic consideration, because simple imitation, they reason, is only a skill. Mimetic artists have included Leonardo, Rembrandt, and Andrew Wyeth—only a skill indeed!

Formalism is an aesthetic theory that finds excellence in the expressive power arising from what are seen to be correct relationships between forms and colors in an artwork. This theory has been championed by a number of noted aestheticians and critics such as Bell, Beardsley, Collingwood, and Greenburg from the early twentieth century until the present. It tends to be a coolly rational approach to art that disregards themes, illusions, and references to the outside world, focusing instead on pure form and on the compositional qualities within a work. Art that is most purely formalist might include the early work of Frank Stella, the color-field work of Joseph Albers, and the work of the contemporary painter Ray Burggraf. (See Color Plate 7, Ray Burggraf, *Jungle Arc,* 1998.)

By contrast, **expressionism** finds excellence in the degree of a work's emotional power, usually through exaggeration of form and color and animated, dynamic treatment of forms. Artists who work in the expressionist mode include Franz Marc (See Color Plate 8, Franz Marc, *The Large Blue Horses,* 1911), Francis Bacon, and Constantin Brancusi. These artists show us more how life feels to them than how it looks. Thus expressionist theories tend to focus on the psychological and the realm of inner experience—the realm of the heart. Among the most important theorists of art as the expression of emotion are Leo Tolstoy and Suzanne Langer.

A more recent development in aesthetics is contextualism. Contextualists— rather than examining the physical qualities of art or its effects on individual perceivers—focus on the circumstances surrounding artistic objects and performances. In essence, pragmatic aestheticians argue that art is art because people in a society, in communication with each other, agree that certain things with certain qualities will be art.

Two theories, at least, should be mentioned as having opened the door for contemporary contextual theory. The first was Wittgenstein's "family resemblance" theory, an open rather than a closed system of definition, which was further developed by Weitz and others in the realm of art. Before Wittgenstein, many

FIGURE 5.1 Example of the mimetic approach. Maria Sibylla Merian, *Banana Plant from Metamorphosis Insectorum Surinamensium,* c. 1750. Watercolor, 12¾ x 9 inches. *Merian traveled to South America from her home in the Netherlands to study and draw exotic plants—an extraordinary adventure for a woman in the 1700s.*

aestheticians argued that something had to have both necessary and sufficient conditions in order to be called art: for example, unity, variety, and dynamic tension. Wittgenstein's theory led others to the idea that art need not have one or several ever-present qualities. Instead, there tend to be some of a larger group of qualities that we can pick from, some of which will be in some artworks, others of which may be in others. But the obvious question that follows, then, is who decides?

This question—who decides?—leads to perhaps the most important recent development in aesthetics: **institutional theory.** Dickie (1974) and later Danto (1988) argued that society decides, collectively, what is and what is not art. This decision is based not only on physical qualities and traits such as beauty, skill, and aesthetic (compositional) appeal, but more fundamentally on how these qualities are seen by the group as making the potential artwork—as Dissanayake would put it—"special" and thus worthy of the status of art. Different groups make different decisions in different times and places; that is why classic Yoruban art has different forms and functions from classic Greek art. In institutional theory, there are no universal forms.

One type of institutional theory, **pragmatism,** focuses on the context in which a work is made, seen, or used. An extensive examination of context is the most important factor in determining the nature and value of a work. This context can include the artist and his or her intentions, circumstances, themes, media, and so on; the larger physical and social circumstances of the making of the work (for example, war or peace and other social conditions); and what place the artwork has in social values, mores, and institutions. For example, what do the form and functions of a Japanese tea bowl tell us about certain Japanese social and spiritual beliefs in the context of the tea ceremony?

Pragmatism is the basic philosophy of contemporary visual culture studies. The context in which art is made and used, and in particular its meanings and effects on society, is crucially important for the examination of visual culture, in which the point is not appreciation but understanding. The point of pragmatism in the study of visual culture is not whether something is beautiful or even whether it is art; rather, the question is what a visually expressive artifact or performance does and how it affects individuals and society.

Conceptualism is another aesthetic theory made possible by an open, institutional approach. It is related to pragmatism in focusing on meaning rather than form. Conceptualism departs completely from the traditional realm of the aesthetic as a response to beauty. It examines the idea embedded in an artistic act or work. The first **conceptual** artist may have been Marcel Duchamp, in the early twentieth century. He signed a urinal (R. Mutt), put it on its back on a pedestal in a museum, and claimed it was art. This claim was based on context: he was an artist of some standing, he said this work was art, and the artistic establishment accepted it and displayed it as art in a recognized art museum. And because it was accepted as art by an institutional authority, it has in fact become art, not for its aesthetic value but for the idea it contains.

Talking about Art

The fourth traditional concern of western aesthetics is how we talk about art. All the theories and arguments described above about the significance of form, the viewer's perception of and response to form, and the social and physical contexts of art and visual culture are concerned with how we define and value art. These issues and other issues of definition and value frame **metacriticism:** how we talk about art.

Aesthetics provides the philosophical foundation for informed talk about art. This informed talk is called **art criticism.** As we will discuss in Chapter 6, art critics have different reasons, different points of view, and thus different structures when they examine and talk about works of art. Their structures come from their aesthetic theories or systems of belief. Art criticism, in turn, provides raw material for the development of aesthetic theory. So theory and practice continuously inform each other. In short, aesthetics provides the theory for talk about art, criticism provides the raw material for theory, and metacriticism—the last of the four functions of aesthetics to be discussed here—provides the structure to make the talk possible. Metacriticism is discussed further in Chapter 6. Here, we will move on to the act of aesthetics. What do aestheticians actually do?

WHAT DO AESTHETICIANS DO?

What, ultimately, do aestheticians do? It's simple in concept but complex in practice. The simple part is that they ask questions about the nature and value of art, of art talk, and, traditionally, of beauty and aesthetic experience. The complex part is that they develop arguments or theories about these issues or about some aspect of the issues. As we said at the beginning of this chapter, there is no final truth in aesthetics: there are only stronger and weaker arguments and theories. A practical example of how theories might compete for your attention in your work as an art teacher might be useful here.

Using Aesthetics in the Curriculum:
Deciding on Your Own Values*

Many art teachers are not certain how to use aesthetics in their own programs. But consciously or unconsciously, teachers do use aesthetic concepts in art curricula. Any lesson or curriculum instituted by teachers comes from what they believe is important. Defining art, determining its meanings and value, and deciding how it is to be approached are core issues of aesthetics. Of particular concern for art educators are the questions that aestheticians ask about the definition, meaning, value, and functions of art, and how to talk about art. Systematically trying to answer these questions results in aesthetic theory. These aesthetic theories shape and direct a curriculum. They are a manifestation of the teacher's values.

As an example, let us consider two aesthetic theories: formalism and contextualism. These theories have been debated endlessly as positions an art teacher could take in forming his or her program. Formalism has been held to be unapologetically essentialist, valuing art for its own sake. Contextualism has been held to be socially engaged and potentially reconstructionist.

Formalism

Formalism emphasizes (1) use of the elements and principles of design, (2) manipulation of materials involving mastery of particular media, and (3) originality, all leading to production of objects that have "significant form," or that look good, look well crafted, and aren't copies of other work—in short, objects that look like art with a capital "A."

In answering the question "What is art?" formalists emphasize form, how objects look, what materials are used, and what skills and techniques the artist has demonstrated. They take an essentialist approach in that they consider art intrinsically important. Art is for art's sake. Art, formalists contend, should not have a primary concern with anything outside itself—not politics, not economics, not the community. The quality that makes art different from everything else in the world, so that it is neither entertainment, therapy, journalism, nor kitsch, is form.

In answering the question "How and why do we value art?" formalism refers to the self-referential quality of art. A good work of art is both avant-garde—a break from tradition—and a continuation of the progression of art. The best art embodies new uses of design elements and media. All this newness reflects the essential

*Much of this section is taken from "A Role for Aesthetics in Centering the K–12 Art Curriculum," Sally McRorie, coauthor. Originally published in *Art Education, 50*(23), 6–14.

FIGURE 5.2 *Reflection,* Tom Anderson, photograph. *Aesthetics, as a branch of philosophy, is reflecting on the meaning and value of art, beauty, and aesthetic experience.*

quality of originality of thought and processes of the individual artist. Art is valued (and judged) for the qualities that set it apart from the rest of the world, the things that make it intrinsically important.

In answering the question "What is the function of art?" formalists maintain that the function is transcendental. Art transcends the ordinary by offering the artist and the viewer an extraordinary experience, beyond the commonplace, and so art is answerable only to a higher standard.

How is formalism manifested in school art curricula? It leads to emphasis on the elements and principles of design. This results in numerous design projects and experiments with cut paper, color mixing, contour lines, texture rubbings, and the like. It also results in an emphasis on experimentation with media.

The formalist emphasis on originality results in mostly individual projects, in which students work alone, following the model of the solitary artist, with a well-crafted, highly creative work of art as the goal. The focus is on the character of the work of art itself as represented in its formal and technical quality and originality, rather than on what it means, stands for, or does beyond eliciting an aesthetic response. The elements and principles and the use of media and related techniques lend themselves to formalist universalism: ideally, they constitute a form that can be read by peers and strangers alike. This form is considered universal and significant.

Contextualism

Contextualists believe that the meaning and worth of art can be determined only in the context in which it is made and used. They think of art as social communication, which, like spoken or written language, requires the artist and the receiver to understand a code in order to understand the work. Since art is communication that requires a shared code within a specific cultural matrix, they believe that there are no universal forms or meanings. A large contingent of contextualists, called **instrumentalists** or pragmatists, think that art is never for its own sake. They hold that the aesthetic response does and should serve extrinsic purposes; that is, it should lead to some concrete thought, action, or activity beyond itself. Some instrumentalists think that this action should be a reconstruction of existing social systems and that the value in art lies in its potential to change society.

As we mentioned earlier, contemporary **contextualism** owes its form to George Dickie, who developed an institutional definition of art based on Arthur Danto's concept of the "art world." Dickie held that art could not be defined by looking at its formal or technical qualities, because no one set of qualities can be found universally in all works of art. Thus instead of looking to the work for a definition, Dickie looked to the people who made, viewed, and used the work. He argued that in a specialized, hierarchical society, cultural institutions speak for various specialties, and that the art world (curators, painters, art historians, gallery owners, art teachers, and so on) collectively defines art.

This argument explains some of the struggles for position we see today. If art is defined by people who are recognized as the art world, then who exactly gets to decide? Women, African-Americans, and other representatives of cultural minorities have been underrepresented in the art world. They have felt left out of the universal formalist agenda and have been the strongest advocates of instrumental reconstructionism. Of particular concern to reconstructionists has been the formalists' devaluing of the narrative, socially communicative, and collaborative aspects of art. Many people have felt that the formalist agenda did not allow their stories to be told and wished to retrieve the narrative function of art. Not satisfied to merely mirror a formalist reality that they saw as overwhelmingly indicative of a white male power structure, they have attempted to reconstruct art and, through art, society. Many contemporary artists now use personal narrative and reconstructionist subject matter in their work.

A contextually oriented art curriculum, then, assumes that art has some purpose beyond being merely decorative or formally adept. Since art is communication between two or more people about things that count, form does not exist for its own sake or for the sake of pure enjoyment. This also implies that form is to be composed in a manner that will be understood at some essential level by both the sender and the receiver. In a pure contextualist curriculum, then, you won't find technique or design for its own sake. Pure aesthetic enjoyment is not an accepted rationale for making art.

Such a curriculum favors skills related to constructing and interpreting meaning; developing signs, symbols, and codes within a mutually understandable social matrix; and analyzing, interpreting, and evaluating images. Contextual programs lean more toward academic aspects than toward experimental or technical studio work. Studio projects involve narrative and other social subject matter. The contextualist curriculum also generally selects against creative self-expression; this is because signs and systems of signs must be mutually understood, whereas creativity often results in works that are individualistic, idiosyncratic, and inaccessible.

In a contextualist curriculum, whether students are interpreting or making artworks, what is most valued is that the work tells us something significant about human experience beyond the art world and in many cases has the power to move us to action. Therefore, a contextually oriented curriculum is based on themes. Fundamental human concerns (themes) are used to organize instruction—as opposed to the common formalist practice of organizing curricula around elements and principles of design, or media and techniques, or both. Ultimately, the defining characteristic of the contextualist curriculum is that it in some way helps us to understand people through their art rather than art for its own sake. (A contextualist philosophy is illustrated in Color Plate 9, *Great Wall of Los Angeles* by Judith Baca, 1976.)

FIGURE 5.3 Betye Saar, *The Liberation of Aunt Jemima*, 1972, mixed media. *In this socially reconstructivist work, the two-dimensional stereotypical advertising images of Aunt Jemima in smiling servitude are juxtaposed behind a three-dimensional liberated Aunt Jemima surrounded by a rifle, a pistol, and the black power salute.*

Useful Eclecticism

It should be clear that neither pure formalism (with its emphasis on elements and principles, exploration of media, and originality) nor pure contextualism (with its emphasis on communication and socially relevant subject matter) is adequate for a comprehensive approach to art for life. Most art teachers include aspects of both approaches and recognize that an exclusive focus on either would be shortsighted. Therefore, we advocate a pragmatic combination of contextualism and formalism to conceptually center K–12 art for life. (An example of a blending of artistic intentions may be viewed in the artwork of Mark Messersmith, *Afternoon of the Faun*, 2002, Color Plate 10.)

The contextualists' idea that art is about something beyond itself and the formalists' attention to technique and design are not mutually exclusive. Rather, they can be combined, allowing an almost infinite range of highly suitable art curricula that are locally specific, include themes to fire individual students' imagination as well as a collective social conscience, and integrate skills and techniques so that students can communicate their ideas visually. Such goals, or values, meet the criteria of both aesthetic approaches: the formalist ideal of the intrinsic importance of art and the contextualist ideal of its extrinsic functions. However, the teacher needs to establish the balance. In practice, most art teachers don't follow—and don't wish to follow—totally prescribed curricula. The diversity of localized needs and resources coupled with individual teachers' strengths and shortcomings works against curricula prescribed from afar. But all art teachers, including those who choose or are forced to work within externally imposed structures, can successfully modify or personalize curricula by answering aesthetic questions in the context of their own schools and communities.

To check your values, consider what your centering concepts say to students, parents, other teachers, the principal, the community members, and other stakeholders about what art is, what its functions are, and why it should be important in the schools. In answering these questions, balance community concerns with issues and skills that you, as an expert, know your students need for a meaningful education in art.

One way to include community values and involve students in meaningful aesthetic activity is to have students participate in answering the aesthetic questions that are a focus of your curriculum. For both the teacher and the students, cooperatively derived themes, functions of art to be investigated together, and agreed-on media and techniques that allow collaborative as well as individual exploration are more meaningful and engaging than those for a curriculum imposed from outside. Using aesthetics collaboratively to shape the curriculum leads directly to students' aesthetic inquiry—which in turn is integral to making, understanding, and appreciating art.

Art teachers, then, must ask themselves aesthetic questions and arrive at their own answers, to meet their own needs in their own curricula and communities.

Aesthetics as Critical Inquiry: A Course of Study*

Aesthetic inquiry in an educational setting has to do with framing questions as much as seeking answers. Much good work has been done in defining the theory and practice of aesthetics for art education. However, from a teacher's point of view, the practical strategies of implementing aesthetics may be the least clearly understood aspect of aesthetics. Therefore, in this section we take a look at aesthetics as critical inquiry in the context of teaching art for life. Content (aesthetic theory) is acquired through critical skills, strategies, and ways of thinking intrinsic to philosophical aesthetics. More important, student teachers discover what they and their peers value in art, and why, as preparation for teaching art in K–12 programs.

Following is an instructional sequence centered on asking questions and seeking answers about (1) meaning and value in art, (2) how we discuss art, (3) aesthetic experience, and (4) beauty. It comes from an introductory course in aesthetics and art criticism for teachers and is used here to illustrate means and methods of aesthetic inquiry for secondary and postsecondary art education. It is not prescriptive. Rather, it is meant only to stimulate your own ideas about developing aesthetic inquiry in your own particular context.

Is It Art? The Case of Sherrie Levine

The first activity in the sequence addresses both the meaning and value of art and how we talk about art. Students consider what appears to be a print by Edward Weston. The usual collective reaction is that the image is awe-inspiring, or that it represents a transformation of everyday things into sculpture, or both. Then more contextual information is given about Weston's use of natural light, his ability to get

---

*This section is largely from an article by Anderson that appeared as "Aesthetics as Critical Inquiry," *Art Education, 51*(5), 49–55.

A CLOSER LOOK — Is Sherrie Levine an Artist?

No

1. It's not an original image.

2. What she does is blatant plagiarism; her work is simply a copy. She doesn't respect the artistic property of others.

3. Her production is only technical. She didn't create the original image.

4. A concept is not art. Art is aesthetic. She didn't produce but only reproduced an aesthetic object.

Yes

1. Her work is not plagiarism. She gives credit, in the manner of a bibliography, to those from whom she has appropriated images.

2. She exhibits technical skill.

3. She makes a strong conceptual statement.

4. She's very creative. It's a very original idea to appropriate images and thereby deny that any particular image is the property of any one artist.

5. Her intent is artistic because through appropriation she changes the meaning of the image.

Questions Generated

1. What is art? (Is appropriation art real art?)

2. What makes art valuable?

3. How do we decide?

4. Who decides? (Who has the right to decide?)

Criteria Presented to Substantiate Arguments For or Against

1. Ethics

2. Emotion, power of expression

3. Skill or technique

4. Composition

5. Artistic process, time, effort

6. Social validation or status

7. Creativity

8. Sincerity

9. Usefulness

10. Artistic intent

11. Communicative power

12. Value of the idea

a range of tones, his concern with the architecture of form, and so on. With regard to evaluation, two camps usually form: some students say that Weston, godlike, helps us to understand our place in the world, profoundly; others, evidently having seen too many postcards and holiday calendars, say "Been there, done that, seen that." This debate leads to a discussion of context as a factor in determining meaning and value. Then the students are told that what Weston did to achieve the original effect really is of only secondary importance in understanding the image, because, in fact, this is a picture by Sherrie Levine.

The instructor explains that Sherrie Levine became famous as an **appropriation** artist, and this is a picture of a picture. While she worked in this mode, Levine held that taking a picture of Weston's picture was like taking a picture of a landscape or a still life. She was making a feminist statement by appropriating the work of dead white men, taking art away from dominant white males and bringing it into the public domain. The instructor also tells the students that Levine's goal, stated while she was in art school, was to be famous, and this was her means of attaining fame. Finally, they are told that she was sued for copyright infringement by the family of Edward Weston, and lost.

At this point, invariably, some students will be outraged and will attack Levine, while others will come to her defense. The heated argument should be allowed to

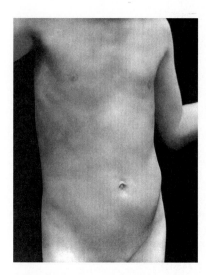

FIGURE 5.4   Edward Weston, *Neil Nude*, 1925. *This is one of the images from a series of* Six Nudes of Neil* *by Weston reproduced by Sherrie Levine. Each of Levine's photographs is titled "after" the name of the artist whose work has been copied. These blatant appropriations question the nature of originality.*
*ROM

build for just a few minutes before being cut off. Then the students are given a one-page homework assignment entitled either: "Sherry Levine Is a True-Blue, Original, Big-League Artist" or "Sherrie Levine Is a Plagiarist, Charlatan, and Con Artist." Students are to produce a reasoned argument: that is, they must support their position with evidence and logic. Research is encouraged.

On the next day there is a debate. Those who think Sherrie Levine is not an artist sit on one side of the room; those who think she is an artist sit on the other side. The students then present arguments. These arguments—though the students may not realize it—are the actual crux of the instructional unit. Thus the instructor should act as a referee, influencing the structure and direction of the debate and occasionally jumping in on the losing side (and switching sides if necessary). Reasons why Levine is to be considered an artist are written on one side of a chalkboard; reasons why not are written on the other side. Space is left in the middle for questions and reasons: the evidence, systems, and context that make up criteria and judgments.

Neither team should be defeated—a defeat would be counterproductive—so the debate should be stopped at a point where the two sides are rather evenly balanced. Students will then frequently ask the instructor for the "right" answer. Whether or not the instructor thinks there is a right answer, he or she should direct the students to the questions and criteria written on the board. The instructor should explain to the students that they have generated questions, criteria, and arguments central to many important aesthetic theories. For example, emotion or power of expression is a premise of expressionism; ethics is central to pragmatism; and so on.

Broader issues can also be addressed. For example, it soon becomes apparent in the debate that whether or not Levine is an artist depends on whether or not what she makes is art. Thus object-centered aesthetics emerges almost immediately. But perceiver-centered aesthetics also arises as students try to determine whether the point of her work is an aesthetic response or something else. Institutionalist aesthetics arises as students try to decide who exactly has the authority to designate Levine as an artist or not an artist.

Considering the students' arguments in terms of particular aesthetic premises and theories begins to establish the idea that aesthetic theory is built on practical inquiry. A second idea is that criteria are premises for arguments. Many different arguments can all be correct when they are based on different criteria. A third idea is that aestheticians undertake the same sort of open-ended, criterion-based searches and debates in addressing the great questions of their subject. The instructor should conclude this session with a fourth idea: that aesthetics consists of questions that are answered as theory, that a theory is not truth but only a persuasive argument, and that for now the question of Sherrie Levine's legitimacy as an artist will remain open.

Meaning and Value in Art

To further address meaning and value in art, the students' homework for the next session is to bring in two objects: one they consider to be a work of art and one they consider not to be a work of art. Again, they are to defend their choices with reasons and criteria. Some students have argued that the following are art: original paintings, prints of masterpieces, drawings, children's art, ceramic mold sculptures, manufactured objects, jewelry, photographs, seashell folk art, Coke cans, paper clips, and twigs. Other students have argued that the following are not art: twigs, Coke cans, paper clips, paintings of Elvis on black velvet, wads of paper, clothespins, and fine art prints. Again, the instructor's role is to record questions and criteria on the board while asking provocative questions to keep the discussion lively.

Given even the few objects just listed, the issues for discussion are virtually limitless. An obvious question is why, say, a painting is art. If it's art because it's unique, then why isn't a tree or a snowflake art? If it's art because of the skill that

Chapter 5 Aesthetics

A CLOSER LOOK — A Student-Generated Position: What Is Art?

Students in a course on teaching aesthetics and art criticism developed the following statement.

"Art must be made by a person. No object not made by a person, no matter how beautiful, no matter how aesthetically it may be viewed, is art. Trees, driftwood, and beautiful shells are not art. Art has to be intended to be art. Maybe this means that art has to have an aesthetic component, but we're not absolutely sure about this. In addition to being aesthetic, much art can be functional, like a quilt or a Coke can. We aren't sure if all works of art everywhere must have a quality of originality, but we are sure that it's important for art to be original in this culture. We think art that can be made up of copies—for example, photographs—is lesser art than one-of-a-kind objects like paintings. Just because it's art doesn't make it good. There may be bad art as well as good art. The best art has a high purpose (for example, commercial art is less good than high art), high skill, and strong composition.

went into its execution, why isn't a haircut or a perfectly thrown pass art? Or maybe they are? If a painting is art because it's unique, how can a photograph be art? After all, a photograph is only a mechanical reproduction. But if mechanically reproduced objects—photographs—can be art, what about a postcard or a fine art print? To return to the painting: if skilled execution by the artist is a criterion, what about the work of Mark Kastabe, who pays other artists to make original Kastabes. If we accept that people other than the artist can make art, what about the Coke can? It's beautifully and powerfully designed but made by a machine. Does it fail to qualify as art because it's mechanically reproduced? What about the prototype, then? Was that art because it was an original object, the first of its kind, and was made by a human being? Does the fact that the Coke can has a function beyond the aesthetic preclude its being art? Why isn't a twig a work of art? It's also a beautifully formed, exquisite design. Can we say it is art because God made it? If we say this, will we have to say that because God made everything, everything is art? And if everything is art, what makes art different from anything else? If everything is art, is "art" even a useful concept? Here's a photo of an "artwork" by an elephant. Does this refute the idea that art is made only by humans? Can we say that the elephant is only a tool used by the real artist, the person who supplies the elephant with brushes and paint?

Clearly, the discussion should be free-ranging, organic, connective, and thematic, considering all the items presented rather than focusing first on one student's objects, then the next student's. As points are made, the instructor should support those that reflect traditional aesthetics, but not too soon to impede give and take and not so authoritatively as to cut off contrary opinions. For example, when a student says that art must be made by people, the instructor might note that this position is supported by Suzanne Langer, who describes art as an embodiment of human feeling in a sensuous form. When a student suggests that art can be functional or instrumentalist, the instructor may note that this position is supported by Suzi Gablik and numerous traditional cultures, in which aesthetic objects are considered useful in calling forth the gods, cementing group values, selling goods, and so on. If a student argues that a work of art—for example, a chair or a quilt—is less valuable because it's functional, the instructor might cite formalists or expressionists who support that position. If a student argues that a work of art must be original, the instructor could mention any number of theorists in various camps, including Collingwood, Dewey, and Langer, who support that idea. This discussion is followed by discussions in small groups and then large groups, and then by a collaborative written paper: "What Is Art?" An example of such a paper is presented in the sidebar.

Aesthetic and Artistic Experience

The students' next assignment is to write a one- or two-page description of their most memorable aesthetic experiences and read these descriptions to each other in class.* The question of beauty always arises in addressing aesthetic experience, since beauty usually is the prime stimulus for an aesthetic response. An additional question that may have more to do with value and meaning of art also can appropriately be addressed at this point: the difference between aesthetic and artistic experience. The primary distinction is reception (aesthetic experience) versus some kind of manipulation of material to achieve an aesthetic effect (artistic experience). This issue is of particular significance to future art teachers.

As students read and discuss their papers, their peers try to identify the significant qualities of aesthetic experience. Each student makes a list of the qualities of each experience. The instructor should be ready to ask some guiding questions: "Well, she felt pretty strongly about that, didn't she? What was her sense of time? Did you notice the detail of her description? What sorts of things was she describing?" And so on.

As homework, each student writes about the qualities of an aesthetic experience. In the next class meeting, students discuss those qualities in small groups. Then spokespeople for the small groups present their agreed-on qualities to the class. Someone lists the qualities on the board. After all the qualities have been listed, there is further discussion and negotiation to come up with a final synthesis. Following is an example of a synthesis.

> Aesthetic experience is a heightened emotional response to some object or experience, whether natural or made by a person, that is perceived through the senses. Usually it's a feeling you get in the face of beauty. It's more intense than mere appreciation. Aesthetic experience is quite individual and is triggered by different things in different people. Aesthetic experience seems to flow in a natural and seamless way, creating a sort of wholeness or oneness of the person with what is being experienced. There's a heightened consciousness, but in spite of that you seem to lose your sense of self. Often you lose track of time. Aesthetic experience requires receptivity to it, but it is often stimulated by surprise or out-of-the-ordinary circumstances. It is considered positive (usually extremely positive) by the person experiencing it—a peak experience—although there can be negative aspects. Afterward, there's always a sense of satisfaction at having really experienced something special. Although it's experienced for its own sake, for the pleasure it brings, sometimes it stimulates changes in life. Finally, it has to start from the senses. Even if it's experienced as a dream, the dream had to have some basis in sensory input in order to exist.

As follow-up, the questions that the students generated in the course of their debate are also noted and then returned to them by the instructor. These questions are intended to be an aid to future teachers in leading their own discussions. A list generated during one class follows.

> What is the overall sense of being? How do you think and feel while engaged in an aesthetic experience? What feelings or kinds of feelings are involved in aesthetic experience? What is the role of intellect (especially in relation to feeling)? How is aesthetic experience different from artistic experience? What is the role of beauty in aesthetic experience? Is aesthetic experience (at least primarily) positive in nature, or can it be dominated by negative experiences and feelings? What is the role of sensation? Must there always be

---

*The assignment, in part, was first presented to Anderson by Paul Edmonston at the University of Georgia.

something sensual to stimulate aesthetic experience? Can a dream, for example, be aesthetic? Are there necessary or sufficient physical qualities or aspects of aesthetic experience? Must it be individually experienced, or can it be collective? Is there a necessary attitude that accompanies it? What are the roles of education, preparation, and surprise? Does the heart of the experience lie in the object or event or in the viewer's perception of it?

Again, students are told that they have generated questions reflecting significant positions in aesthetics: centered on the object, the viewer, the interaction between them, and the physical and psychological context. This also should stimulate further reading and discussion about traditional aesthetic theories, such as expressionism, mimesis, formalism, and pragmatism; the premises and assumptions of each position; and the criteria applied in each theory to define artistic excellence and aesthetic experience. These theories are not to be thought of as "truth"; they are merely positions arrived at through the same processes that the students have just followed. At this juncture it is good to reinforce the notion that the students are functioning as aestheticians; point out to them that they have individually analyzed and synthesized experience, argued for or cooperatively developed criteria, tried to convince the class of their position, revised their position as necessary in the face of new evidence or stronger arguments, and finally tested it against previously established aesthetic theory.

Finally, students frequently confuse the word *aesthetic,* used to describe a type of response, with the discipline of aesthetics. To clear up this confusion, the instructor should note that *aesthetics* is a noun, as in "the discipline of aesthetics." *Aesthetic* is an adjective used to describe an experience or a quality of being. A traditional goal of art education has been to heighten students' aesthetic awareness through experiences in which students attend to aesthetic qualities in nature and in the built environment. As students become sensitive to the beauty of common experiences, such as an unusual crack in the pavement or the texture of a pinecone, they begin to accumulate visual experiences that enrich their enjoyment of daily life and help them find meaning in a work of art.

Although aesthetic responses to nature or art are based on the students' perception of beauty, such responses may also be culturally specific. Western art teachers have typically encouraged aesthetic awareness of nature and art through the study of formal qualities: line, shape, color, and so on. In this way students come to implicitly understand the meaning of the formal concepts and qualities in art and in everyday visual experience that are culturally desirable, through what they are encouraged to focus on and the language they use to describe their aesthetic responses or experiences. For example, the strong horizontal lines of a landscape in Kansas may suggest welcoming spaciousness to a flatlander but at the same time may appear dull and uninteresting to a tourist longing for the dramatic diagonal ruggedness of the Rockies or the soothing, rolling curves of the Appalachians.

Interpretations of visual experience may depend on personal and cultural contexts, but the importance of attending to the visual environment should not be underestimated. Habitually attending to visual experience and developing meaning from that experience enhance students' understanding of the visual world and culture. Noticing the visual environment enhances students' critical consciousness and awareness by asking them to reflect on what they see. A teacher who encourages students to focus on their aesthetic response is asking them to notice and enjoy beautiful, pleasing, or interesting aspects of the visual culture, which is often discussed within the discipline of aesthetics.

ADDITIONAL ACTIVITIES

ACTIVITY   In art education, there is no clear division between aesthetic inquiry and art criticism. These two processes often overlap, as do the other disciplines of art.

However, it is convenient to describe each group of strategies separately, by discipline. Here we present some strategies for aesthetic inquiry.

ACTIVITY   The instructor or students collect cross-cultural images (a totem pole, a painting by Botticelli, a *ukiyo-e* print, an African drum, and so on). Discuss who might have made each one, why, and what it might have been used for. Describe and analyze the qualities of the objects to support ideas about their functions. Do research to learn how the objects are or were used and valued in their original contexts and report back to the group.

Conceptual Purpose   To understand that form follows function, which is culturally determined and varies over time and from place to place.

ACTIVITY   Keep a list, by category, of all types of artwork brought in, discussed, and produced during the year: jewelry, masks, furniture, paintings, and so on.

Conceptual Purpose   To understand the broad range of aesthetic objects and their functions cross-culturally.

ACTIVITY   Students critique examples of formalist, expressionist, mimetic, imitationalist, and pragmatist art. (See R. Anderson, 1990, for more on these categories.)

Conceptual Purpose   To understand broad underlying reasons for making art as clues to forms, and vice versa.

ACTIVITY   "What was designed by an artist?" In this game, students look around the room, noting in turn one thing each thinks was designed by an artist, and why.

Conceptual Purpose   To realize that almost all things made by people are designed and that artists are the people who do the designing, therefore, to understand the importance of art and visual culture in the everyday world.

ACTIVITY   "Token response." (Erickson & Katter, 1991) For this game, a "print gallery" is set up in the art room by the instructor (or students may visit an art gallery). Students put tokens in front of images to indicate their aesthetic judgments: a heart in front of the image they like best; a lightbulb in front of the image they think is most original; a clock in front of the one they think took the most effort or time; a blue ribbon in front of the one they think is best; a hand in front of the one they think was best crafted; a dollar in front of the one they think is worth the most money; a downturned thumb in front of the one they think is bad art; a "yuk" face in front of the one they most dislike; a house in front of one they'd hang in their home.

Conceptual Purpose   To encourage making aesthetic decisions on the basis of defensible criteria, and to discover the difference between an aesthetic judgment (blue ribbon, lightbulb, hand, clock, thumb down), which requires substantiating criteria, evidence, and argument, and a personal preference (heart, "yuk," home), which does not require substantiation. Variation: Tokens may used to represent compositional qualities, (jagged line, undulating line, various shades of blue, and so on).

ACTIVITY   "Synesthetic recognition." In this game, the students feel the texture of items placed in paper bags that correspond with the painted textures of prints placed around the room. They write on a slip of paper which print they think is represented by each bag.

Conceptual Purpose   Recognition that stimuli are often multisensory and that the arts are often cross-disciplinary. Variation: Use sounds or musical passages rather than textures.

ACTIVITY   Have students explore symbols in art by finding examples of symbols in the print media and bringing them to class. Discussion should center on the meanings of symbols in so-called fine art versus advertising or popular art. What forms do symbols take, and why?

Conceptual Purpose   Understanding symbols in the history of art as representing what people know, believe, think, and feel. Variation: Compare symbols over time and cross-culturally in traditional and high arts. A collection might be started that could be sorted categorically by subject (sun, moon, wolf, bird, etc.), culture, time period, and so on. The collection might grow all year.

ACTIVITY   Give the students a theme (boating, love, horses, families, etc.). Have them come to class on a given day with three to five artistic images illustrating the theme. Students should note the artist, date, place where the work was executed, and style. Discussion should ensue about how the subject is portrayed differently by each artist.

Conceptual Purpose   Students begin to distinguish between subject matter and style, each of which contributes to the expressive quality of art.

ACTIVITY   Look in the telephone directory under "art." Discuss whether what is found there is in fact art. Why or why not? Who decides?

Conceptual Purpose   To get students to examine art as a manifestation of visual culture and recognize that various social institutions define art in various ways.

CONCLUSION

In art for life, aesthetics as critical inquiry is a process of teaching students to use the strategies of professional philosophers to develop aesthetic content and in that way to develop their own meanings and values related to art and aesthetic experience. The procedural core of aesthetics lies in the questions put forward and the arguments and positions generated as a result of trying to answer those questions systematically and in relation to some defensible criteria. A sequence of activities addressing four major questions of aesthetics was presented in this chapter: What is beauty? What is the nature of aesthetic experience? How do we define and value art? How do we talk about art? Critical inquiry can be constructed around these four questions.

Critical inquiry gives students a sense of ownership and accomplishment with regard to the methods and content of aesthetics. Students who participate in developing aesthetic theory discover the strategies and the resulting theoretical content of the discipline of aesthetics; they also apply higher-order thinking and gain the confidence to use such thinking for intellectual and social empowerment. This may be the most important educational aim: aesthetics as critical inquiry can make students "players" who decide where and how to move rather than pawns that are moved by others. It gives them the tools they need to be decision makers in the larger world of socially constructed ideas. That is a primary purpose of art for life.

In Chapter 6, we examine art criticism.

QUESTIONS FOR STUDY AND DISCUSSION

1. What are the four categories of questions discussed in the text as being addressed by philosophical aesthetics? Which of these is most interesting to you? Why?

2. What is beautiful to you? Why? Do you feel you need to justify your answer? Why or why not? Discuss with your peers how your tastes are different and the same. Go online to find students your age in a culture other than your own and ask and discuss the same questions.

3. Think of an aesthetic experience you've had and describe it to your group. Discuss its qualities. Are they similar to what students in the example in the chapter found?

4. During the Renaissance in Europe, art changed from serving extrinsic functions (holding things, teaching, and so on) to serving intrinsic functions (self-expression). Today, contextualist aestheticians once again consider function the most important quality of art

and visual culture. Which purpose do you think is more important? Why? Can artworks serve both purposes equally?

5. Describe the following traditional western aesthetic theories: mimesis, formalism, expressionism, and pragmatism. Which one is most appealing to you? Why?

6. Addressing the context in which artworks are made and used gave rise to institutional theory. Describe this theory. Do you think it is appropriate to ignore

the qualities of the work and focus instead on the institutions that define it and assess its value?

7. Discuss why, as the text says, visual culture studies rely on pragmatic theory in discussing and evaluating art and visual artifacts.

8. In a group, discuss the activities described in the chapter in terms of their potential success in a teaching situation in which you might see yourself. Think about age appropriateness. Can you devise another activity designed for a particular grade or skill level?

FURTHER READING

Anderson, R. (1990). *Calliope's sisters: A comparative study of philosophies of art.* Englewood Cliffs, NJ: Prentice Hall.

Anderson, T. (1998). Aesthetics as critical inquiry. *Art Education, 51*(5), 49–55.

Anderson, T, & McRorie, S. (1997). A role for aesthetics in centering the K–12 curriculum. *Art Education 50*(23), 6–14.

Bell, C. (1981/1914). *Art.* New York: Putnam.

Dewey, J. (1958/1934). *Art as experience.* New York: Capricorn.

Dickie, G. (1974). *Art and the aesthetic: An institutional analysis.* Ithaca, NY: Cornell. (Seminal work in institutionalist theory.)

Dissanayake, E. (1988). *What is art for?* Seattle: University of Washington.

Erickson, M., & Katter, E. (1991). *Token response* (2nd ed.). Tucson, AZ: Crismac.

Hamblen, K. (1985). Developing aesthetic literacy through contested concepts. *Art Education 38*(5), 10–24.

Jeffers, C. (2000). Drawing on semiotics: Inscribing a place between formalism and contextualism. *Art Education, 53*(6), 40–45.

Journal of Aesthetics and Art Criticism. (All issues, published by American Society for Aesthetics.)

Kaelin, E. (1989). *An aesthetics for art educators.* New York: Teachers College Press.

Langer, S. (1980). *Philosophy in a new key: A study in the symbolism of reason, rite, and art.* Cambridge, MA: Harvard University Press.

Lankford, L. (1992). *Aesthetics: Issues and inquiry.* Reston, VA: National Art Education Association.

Lipman, M. (1988). *Philosophy goes to school.* Philadelphia, PA: Temple University Press.

Parsons, J., & Blocker, H. (1993). *Aesthetics and education.* Urbana: University of Illinois Press.

Pirsig, R. (1999/1974). *Zen and the art of motorcycle maintenance: An inquiry into values.* New York: Morrow.

Risatti, H. (1990). *Postmodern perspectives: Issues in contemporary art.* Upper Saddle River, NJ: Prentice Hall.

Sartwell, C. (2000). Teaching non-Western aesthetics: Teaching popular art. At *http://aesthetics-online.org/ideas/sartwell.html*

Sarup, M. (1995). *An introductory guide to poststructuralism and postmodernism* (2nd ed.). Athens: University of Georgia Press.

Thompson, J. (1990). *Twentieth century theories of art.* Ottawa, Canada: Carleton.

Art Criticism

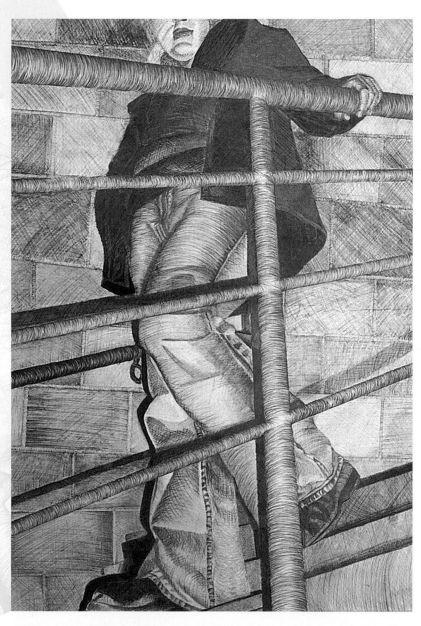

Lakia Porter, *Descending the Staircase*, Druid Hills High School, DeKalb County Schools, Decatur, GA. Betsy Epps, Art Teacher. *This unusual view of a descending figure creates suspense in a visual mystery that invites the viewer to interpret or speculate on what will happen next.*

WHAT IS ART CRITICISM AND WHY DO WE DO IT?

What is art criticism and why do we do it? The simplest answer is that **art criticism** is talking or writing about art, and we do it because we want to know the meaning and significance of artworks. Because art reflects human values and understanding, at a deeper level we engage in criticism to understand our own existence. In their form and content, art and expressive visual artifacts are a primary way we send messages to ourselves about who we are, what we believe, and what we feel.

In most cases, the meaning of works of art and other visual expression is not as self-evident as the meaning of written communication. Art—unlike written or spoken language—is normally not discursive, or explanatory. Rather, it is presentational: it presents us with a feeling, a visual worldview, suggesting or implying what is or what may be but not giving an explanation. The meaning of a work of art is carried by aesthetic components that modify and shape the literal content. As a result, the meaning of art is frequently obscure; literal meaning is difficult to ferret out or is even nonexistent.

Reduced to an abstract formula, art can be described as content (for example, an image of a horse) carried by aesthetic form (the horse may be executed expressionistically, using exaggerated form and arbitrary colors) that together make up the expressive presentational meaning and quality of the work (such as elegance, power, and speed). But how this works is understood best not in the abstract but through repeated practical art criticism.

Looking at the Work: The Question of Style

In an artwork, presentation, or style, has both intellectual and emotional qualities. Through artistic style, artists tell us something about what they both think and feel. Art reflects the artist's view of life, whether or not the artist intended it to do so. Thus similarities and differences between artworks are not a matter of style alone, or of style for style's sake. Rather, style carries meanings. Artistic expression, and the style that transmits it, is communication, intentional or unintentional, from the artist to other people about some aspect of his or her being, seeing, and valuing.

It is generally understood that art criticism addresses the form and composition of artworks, but what may not be as widely understood is that mature art criticism goes further, looking at style as a container of meaning. Art critics see art as personal and cultural artifacts that shed light on the human condition. As we attempt to understand ourselves and others through art, we need to consider context—the conditions in which a work or artifact is made, used, and valued.

Looking beyond the Work: Determining Meaning in Context

The worldview presented by an artist is in many ways unique. For example, the Mexican artists Frida Kahlo and Diego Rivera were married to each other, lived in the same places, had many of the same experiences, and yet made art that in form and content was very different. As individuals, they had different things to say, and so their artwork took different forms. Even in indigenous cultures where originality is not valued, differences in skill, craft, and approach can be detected from one handmade artifact to the next. Clearly, artists put something of themselves into their work, so that the work suggests what they think, feel, and believe. Art is in this sense a window into the artist's soul.

Artworks also reflect a collective soul, sensibility, and culture, because an artist is part of his or her place and time. Thus the works of Rivera and Kahlo, despite their differences, also share many qualities; in fact, they are very similar to each other in the larger scheme of world art. For the same reason, the works of Hiroshige and Hokusai, artists who lived a hundred years earlier in Japan, are similar to each other and different from those of Rivera and Kahlo. In spite of their individuality, the Mexicans cannot help being Mexican and the Japanese cannot help being Japanese. Artists' culture, place, and time are a huge factor in their work. Through their work, artists speak about their culture. We might even say that the culture speaks through the artist. (Sometimes contemporary artists present more than one culture in their artwork. See Color Plate 11, the work of Roger Shimomura, *Untitled,* 1985).

Artwork is never only its surface qualities; its qualities and its style always refer intellectually and emotionally to something beyond themselves. Artists always tell us something about what they think and how they feel, and their thoughts and feelings arise in part from their particular place and time. Therefore, artworks and other expressive visual works must be seen as cultural artifacts. They are cultural statements expressing shared assumptions, premises, forms, and ways of doing things. However, they also illuminate the artist's individual values and sensibility and so are also personal artifacts. They shed light on the human condition. Accordingly, the purpose of criticism in art for life is to understand and appreciate art as visual culture in order to understand and appreciate people—ourselves and others.

SOME PREMISES OF ART CRITICISM

The art critic looks at works of art in context to see what they tell us about the human condition. Critics examine aesthetic, formal qualities and symbolic, meaningful qualities and approach art as both personal expression and cultural artifacts.

This process of criticism results in more or less informed opinion, based on evidence and arrived at within a cultural context. The process itself and conclusions reached are determined by what the critic is looking for and by his or her beliefs, values, and point of view. Professional criticism is usually impelled by aesthetics: that is, professional critics usually consciously subscribe to one or more aesthetic theories. Whether critics are formalists or contextualists, for example, will determine what they look for, how they examine a work, what they find, and what value they give to the work. Likewise, a mimetic critic will find different meaning and value from a pragmatist critic.

Over time, critics (professional and other) have asked four basic questions: (1) What is this? (2) What is it for? (3) What does it mean? (4) What is it worth? The most difficult question is the third: What does this mean? That question can be answered only after questions 1 and 2: What is this? What does it do? The fourth question—What is this worth?—almost always arises from the discovery of what the work is, does, and means.

Question 2—What is it for—has only recently been rediscovered by the majority of western critics. This is the question that leads to an examination of context, which is a crucial strategy in art for life.

EDUCATIONAL ART CRITICISM

The most basic goal of educational art criticism is to help students understand and evaluate individual works of art and visual culture and their own response to these

FIGURE 6.1   David Hammons, *Higher Goals*, 1990 (size, medium). *Hammons combines traditional cultural forms and patterns with a contemporary social concern to create totem-like sculptures with a message particularly directed at inner-city African-American youth. The message challenges them to aspire to life goals beyond the basketball court.*

works. Beyond that, the goal is for students to engage in art criticism in order to find meanings for their own lives and to understand the authentic meanings of others. Edmund Feldman (1971) argued that the ultimate objective of educational art criticism is to help students become members of the human community through understanding art. To achieve this understanding, students should have frequent and sustained critical encounters with artworks other than (or at least in addition to) their own. Such criticism is not a technical critique of the students' own work. Rather, it frequently takes the form of description, analysis, contextual examination, interpretation, and evaluation of the work of others. In art for life our social reconstructionist goal of improving the world through the study of art defines most or all of the activities in this book involving criticism. We believe that art is more than an object of aesthetic appreciation.

An important model of instrumentalist reconstructionist criticism is that of feminists. They seek to deconstruct the modernist patriarchal, hierarchical categories of art and offer instead a more fluid understanding of art in relation to life. Feminist educators frequently extend their humanist concerns to all people and advocate cross-cultural and multicultural critical strategies and content. Congdon, for example, suggests that educators should recognize both contemporary innovation and traditional cultures; otherwise, they will perpetuate hierarchy and the notion of "others" as powerless outsiders.

The feminist approach described here is nonhierarchical; it involves conversation, narrative, or other cooperative strategies for discussion rather than presenting lectures or competitive strategies such as debates. The analytic model we present, as well as the principled model, should also be approached nonhierarchically. Conversational approaches help students realize that there is more than one right answer, more than one possible meaning, and that the instructor and other authorities do not stand at the apex of knowledge. Rule-governed conversation about art can empower everyone engaged in it.

Art criticism as presented in the models that follow develops students' ability to make systematic critical choices. Wilson, in *Toward Civilization*, considers critical judgment essential to competence in life, effective communication, creativity, and a sense of civilization.

MODELS FOR INSTRUCTION

An Analytic Model

In analytic models of art criticism, the process almost always results from asking these three questions: What is this? What does it mean? What is it worth? In the art for life model, a fourth question is essential for stimulating contextual examination: What is it for? Answering these four questions results in the basic critical processes: description (which tells us what an object is and what it is for); interpretation (which tells us what the object means), and evaluation (which tells us what the object is worth). Interpretation is the main outcome of criticism, since it answers the question, What is this work all about? As a result, the most important of the four questions is, What does it mean? Since this is also the most difficult question critics first ask, What is this? and What is it for—and try to find answers through description (including contextual examination). The answers provide evidence of and a path toward meaning. The answer to the question What is it worth? almost always becomes clear from the answers to the other three questions.

Even a glance at *Art in America* or *Art Forum* will show that professional art critics usually do not separate these questions and answers; instead, the questions are allowed to flow together as seems most appropriate for the critique at hand. That strategy is used later in the section on the "principled" approach. In educational art criticism, however, a strong argument can be made for ordering the processes of description to avoid any confusion of categories and to facilitate systematic teaching and learning.

The analytic model presented here was introduced fifteen years ago, tested with K–12 as well as university students, and modified as a result of practical experience. It has been found to work well at all age levels. It consists of four primary processes or stages: (1) An initial, general, intuitive reaction. (2) Description, consisting of representation of the obvious thematic and formal qualities, examination of the relationships between the forms and figures, description of what seems to be the intended emotional impact of the work on the viewer, and contextual examination of the qualities outside the work itself that affect its meaning. (3) Interpretation. (4) Evaluation. Let's look at these stages in more detail.

Reaction When we encounter anything new or not understood, we all ask ourselves, What is this? Most fundamentally this judgment, as Dewey (1934) would call it, is a means of survival. Once we have discovered that the thing won't eat us or run over us, we typically have some sort of overall response: it's big; it's pretty; it's ugly; it's weird; it looks like circus colors; or perhaps, with Munch's *The Scream,* it's threatening or disturbing. We all begin with this rudimentary response to art, and for many of us that is also where the response ends. To go beyond it requires some strategy. One strategy is to use the response to direct our inquiry. Our biological instinct to construct meaning (it's threatening, it feels sterile, it reminds me of Indiana) can be put to use for further examination if we will trust it to guide us. The initial reaction should become a reason to look further, to see what in the image caused the reaction.

Description Using our first reaction as a guide, we can begin the task of description as the first step toward determining meaning and value. For example, what about *The Scream* is disturbing? We can begin to find answers by describing the work, both in terms of

FIGURE 6.2 Edvard Munch. *The Scream,* (1893, 36 x 29 in., tempera and casein on cardboard). *The terror conveyed in Munch's image exemplifies the Expressionists' goal of portraying anger, anxiety, or other strong emotions through art.*

its form—how it looks—and in terms of its context, its place in the world of human affairs. Usually, though not always, the first part of description is an examination of the appearance of the work. If a work is remote to students either culturally or in time, it may be better to start with some contextual examination. If you start with appearance, you should begin with obvious features, such as representational and illusional qualities. In *The Scream,* for instance, a person is crying out. Surface features also include elements of design (color, line, shape, and so on), obvious technical effects (the fact that something is a painting), and other physical features (size, setting, and so on).

Formal description usually starts with the obvious and works its way to more subtle features, finally analyzing composition and its emotional effects. The most effective conceptual tools for formal analysis are the principles of design: unity, variety, focus, rhythm, and so on. Wherever there is focus for any reason (such as a change in rhythm), there is significance, or meaning. At this point, if you reconsider the emotional effect you will either confirm your initial reaction or discover that new evidence is leading you elsewhere. In either case, reconsidering your emotional response serves as a bridge to interpretation.

The second step in description is an examination of the contextual qualities that help make the work meaningful and expressive. These qualities are not actually visible; rather, they "surround" the work—they have caused it to come into being and have influenced its forms and its place in the larger scheme of things. Contextual description is focused on the artist's life and intentions; the circumstances of the making of the work; the function or functions of the work (ceremonial, utilitarian, educational, decorative); and its place in society—its symbolic meanings, its reflection of beliefs, and so on. For more on how to engage this contextual examination, look at Chapter 8.

Interpretation   Determining meaning is the heart of art criticism. To arrive at a meaning, it is important to gather as much evidence as possible. The purpose of description is to let us venture an interpretation.

Interpretation is our best guess about what the work means, based on the evidence: forms, composition, technique, aesthetic and emotional impact, and contextual information. In one sense interpretation itself is an art, since it relies on the critic's sensitivity and his or her ability to synthesize and to distinguish between the relevant and the irrelevant. Since interpretation is creative activity, multiple interpretations should be included in interactive educational critiques. Whether an interpretation holds up depends on whether it can be justified in light of the evidence.

Typically, a professional critic will make tentative guesses about meaning throughout the process of description. Students will be tempted to do the same, but it's up to their teachers to decide if tentative interpretations are appropriate at every stage. The advantage of such interpretations is that they may stimulate further examination of the evidence in an attempt to justify them. However, a potential problem is that premature interpretations can derail the critique by pursuing irrelevancies and ignoring further evidence. Still, if the teacher feels confident about keeping the group focused on descriptive evidence, tentative interpretations may be entertained throughout the process of discovery.

Evaluation   In the fourth stage, evaluation, we use all the work done in the previous stages to reach a conclusion about the value of the work and of the experience of encountering it. Again, most people, professional critics and students alike, will be developing a sense of a work's value throughout the process. The value of the work is almost always already known by the time we're ready to talk about it. The key to successful evaluation is criteria. That is, it is important to give reasons for assigning value and significance. The distinction between mere preference and aesthetic judgment is that the latter is based on reasons having to do with observable criteria. In professional criticism, these reasons come in part from aesthetic theory: expressionist (Is the work highly expressive?), mimetic (Is it realistic or naturalistic?), formalist (Does it seem "right" in terms of color, composition, and so on?), and pragmatist (Does it do something important? Does it do this well?). Other criteria for evaluation include whether the work is well made (skill and technique), the strength of the ideas driving the work (concept), and its overall aesthetic impact.

Summary: The Analytic Model   Professional critics undertake reaction, description, interpretation, and evaluation to determine the meaning and significance of works of art. They do not separate these processes but instead use them, often instinctively, as seems appropriate. For educational purposes, however, it is useful to distinguish among the processes or stages of criticism; this facilitates information gathering and enhances the students' understanding, not only of content but of cognitive processes. The educational structure for art criticism presented here is (1) reaction to the work, (2) description of how a work looks (images, themes, composition, embedded ideas and emotions) and its place in society (personal and social functions, history, and circumstances); (3) interpretation, or what the work means; and (4) evaluation, or what the work is worth. The following sample questions provide a structure for analytic art criticism.*

I.   Reaction (This stage should be brief, only long enough for overall responses.)

    A.   General questions

        1.   What's your first response to this work?
        2.   How does this make you feel?
        3.   What does it make you think of?
        4.   What does it remind you of?

II.   Description (Let's find out why you have this reaction by beginning to describe what we see.)

    A.   Obvious thematic, formal, and technical qualities

        1.   What images (illusions, pictures of recognizable things) do you see?
        2.   What colors (shapes, textures, etc.) do you see?
        3.   Are there any outstanding or unusual features you notice?
        4.   What else do you see? (Encourage increasingly subtle discriminations.)
        5.   Are there any dark (light) areas? Rough or unusual textures? Large or small shapes? And so on.
        6.   How do you think this work was made? (What was it: a painting? a sculpture? a photograph? something else?)
        7.   Why do you think so? What types of brush strokes (sculptural finish, photographic technique, etc.) do you see?
        8.   What is the artist's (physical) point of view? What are your clues?

    B.   Formal relationships of shapes and images to each other. (The key in formal analysis is to look for relationships between forms and images. Differences such as changes in rhythm or one thing's being bigger, darker, brighter than another are particularly significant clues for meaning. The focus here is on principles of design.)

        1.   What (colors, shapes, textures, lines) dominate the image? Why?
        2.   Are there significant negative areas or spaces in the work? What makes them significant?

---

*These questions first appeared in an article by Anderson (1997) entitled "Talking with kids about art," *School Arts, 97* (1), 21–26.

COLOR PLATE 1 Lynne Hull, *Flowing Water Moon, Hydroglyph: a water capture basin for desert wildlife,* 1992-95. Utah. *Hull integrates her knowledge of the environment to create art with the primary purpose of sustaining nature. In this piece the hydroglyph collects moisture and rainwater to support wildlife in an arid climate.*

COLOR PLATE 2 Nam June Paik, *Electronic Superhighway,* 1995. *Paik utilized multiple television monitors, laser discs, neon and other media to create a work that blends contemporary visual culture with both modernist and postmodern flair.*

COLOR PLATE 3 John Ahearn and Rigoberto Torres, *Banana Kelly Double Dutch*, 1981-82. *The signature characteristic of art for life is the continual search for real-world connections. This relief sculpture was constructed from a fiberglass casting of children in the South Bronx by community artists, John Ahearn and Rigoberto Torres. Banana Kelly Double Dutch was made in cooperation with a local city block association. Displayed on a building where the children live and play, this work celebrates the identity and self-esteem of the community.*

COLOR PLATE 4 *Billboard Painting,* 2002. Photo courtesy of Kirby Meng, art teacher, Hickory Flat Elementary School, Stockbridge, GA. *Fifth grade students investigated advertising and trademarks before visiting a billboard company to create a mural of personal logos during Youth Art Month 2002.*

COLOR PLATE 5 *Las Vegas at Night. The dazzling glitz and glamour of neon lights and signs fill Las Vegas, Nevada streets. Such exciting spectacles of color and lights provide a visually stimulating backdrop for the thousands of tourists visiting this nocturnal playground.*

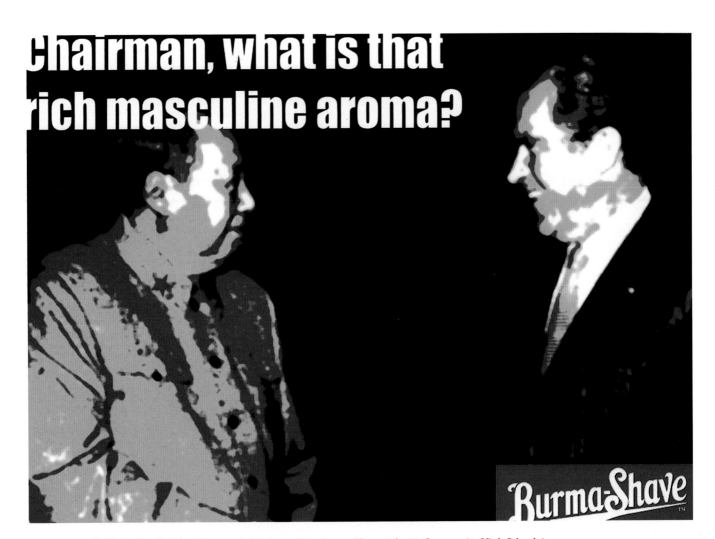

COLOR PLATE 6 Eric Barkin, *Nixon meets Chairman Mao, Burma Shave.* Atlantic Community High School, in Delray Beach, FL. Genia Howard, art teacher. *With the old Burma Shave signs, once set up along the road in the Midwest, as his inspiration Barkin appropriated images from the media and turned the tactics of propaganda and manipulative advertising against themselves to create this clever socio-political critique.*

COLOR PLATE 7 Ray Burggraf, *Jungle Arc*, 1998. *Formalist artwork communicates a message through a composition of pure form, as demonstrated in this exciting non-objective painting.*

COLOR PLATE 8 Franz Marc, *The Large Blue Horses*, 1911. Expressionism finds excellence through the strength of a work's emotional power, often created through exaggeration of form and color, as in this portrayal of horses. The additional dynamic movement expressed through the repetition of strong curved lines adds to the emotional impact.

COLOR PLATE 9 Judith F. Baca, *Great Wall of Los Angeles*, 1976. Chicano artist, Judith Baca, initiated the Citywide Mural project in 1974. Nearly 400 inner-city youths, many from the juvenile justice system, designed and painted the one-mile long Great Wall. During the citywide collaborative project 250 murals were completed and lives of the young artists were transformed.

3. What movement do you see? What elements (line, shape, etc.) and principles (rhythm, proportion, etc.) cause movement?
4. Where do you see contrast? What causes it?
5. Where are the figures looking/leaning toward/pointing? (The emphasis here is on implied movement.)
6. What is the focal point in this work? What causes you to look there? (Is there a single focus? Why? Why not? What features cause us to see it that way?)

C. Formal characterization (Intended impact of the forms, colors, theme, and their relationships.)

1. What mood is presented? How are we meant to feel in the presence of this piece? Why? What's the evidence?
2. Why are we meant to focus where we do? (Why is there no central focus, or why is there a central focus?)
3. Is this work realistic? Formalistic? Expressionistic? Some combination?
4. Would you characterize it as primitive, slick, aggressive, bold, intellectual, overpowering, timid, monumental, fluid, abstract, cool, static, rhythmic, hot, etc.? Why? What's the evidence?
5. (Sometimes you need to ask opposites to get at the character of a piece.) What if the background were a different color? What if this work were realistic instead of having exaggerated forms? What if it had soft instead of hard edges? And so on.

D. Contextual examination: historical and cultural context (These questions will normally be answered by the teacher or through outside research. All or parts of this stage can come before a physical description of the work if the work is very foreign to the students. Physical description should start the process only if a work is from the students' own culture.)

1. Who did the work?
2. What was the artist's point or intention?
3. What is the title?
4. When and where was the work done?
5. How does it reflect that place and time?
6. What style is it considered to be?
7. Does it have or has it ever had a functional purpose? What?
8. What influenced its production (social context, other art, technology)?
9. What impact has the work had on work that came later or on society in general?
10. What does the work tell us about the people who made and used it?

III. Interpretation (This is the most difficult but ultimately the most significant stage.)

A. General questions

1. What do you think this work means? (Remind students of the subject matter, qualities, and character as described earlier to stimulate interpretations.)
2. If you were inside the work, as a particular character, abstract form, or figure, what would you be thinking and feeling?
3. (In the face of a nonobjective or highly abstract work.) What does it remind you of or make you think of?
4. What title would you give this work if you were the artist? Why?

IV. Evaluation

A. Personal experience

1. What was the quality of your experience in critiquing this work?

2. Have your perceptions or feelings changed since we started? How?
3. Would you like to own this work? Why or why not?
4. Do you feel a need to resolve what you found through personal critique (looking at the work) with what you found in the contextual examination? Can this be done? If so, how?

B. Aesthetic judgment

1. Is the work well made? (Does it indicate a high degree of technical, compositional, or conceptual skill?) Do you think its form, composition, and technique are good? Why or why not?
2. Does it clearly express a point of view?
3. Overall, is it beautiful, visually satisfying, complete in and of itself?

C. Contextual judgment

1. Does the work address some significant human problem or need? If so, does it do this well? Why or why not?

D. Final judgment

1. Is the work clear? (Does it do what it seems to be trying to do?) Is it up to the task we have determined that it set for itself? Was it worth making?
2. Finally, does it move you? Does it have the aesthetic power to make you feel something strongly, or think something new, or move you to action in any way?
3. Ultimately, was it worth examining? Why or why not?

Finally, some words of caution about this analytic model are in order. First, critiques of students' work are not art criticism as it is defined here. The purpose of such critiques—technical, compositional, or conceptual—is solely to improve students' work on future projects. Art criticism is the examination of the work of others to find what they can tell us about being human. The second caution is that art criticism is best when it is organic: when the critic is constantly making sensitive connections among description, interpretation, and evaluation. The structure suggested here for educational purposes is merely a guide to help both teachers and students understand the kinds of thinking and speaking that go into art criticism. The final guide for the process of art criticism should be the work itself. Take the time and energy to look sensitively and deeply, and the work will lead you.

A Feminist Conversational Model

Feminist art criticism seeks to reflect women's ways of knowing. It is highly sensitive to gender issues in both content and structure. In this regard, we should understand that (biological) sex and gender are different. Gender, although it has its roots in biology, is a product of socialization. Likewise, sexuality is understood through language and representation. Also, form and its interpretation are cultural rather than given. Feminist art critics, arguing that women are socialized differently from men and so have different ways of seeing and describing the world, consider how femininity has been constructed and reflected through art and the mass media.

Unlike analytic criticism, feminist criticism has no predetermined structure. Feminists do not believe that any one structure is universal or adequate for all works in all situations at all times. The structure of feminist art criticism is situationally specific, changing from one critical undertaking to the next. Other characteristics of feminist art criticism are that it is personal and subjective in nature, usually conversational and cooperative in format, and thus most often narrative rather than definitive in form. Not surprisingly, it most frequently examines content that is of concern to women.

FIGURE 6.3   Sally Mann, *Naptime,* black-and-white photograph, 1989. *This artwork is one of a series of black-and-white photographs called* Immediate Family. *Mann has been criticized for presenting her children in a sensuous manner, but she feels her photographs document a typical summer of natural and candid moments in her family.*

The Content of Feminist Art Criticism   Most feminist art criticism is directed to content it considers to be lost, ignored, or peripheral artists and movements, especially women. Its aim is reassessment based on feminist or feminine criteria and standards, in contrast to what feminists see as the normal male standards and criteria. If we are used to mainstream (male-oriented) criticism, it is easy to dismiss this aim as unfounded and self-serving. And even if we recognize the merit of questioning given values, such questioning is frequently very uncomfortable. Our values are rooted so deeply in language and customs that words and practices become our reality. For example, Anderson recalls that when his two daughters were quite young, he and their mother taught them to sing "America the Beautiful" with one small change: "God shed *her* grace on thee." It was instructive, to say the least, to see the reactions—ranging from surprise and amusement to indignation—of friends and acquaintances.

Feminists seek to reveal tacitly male assumptions—such as "God the father" in the anecdote above, and the male as the generic human subject. They want to position women with men at the center of what it means to be human. An example is the work of the artist Miriam Schapiro. Schapiro and the feminist critics who interpret her work consciously deconstruct stereotypes, images, and iconography of women as somehow inferior to men. Thus although most art critics (with reputations to protect) see hearts or flowers in professional art as maudlin and sentimental, Schapiro and her critics attempt to reposition them as a meaningful expression of some aspect of the human condition.

The question to be asked and answered is, why have hearts and flowers been peripheralized and automatically demoted to stereotypes? Schapiro would say that it's because hearts and flowers are associated not with boys and men but with girls and women, thus with women's qualities: sentimentality, emotionalism, tenderness, and affection. And whether we're men or women we tend to accept these qualities as somehow being of less value than intelligence, discernment, or reason: qualities that for some reason we've traditionally associated with men. We—all of us—have accepted qualities associated with men as being privileged over those

FIGURE 6.4 *Students at Georgia State University engage in an interactive critique of a contemporary painting. It's important that students present evidence from the image for the meaning and value of a piece, and in that context every student's opinion about the piece should be acknowledged and respected.*

associated with women without ever really thinking about it, simply because we are socialized into it. Thus hearts and flowers, which represent women's ways of knowing, easily become dismissed as second-class symbols, the symbols of less serious artists and consumers, those who are not intellectually engaged.

But Schapiro seems to ask in her work, what in essence makes hearts and flowers less interesting, challenging, powerful, or meaningful than for example Jasper Johns' targets and flags or Charles Sheeler's buildings and machines? And what makes the mind superior to the emotions, anyway? A feminist critic, in support of Schapiro's work, might claim, "Nothing!" She or he might make a (personal and emotional as well as intellectual) argument that Miriam Schapiro's heart motifs and domestic materials collages represent a position not of peripheral importance but of central importance, because they reflect women's experience and women's ways of knowing, because they represent the subjective and the personal, because that subjective and personal way of seeing and being is of great value in the world. Schapiro seeks to communicate a seamless transition from her personal experience to her art.

Traditional high art—defined by men—asks women to use language and constructs that do not represent their subjective reality. Feminist artists like Schapiro resist this demand. They prefer to express the feminine experience: household concerns; domestic knowledge; forms such as basketry, interior design, and quilting; and subjective qualities such as caring. To feminist critics, women's concerns are as central as the concerns of the traditional (male) "high" arts.

Discussion and Dialogue as Strategies for Feminist Art Criticism   We are born as biologically male or female, but we are socialized to take on gender roles. The way we see and do things as females and males is largely a result of how we are raised and what is expected of us. Feminist aestheticians and critics argue that the differences in the way men and women, in general, tend to see should be reflected in the structure and strategies of art criticism.

For example, many feminists might argue that analytic art criticism is not ideologically neutral but represents men's ways of knowing. They might argue that men tend to separate and analyze qualities rather than seeing and feeling them holistically. They might also argue that such an approach artificially separates cognition from emotion. They might suggest that analytic criticism facilitates men's typical strategy of dominating by defining, establishing, and defending a position, rather than women's typical approach: cooperative discussion arising from intimacy with a form, not for the sake of dominance but for the sake of self-fulfillment or personal transformation. If the point of feminist criticism is personal engagement or fulfillment through an encounter with art, then the universal, definitional analytic strategy is inappropriate.

From a feminist perspective, a more appropriate strategy is narrative dialogue and discussion. A reader used to the male way of doing things might at this point say, "Discussion? Narrative? Dialogue? That's not a method at all!" But it is a method, an open-ended, situationally specific, conversational method. Like conversation, it is sensitive to the situation, the dialogue, and feelings generated during the dialogue, so it has no predetermined structure.

Feminist art criticism is subjective and personalized, reflecting women's ways of knowing. Congdon maintains that in general women are socialized to seek personal and subjective *meaning* whereas men are encouraged to seek universal *truths*. In other words, women's motivation may be characterized as inner or subjective, men's as outer or objective. By extension, women, as a group, appreciate the inner or subjective life more than men do. Accordingly, feminist art criticism will be more subjective than the standard analytic model. The critic will approach a work from a personal perspective, considering how she herself feels about the forms and meanings in it. She will not attempt to neutralize her personal perspective by using, for example, value-free language or the third-person point of view. This explains why a feminist model of art criticism will not be as highly structured as the analytic model. Feminist criticism will be guided by the critic's intuitive sense of what is personally and situationally appropriate in reference to that particular work. The point is to find meaning—usually a personal meaning—rather than a defined truth.

FIGURE 6.5   Maria Martiniz, Pottery of the San Ildfonso. *Maria's techniques for hand-building pottery were passed down orally through generations of San Ildfonso people. The meanings in feminist art criticism also engage this communitarian oral perspective.*

Nonhierarchical Interactivity, Narrative, and Personal Engagement   When art criticism is done interactively in a group, the feminist model encourages conversation and dialogue rather than the more linear, definitional strategy of staking out a claim and defending it. In feminist criticism, people do not dominate each other or impose a "correct reading" or a form. Rather, personal meaning is established cooperatively, in relation to the form. This encourages openness and receptivity to new ideas about meaning and significance; the point is to expand one's possible relationships, not defend one's own interpretation. Ideally, when the feminist model is used, no one is trying to prove anything, so there's little or no risk of failure in exploring multiple possibilities and points of view. Criticism in this sense is like a conversation. The participants don't know where it will end up, but they do know that if they are open, receptive, and engaged, the destination and the process will be valuable.

This open dialogue encourages narrative, or storytelling related to the image, as a primary critical strategy. Often, storytelling is related to the critics' life experience. A critic may say something like, "This reminds me of . . ." The image not only contains meaning but also stimulates understandings beyond itself. Rather than being the end point, it serves as the starting point for an expanding dialogue. In this conversational mode, there are no predetermined guidelines for what may be addressed or how. All that's required is that the dialogue should make sense in terms of webbing or building on what has come before. Reflection, storytelling, projection, memory, and bodily as well as mental insights are all appropriate strategies.

In this conversation, feminist critics use (at least) nonsexist and sometimes overtly feminine self-affirming language. One hallmark is that the language, to support the cooperative strategy of understanding meaning rather than establishing position, is nonaggressive. Women are socialized to connect rather than separate and analyze. So a feminist, conversational criticism is personal (rather than theoretical and focused on disinterested aestheticism), subjective (rather than autonomous and analytic), and inclined toward bonding (rather than toward objective analysis). Cognition and emotion are not artificially split; rather, emotional language is allowed and even encouraged.

A CLOSER LOOK — Elizabeth Garber's Principles of Feminist Art Criticism

1. Study all artworks in their authentic social and cultural contexts.

2. Include women artists from various cultures, classes, nationalities, races, ethnicities, sexual orientations, and regions, including rural and urban.

3. Look at artwork by women in relation to women's lives and experiences.

4. Use narrative and conversation as techniques rather than debate or lecture.

5. Consider the social ramifications of an artwork's physical properties.

6. Practice sensitivity to language.

7. Allow for personal associations.

8. Explore a variety of possible interpretations by comparing differences.

9. Explore how change in art and society might occur.

   In undertaking feminist criticism, be open to your goals for social change.

As Frueh (1994) suggests, overemphasis on the intellect denies our full being. As conversation, feminist criticism is not speaking or writing to prove yourself right and someone else wrong. It is speaking or writing to be heard and understood. Interpretation is neither "this" nor "that" but usually a compromise allowing for both. In feminist criticism, the most important result is not judgment but meaning. The final goal is interpretation, not evaluation.

Why Engage in Feminist Art Criticism? Who should use feminist art criticism? When? Why? From a feminist perspective, the question *why* cannot be answered through traditional stylistic analysis. The answer requires a deep responsiveness to feminine (and masculine) socialization as manifested in art. Thus in the end, despite its nonconfrontational method, feminist art criticism challenges traditional (men's) ways of seeing and doing things. This revisionist stance is uncomfortable for men and women who have integrated traditional values, ideas, and emotions, since it entails looking at old material in new ways. But anyone who wants to understand where forms come from in society, and how they reflect on and affect us all, can benefit from the feminist conversational model of art criticism. It can be used not only to understand women's forms, issues, and ways of being but to understand all peripheral and marginal people. The feminist conversational model is effective in enhancing cross-cultural understandings and an understanding of people who may not share your own values.

In addition, the feminist model promotes dialogue in which teachers and students are partners in problem solving, rather than an authoritative top-down presentation of material by teachers. Such an approach empowers students by giving them a stake in the content to be discovered and in the process of discovering it. It therefore encourages active continual involvement and so provides a good context for aesthetic education. Conversational inquiry fosters the ability to distinguish important points from background information, as well as the ability to make important points clear and support them with pertinent information. During

FIGURE 6.6 Prayer rug. *The geometric composition of this Persian rug is visually beautiful but also contains highly contextual symbols representing the gardens of Paradise. A feminist conversational art criticism model offers an effective approach to interpreting and understanding cross-cultural values and beliefs.*

such inquiry there may be frequent repetition of ideas within a group, but this is a good thing, signaling engagement in the conversation and active listening. According to McRorie, in cooperative inquiry the teacher's role is to model and moderate active listening and collaborative comments so as to respect and support the contributions of all students. Traditionally, girls have been perceived as quieter or less willing to talk, and boys have been seen as more argumentative than collaborative. However, knowledgeable teachers may intervene to facilitate conversations that discourage the perpetuation of these stereotypes.

A Principled Approach to Art Criticism

Seung-Ryul Shin (2003), relying on Terry Barrett's principles (1994) for interpretation of a work of art, developed a "principled" metacognitive approach to art criticism. That is, he examined how we think about the process of art criticism. Shin devised "what to know" and "what to do" cards, modeled after Barrett's studies in art education lecture, "About Interpretation for Art Education." Shin's structure, incorporating the steps of planning, implementing, and evaluating the critical act, informs the following practical strategy for interpretation.

ACTIVITY   **Art Criticism**

Step One   •   Planning Art Criticism

What to Know

1. Artwork is about something.
2. Feelings are guides to understanding artworks.
3. Basic reactions to the artwork are important but subject to change.

What to Do

1. Note your first impressions and what triggers them.
2. Note your feelings about the work.
3. Ask questions about the work, think about it, and jot your thoughts down on paper.

Step Two   •   Implementing Art Criticism

What to Know

1. Good description includes both internal and external information.
2. Good description should be relevant to the work.
3. Good interpretations are persuasive arguments.
4. There can be different, competing, and contradictory interpretations of the same work.
5. The steps of description, interpretation, and judgment are circular and interactive. Each can be used to lead to the others.
6. No single interpretation covers the whole meaning of an artwork.
7. Good judgments are based on reasons or criteria.
8. The value of an artwork and your preference for it are distinct and different.

What to Do

1. Give attention to the details of the work and to external (social, historical, cultural) information.
2. Describe the work itself and collect external information.
3. Think about and incorporate some unified theory of the meaning of the work.
4. Keep an open mind as you develop your hypothesis.
5. Be flexible in your thinking. Allow what comes up to come up, whether it's descriptive, interpretive, or evaluative.
6. Be open to the interpretations of your classmates and others even if they are different from yours.
7. Collect evidence all through the process, both from the work itself and from the contextual information.
8. Base your judgment of value on the criteria and reasons you have established, knowing that you can like or dislike a work whether it's good or bad.

ACTIVITY   **Art Criticism**

Step Three   •   Evaluating and Modifying the Critical Performance

What to Know

1. Good interpretation relies on accurate, in-depth, sensitive seeing and fits the work being examined.

2. Good criticism, as persuasion, is consistent in form and argument.

3. Good criticism is usually not final but open to modification.

What to Do

1. Pay attention. Look carefully over time, all the while seeking meaning from multiple perspectives. When you think you're done looking and writing, look again. Have you missed something? Does what you've said or written correspond with both the appearance and the intention of the work?

2. Be sure your interpretation is based on your established criteria and reasons. Remove irrelevant or distracting ideas. Supplement your weak points or remove them. Be sure that description, interpretation, and evaluation are interconnected and mutually supporting.

3. Stay open, even in the end, to new ideas.

Three Models of Art Criticism: Which to Use?

In this section we have presented three strategies for art criticism: an analytic model, a feminist model, and a principled model. Each of them is useful for authentic instruction and art for life. The inner, subjective awareness emphasized in the feminist model is actually important in the other two models as well, since art itself seeks meaning over truth and presents its meanings as a combination of the emotions and the intellect. But objective qualities identified through analysis can also be very important to understanding art. Neither the male universalist nor the female subjectivist strategy will give a complete picture. Therefore, we recommend that they both be used. When you feel adept at leading both kinds of criticism, both can be incorporated into the principled approach. Art melds the cognitive and the emotive, the intellect and intuition, and form and spirit—and good criticism will follow from that fact. In art for life, the purpose of criticism is to understand people through art, not to understand art for its own sake.

ADDITIONAL ACTIVITIES   *Art Criticism Strategies*

ACTIVITY   Students act out an image, taking the positions of the figures they see. This works well with abstract art and with thematic art.

Conceptual Purpose   To gain an understanding of feelings projected by a work through kinesthetic reenactment of its qualities. For many students, body-centered understanding is more integrated and deeper than intellectual understanding.

ACTIVITY   Comparative analysis. Have students critique two artworks or aesthetic objects to find similarities and differences between them.

Conceptual Purpose   To understand how form carries expressive meaning, which is connected to the qualities and purposes of the aesthetic object. This may sharpen students' ability to distinguish types, styles, functions, and themes in art. Many different aspects of art can be compared and

ACTIVITY

contrasted: media (sculpture versus stained glass, water-color versus oil paint); treatment of themes, such as war and peace (Eugene Delacroix's depiction of war versus Francisco Goya's); compositional and technical qualities and what they portray (focused versus unfocused, arbitrary versus local color, exaggerated versus naturalistic form); functions (a carved wooden chair versus a mural painting, an ad versus a ritual mask); and so on. This activity may also be used in conjunction with studio production to illustrate how artists have solved the problems students are facing.

ACTIVITY   Each student writes a critique of a work of art of his or her choice using a given pedagogical method and then reports on the work to the class.

Conceptual Purpose   To develop a profound understanding of specific works of art, and vicariously, through listening to the reports of others, a broad knowledge of a range of artworks. This may contribute to a breadth of understanding about art in relation to human consciousness, and less broadly to aesthetic theory. Art criticism of this sort also develops skills of critical thinking, writing, and reporting.

ACTIVITY   Sorting games. Students may sort art reproductions (ideally, postcards) into categories using opposites (light–dark, busy–calm); similarities (all landscapes, still-life paintings, and portraits together; or all warm-colored images together; or all radial patterns together; or all works with implied social relationships together; and so on). Simple categories may be used for beginners (all with blue in one pile, no blue in another). Very complex categorical problems may be used at high levels (all that show influences of nonwestern art in one pile, all that have instrumental intent, and so on). Images may be sorted by style, theme, aesthetic theory (formalist, expressionist, mimetic), or compositional qualities (elements, principles, and overarching concepts such as closed versus open form or contained versus uncontained composition).

Conceptual Purpose   To master aesthetic concepts by making distinctions of form and content in artistic and aesthetic objects.

ACTIVITY   Creative projection (the "what if" strategy). The instructor asks or students ask each other "what if" questions that require creative projection into the image examined. Examples: "How would it feel if you lived in this image? What would you do next if you were this character? What kind of cage, home, platform would that animal, person, vase have? What would you name this picture? Make up a story about this image: who are this person's friends? If you were standing next to the artist and turned your head left or right, what would you see? If you painted this picture another color (name one), how would it change in feeling? How does this work remind you of your life?" Each of these questions requires the students to refer to the image or aspects of the image and formulate a creative response. Thus the teacher's follow-up question should always be, "Why?"

Conceptual Purpose   To develop the ability to make creative and interpretive statements based on criteria and referring to the image.

ACTIVITY   Have students critique print or television ads for form, content, meaning, and interest in relation to the consumer.

Conceptual Purpose   To understand the commercial images that attempt to manipulate our behavior, often through devious and subliminal means. (See Chapter 3 for more details.)

ACTIVITY   "Twenty Questions." In this game, one student can see a work that the whole class should be familiar with. No one else can see it. The point is to guess what the image is. The class may ask only questions that can be answered yes or no in trying to determine what the image is. Questions may be about style, theme, function, historical context, and compositional or technical qualities.

Conceptual Purpose   To reinforce visual memory and develop critical thinking.

ACTIVITY   "The Art Critic" (A Picture Is Worth a Thousand Words). An art critic in a local newspaper may often describe works in a gallery that the readers cannot see. In this game, the student chosen to be the "critic" exhaustively describes a work the rest of the students cannot see, until he or she cannot think of anything else to say. The rest of the students may ask the critic questions and should imagine the image as it is being described. Without actually seeing the image, they are to make a line drawing, placing items where they have imagined them in the composition. The image is then shown, and they compare what they imagined with the image the critic described. Follow up by showing Albrecht Dürer's drawing of a rhinoceros, which he drew only from descriptions, never having seen one.

Conceptual Purpose   To develop visual imagination and the understanding that descriptions, while they can help us see, can never replace the visual image itself. Also, to understand that art is subjective; each of us has a different inner vision.

ACTIVITY   "The Gallerygoer." In this game, students look at an image for 7 seconds—about the time the average viewer normally spends in front of a work in an art gallery. The image is then put away. One by one, students name or describe one thing they saw, until no one can name anything else. Now reexamine the image to see what was missed and what was imagined but not there.

Conceptual Purpose   To develop visual memory; to realize that works of art, like books or other forms of communication, take some examination before they reveal their secrets. *Variation*   The instructor flashes a slide on a large piece of white paper for 3 seconds at a time. Students go up in turn after the projector is turned off and draw in one form in the place they saw it, until the whole composition is completed.

ACTIVITY   "Finding the Lost Masterpiece." In this game, students "find" an old trunk (perhaps a shoe box) that's been hidden away "for years." In the trunk are mysterious pieces of paper, clues to the lost masterpiece. Each piece of paper has one word or a short phrase written on it. The categories of the words are style (realistic, atmospheric perspective, and so on); context (Italian Renaissance, artist was an inventor, and so on); formal qualities (cool colors, painterly, contrasting textures, etc.); and theme (woman, portrait, landscape, famous smile, etc.). Students pull the clues out one at a time to try to find the missing masterpiece by guessing what it is. Have you guessed the *Mona Lisa* yet? Students might form teams to write descriptors for the given works to see if other teams can "find" their work from the clues.

Conceptual Purpose   Visual and verbal interactive development of descriptive skills and ability to categorize artistic traits, as well as reinforcement of aesthetic concepts.

ACTIVITY The instructor creates puzzles by cutting up reproductions of various works of art (three or more) and mixing them together. Students may work on the puzzles as preparation for a further activity or after finishing another activity.

Conceptual Purpose Recognition of style.

CONCLUSION

The focus of this chapter has been on art criticism as a strategy for understanding artworks and visual culture, and on art criticism in art for life. In particular, we presented an overview of art criticism in the world and in education and introduced an analytic model, a feminist conversational model, and a principled model as three strategies for art criticism in education. We suggested that each has merit and recommended that you try them all. Finally, we provided some activities compatible with art for life. In Chapter 7, we focus on art history.

QUESTIONS FOR STUDY AND DISCUSSION

1. Why do people engage in art criticism?

2. Why is it important to look at works of art in their authentic or original contexts?

3. What are the four guiding questions that art critics ask? What processes does each question stimulate?

4. How is art criticism different from critiquing your own artwork?

5. Explain how style in an artwork reflects understandings about life.

6. What are the defining characteristics of analytic, feminist conversational, and principled art criticism? What do you think each does best? Which ones are you more comfortable with? Why?

FURTHER READING

Anderson, T. (1995). Toward a cross-cultural approach to art criticism. *Studies in Art Education, 36*(4), 198–209.

Barrett, T. (1994). *Criticizing art: Understanding the contemporary.* Mountain View, CA: Mayfield.

Barrett, T. (2004). *Interpreting art: Reflecting, wondering, responding.* New York: McGraw-Hill.

Blandy, D., & Congdon, K. (1991) *Pluralistic approaches to art criticism.* Bowling Green, OH: Bowling Green State University Popular Press.

Dewey, J. (1958/1934). *Art as experience.* New York: Penguin. (Hard reading, but worth it. In Chapter 13 you will find the conceptual foundations of many of the analytic methods used today. A classic.)

Feldman, E. (1970). *Becoming human through art.* Englewood Cliffs, NJ: Prentice Hall. (The gold standard of modernist methodology in art criticism.)

Frueh, J., Langer, C. L., & Ravens, A. (Eds.). (1994). *New feminist criticism: Art, identity, action.* New York: HarperCollins.

Garber, E. (1996). Art criticism from a feminist point of view: An approach for teachers. In G. Collins & R. Sandell (Eds.), *Gender issues in art education: Content, contexts, and strategies* (pp. 21–38). Reston, VA: National Art Education Association.

Geahigan, G. (1998). From procedures to principles and beyond: Implementing critical inquiry in the classroom. *Studies in Art Education, 39*(4), 293–308.

Keifer-Boyd, K. (1996). Interfacing hypermedia and the Internet with critical inquiry in the arts: Preservice training. *Art Education, 49*(6), 33–41.

Shin, S. (2003). *The effects of a metacognitive art criticism teaching strategy that incorporates computer technology on critical thinking skill and art critiquing ability.* Dissertation completed at Florida State University.

Stout, J. (1995). Critical conversation about art: A description of higher order thinking generated through the study of art criticism. *Studies in Art Education, 36*(30), 170–188.

Art History

Visual Timeline, Sarah Workheiser and Kenneth Humphries, Grayson High School, Loganville, GA. Janet Felts, Art Teacher. *Students researched art movements, events in U.S. and world history, science, and technology as facets of society from 1850-1975 to construct a timeline of contextual background for their study of the history of photography.*

THE SOCIAL CONSTRUCTION OF ART HISTORY

It has been said that the social function of art is the resolution of the unconscious. Ancient people tied knots in a cord to record the waxing and waning of the moon; similarly, art is a means of recording individual and collective feelings and events. Recorded stories become historic **narratives** deeply engraved on the collective human consciousness, serving to maintain and transmit culture. Through art, a history of people and events records not only facts but also the spirit and emotions of a time.

Because each culture records its own history in its own way, the study of **art history** gives us many perspectives on the moral and spiritual character of humankind. Although all people everywhere have certain overarching concerns, each culture has a different sensibility. As we will discuss later, aesthetic artifacts and performances convey particular observations of human nature and can provide opportunities to discuss themes that are important in many times and places.

Art history was once dominated by a fundamentally conservative and restrictive definition of high culture and controlled by the western male social order, but over the past twenty years it has been influenced by revisionist postmodernism. For example, the French historian Michael Foucault rejected the western linear organization of history and suggested that history should be constructed in a cultural context of unrelated chronological events to better understand differences as well as similarities. Today, many art history texts and museums present artworks and artifacts clustered by themes for cross-cultural comparison, rather than in a strictly linear, chronological format. This approach allows us to hear personal, idiosyncratic, and autobiographical narrative voices that were muffled by the grand linear narrative of the western tradition. As art itself challenged traditional boundaries, the role of the art historian also shifted to acknowledge multiple views rather than one absolute truth, emphasizing the **social construction of meaning** in individual self-expression.

Typically, art historians focus on a work, artifact, or performance to identify its context: how it was created, by whom, when, and why. They try to determine the work's original appearance and the artist's intended meanings. Accordingly, the patrons and the intended audience are also are among the art historian's concerns.

The civil rights movement and women's movement affected traditional institutional practices; who decides which artworks are credible and worthy of public attention and public funds is an increasingly contested issue. However, art critics, museum and gallery curators, and institutional art historians are still the primary gatekeepers of the arts establishment. In general, contemporary art that is consistently noticed by the arts establishment begins to be viewed as part of the continuum of western art and is eventually placed in that context. Western

FIGURE 7.1 *Ganesh,* decorated with hibiscus flowers, Ubud, Indonesia. *This statue of Ganesh represents one of the most popular deities of wisdom and good fortune in the Hindu tradition.*

institutions do not yet give much attention to contemporary non-western art, but the international market is growing, and various new definitions of art in relation to both the local and the global community may emerge.

Some artwork may not be valued by the general public or by critics at the time it is produced, but art historians may later consider it as an important influence on other artists or as having opened the doors for new forms, so it enters the halls of art history for that reason. In recent decades a number of artists have created satires or parodies, appropriating art within the western canon in order to circumvent and comment on the traditional institutional process. Some of this artwork may be difficult to understand without previous art historical and other cultural knowledge. Contemporary appropriation artists copy or borrow images from other times and cultures and challenge us by recontextualizing historical western images. No doubt some of this work will itself become part of art history, although other work will fade from memory. Questions for students to consider are not only why artists appropriate images, but also how images are constructed and used to influence decision making or to communicate group identity, status, or power.

Appropriation in art is based on historical tradition. It is not simply borrowing or copying; it may also be a cultural tool for achieving power and a form of social commentary. It raises legal and ethical issues as well as issues of originality in the art classroom.

Sometimes we have difficulty distinguishing between appropriation and inspiration. We can find themes and images that have been copied repeatedly almost since the beginning of recorded history. For example, the gesture of the left hand in an early relief

FIGURE 7.2 Robert Colescott. *George Washington Carver Crossing the Delaware.* Acrylic on canvas, 7 x 9 ft. *In this satirical appropriation of a well-known American painting, Colescott critiques the historic stereotypical portrayal of race, culture, and history.*

Appropriation and the Law

Artists who appropriated images and then were accused of infringing copyright laws include Andy Warhol, Jeff Koons, and Sherrie Levine. Andy Warhol appropriated many images. His *Campbell's Soup Can,* perhaps his most famous image, was taken directly from the actual can. His disaster paintings were a series based on actual events such as automobile accidents, and he created them by using photographs copied directly from newspapers. Warhol also appropriated artwork from master artists such as Leonardo da Vinci and Edvard Munch. For his 1966 *Jackie,* silkscreen images related to President Kennedy's assassination, he used eight copyrighted images without obtaining permission. In some of these instances lawsuits were filed, but all these suits were settled out of court. Warhol's strategy seems to have been to ask forgiveness rather than permission and negotiate a financial settlement.

Jeff Koons, a businessman turned artist, was involved in a suit that was tried in court. In 1988, Koons exhibited *Banality,* twenty sculptures made from a variety of materials. These pieces had been created from existing images collected by the artist. One of the large carved wooden pieces was called *String of Puppies.* For this work, Koons found a photograph of a couple holding eight puppies. The photographer was Art Rogers. Koons had bought the photo at a souvenir shop and, since it was sold as a commercial product, considered it part of the public domain. *Banality* makes a comment about the use of trite images in the mass media and about the trappings of the upwardly mobile, so this photograph suited his theme. Like the other pieces in *Banality, String of Puppies* has the look of popular culture or even kitsch. Koons had an Italian company carve the photographic image of puppies to create a three-dimensional piece from a two-dimensional photo. The artisans were instructed to change the puppies' color from black to blue, make the puppies' noses white, and add flowers in the woman's hair.

In 1991, Koons went to court to see how the court would interpret copyright laws with regard to the appropriation of widely distributed items, such as note cards, in postmodern art. The judge ruled that Koons's work infringed on the copyright owned by Rogers. While Koons's piece could be considered conceptually original, there was no product identifiable as Koons's work, so the "originality threshold" for a tangible product had not been met. Although Koons's work was a satirical comment on trite images in the mass media, he was not referring to a specific original work, since Rogers's photo was relatively unknown. Therefore, Koons's sculpture could not be considered a parody, and parody was not a valid defense.

In another, similar case, Koons created *Ushering in Banality,* a sculpture of two boys pushing on a pig, based on a work by Barbara Campbell. In this instance Campbell and Koons reached a settlement for the use of the image, and the work remained in the catalog.

Many lawyers specializing in this area understand that the concept of copyright to regulate the use of visual imagery is alien to the tradition of art, which has evolved over thousands of years using the principle and practice of copying. Unauthorized copying, for which no fees are paid and no licenses are obtained, is the basis of artistic apprenticeship. But regardless of thousands of years of tradition, new case law has now emerged that imposes fines for copying.

---

sculpture, the *Venus of Laussel,* is very similar to gestures in later figures of Venus in western art, such as the *Sleeping Venus.* A painting begun by Giorgione, who died in 1509, was said to have been finished by Titian. Later, in 1538, Titian created his own *Venus of Urbino,* in a very similar pose. Manet's *Olympia* was completed in 1865 as a satire on Titian's *Venus.* Even in these few works we can see various applications of appropriation: the appropriation of style and technique and the appropriation of a theme for purposes of satire or social commentary.

Historically, and until the modern era, the teaching of art was based on the apprenticeship model, which generally encouraged imitation and the appropriation of style and technique. With the advent of modern art, originality and creativity became important, and copying or appropriating artwork for any reason was disparaged. However, appropriation has generally been acceptable for the purpose of parody or satire, in which one artist closely imitates the style of another, creating a new work that ridicules the original. Parody and satire are valuable forms of criticism that actually foster the creativity protected by copyright law. They are said to be transformative, shedding light on earlier works and in the process creating new works.

Contemporary artists who use satire and parody for social commentary include Robert Colescott, Cindy Sherman, Renae Cox, and Jeff Koons. They appropriate existing images—from advertising, art, or other sources—and reconfigure these images in new contexts to create new art. Their intention is to give new meanings and associations to both the original work and the copied version. Some appropriation artists go so far as to challenge the laws against plagiarism. Sherrie Levine, for instance (see Chapter 5), became involved in a lawsuit. We look at some legal issues in the sidebar.

THE PRACTICE OF ART HISTORY

What Do Art Historians Do?

In practice, we cannot separate art history form art criticism. However, it might be said that art historians look more for information *about* a **visual artifact or performance** whereas critics look for information *within* the work of art. Art history has to do with external, contextual information; art criticism has to do with internal, formal information. Art historians want to know (1) who made a work, when, where, why, and how; (2) what the style of the work is; (3) what influences (artistic, social-cultural, technological) affected its production; and (4) what impact the work had on other works or on society.

What art historians do depends on what they are looking for, and what they look for depends on their philosophy. Various approaches may be taken. Some art historians set out to develop a chronology. Others look for an evolution of form, style, or symbols—this is called iconography. Some seek to ascertain the place of a work or movement within the history of ideas. Others attempt to place a work in a cultural context. Still others look at the lives and personalities of the artists. Another aspect of understanding art is the impact of a work or performance on other artists and the larger public, both at the time of its creation and thereafter. In the late twentieth century, many art historians reacted against formalism, connoisseurship, and what they see as simplified iconography. These historians see the artist and artifact as representing an ideology and the construction of history as ideological problem solving. Others focus on semiotics: the use of artistic "language" (signs, symbols, signifiers, and signifieds) in the construction of meaning. Addiss and Erickson summarize the purposes of art historical research as (1) formal analysis, (2) biographical information, (3) knowledge of patronage and audience, and (4) understanding of cultural context.

For our purposes, social approaches to art history are more useful than formalistic or purely chronological approaches. We advocate taking a social perspective in studying a work. This contextualist approach entails critical investigation of social setting, mood, economic conditions, and other circumstances in which the work was produced in order to interpret and evaluate the work. Such cross-disciplinary research may require the art historian to consider sociology, anthropology, economics, and other disciplines as well as traditional art history.

In addition to style and artistic tradition, ideological sources of cultural and aesthetic values are important for the art historian to understand if the artwork is to be placed in a larger human context. Such placement encourages investigation of and speculation about connections between art and actual events, other artists, philosophers, scientists, and ideas. Because humans are similar in some respects over time and across cultures, once an artwork is understood in its original context, students may compare and contrast its meaning with the aspects of their own lives.

What Are Art Historians' Tools?

Art historians use both primary and secondary sources. Primary sources include objects and performances (for example, paintings, masks, sculpture, votive objects) as well as written sources from the same time and place as an object itself—that is, sources written by someone who was actually present when the object was made or when an event connected with the object took place. Michelangelo's paintings and journals, for example, are primary sources, as are Van Gogh's letters to his brother, photographs of artists in their studios, and firsthand accounts of artists' lives, such as Anne Truitt's daybooks or Vasari's biographies of artists he actually knew.

Secondary sources are all sources other than primary. For example, if someone incorporated Vasari's account into his or her own biography of an artist, that biography is a secondary source. Most of the readily available print sources are secondary sources; but increasingly, primary sources are available to student researchers online in the form of images, statements, and interviews. Professional art historians pride themselves on finding and using primary sources, which offer greater accuracy than secondary sources. Mistrust of secondary sources is well founded—as you can see by thinking of the "telephone game," in which one person starts a message by whispering it in the ear of the person next to him or her, and the message then goes around a circle of other people. Frequently, by the time the message gets all the way around the circle, it's hardly recognizable to the primary source, the person who originated it.

But art historians don't take even primary sources as necessarily accurate. For example, an artist talking about his or her work may have reasons not to tell the truth; a person giving a firsthand account may be mistaken as to what was seen or heard or may have reasons for deception. Art historians attribute more or less significance to their findings by applying the strategies of internal and external verity and provenance.

Verity is a word used by historians to mean "the truth." **Internal verity** is an examination of a work itself, or an account of a work in its context, for flaws that suggest deception or misinterpretation. For example, a work may be attributed to Van Gogh, but a close examination reveals clumsy brush strokes of a sort that Van Gogh would never make in his mature period, suggesting that the painting is a fake. Or perhaps some strokes seem like the mature Van Gogh but others seem amateurish, suggesting that the work has been retouched. However, if the strokes seem true throughout and in harmonious relation to one another and to the apparent intention of the work, there is internal evidence that the painting may be authentic. Likewise, if an eyewitness account places a certain event at a certain date or place, then contradicts that date or place later, there may be problems with internal verity. Internal verity, then, has to do with the internal relationships of an object or account.

External verity involves seeking confirmation from sources outside an account or object. For example, if a work is supposedly Byzantine, but the style looks like the early Renaissance when the work is compared with similar objects, or if one account says one thing and three other accounts contradict it, there are problems with external verity.

Provenance is another important tool in determining verity. Provenance involves an examination of the history of a work by determining an owner or successive owners in order to establish its authenticity. Suppose it has been suggested that a work said to be by Tintoretto is a fake. If the historian can establish the record of its being bought, sold, and traded all the way back to Tintoretto, its authenticity can be established almost beyond a doubt. But if the painting was lost for twenty years and then reappeared, how are we to know it isn't a fake? Art historians must then use other methods to determine authenticity: internal and external verity, primary sources, and—if primary sources are not available—secondary sources.

In the end, though, the most important tools of the art historian are his or her own intuition, sensibility, ability to nose out the truth, and integrity and skill in reporting, analyzing, and interpreting findings. Art history is selective and interpretive; it is not merely a matter of recording and reporting objective facts. It is a **narrative,** a story composed by the historian that gives his or her best account of what happened and what it means.

Therefore, even when historical accounts seem to be based on reasonable, factual information, there are sometimes disagreements about what the facts are, who the experts are, and what conclusions are to be drawn. In the past century many new historical facts have been uncovered and documented, leading to new interpretations of events and artworks. Because art historians develop meanings based on intellectual speculation about historical evidence, any claim to scientific neutrality is questionable. So that they will not seem to be claiming omniscience, many art historians announce their point of view, assumptions, and agenda. This allows the reader to consider their findings in light of their positions and adds immensely to the integrity of research and of the meanings developed.

ART HISTORY IN EDUCATION

The Practice of Art History and Art for Life

With regard to art for life, this description of current practices in art history has three implications. First, art history—like the making of art—is a social construct, and as such is continually changing. Art history is not written in stone. Human meanings and human experiences, including aesthetic representations and art history, are constructed daily. Today, art historians investigate not only the great artworks of older cultures but also art of contemporary society and of artists and cultures that were once considered peripheral. For example, since the 1980s folk art, crafts, and so-called outsider art have gained acceptance as areas of study for serious art historians. Likewise, film, video, digital imagery, and visual culture are now a part of the contemporary institutional mainstream in art museums and galleries. Everything from automobiles to Manga can be studied.

The second implication is that artworks and performances should be understood in their authentic cultural context. Art for life helps us understand people through their art rather than understanding only the form of the art. Because cultures and artists have specific characteristics, art for life facilitates a multicultural approach. This is entirely appropriate; no one culture can provide all the important insights on what it means to be human. It's also appropriate for this text, which is designed to serve the multiple contemporary cultures of North America. We believe that everyone can benefit from an awareness and appreciation by the dominant culture of those who are perceived to be outside the mainstream, and from an understanding of the dominant culture by those who seem to be on the periphery.

The third implication is that although art history must be defined in terms of its distinct qualities, it does not really stand apart from the other disciplines of artistic inquiry. Rather, it overlaps with and utilizes aesthetics and art criticism. In practice, then, it is yet another tool to help us reach the goal of thematic interdisciplinary understanding.

Art History and Students' Constructed Meanings

In art for life, the most valuable instructional strategy is usually personally motivated, personally responsible art historical investigation of contemporary art and the art of the past. The sort of art historical inquiry we advocate blends with aesthetic inquiry, art criticism, the social sciences, and so on. We believe that such inquiry is possible because so many primary sources are available to students—especially now, when technology gives them ready access to contemporary art and artists. In our media-driven culture, contemporary artists are often featured in art magazines, periodicals, and interviews, and online. This exposure leads to celebrity

A CLOSER LOOK   The Interview as Research

Written narratives are a consistently valuable resource for teaching about the social context and personal circumstances of artists. Historically, artists have kept journals and written about their work in letters and books. Van Gogh's famous letters to his brother Theo reveal his struggle to survive, his emotional turmoil, and his despair. Such letters add a human touch that can immeasurably enhance our appreciation and understanding of art. If students are encouraged to read autobiographical narratives and other primary sources, they may find more revelations about the human beings behind artworks than a textbook can provide.

A study of contemporary art offers a very appealing way to obtain information from primary sources: an interview with an artist. Such interviews are readily found in many popular art magazines and journals. Several interviews with artists over a period of years will provide an interesting comparison of works and comments. In this text (Chapter 12) you will find a long interview with Nancy Merrill, who worked with Ciel Bergman to create an interactive installation as a critique of environmental conditions.

Artists can often be contacted through their websites, by telephone, or face to face for interviews in which information is gathered about their processes, ideas, and motivations. Walker (2001) interviewed Chandra McCormick and Keith Calhoun, two African-American photographers in New Orleans, to discuss their art in relation to their cultural heritage and community commitment. Walker suggests interviews as "a practice for art teachers who are striving to understand their students and the communities they live in and who want to integrate concepts into their art curricula that are relevant to students' lives and that challenge notions of White supremacy" (249).

This idea was explored in a summer session at Georgia State University in 2002. As the city of Atlanta prepared to celebrate a biannual Black Arts Festival, the university's art education department offered a two-week seminar on African-American art. This seminar included visits to museums to highlight the rich tradition of African-American art in Atlanta; in addition, seven African-American artists spoke with students about their work. The students had developed a set of general questions that a spokesperson asked each artist, along with specific questions that came up in the course of each presentation. At the end of the seminar the students analyzed and compared the remarks of the artists. Although the artists were all African American and most of them were men, their works and comments were quite varied. The students' interaction with the artists helped them break away from stereotypical views of African-American artists and revealed a rich array of community resources.[1]

Wigginton (1989) helped elementary school students develop questions and interview community members to create an oral history. This technique could be easily adapted for students of any age so that they could interview local artists. The result would be authentic learning, and the connection with community artists would deepen students' understanding of the role of art and artists in a specific place. Commercially prepared materials might not do this nearly so well.

Teachers and students may want to gather reviews, interviews, opening statements, and so on related to an artist's work as a comprehensive form of art historical research. As students become acquainted with critiques in magazines, in exhibition catalogs, in advertisements in *Art in America,* and online, they may come to understand that although the quality of observations and judgments may vary, reviews and critics serve as gatekeepers of contemporary art. Through primary personal inquiry, students may gain insights into contemporary artists' views, values, and functions in society. Depending on the age of the students and their ability to work independently, the teacher may have the role of lead researcher or simply of facilitator.

---

[1]Artists who participated in the seminar were Larry Walker, Radcliffe Baily, Charnelle Holloway, Donald Locke, Toby Martin, Gerald Straw, and Kevin Sipp of the Hammond House. Students visited art galleries at Spelman College, Clark Atlanta University, and the High Museum of Art.

in the art world that in turn often generates more and more written information. Many artists also maintain their own websites and will sometimes give interviews or answer questions online.

Student researchers are less likely to gain new insights on traditional works and artists that have been through the art history mill. But motivated students can still find new meanings in the old masters that may shed light on their own personal situations, and we encourage that.

FIGURE 7.3 Jacques Bordeleau, *Installation* (2002). *Bordeleau gives new meaning to traditional art and the art of old masters through recontextualizing them in this contemporary piece.*

Art Historical Research as Authentic Education

Many goals of authentic art education may be reached through teaching and learning art history. Addiss and Erickson note that in a democracy, it is necessary for art history to reflect and serve the diverse cultures of the population. Beyond a familiarity with names and dates and a fundamental ability to recognize images, an important aspect of art history is the use of images as paradigms to help students understand concepts and people of other cultures and times. Individuals and cultures develop their understandings from the understandings of those who preceded them. Art history helps us understand that artistic concepts were developed in specific places and at specific times to meet specific conditions and needs. Thus it gives artistic forms and aesthetic ideas a context that makes them meaningful and real.

Also, art historical inquiry can be used to develop students' critical thinking and problem solving. Such inquiry teaches students to ask questions, seek information, develop hypotheses, and draw conclusions about the meaning of artworks from other times and cultures. As students become able to move beyond the curriculum and investigate topics independently, they may generate their own questions and approaches. This type of authentic research may be more interesting and more appealing than traditional teacher-directed methods.

In the South Bronx a group of high school students called Kids of Survival (KOS) has gained a national reputation for their collaborative murals. Their teacher, Tim Rollins, says that he provides many books with images from art history for students to look at and then lets the students' interest guide his and their research. He urges students to become aware of the power of art history and how they can use this power to make their own history, not just following tradition but starting new traditions. Rollins also stresses helping students to learn for themselves, take over their own education, and demand more information.

In art for life, the educational role of art history is to inform students about what has been done before and what ideas have been explored—how, why, when, where, and in what context. Ultimately, this information should serve their own drives and needs. Investigations in art history can help students understand the importance of the historical narrative in all cultures and societies, past and present. Cultural, national, and ethnic narratives provide a basis for our individual and collective identity. Art as communication depends on a shared symbolic code, which in turn depends on critical inquiry and examinations of context to arrive at valid interpretations or speculation about meanings. A study of art history can help students understand how and why some events are remembered, commemorated, or celebrated and others are forgotten. Inquiry in art history also helps students synthesize information from many sources as they continue to develop their perceptual skills as viewers and artists.

Authentic instruction and assessment can be easily implemented within art historical inquiry. If students are responsible for contextual research about an artwork or artist, they are challenged to deepen their knowledge. This research can be done individually or collectively, although collective inquiry is likely to lead to more sophisticated and more profound results. The teacher may assign groups of students to work collaboratively on comprehensive research that crosses disciplines and connects various views—economic, political, social, religious, and so on. Such a comprehensive approach may deepen students' understanding of art in its historical and cultural context and of the connections and interactions between contemporary art and society.

Art history also entails substantive discussion about the relationship between an artwork or artist's life and philosophical or aesthetic questions, the mores and traditions of a society, and students' own values and beliefs. Artists often deal with themes such as justice, fairness, compassion, love, hate, clarity, and delusion. Their works may reveal a civilization's moral tradition by celebrating moments that affirm social values or by pointing out discrepancies. Such concepts are basic to the democratic legal system and deserve exploration and discussion so that students can develop their own understanding of morality and moral reasoning. Narrative stories that inform, engage, and inspire may emerge from art history.

FIGURE 7.4   KOS, *Amerika—For the People of Bathgate,* 1988. *Tim Rollins and Kids of Survival (KOS) collaborated with students and staff of South Bronx Elementary School #4 to create this mural of twenty-eight golden horns.*

THE BAYEUX TAPESTRY: AN EXAMPLE OF AUTHENTIC ART HISTORY

In art historical research, the teacher may be a facilitator, helping students connect their own themes to images and artifacts that shed light on the problems they are trying to solve. Such themes arise from life. They include the terrorist attacks of September 2001, the bombing of Afghanistan, the continuing conflict in the Middle East, and the seemingly random violence on the streets and in the schools of America. Debate persists regarding the pathology of violence, the relationships among people and nations, the impact of popular culture on human behavior, and social values that contribute to conflict and brutal confrontations. If contemporary social issues can be connected to aesthetic artifacts, the connection may give students a new perspective.

The Bayeux Tapestry, for example, can be used to address concerns and issues related to violence that touch students' daily lives. (See Color Plate 12, *Bayeux Tapestry,* 1066). The Bayeux Tapestry—so named because it is housed in the town of Bayeux in France—depicts one of the most important events in English and French history, William the Conqueror's invasion of England and the battle of Hastings in 1066. The battle of Hastings was one of the most significant military achievements in the history of western civilization, but equally compelling is the more personal story of loyalty, friendship, and betrayal that led to the Norman invasion.

The artwork is actually not a tapestry but an embroidery; it is 230 feet long and 20 inches wide and consists of a linen background sewn with woolen thread of red,

FIGURE 7.5 *Bayeux Tapestry,* 1066, embroidery on linen, 230 ft. x 20 in. *Each scene of the Bayeux Tapestry is accompanied by Latin text. In this section of the narrative Harold, duke of the English, rides to Bosham with his men-at-arms. Notice the border symbols that appear throughout the narrative. Many art historians believe that these symbols were used to communicate attributes of the principal characters to the masses through animals from well-known fables of the day. For example, peacocks (representing royalty because of their colorful, showy plumage) are often seen in the border when Harold and William meet. How might we read these images today? Detail from the Bayeux Tapestry—11th Century. By special permission of the City of Bayeux.*

yellow or buff, gray, and several hues of green and blue. Nine linen panels of unequal lengths were sewn together to create the work. The narrative covers seventy-five scenes with 623 figures, only three of whom represent women. Much of the visual narrative is supplemented by a Latin text.

The story of the Bayeux Tapestry began about 1064. Edward, king of England, was growing old, and the question arose who should be his successor. Edward and his wife, Queen Edith, had no children, but several relatives were contenders for the throne. Edward decided on his distant cousin, William, Duke of Normandy. He asked one of the other contenders—his wife's brother, Harold Godwinson, Earl of Wessex, who was one of his wealthiest subjects—to deliver the message to William.

Harold set off, stopping with his small troop at his castle on England's southern coast to feast and pray for a safe voyage across the English Channel. Although their crossing went well, they were blown off course before landing and arrived on the shore of an unfriendly Norman count. Harold tried to explain his mission, but when the count realized that the intruder was rich and important, he decided to hold Harold for ransom. William was notified and paid a high price for Harold's release.

Harold was therefore indebted to William and swore allegiance to him. William formalized their relationship by giving his daughter (the first woman in the tapestry) to Harold in marriage. Harold delivered the message from Edward, and a new relationship seemed to have been formed. When William received news of an attack on one of his allies, Harold offered to ride with him and his knights into battle. Along the way, Harold single-handedly saved two of William's knights who were caught in quicksand. Later, he proved himself as a warrior in battle, helping to defeat the enemy.

Harold returned to England to report to the king. Soon after Harold's return, the tapestry records the death of Edward on January 5, 1066. The tapestry shows Harold and Queen Edith (the second woman in the tapestry) at Edward's bedside. On his deathbed, Edward supposedly reconsidered his choice of William as his successor and asked instead that Harold become king. Harold immediately claimed the throne. Although Harold was not of royal blood, his claim was supported by Edward's deathbed wish; by Harold's relationship to his sister, Queen Edith; and by encouragement from elders in Edward's court.

When William received word that Harold had accepted the crown, he immediately began to build a fleet to cross the channel and invade England. This was the largest military operation undertaken in northern Europe to that time. The tapestry portrays an enterprise in which at least 600 vessels transported 8,000 to 10,000 troops, including 3,000 to 4,000 knights and horses. On September 28, 1066, the fleet set sail, with William in the lead ship, commissioned for him by his wife, Matilda.

Once they landed in England, the Normans established camp. They pillaged the surrounding area for food and supplies during the two weeks before to the battle. A woman (the third woman in the tapestry) and a child are depicted in the tapestry fleeing from a house burned by the Normans. As William and his troops feasted the night before battle, he reminded his soldiers of the importance and justice of their mission and urged them to "fight valiantly and wisely." William's half-brother, Odo, who was a member of the clergy, led William's personal troops. William carried only his commander's staff, and Odo was armed with a three-headed mace (a sword that could draw blood was thought unseemly for a member of the clergy to carry). William sent a monk to ask Harold to relinquish his claim, but Harold refused, so the troops engaged in battle.

The battle lasted all day. The Normans sent in men on horseback, followed by rows of archers. The English formed a wall of foot soldiers with overlapping shields that presented an impenetrable barrier to their enemies. Although the English suffered losses, including Harold's two brothers, the wall of shields held, and the French began to lose soldiers and mounts in the marshy ground at the base of a hill, which Harold's forces had lined with sharp stakes. Believing that William had been killed, the French started to flee. The English broke their wall of shields and chased the French down the hill. William then raised his helmet so that his troops could see his face, and Bishop Odo stood in his stirrups and shouted encouragement. The French then once again took up the fight. Since the English were no longer holding their shield wall, the battle turned in William's favor. When Harold was killed, his troops began to scatter, and the battle was over. The story of the tapestry ends as William's troops advance on the fleeing English.

William was crowned king on December 25, 1066, but this section of the tapestry is missing. It is generally assumed that the missing section depicted the coronation of William as a mirror image of King Edward the Confessor at the beginning of the tapestry, suggesting the ongoing royal lineage and the stability of the lawful English monarchy.

Look at Color Plate 12 and ask yourself the following questions. How does the artist convey the agony of this battle? How might you identify which army is which in this scene? (Normans are on horseback or clean-shaven or both; Saxons wear moustaches.) How does the designer of the tapestry convey action and violence? How are the actions like or unlike some contemporary cartoons? By today's standards, do you think this scene is very violent? Explain why or why not. Is the depiction of violence justifiable? Do you think it was right for William to sacrifice so many lives to gain power? What about Harold? Do you feel that violence is acceptable in art? Do you think that violent images contribute to violent behavior, particularly among young people? Do you think artists need to take greater responsibility for the violent images they produce? How does this question relate to the concept of censorship in the arts?

Regardless of their age, students may recognize in their examination and discussion of the Bayeux Tapestry authentic, universal issues that remain current. Some students may want to discuss instances when they failed to keep a promise or violated a friend's confidence, or when a friend betrayed their trust. How does betrayal of a trust affect a friendship? Some students may be willing to share their experiences. What are some other causes of conflict between people? Why do such conflicts sometimes become violent? Do you consider acts of personal aggression or violence different from acts of group or national aggression or violence, such as war? Explain your view. If you feel that you have hurt a friend or have been betrayed by someone, what might you do to resolve the conflict? What might you do to disengage yourself from a potentially violent situation?

One benefit of winning a war or battle is that the victor typically has control of the media. In this case, the tapestry suggests that William was probably a more moral man than Harold, so he deserved to win the battle and become king. Are the morally "best" people always the victors in battle? Doesn't every contestant say "God is on our side"? How can this contradiction be resolved? Can you think of examples to support your answer? Are viewpoints ever totally objective? What point of view does the Bayeux Tapestry take? Who are the good guys and bad guys? Were they really? How might you determine the historical accuracy of events? Explain.

Students may also ask themselves about relationships having to do with power, not only in the main content of the tapestry but also in its unintended themes, such why there are only three women depicted and what their relationship is to men and to power. The students may recognize in this story from the eleventh century some of the same issues—inequality, trust, betrayal, justice, injustice—that we find today in violence at school or the destruction of the World Trade Center. They may then realize that although we are all different, we have had many of the same human concerns over time and across cultures.

The Bayeux Tapestry has survived fire, pillaging, and several wars. It left Bayeux for the first time in November 1803, to be exhibited at the Louvre at the request of Napoleon when France was at war with England. It was stored in Switzerland during World War II but was returned to Bayeux in 1945; it is on display there today. The lessons of the tapestry's story in the context of its style (which provides a slant on the story) have to do with themes—greed, conflict, destruction—that are still relevant today, not only in the western tradition but in myths and legends of cultures around the world. Whether such stories are from an oral, visual, or written tradition, they convey valuable lessons about life. As students discuss the Bayeux Tapestry, they may also examine their own reactions to and understanding of confrontation and violence, war and peace, love, loyalty, betrayal, and loss. Through this process they may come to understand how meaning is constructed in art history and in society.

DEVELOPING SOCIAL CONSCIOUSNESS THROUGH ART HISTORY

In a survey conducted in 1999, art educators in Georgia reported that they routinely taught lessons addressing social themes or issues, most often through art history. Through discussing an artwork and its context, teachers guided students to think about large issues and social concerns. For example, *Guernica*, by Pablo Picasso, is often used to discuss the horrors of war or violence. The Guernica Children's Peace Mural Project (see Chapters 1 and 15) was inspired by this work. Racism and poverty are themes addressed in work by Jacob Lawrence, Romare Bearden, and Käthe Kollwitz. Issues of power and identity are addressed by Barbara Kruger and Cindy Sherman (see Chapter 9) and by Krzysztof Wodiczko and Fred Wilson (see the curricula in Part Three). These artists and many others can be important role models because they have used their art to seek resolution to a problem or an injustice. Through looking at and discussing images that express strong emotions or moral concerns, students are given opportunities to develop meaningful ideas, reflective thinking, and moral reasoning. As Lanier (1974) noted,

> What are required are a critical consciousness, an informed awareness of those social forces that oppress our lives, confine our growth, and defile our dreams, and an additional awareness of what we can do to combat them. . . .
> If education is seen in any measure as the development of a critical consciousness, then art education should contribute to this process. (116–117)

FIGURE 7.6   Kara Walker, *Slavery! Slavery!* Walker Art Museum, Minneapolis, 1997. *Walker uses the traditional cut-paper silhouette to confront and challenge historic African-American racial stereotypes that still affect racial relationships today.*

Controversial Topics

Artworks frequently address topics that are controversial or even taboo at school, such as religion and sex. Examination of such works may lead students to question their basic assumptions about life. For example, since art has for most of its existence been related to belief, it is almost impossible to study art history without taking up world religions. Artworks that serve religious functions are often neglected by art educators who lack sufficient knowledge of world religions or fear controversy or do not want to seem to be proselytizing. But if religious ideas are avoided, students may not understand the meaning of artworks with religious subjects, whether from the western tradition or from other cultures. As a result, they may be less and less tolerant of artistic expression outside their own system of preferences or beliefs (Eaton, 1998). Religion is often fundamental to an understanding of a culture. Think about trying to understand Saudi Arabia without some knowledge of Islam, or trying to understand North America without the context of the Judeo-Christian tradition.

Avoiding discussion of religion and other difficult topics leads to ignorance and conflict. The more controversial the topic, the more relevant a discussion would be to the real lives of students. Racial issues, violence, and sex are among the forbidden topics in contemporary education, yet students continue to feel a need to discuss these topics honestly. Artists address issues that directly affect their lives, issues such as sex (Barbara Kruger and Adrian Piper), injustice (Robert Colescott and Fred Wilson), war and peace (Picasso and Goya), power (Krzysztof Wodiczko and Sherrie Levine), and belief, whether that involves sand mandalas or the Christian murals of Giotto. These social concerns are part of the context necessary to fully understand the artwork. For example, *American Gothic, Washington, D.C.* by Gordon Parks reveals American values from the

FIGURE 7.7   Gordon Parks, *American Gothic, Washington, D.C.*, 1942. Photograph. *When this photograph was taken in 1942, the job of cleaning woman was the only one open to this educated woman in Washington, D.C. Why did Parks make American Gothic part of his title?*

point of view of a well-educated African-American woman who has been forced to accept a menial job because of prejudicial hiring practices. *The Chair,* by Andy Warhol, raises the issue of capital punishment and our culture's ideas about what is considered "acceptable" violence. *We Don't Need Another Hero,* by Barbara Kruger, points out stereotypical gender roles apparent in Americans at a very early age. As a graphic designer and managing editor of a women's magazine, Kruger developed an intense sensitivity to women's images in the media. Art teachers must not be naive regarding their school and community, but they should work to gain the support of parents and the administration for open, honest discussions in the art classroom.

Difficult Topics and Strategies for Authentic Discussion

Sometimes social concerns from the world beyond school enter the classroom itself. The First Amendment to the Constitution safeguards freedom of speech and self-expression, but such issues may create conflict, and so teachers are somewhat hesitant to address them. Still, people have a right—some would say a patriotic duty—to disagree when they see injustice, and dealing with controversial topics need not be confrontational. The art classroom may be a particularly good educational setting for students to learn to pursue their own goals without disregarding the rights of others.

Kirschenbaum (1994) suggested three basic ways to prevent conflict over difficult topics. The first two of these are already used routinely in art classrooms: (1) an environment in which cooperative learning and teaching are well established; (2) an understanding and appreciation of diversity and multiculturalism. The second approach entails presenting a variety of positive multicultural role models, presenting cultural diversity as a national strength, and teaching students to oppose stereotypes in thought, word, and deed.

Managing anger is also a valuable skill that helps students deal with conflict. This may not be an established part of most discussions in the art classroom but may be worth adding. It can help students realize that while anger is a natural reaction, it can be channeled or managed in numerous nonviolent ways, such as making and talking about art. Time out, "self-talk," deep breathing, and regular exercise to reduce stress may help students manage their strong feelings productively as they make art and talk about art.

In potentially controversial discussions about the context and meaning of art, teachers may want to consider conflict resolution as a problem-solving skill. They may also consider mediation. It's important in this regard to teach students to develop their own ideas based on evidence and criteria rather than on emotion and to listen to opposing views respectfully. Kirschenbaum's advice for facilitating discussions that engage students in developing their own ideas and moral values includes asking open-ended questions that require reflective thinking or have more than one plausible answer. He also suggests that teachers should not telegraph their own answers. If you want students to respond honestly, try not to let your own opinions dominate the discussion. But do participate. Many students value comments from the teacher, but remember to listen well and respectfully and share your viewpoint without preaching. Also, treat all responses with equal respect. Avoid overly positive and overly negative reactions so that students will continue to think for themselves. Insist on equal respect for all participants. If you must shift to inculcation, do so advisedly and with awareness. Sometimes you will need to clarify an important point or position, but be aware of the students' responses and return to the discussion to the students by asking another open-ended question if possible. Don't let the group discussion wander off the track for extended periods; stay on the topic.

Another important strategy is to vary the discussion period. There are many formats for large- and small-group discussions, time limits, and so on. Vary your approach to group discussions to keep them interesting. Also, go beyond the superficial. Relate discussions to art history lectures, research, and studio projects:

compare and contrast themes, issues, and forms in terms of students' concerns and broader human concerns.

Finally, respond appropriately to irresponsible statements. Most students can be impressively serious and thoughtful, so high-quality responses and discussions should be expected, not a rarity. Understanding the demographics and cultural values represented in each classroom is a first step for teachers who are planning topics and questions for discussion. Because situations vary, there isn't one right way to respond to students' negative or antisocial comments. Each case must be assessed specifically. As in any other teaching situation, teachers first have to decide whether or not to take an infraction seriously. Often, other students will contradict a negative statement themselves so that the group becomes self-correcting. At other times you can voice a different opinion, or correct the student during the discussion or in private.

When students are encouraged to debate issues respectfully and openly, they may develop a better appreciation of both sides of academic and social controversies; in consequence, they can advance the cause of "peace education" through studying works of art (Kirschenbaum, 1994). Once the art teacher has established respectful ground rules, significant issues arising from works of art can be discussed without time-consuming preliminaries. Additional resources for controversial issues and conflict resolution in the classroom are listed at the end of this chapter.

ACTIVITIES   *for Authentic Art History*

Activities in authentic art history address information about a work and its context rather than formal concerns. Authentic information includes who, what, when, why, and how; style as related to other, similar works; what or who influenced the work and what or who it influenced; and the impact an artwork or body of work has had on other artists or society in general. Art history overlaps with art criticism, aesthetics, and other disciplines, and the activities that follow reflect this fact.

ACTIVITY   The instructor gives each student an unidentified print and has him or her find out about it and identify it by searching through art historical materials. Less popular works may be best for this exercise, since students will need to recognize stylistic resemblances rather than find the print itself.

Conceptual Purpose   Recognition of stylistic features through broad and careful examination of historical sources.

ACTIVITY   At the media center, or on the Net, or using art history sources in the art room, have students find three works of art from the same time period but from different countries. Each student should return with basic information on the images and be ready to share this information with the class. Discussion should ensue. Variations: Three works from the same country but different centuries; or three works from the same time and place but in different media; or different types (such as a chair, an ad, and a painting).

Conceptual Purpose   Understanding cultural and personal differences reflected in art, as well as different functions of art reflected in various forms.

ACTIVITY   Students are encouraged to find an image in an art history text or some other art text that stimulates them. They are to bring a five-minute report to class, to be delivered orally, about the artist. The report should cover items 1 through 4 under "What Do Art Historians Do?" (page 120).

Conceptual Purpose   Students will increase their fundamental information about art history. More commitment will develop if images the students are fond of are chosen. A broad range of art experiences will no doubt be covered.

ACTIVITY   "How Did It Look When It Was New?" Have the students do research on famous ruins (the Parthenon, the Sphinx, Pompeii, Tikal, etc.) and try to reconstruct how these sites would have looked in their prime, through drawing or sculptural modeling. In drawing, students might work by overlaying drawings on reproductions of ancient images. Discuss how the artifacts seem different from each other and different when they have color. Does color change our idea of the ancients as austere and elegant? How would some of our sites look as ruins in 2,000 years? Variations: Constructing and painting classic Greek statuary in its full original polychromatic form; or using local architecture to find out how older architecture looked long ago.

Conceptual Purpose   Bringing art historical images alive as artifacts that represent people's labors and ideas, like art and architecture today.

ACTIVITY   Have students choose specific periods or styles in art history to report on (romanticism, abstract expressionism, high Italian Renaissance, etc). They should include reasons why things looked as they did. What did people value? Possible follow-up: Have students design a CD cover, ad, web page, or the like in the style they studied. Discuss how that style changes the item designed. Variation: Reports on individual artists from the same period and style, to reveal commonalities and differences. How does individual sensibility affect a style and relate to the larger sensibility of the time?

Conceptual Purpose   General knowledge of periods and styles and how they reflect the values of their time.

ACTIVITY   Have students do research on an architectural style, then design a school, home, office, or retail space in that style, using its distinctive elements. Discuss how substance becomes style and vice versa. Variation: Use advertising, clothing styles, automobile styles, or other manufactured items.

Conceptual Purpose   Recognition of architectural style as a reflection of sensibility.

ACTIVITY   Have each student find one aesthetic object or reproduction from a culture other than his or her own. Research should be done on where the artifact comes from, who made it, for what purpose, and any other enlightening facts. Five- to ten-minute reports should be made. The instructor should have a world map on which pins are placed to locate each artifact geographically. Reports might be made at the rate of a couple a week throughout the semester. A reproduction of each image should be placed on the art history time line (see the next activity).

Conceptual Purpose   Understanding that art is made in all cultures at all times; that it has very different forms and functions from time to time and place to place; and that aesthetic form tends to follow function.

ACTIVITY   Develop an art history time line that will stay on a wall in the art room throughout the year. Have it cover 20,000 years ago to the present. After every activity, locate the image on the time line; put up a reproduction of it with basic information about it. Additionally, for context, students may be required to find and depict a significant non-art event from the time.

Conceptual Purpose   Understanding art developments in relation to each other and to significant world events over time and cross-culturally. Knowing that Hiroshige and Daumier were contemporaries or that Mayan temples and Byzantine painting and the development of Arabic algebra were concurrent gives a broader perspective.

ACTIVITY   Students will first be asked to name the women artists they know (typically about half a dozen will be named). Students then will be assigned a 10-minute report on any other woman artist and asked to think about Linda Nochlin's question, "Why have there not been any great women artists?" The teacher may first need to ask students to consider the question and perhaps reword it according to their findings. (A more appropriate question might be, "Why do we not know about many of the women artists of the past?")

Extension   After students present their reports on women, ask them to discuss, in writing, why each woman creates art. Many artists have chosen to comment on their gender or racial or ethnic heritage through their art, but some artists may use their work to express other ideas. Students could compare and contrast feminist artists with other women artists and consider whether the artist's gender is important to the work.

Extension   This research project might also be done with other groups, such as African-American artists, African artists, Asian artists, and Latino artists, to point out that there are many productive artists in these groups (past and present), not just the few artists who are included in western art history texts. Work by many of these artists presents the point of view of a member of a specific group, but many contemporary artists in these groups attend to more formal considerations. Internet resources or other specialized texts may be necessary for this research.

Conceptual Purpose   To expand students' knowledge of the contributions of women artists and increase their awareness of the barriers that women have had to overcome to achieve recognition as artists. Students should also examine gender roles today and discuss the ideal of equality. Do contemporary social roles affect women's achievements in our society? Why or why not?

Conceptual Purpose   Students should understand that some artists choose to express and emphasize the viewpoint of a woman. They should also understand that some artists choose to create work that does not emphasize a particular gender or racial point of view, and that this too is a valid artistic approach.

Conceptual Purpose   Same as above.

ACTIVITY   Ask students to bring in newspaper clippings throughout the year that deal with local and national art news. Discuss these articles as current events, but then at the end of the year compile a historical overview. Did certain new artists, exhibits, or controversies dominate the news? If so, why? Notice any apparent trends: for example, more exhibits of photography, computer graphics, or folk art; more women or men in major art exhibitions; artwork from nonwestern nations; artwork that addresses specific social issues. Keep class "art histories" as resource files for future art classes and continue to build reference volumes.

Conceptual Purpose   This activity reinforces the ideas that art is continually becoming art history and that art history is a social construct. Students can begin to think about contemporary art as a part of that evolving historical context. The activity also shows that art is connected to local communities and is a part of daily life for thousands of people in our nation and the world.

ACTIVITY   Arrange for students to do volunteer work during a local arts festival or in some artistic capacity at a youth or senior center, keeping a record of their activities and of the larger events.

Conceptual Purpose   Authentic connections to the local arts community can help students understand the importance of the arts for the quality of life and for individuals in their own community. They also learn that art history is made not only on the grand professional scale but also outside the mainstream and locally.

ACTIVITY   Use art history as a tool for enhancing studio and aesthetic conceptualization and general studies. Following are some activities that stress examples.

Conceptual Purpose   Art history may connect and support art criticism, aesthetics, studio activities, and social sciences. It may provide examples of excellence in particular concepts or techniques. Art history can be used to illustrate style as well as solutions to design problems in aesthetics and in the studio. Examples of excellence can connect students' studio experiences to their cultural heritage so that they need not reinvent the wheel. Art history also gives us a sense of the times in which art was made, enhancing written accounts in general studies.

ACTIVITY   Each student chooses an artist who has moved him or her and prepares a 5-minute (two-page) research paper (when, where, why, how, what artistic and aesthetic point was being made, what technical problems were being solved, what materials were used, what influences were felt). From classmates' presentations, students will then select one other artist's work and combine it with the style, content, or palette of their original artist to make a new work. Students should make a work of art focused on the content of one artist but the technique and style of the other artist. For instance, they may do the ballet dancers of Degas in the style of Picasso or Dalí. After presenting their papers in class, students should keep them, along with class notes on other artists, in an ongoing journal of ideas. Students should be encouraged to gather as much information about artists as possible and use these resources as inspiration for ideas, techniques, and so on.

Conceptual Purpose   To acquire, through various means, the strength of purpose, sensibility, and compositional and technical expertise of actual artists. Maintaining a book of inspiring ideas can help students identify artists and themes that have special meaning and appeal for them.

ACTIVITY   Students will consider the historical use of appropriation in art, then do research on an artwork and the artist and satirize the work by appropriating the image and altering it in some way to create a new concept, statement, or point of view. Students should discuss the identity of the artist as an important aspect of satire and political cartoons as popular forms of contemporary satire. Students might appropriate an artwork to make a comment on an environmental, consumer, or economic issue. Robert Colescott's work is a good example of this kind of activity.

Conceptual Purpose   To realize that satire is an important, recognized means of social commentary used in literature and art to draw public attention to an issue or problem through humor.

ACTIVITY   Students will do research on artists of any time period who have a local, state, or regional reputation. They will develop an understanding of how place can influence an artist's work. Students should include research that describes the economy of a community or region, important political concerns, and historically significant events of the time as they reflect on the artwork chosen. Museum holdings and catalogs may offer information about regional artists of the past. Interviews with and talks by artists may help students understand the connections of contemporary artists in their area to a specific location or place.

Conceptual Purpose   Understanding that some artists choose to produce work that reflects the place where they live or memories of an important place. A person's sense of place may be commemorated and shared through art. These works may also become a part of the identity of a region or community in relation to the larger culture.

ACTIVITY   Hang a large map of your community (adjust it according to what is feasible for students to see and discuss in your situation) and a sheet of white paper alongside it. As appropriate during a lesson, discuss past and present architectural styles in your community (Greek or Roman columns on buildings; domes; modernist elements; Art Deco; and so on), religious art (stained class; statues; paintings), public art (sculptures; murals), commercial art (store displays; billboards) and fine arts (exhibits; art fairs; galleries; museums). Throughout the year, whenever students are able to identify particular art forms discussed in class, they should pinpoint them on the map with a colored or painted tack and then label them on the key with a corresponding color code. As students discuss a broader definition of art (landscaping?), the observed elements should be included on the map.

Conceptual Purpose   To develop a heightened awareness of art in students' daily lives.

ACTIVITY   Do research on artists who are self-taught. Provide students with a variety of folk art or outsider art from contemporary western culture and other countries. Ask students to do research on the iconography used by these artists and its meaning, then compare and contrast these works with high art of the same culture and time period. Discuss how folk art is related to its local setting and how local traditions and values and the local economy have influenced the work. Ask students to explain why the work is successful or not. Variation: Ask students to interview local artists, folk artists, and hobbyists and find out why art is important to them.

Conceptual Purpose   To help students understand that artists live and work everywhere and produce work that reflects all aspects of a culture. Context is important to understanding folk art as a part of the larger visual culture.

ACTIVITY   Provide students with a variety of indigenous cultural artifacts or images, such as amate cloth from Mexico, molas from Panama, sand paintings from New Mexico, aboriginal bark paintings, and Native American ceramic storytellers. Ask students to do research on the historical roots of these art forms and their uses, functions, and value in their original contexts. Consider the impact of the tourist trade on these art forms today. For example, in the case of the Native American storyteller, the history is relatively recent. Helen Cordero, a Pueblo potter, began producing open-mouthed ceramic figures with numerous children in 1964 at the request of Alexander Girand, a well-known collector of folk art, to commemorate the Navajo oral tradition. Ask students: Is art made primarily for collectors or tourists as valuable as art made for other reasons? Is it even art? What makes an art form authentic to a culture? How are traditions created? What if a family or group creates works? Does it matter who creates a work? Compare tourist patrons today with artistic patrons of the past. How are they alike and different? Have you or has anyone you know established any rituals or traditions? What is the difference between in a ritual and a tradition? What traditions do you find valuable in your family or nation? How can you relate them to traditions in art?

Conceptual Purpose   To focus on the impact of economics on traditional art forms and help students again consider the purposes and economic and social context of contemporary art or artifacts in their indigenous contexts as well as in the larger context of the art world. This activity also may help students understand cultural traditions, with a realization that people continue to develop traditions daily.

CONCLUSION

Art history gives students a sense of the standards, sensibilities, values, mores, and practices of past peoples through examining the functions and forms of artworks and performances in their indigenous contexts as well as in the larger context of world culture. Art history offers a variety of circumstances that motivate students to reflect on present conditions from multiple perspectives. It also helps students understand what is possible in art by informing them about what has already happened. A sense of artistic traditions leads students to respond to the past—to ask, What if changes were made? What if the artwork were structured differently, the palette were altered, the subject were revisited? Understanding that artists have revised and reinvented artistic traditions enables students to examine a greater range of possibilities in order to make more informed artistic decisions and synthesize selected elements of the past in a contemporary response to lived experience.

Art historical inquiry also may be applied to objects in popular visual culture that students themselves value, in contexts that are familiar to them. Philosophical discussions regarding the nature of art may be combined with historical research to understand how our own society values art and how art is of value in our understanding of society. America has increasingly become a society oriented toward the visual market, and the history of advertising and design may also lead to more literate and responsible

FIGURE 7.7 Barbara Kruger. *Untitled: Surveillance is Your Busy Work*. 1983. Black-and-white photograph. *Barbara Kruger often directs her message to "you": the dominant male culture. Looking at art in context may help students understand life issues from multiple perspectives.*

consumers. One important justification for teaching art history is its ability to help students make personal, social, and professional choices. The educational role of art history, then, is to inform students as to what has been done before, what ideas have been explored, how, why, when, where, and in what context. This sort of exploration gives students a head start on knowing where they fit into the scheme of things both as perceivers and as artists.

John Dewey argued that education is a reevaluation of experience, meaning that we learn through reflecting on our experience with the world. Teachers want to share our experiences, to help students gain insights about events that have molded our attitudes and beliefs. But we need also to respect their experience, knowing that what becomes history is not given from above but is constructed by all of us. As art teachers, we enter the domain of art in its authentic contexts. We enter a collective history by sharing, recording, and confirming narratives that address the role art has played in our own lives and our students' lives. Art history is constructed narratives, not only of high art but of all visual culture, providing stories of artists and artifacts in their own time and afterward, and of those they touch. It is meant not only to inform but to provide models and discussions that inspire students to engage in the arts as a means of celebrating human experience and achievement.

In the next chapter we look at making art.

QUESTIONS FOR STUDY AND DISCUSSION

1. Through what mechanisms does art history reflect society's values, mores, and sensibilities?

2. Find an art history book and look at the chapter headings. Skim a bit and look at the pictures. What slant, bias, or point of view does the book have? Who is included? To what extent? Who is left out? Who is spoken of highly, and who is disregarded?

    What do you make of this? Who do you think should be included? Why?

3. Art historians consider who, what, where, when, why, and how. Which of these considerations do you think is most important in finding the significance and meaning of a work? Explain.

4. How does art become history, in your opinion? Who decides?

5. What is a primary source? A secondary source? Do you think it's ever all right to use only secondary sources in art history? If so, when and why?

6. What is provenance? How does it help us determine the validity of a work?

7. What are internal verity and external verity? How do they help us determine the authenticity of a work?

8. Discuss in a group how students can be helped to go beyond traditional interpretations of artworks and find meanings that apply to their own lives.

9. Foucault suggested that not only the great and grand should be represented in art history: peripheral figures should sometimes be brought to the center. The Bayeux tapestry of the battle of Hastings and events leading up to it is filled with deeds of kings and other leaders depicted on a heroic scale. Can you construct an alternative story line from the point of view of one of the three women represented? What about the point of view of a common foot soldier? Are there other characters that could be focused on? As a group, would you like to make an image of (draw, photograph, generate on the computer, paint, collage) an alternative story? Consider some current or recent event, like September 11 or the Middle Eastern conflict, or—perhaps even better—something local: a pileup on a freeway, a springtime festival, a social conflict. Be sure to choose a point of view, preferably of someone not at the center of decision making. How does that perspective change the event?

10. Do you think it's possible to address controversial issues such as sex, violence, abuse, power, or religion through art in a typical school setting? Do you think it's a good idea? Why or why not? What guidelines would you put into place?

11. Can you think of some art history activities beyond the ones we've suggested?

12. How important will art history be to you in constructing your own curriculum? Why?

FURTHER READING

Addiss, S., & Erickson, M. (1993). *Art history and education.* Urbana and Chicago: University of Illinois Press.

Bayeux Tapestry. Website with images and text telling the story of the Bayeux Tapestry. http://www.sjolander.com/viking/museum.

Berger, M. (1992). *How art becomes history.* New York: HarperCollins.

Erickson, M. (1998). Effects of art history instruction on fourth and eighth grade students' abilities to interpret artworks contextually. *Studies in Art Education, 39*(4), 309–320.

Freedman, K. (1991). Recent theoretical shifts in the field of art history and some classroom applications. *Art Education, 44*(6), 40–45.

Jones, L. S. (1999). *Art information on the Internet: How to find it, how to use it.* Phoenix, AZ: Oryx.

Raths, L. E., Harmin, M., & Simon, S. B. (1978). *Values and teaching: Working with values in the classroom* (2nd. ed.). Columbus, OH: Charles Merrill.

Rees, A. L., & Borzello, F. (Eds.). (1991). *Rethinking art history.* London: Camden.

Slatkin, W. (2001). *Women artists in history: From antiquity to the present.* Upper Saddle River, NJ: Prentice Hall.

Staniszewski, M. A. (1995). *Believing is seeing: Creating the culture of art.* New York: Penguin.

8

Making Art

Kim Kensinger, a student at Florida State University, develops a self-portrait collage constructing her work from images that represent meaning and value in her life.

In this chapter, we consider the act of making art. The disciplines of aesthetics, art criticism, and art history all examine art from the receiver's perspective. But without artistic production there would be nothing to perceive. Only from the perspective of production can we understand the artist's problems, processes, issues, and rewards.

Here, we look at the making of art primarily as a behavior—as experience—looking at the artwork, the object, only when it helps us understand the process of making art. We begin with the personal (essentialist) and social (contextualist) reasons for making art, and we argue that both reasons are crucial to art as communication. We turn next to the nature of that communication, then to the actual process of making art, and finally to making art in the educational context. The point is to understand what can motivate students in the practice and achievement of art and visual design for life.

MAKING ART FOR MEANING

Why do people make art? Basically, we make art to make sense of things, to give meaning to our existence. When we express ourselves through making art, we create something tangible to look at, hold, reflect on, feel, and try to understand mentally and physically. Artists as diverse as the abstract expressionist Mark Rothko and naturalist-environmentalist artist Andy Goldsworthy agree that when they make art, they create meaning. Artists connect ideas and emotions through the physical act of making aesthetic forms to represent their meanings. Kinetics and intellectual consciousness—body and brain—coincide. The eye, the mind, the heart, and the hand interact when we make art.

http://www.mhhe.com/artforlife1
The work of both Rothko and Goldsworthy can be accessed through the McGraw-Hill website.

What Kinds of Meanings Do Artists Make?

What kinds of meanings do artists make? One type has to do with self-gratification. That is, one reason we make art is simply for ourselves: to get a sense of who we are, or even just to give ourselves pleasure. This is a personal, psychological motivation. People who think of art in these terms are called essentialists. The second type of meaning has to do with communication: we make art to communicate something important to someone else. This second motivation is social. People who take a socially instrumentalist view of art are called contextualists. Almost invariably, artists have both psychological and social motivations. It is useful, however, to discuss essentialism and contextualism separately because in art education they have traditionally been analyzed as distinct. We described **essentialism** and **contextualism** fairly extensively in Chapter 5, but the basic premises bear repeating with regard to making art.

The Essential Language of Art

Essentialists believe that art is intrinsically valuable and is best understood as existing for its own sake—for its own innate qualities and their aesthetic and emotional effects. Art is made, viewed, and valued for its intrinsic, self-contained,

FIGURE 8.1 *Old Man,* Liu Nan, 1995. *Chinese bamboo brush and ink on Xuam paper. As with western gestural drawing, this painting in the Xie Yi style is an attempt to capture the emotion of the moment spontaneously. According to the artist, this work captures the emptiness of solidity.*

self-explanatory properties. The artist who says, "The work should speak for itself" is taking an essentialist point of view.

In considering the making of art, essentialists are concerned with whether intrinsic properties such as medium, composition, and technique achieve specific expressive ends. Their primary concerns are, for instance, how well paint is used, whether a composition fits a canvas, and whether a work is executed in a manner that is aesthetic and appropriate to the criteria the work sets for itself.

From an essentialist perspective, the language of art consists of understanding and using the elements and principles of design, media, and tools to create a compositionally satisfying and skillfully controlled product. In other words, artists arrange and manipulate physical materials to create artistic meanings. At the turn of the twentieth century the philosophers Roger Fry and Clive Bell described this act of composition as the attempt to achieve what they called significant form. At about the same time, Arthur Wesley Dow held that significant form, or artistically meaningful design, relies on how well compositional qualities are put together. He called these qualities the elements and principles of design.

The elements and principles of design have been with us ever since as an approach to teaching art. Visual elements such as line, color, value, texture, form, mass, and space are arranged according to principles such as unity, variety, balance, rhythm, proportion, and contrast to make visually meaningful statements. If we think of artistic activity as communication, we can make an analogy with written communication: the elements are analogous to words, and the principles are analogous to sentences, or the way words are put together. Artistic style is the compositional choices made by the artist—the ways he or she combines elements by using the principles of design.

But the style of a work is only one aspect of its communicative quality. The other is its content, or thematic component. The thematic content of a work may be objective: for example, forms and colors that are constituted to represent a horse, a person, or a tree. Or the content may be nonobjective: forms and colors used for expressive compositional purposes only, representing nothing beyond pure expression. In either case, the way style carries content makes up the expressive quality of the work, which is its heart and soul. The artist's skill in using materials, creating a composition, and integrating content and style determines the expressive power and excellence of the work. And it is precisely this expressive quality that makes the content of art different from, and some would say qualitatively richer than, social studies or history.

The Contextual Uses of Art

Contextualists believe that the meaning and worth of art can be determined only in the context in which it is made and used. They think that art is or should be made and used for something beyond itself. Art is a manifestation of culture and should at the very least communicate something about its cultural context. Better, like a mural by Giotto or Judy Baca, it should tell a story, indicate what is valued, reinforce social beliefs, or perform some other obvious extrinsic function. We advocate contextualism throughout this text, but here we would also like to make the case that contextualism and essentialism need not be at odds; in fact, both are important in making art for life.

Bridging the Gap between Essentialism and Contextualism

The split between essentialism and contextualism has a counterpart in the split between so-called high arts, whose sole purpose is to communicate an aesthetic state, and utilitarian arts—the so-called crafts. From an extreme essentialist perspective, the high or fine arts are superior to crafts such as pottery, furniture making, and product design, because crafts have obvious extrinsic functions—a vase or a chair holds something; a heritage mural or a picture book tells a story; an ad on television sells something—and thus are not "pure." This distinction persists today in schools where the classes in fine arts (painting, drawing, and sculpture) are frequently separated from and elevated above classes in the practical crafts (ceramics, design, and illustration).

But as Rudolf Arnheim tells us, if we agree that the forms of artistic expression carry meaning, there is no art without function. If we agree that making meaning is functional or purposeful, the wall between essentialism and contextualism breaks down. The entire essentialist premise of functionless art is false. The modernist painter Adolph Gottlieb, for example, said that all art must be about something beyond itself. Mark Rothko said of his works: "They are not pictures; they are the whole of my experience." The high modernist art critic Clement Greenberg saw the function of high art as a bastion in the defense of high culture, keeping out the rabble of common taste—kitsch, as he called it. These statements by three formalists suggest why art is more than form for its own sake.

On the other hand, even the strongest advocates of contextualism, such as Ben Shahn, Suzanne Langer, and John Dewey, agree that ultimately aesthetic form—the rightness of means, ends, and expression—makes art different from, say, social studies. They would agree that even a great idea is not great art if it is poorly formed. However important the content, art relies on skilled execution in a medium, an intrinsically aesthetic task.

It seems, then, that there is no real conflict between essentialism and contextualism. All art is functional (contextualist), even if its function is simply aesthetic pleasure. And art is also by nature expressive form (essentialist), skillfully crafted to be at one with the content it carries.

In fact, art reaches its full potential in school, as in life, when essentialist and contextualist purposes are both consciously sought. That potential has to do with the creation of meaning. Through making art students synthesize their own experience and think about that experience and the meaning it produces. Zurmeuhlen (1990) argued that through self-reflection we may recognize ourselves as "originators, transformers, and reclaimers" of our individual and collective life stories. Making meaning expressively is the core of art education for life.

Developing a Curriculum for Making Art

In art for life, a good program will combine the intrinsic, essentialist, personal, psychological aspects of making art and the aspects that are social, community based, extrinsic, and instrumentalist. The essentialist-psychological aspects have to do with understanding forms, materials, and techniques and the expression inherent in those forms, which reflect the artist's state of mind. The contextualist aspects have to do with what **artwork** does: how it reflects society, how it serves our purposes, and what it says about our values, mores, and institutions.

The connection between essentialist and contextualist purposes for making art is apparent when we understand that the joy and satisfaction of making art for its own sake are crucial whether the instrumentalist goal is environmental activism (as with Merrill and Bergman in Chapter 12), self-development (as in the notebooks in Chapter 10), or challenging social injustice (as with Fred Wilson's work in Chapter 13). In practice, the social and the psychological cannot be separated. In art for life, contextualism is usually the motivation for making art and for using the finished work, while essentialism drives the artistic process.

MAKING ART AS A SYMBOLIC COMMUNICATION IN A MEDIUM

Making meaning is the overarching reason for **art making.** It is important, then, to understand how we make art make meaning. John Locke identified two purposes for the construction of signs: to understand things in their own right, and to convey knowledge to others. Art is a communicative activity involving both purposes; in art, we produce exact descriptions of our sensual experiences of the world.

Making art is not an intellectual abstraction. An artist thinks and feels in, and shapes the visual elements of, a medium. The artist's memory of qualities in the world and his or her capacity to translate them into visual symbols are equally important. One of the most important tasks in art as **symbolic communication** is to make the intrinsic connection between form and meaning—between a sign or symbol, with its nuances and particularities, and actual experience.

Making Art as Qualitative Thinking

David Ecker (1966) calls this act of thinking in an artistic medium "qualitative problem solving." Howard Gardner (1994) holds that the content and the means of expression develop throughout life and are based on modal-vectoral (bodily) understanding, increasingly sophisticated understanding of the cultural code, and increasing skill in presenting it.

This qualitative problem-solving process has three components: (1) intentionality (boredom, intensity, focus, and so on); (2) the artist's skill; and (3) the materials used, particularly their appropriateness to the intention of the artwork. These three features can be enhanced through teaching. Their quality is not a matter of luck or of the artist's inborn capacities. Art is a way of knowing and doing that can be developed through art education. Making art is not an activity just for the gifted.

Inspiration, Craft, and the Creative Process

According to Gardner, both inspiration and disciplined craftsmanship are essential to the artistic process. Artists' solutions to creative problems may seem spontaneous but usually come about as a result of a close relationship among the material, the particular art form, and the code of expression—and as a result of sustained effort and sustained practice. After the initial inspiration, the content of the work usually changes during the artistic process. Therefore, artists typically cannot specify a solution ahead of time; rather, they begin with vague notions and explore possibilities as they go along, finding new possibilities but also new constraints dictated by the work in progress.

This creative, open-ended process makes art different from crafts. In a craft, the solution is generally already known and the only problem lies in how to apply skill to achieve it. In art, the problem continues to change in response to the demands of the work in progress, and the work changes as the problem changes. Sometimes no direct solution presents itself. Then, the artist may experiment with fragments, allowing for the undirected shifts characteristic of play, until a direction again becomes clear. Eventually the artist reaches a point where every possible change is for the worse and realizes that the work is done. A final work is thus almost always a result of taking pains with the details of form and composition—in other words, a result of disciplined craftsmanship.

The Social Aspect of Making Art as Communication

The social aspect of making art is the artist's communicative problem: how to convey his or her affective insights to others symbolically. Such insights are conveyed not through affective qualities (e.g., longing or love) as such, but through manipulation of a symbolic medium, such as paint on canvas. To recreate what is in his or her heart and mind, the artist must find ways to embody it in a medium. To do that, in turn, the artist must be sensitive to the signs and symbols of the culture, the ways people communicate with each other visually. (A student's expressive use of the contemporary medium of technology to communicate a social concern can be seen in Color Plate 13, *Child Abuse* by Sarah Bernstein, 2003.)

To a certain degree, this sensitivity is a birthright; it comes from being born in a particular place at a particular time. But to manipulate cultural symbols in a sophisticated way, the artist also needs intuition, reflection, study, and practice. Cultural understanding contributes to the difference in form and expression between,

FIGURE 8.2 *Replacements,* Kerry Hill, Druid Hills High School, DeKalb County Schools, Decatur, GA. Betty Epps, Art Teacher. *In this conte crayon work, Kerry uses metaphorical imagery to represent beginnings and endings. She says that through this work she has come to realize that when one thing ends in life, another begins.*

for example, Norman Rockwell and Pablo Picasso, two artists who lived at approximately the same time but in very different worlds. Individual understanding and individual motivation contribute to the differences between, say, Picasso and Matisse, artists of the same time and the same artistic culture.

Personal Pleasure and the Survival Function of Art

Everyone who has made a work of art recognizes the pleasure that may come from the process. In this sense, the experience of making art is intrinsically significant. But it has been argued that **art making** and play come from similar pleasure-seeking centers in the psyche and that the pleasure associated with them entices us to engage in something conducive to our survival. The survival function of play and art is that they allow us to learn, in pleasurable, nonthreatening circumstances, what things are like and how things work. Zurmeuhlen describes a sensitive art teacher who lets children inexperienced with clay start by simply playing with the material, pushing their fingers in and out and pounding and rolling the clay, letting it eventually suggest something to be made from it. She engages them in art play as a step toward the goal of creating meaning.

Making art can certainly be daunting (we examine the fear of making art later in this chapter), but we engage in art in the first instance for pleasure, and many things that we instinctively find pleasurable help us survive. Once we recognize the survival function of art, we may go one step further and suggest that making art may reveal the social and psychological substance which underlies and motivates it. That substance, according to Dissanayake, is to express and hold out to public view our human beliefs, values, and mores. The pleasure we get from art causes us to focus on communicating something significant about life, giving order to otherwise inexplicable physical and social realities.

Art as Personal Development

Although art has social functions, personal engagement is the key to making art and to the potential contribution of art to individual development. According to John Dewey, art helps us recognize and order our own growing experiences.

Making art is potentially a way of making a personal world. When we make art, our whole being works to achieve the goal.

How exactly do we learn about ourselves through art?

Since art involves communicating subjective experience, its symbolism is based on body consciousness, a prerequisite of the artistic process. In art, affective symbols carry the expressive message. We begin to communicate symbolically when we separate ourselves from others and from the world and recognize, for example, that a picture (symbol) of a dog is not the dog itself. We can express the affective qualities of "dogness" as we learn about our own essential affective qualities at a bodily level, through what Gardner calls modal-vectoral activity. After we have integrated sadness as a bodily ache and crying, or happiness as laughter or a friendly face, we may move to the symbolic level. Here, the essential aesthetic element is empathy for the affective qualities of the symbol. It's not just a dog; it's a friendly dog, a nice dog, a dog we may want to pat. How do we know this? It has a friendly face and posture. Its friendliness is, modally-vectorally, in the image as affective symbolic qualities that we first understand through our own bodily intelligence.

The ability to manipulate affective symbols is the heart of artistic performance. Affective understanding is the key to making art. Gardner holds that, biologically, the "making system" is one of three systems that develop concurrently in human beings, the other two being the perceiving and feeling systems. These three systems first develop more independently and later develop more interdependently. The making system consists of acts, or actions. It "involves the limbs and muscles of the body combined in numerous ways and the gradual internalization of these actions into mental operations" (Gardner, 1994, p. 64).

During our long childhood, through our continual practice and repetitive activities, we learn to generalize our motor movements and to transfer skills from one activity to another. For instance, when we make a sensitive line drawing, the making system becomes increasingly responsive to input and feedback from the environment as it becomes increasingly interactive with the other systems of feeling and perception. According to Gardner, though, "Perhaps the most striking characteristic is the tendency of the making system to combine isolated acts, once they have been . . . mastered, into more complicated sequences, often ones that are hierarchically arranged" (p. 59). This is obvious if we think about carving, rendering, or creating a computer image with mouse and keyboard. Certain actions dominate and others are subservient in the overall aesthetic design and intention, yet all must be brought together to cooperate.

Students Making Their Own Meanings

If students are to grow and develop both psychologically and socially through making art at school, they need to be helped and encouraged to construct their own meanings rather than passively accept meanings from authorities such as teachers and texts. Zurmeuhlen, working with ideas of Beittel's, called this artistic causality. That is, making art should begin with and come back to students' own identities and what they do in the world. Students' construction of meaning, a recent strategy in general education called constructivism, has been understood and practiced by art educators for some time and continues to be important in comprehensive art education. In art for life, the goal of making art at school is to create meanings based on the real world.

If making art opens a window to the world, the worldviews developed through this process should not be left to chance. We don't believe in traditional school art based on meaningless goals, imposed by the demands of composition and media, and you won't find us advocating design activities for their own sake. We recognize that certain skills have to be developed, but this book has no instructions for drawing, painting, or using papier-mâché, because these mechanical aspects of art are covered in numerous other sources. In advocating art for life, we advocate making meaning. Accordingly, Part Three provides strategies that begin with real life; utilize art criticism, art history, and aesthetic inquiry; consider visual culture and new technologies; and are driven by ideas conceived as themes, which result in creativity and interpretations that are really meaningful to students. But to facilitate meaningful art with your own students, you should not follow our formula or any formula. Rather, you should take the activities we suggest simply as a guide.

You'll need to help your students become aware of the artistic process as they engage in it and recognize their own role as both producer and perceiver. Making art consists not only of doing (making) but also of undergoing (receiving), not in alternation but continuously. The artist must be a producer and a perceiver simultaneously, thinking of what is to be expressed and whether the artwork truly expresses it. Ben Shahn said that an artist has to be two people at once: the imaginer and the inner critic.

The real task has to do not with the form itself but with how well the form represents experience. What is expressed should reflect the artist's emotions and understanding. You need to help students realize that their materials and the ways they use these materials must fit with what they're trying to express. They need to test materials and forms against the pervasive emotion and meaning of the work. A work is artistic when the inner and outer materials are transformed by an act of organized expression. Dewey held that what most of us lack as artists is not emotion, drive, or technical skill but the capacity to work out a vague idea or feeling in terms of a specific medium. To help students in this process, the teacher's most important contributions are sympathetic critique and dialogue.

THE PROCESS OF MAKING ART

Laura Chapman suggested that the artistic process begins with an idea, proceeds through elaboration and refinement, and culminates in execution in some medium. But the artistic process can also begin with a medium. For example, an artist might begin by doodling with chalk, graphite, or paint on paper and then elaborate and refine the scribbles until an idea that can direct the process forms.

In any case, the artistic process begins with a compulsion, or hunger, to engage some medium in order to express something from one's own perspective or experience. Dewey described this impulse as like a sense of disequilibrium, or like physical hunger. If the impulse continued unobstructed, it would eventually peter out, thoughtlessly and meaninglessly. But when it meets an obstacle, that causes the artist to reflect on it: "How shall I deal with this hunger, with this feeling I have?" The artist's own cumulative experience then suggests, "I could do this or that." Next comes some direction or purpose, which the artist expresses by forming a medium into a perceptible object.

The process is not a straight line but involves starting, stopping, and sidling toward a goal that changes as the work speaks back to the artist. Making art is unrehearsed and open-ended, a process of seeking and trying in which the result cannot be known ahead of time. Still, although there can be no artistic expression without turmoil, hunger, and excitement, those emotions must be channeled so that materials can be shaped to convey meaning. Otherwise, the process is not self-expression but merely venting. As Langer observed, making art must be symbolic, not just symptomatic, behavior.

The process is complete when form and content are unified and controlled by the expressive purposes of the artist. Technical proficiency is vital to this process, as are ideas and context, since in the act of making art, form and idea should be one. Students' ability to express themselves in art requires not only their own commitment but sensitive guidance from the teacher. We discuss such guidance in the section on qualitative teaching.

What processes we follow when we make art depend on who we are and what type of problem we want to solve. In education, there are many rationales for

FIGURE 8.3 *The Rock Show,* Mathew Montgomery, Duluth High School, Gwinnett County, GA. Brooke Richards, Art Teacher. *Matthew expressively recorded an event from his experience outside of school that held personal meaning.*

making art, including the development of symbol and metaphor, general perception, creativity, visual thinking, and the ability to identify and solve open-ended problems (both conceptual and related to form and content). Two other reasons are self-expression and critical thinking. Clark, Day, and Greer suggest that making art from conception to conclusion involves a full range of processes and capacities including thought, perception, feeling, imagination, and action.

One of the most common reasons for making art in the classroom is simply to study something visually, to see how it looks and perhaps how it works and how it fits with other things in a larger context. We may make art in order to study and understand specific forms: trees, Greek temples, or microbes (to understand their structure); or all the buildings on your block (to understand your neighbors); or a series of self-portraits (to understand facial structure or shadows).

In addition to working from life, copying another artist's work is a way to understand form. Perhaps you want to understand a Celtic knot, or how Edward Hopper painted buildings, or three-point perspective. Art is cultural, and its formal conventions are transmitted form generation to generation. There's no more direct route to understanding form than copying it.

A benefit of all this is that through truly looking at things, we can get past labels. We think of a door as rectangular, for example, but from most points of view a door is usually a nonrectangular parallelogram. The more we look, especially with drawing or painting tools in hand, the more we really see. As we become more sophisticated, we can begin to see that not all black people, white people, Asians, Jews, or Arabs look alike after all. Careful observation to overcome visual stereotyping can be a first step toward overcoming cultural stereotyping. The sculptor Anne Truitt (1982) says, "Unless we are very, very careful we doom each other by holding onto images of one another based on preconceptions that are in turn based on indifference to what is other than ourselves" (p. 46).

Another reason for making forms is to stimulate memory and reflection. For example, you may choose to draw an old pair of shoes to help you remember where you've been in them, how you felt, and what you thought while you were wearing them. The exploration of inner feelings is a logical outcome of this sort of visual exploration. Abstract expressionist works such as Arshile Gorky's or Mark Rothko's and postimpressionist works such as Van Gogh's are good examples of exploring feeling through form.

The quest for formal order is another sort of motivation, typified by artists such as Georges Seurat and Piet Mondrian. The formalist quest has to do with correct visual and conceptual relationships between forms and between forms and their contexts.

Another motivation is the pure joy of decorating or of simply working with the materials of art. Although this kind of activity is at first undertaken for its own sake, it can be a launch pad when artists are stuck for ideas. Doodling and experimenting with media are good ways to get the creative juices flowing. What do ink and watercolor and crayon do together? What will happen if I cut holes through this page to see part of the next? Could I make origami animals? Suppose I cut butterflies that still hang to the binding in my sketchbook? With visual ideas like these, you don't have to think of something and then execute it: execution is often part of the idea itself. Play freely, then come back later and ask, "What did I do here?" "What does it mean, or what could it mean?" "What can I make of it?"

Creative self-expression is also important (see Chapter 4). Examples of creative self-expression include the surrealist art of Salvador Dalí, Joan Miró, and René

Magritte. Their creativity involves making unexpected connections among processes, contexts, and images. This is different from, and more profound than, cutting butterflies from the inner pages of a notebook or simply juxtaposing unusual color combinations, because of the level of thought, feeling, skill, composition, and elaboration the artist has reached.

Only a few instances of truly creative expression can be expected in school or, for most of us, in our activities as artists. Still, that is what artists strive for. If highly creative work is achieved, it is usually a synthesis of visual research; faithful adherence to the artistic process; practice, practice, and more practice in a medium; critical, cultural, and historical inquiry; critiques; and reflection.

Finally, there is an overarching motivation in art for life: a symbolic, aesthetic search for meaning. Other motivations build toward this or are derived from it. We discuss this search throughout the book and need not elaborate on it here, except to note that human beings have a fundamental need to order and make sense of their lives, to create and discover meaning. That, we believe, is the primary reason for making art in school and outside of school. To repeat: art for life should be based on themes, ideally generated by students. Skills and concepts will come to the fore and will be explored as they relate to students' need to make meaning through aesthetic forms.

TRUSTING YOUR KNOWING HANDS

The search for meaning doesn't take place only in the artist's mind. As Zurmeuhlen remarks, making art gives primacy to doing and making over conceiving or naming. Solving artistic problems involves the eye, the heart, and the hand as well as the brain and always entails doing something with some material. It involves working with our hands. Most academic disciplines lose sight of the fact that our hands want real work to do—meaningful work making things, work in which the hands rather than the head can take the lead and decide where to go and what to do; not work like typing, in which the hands follow the head, but work based on the rhythms and habits of the hands. In other words, the hands want work like making art.

We learn differently and learn different kinds of things when our hands, rather than our intellect, lead. Artistic work directed by the hands is open-ended and divergent; one line or color laid down suggests the next; the process is fluid or seamless, almost superconscious, almost seeming to bypass the brain, or at least the frontal lobe. What happens seems to come from our instinctual, intuitive, reptilian brain stem without ever reaching verbalized consciousness. It is activity—feelingful thinking—in which the cells, sinews, muscles, and tissues of the body and the hands sense what is to be done and do it.

When we use a tool, the tool in a sense becomes part of the hand, an extension of the body and the will. Tools vary in their immediacy. Pencils, for instance, are more immediate than video cameras and computers. Computer imaging involves using a keyboard and producing marks on a screen; such marks are a product of the frontal lobe more than of the hand. Using a pencil, on the other hand, involves the hands in tactile, visceral, direct, cause-and-effect relationships. A pencil is more primitive, closer to bare-handedness. It is a short, direct extension of the hand, closer to what the hand actually evolved to do. If you push down hard, the pencil makes a dark (strong) line; if you're tentative or uncertain, it makes a timid line; if your muscles move aggressively, it makes an aggressive line. You can feel these processes viscerally, both kinesthetically and emotionally. Each mark expresses your state of being and physically suggests the next move. When you've reached the stage of completion, the marks suggest that too.

Making art has to do with bodily knowledge, and the more you believe that you have this knowledge—that your body and hands know something direct and meaningful—the better you'll express yourself. This bodily knowledge gives you another way to know yourself: who you are, what you like and don't like, what feels right and true. It's also another way to understand meaning and value, to gain

A CLOSER LOOK   ## Making the Time and Space for Knowing in Art

Solitude and time for reflection and incubation are vital components in the artistic process. Frequently we say that students are not "on task" if they're talking to one another or just sitting and looking out a window. In the art room, so-called off-task behavior may not be off task at all, though this may be hard for teachers to accept. It's important in making art to collect ideas, brood, and dream. Students need to be given time, space, and encouragement to make meanings take form in art. Sensitive teachers will sometimes provide a place set apart from the rest of the lab, a "time-out" area where students can dream, brood, converse, and plan. Schools usually are not designed to provide such places, either in their physical structure or in the structure of the day. The art room, however, may offer a safe place for students to think and feel, as a way to begin making art.

a sense of your relationship to the world. Sensitive art educators can help their students to discover in making art that the hands, too, are windows of the soul.

QUALITATIVE INSTRUCTION IN MAKING ART

Unifying form and idea is not easy for students and often requires sensitive guidance from the teacher. As students develop visual meanings, the teacher should not accept superficial solutions or products that are just barely good enough. The teacher's job is to provide enrichment, stimulation, and challenges so that students will see more, sense more, remember more, and put their own visual imprint on ideas. Not every solution is adequate. Student artists must be encouraged and helped to express themselves in the language, structure, and forms of art. They should be urged to go beyond factual visual reports to include meaning through expressive choices and discrimination of proportions, colors, rhythms, and so on that create artistic form. Thus the teacher must go beyond simple stimulation, keeping the art students involved in processes and problems that will result in good works of art.

The teacher needs to be engaged in ongoing formative evaluation, giving students feedback and guiding them toward continuous self-reflection. The goal of expression is always kept in mind, and forms and composition are considered in terms of how well they contribute to that goal.

Facilitating Skills

To express a vision, command of a medium is required. This is acquired through intensive work with the system of symbols within that medium—its qualities, potential, and limitations. In most cases, even if a child is interested, skills do not evolve naturally but must be developed. The teacher can either create a problem in which the skills are needed or give explicit instruction in the skills. In art education, it is better to demonstrate and model artistic skills than transmit them as abstractions.

Another requirement is the acquisition of sufficient motor dexterity so that the students are not self-conscious about making art. This requires enough practice in a medium to ensure mastery and flexibility. Practice may involve rote learning and overlearning of manipulative sequences that can then be used appropriately even under the pressure of creation. Instruction usually includes technical advice about a medium, but it is most effective when it addresses the student's need for expression.

An important aspect of acquiring skills is immersion in and familiarity with existing traditions. Looking at other work can sharpen students' awareness of style and lead them to attempt to develop similar qualities in their own work.

Skill alone is not enough. Lack of affective qualities in art-works is a weakness, so Gardner suggests providing a stimulus for affective content. The development of the student's emotional life, as important as it is to artistic expression, cannot, however, be addressed directly. Therefore, Gardner recommends a general enrichment of the student's experiences.

Facilitating the Connection between Process and Meaning

If students are to make meaning through art, much of the responsibility for the process falls on their own shoulders. But teachers need to understand that process and facilitate the students' development. Sydney Walker (2001) identifies at least six factors in students' need for guidance. First, the impulse driving the process is a big idea or conceptual focus. Second, the students are involved with technical, visual, conceptual, and practical media and concerns in addressing the big idea; Walker calls this problem solving. Third, the students' knowledge base is involved. Fourth, students should be able to make personal connections to enhance the relevance of making meanings. Fifth, there are boundaries in making choices about media, subject matter, and so on. Sixth, certain ways of working require the students' willingness or ability to play, experiment, delay closure, and take risks. This sixth issue—the need to take risks in order to create art—contributes mightily to students' fear of art. Students' gnawing question, whether acknowledged or unacknowledged, is frequently, "What if I don't get this right? What if what I do is ultimately foolish or meaningless?"

FIGURE 8.4   *Schools*, Tim Van De Vall, Northview High School, Fulton County, GA. Jessica Booth, Art Teacher. *The subject of this student work is the impersonal and restrictive nature of the educational system. This social critique was created in a beginning-level computer graphics class.*

Dealing with Students' Fear of Making Art

Many people, including students in art classes, are afraid of making art. They may say, "I'm not talented," "I'm not creative," or "I don't have the skills," As Bayles and Orland (1993) put it: "If making art gives substance to your sense of self, the corresponding fear is that you're not up to the task—that you can't do it, or can't do it well, or can't do it again; or that you're not a real artist, or not a good artist, or have no talent, or have nothing to say" (p. 13). They therefore remind us that although a genius like Picasso comes along only rarely, good art is made all the time. Making art is a normal activity, not heroic, magical, or extraordinary. Artists are normal people with weaknesses and foibles who face normal, familiar, universal, difficulties in making most art. Talent does exist—and, rarely, genius—but what happens to all the talented prodigies? Where do they all go? Mostly, they quit. Unlike Paul Cézanne and Ansel Adams, who had ordinary talent, they don't keep working. Many quit from fear.

Art teachers who are sensitive to this fear of failure can remind students that the primary difference between an artist and a nonartist is not talent or ideas. It is that the nonartist allowed his or her self-doubt to rule, and quit. Bayles and Orland note that making art will always be an uncertain proposition. Your vision will always be ahead of your execution. You'll always wonder if you can pull it off. Art teachers can suggest to students that self-doubt should be considered a virtue: uncertainty keeps you moving forward.

You can remind your students that failure and fear of failure are common in making art. So is a fear of starting the next work, after either success or failure. But insisting on perfection leads to paralysis. Overcoming fear is a matter of experiencing the process of working with materials; thinking in terms of paint, graphite, or pixels; and letting the medium itself take over, allowing the flow of materials and ideas to lead you, rather than feeling that you must arrive at a predetermined place. Let the potential of the medium seduce and inspire you—the juicy yellowness of

FIGURE 8.5   *The Pain Is Just Too Real,* Katherine Stockton, Duluth High School, Gwinnett County, GA. Brooke Richards, Art Teacher. *Along with the development of technical skills, students need the opportunity to express emotions and ideas that are personally meaningful.*

paint, the pebbly texture of the paper, the warm malleability of Georgia red clay—but also let it sensitize you to the limits of what you can express in any given medium. What shapes will clay hold or not hold? Is paint translucent enough or should you be working in tissue paper?

The only certainty in art, according to Bayles and Orland, is the materials you use. The materials are what you can control. They are your contact with reality. The key to overcoming the fear that you can't do it, or that your work won't be accepted, is simply to keep doing it. You make good work by working frequently in a medium and failing much of the time, because failure offers good feedback about what works and what doesn't. Thus you slowly develop your own vision. Good instruction lies in part in helping students to see "failure" as necessary to the experimental, hands-on, exploratory nature of making art—in short, to see it not as failure at all but as a learning experience.

The Relationship between Skills and Expression

The two kinds of objectives for instruction that we described in Chapter 1 are also objectives in making art. The first type—closed-ended objectives—are focused on helping students develop skills and concepts: for example, the ability to make a contour line with varying pressure to indicate forms coming forward and going backward in space, or to create the appearance of a shadow; the ability to lay a translucent top coat on an oil painting to create the illusion of water; the ability to use Adobe Photoshop to create a seamless montage; and so on. The second type—open-ended objectives—has to do with students using the skills they have learned to express something meaningful to them. Both types of objectives are crucial to effective teaching and learning in **studio art,** and both should be part of the curriculum in art for life. Without skills, students cannot make meaningful communicative images. Without ideas and the drive to express them, students' forms become vacuous.

Facilitating the Growth of Artistic Intelligence

There are several forms of **artistic intelligence,** and research has found that they can be enhanced through education. Art teachers need to realize that nurturing must be appropriate to a child's inherent intelligence, developmental stage, and learning style. It is beyond the scope of this chapter to discuss developmental stage theory and its application to making art, though we do address stage theory in Chapter 3 and you can find some good resources on that topic at the end of this chapter.

Briefly, according to Gardner there are two basic stages of human development: presymbolic and symbolic. Children have normally attained the symbolic stage by the time they enter school, so that is the stage which concerns us. At the symbolic stage, students' making of meaning can and should be enhanced through instruction, dialogue, and studio activities. To repeat: nurturing must be appropriate to a child's developmental stage. At the symbolic stage, after age seven or so, children can be introduced to cultural codes, master domain rules, and finally apply these rules in a sophisticated manner and take risks within the domain.

An important idea is that art engages in all three biological systems: making, perceiving, and feeling. Thus the art teacher should involve students continually in activities and conversations that develop and enhance all three systems: their perceptions, their feelings about things, and their skill in making art.

In western culture, particularly among adolescents, creativity tends to wane unless a child is highly motivated. However, the ability to acquire artistic skills is impressive at this time. Gardner describes adolescence as a time of eagerness in which kids can do just about anything and will devote themselves compulsively to achievement in realms they value. During this period, youngsters become increasingly conscious of the subtlety and complexity of art and begin to feel some of the same satisfaction as an adult artist in working through the artistic process. It is in adolescence that the intellectual gap between childhood and adulthood closes. Adolescents increasingly understand the rules of human relationships, and that understanding increasingly influences their behavior.

Because our culture emphasizes logic and abstract reasoning rather than sensitivity to aesthetic nuances as a means of expression and understanding, the art teacher must be sensitive and thoughtful in directing the development of young artists. Art teachers need to be careful in this, since heavy-handed formal education may thwart rather than facilitate development. London, Lowenfeld, and Gardner all suggest guiding children with tasks that are suggestive rather than formally restrictive and that convey a principle. Giving a young artist appropriate materials and posing appropriate questions at the right time may be one of the most effective procedures for building skills and confidence, according to Gardner. The key may be to understand what a youngster wants to express and help him or her do that through the development of motor skills and conceptual strategies.

Again, we emphasize culture. We do not agree with the idea of hands-off practice and so-called natural growth. Usually, adolescents have some interest in styles and works of the past, and when they are given choices they will find work they esteem and be inclined to take it as a model. Sensitive integration of the young artist into the artistic and cultural tradition will give him or her more tools for personal expression. The capacity to appreciate the code of art enables a student artist to make discriminations that result in having tools for expression. Also, during adolescence, as in earlier periods, there is no substitute for extended practice: "it is only through considerable experience with a medium (and considerable experience in living) that a distinctive style can develop" (Gardner, 1994, 263).

Developing Talent versus Art as a Way of Knowing

Unlike language, art requires a child to learn complicated manual skills. It begins with pure kinesthetics but moves to symbolic, representational activity. At first, physiological forces guide the making of art; soon, though, the process comes to serve emotional and communicative needs. From ages four to nine, children increasingly master the technical aspects of drawing and painting, but by the time they reach the middle grades, or certainly by adolescence, there seems to be a general regression of skill, imagination, and even interest in drawing and painting. Gardner suggests this is because increased verbal skills coupled with insecurity about their visual work make language students' preferred mode of communication. Insecurity may increase, too, when the child discovers other work, maybe the work of mature artists, and realizes that his or her own work is inferior to it. Some children rise to the challenge and become accomplished in art; others, fearing failure, simply stop trying.

The attitudes of adults are also a factor in young people's artistic development. Contrary to what Piaget and Lowenfeld claimed, the current theory is that we don't evolve naturally, on our own, beyond a certain point, described variously as being anywhere between three and seven years old. Rather, early on we enter the realm of culture; and after we reach the stage of symbolism at around age seven, growth in art requires exposure to artworks, training in perception, affective responses to art, activities, and guidance regarding how these activities are related to cultural codes. Research has found that tutelage in these areas can enhance children's powers of discrimination, increase the amount of information they include, and increase their ability to pay attention to sensory and qualitative aspects of art. In art, as in other cultural activities, we don't unfold naturally like flowers. Rather, we grow through teaching and learning, according to cultural codes.

Sadly, what this implies for the many of us is that we don't develop much, aesthetically or artistically, beyond our capacity as children, because we simply don't receive guided instruction. Just as some people are naturally better at playing baseball than others, or at reading, or working with numbers, some people are more gifted than others in art. But we all can learn to hit a baseball; read; and add, subtract, multiply, and divide. Similarly, we all can engage in art, if we are taught certain skills, attitudes, and ways of perceiving. This is significant for instruction in art, since it suggests that not only the talented should be helped as they "naturally" unfold. Rather, with instruction, all children can engage meaningfully in art. Given the goal of art for life—making meaning—in conjunction with the qualitative instructional strategies described here, all students should meaningfully engage in art as part of a larger quest for encountering and understanding life.

CONCLUSION

Making art is an attempt to bring order into being, to create something meaningful where nothing existed before. This requires the mental, emotional, and physical ability to create and use symbols in the context of a culturally constructed system. Making art is a form of contemplation but also involves the eyes, heart, and hand. The artist's goal is to see with his or her own eyes the nature of things—a truth, if not "*the* truth"—and to depict in paint, stone, or pixels meanings associated with people, events, and things.

Authentic teaching and learning in making art are specific to the expressive needs, understanding, and stories of the teachers and learners—what Zurmeuhlen calls idiosyncratic rather than formulaic activity. Teachers and students gain power over their lives when they are given the power to construct meanings through making art that counts.

As Dewey showed us, we learn best and most deeply through doing. The key process in making art is repeatedly doing and reflecting. This process fuses the subjective and the objective. Your spirit and emotion are made visible to and recognizable for others. It's a dialogue between having a feeling or idea and making marks or forms that express and constitute that feeling or idea.

Making art is a controlled but open-ended process of making marks, carving forms, creating symbols and signs, and then allowing those marks, forms, or symbols to speak back, pushing the original idea or emotion in another direction or eliciting a new one. A balance is struck between imposing formal reason and allowing form to emerge from its own emotional realm. Thus making art is a combination of instinct and thought. The process must be allowed to take its course, since the outcome of creative drawing or painting cannot ever be fully determined ahead of time.

Artists use physical materials to express the body's sense of itself. Making art is a form of bodily intelligence. An artist has to feel the artwork both internally (for example, as a kinesthetic sense of an abstract mark) and as a projection (for example, as the heaviness of a dreary day). In making art, the physical body carries out what the mind imagines. Art is a form of concentration that engages the whole of oneself. The artist's quality of attention and state of being show through. As Franck (1993) put it, unlike words, which can "weasel and betray truth . . . [drawing is] as nakedly truthful as the movement of the hand" (xvii). Making art is intuitive and physical, but it is directed by the intellect—it is subjective intelligence.

There is a difference between making art and, say, writing a report in social studies. Ideally, both activities are communicative, but the content of art is carried by aesthetic form. Artists meld form and content into aesthetic, symbolic expression. To do this they use and integrate three bodily systems: making, feeling, and perceiving, which might be called holistic intelligence. This expression of content carried by style says more than either could say separately.

We make art for pleasure as well as meaning, but we care about the expressive outcome. Making art usually entails taking a risk. And because artists don't know what will result from the artistic process, it can also arouse fear. Such fear comes from focusing on the end product and how it will be perceived. Freedom from fear comes from being intensely engaged in the process and materials and the pleasure they bring.

Making art is a form of problem solving undertaken to find and construct meaning in life. Good teaching will engage the eye, the brain, and the heart as well as develop the skill of the hand. In art for life, the making of art is intended to promote the students' own meanings and understandings beyond the classroom, for the sake of their success in life itself. Direct training in this process is impossible, but a conscientious art teacher can devise motivations and activities as well as provide guidance to help students develop the skills, attitudes, and patterns of work that allow them to express themselves meaningfully in art and life.

In Chapter 9, we discuss new technologies and their uses in art for life.

QUESTIONS FOR STUDY AND DISCUSSION

1. Describe the connection between the essential language of art and its contextualist functions. Which do you think is more central to the artist's concerns in actually making art? Why do you make art? Do you think, given the reasons you've described, that you are of an essentialist or a contextualist?

2. What are the processes you go through when you make art? How are they the same as or different from what's described in the text?

3. Describe how artistic communication relies on both content and style, and how that fact makes it aesthetic expression.

4. How is aesthetic expression different from normal communication?

5. Describe how understanding your body sense is important to artistic communication.

6. What are the three body systems that go into making art as communication? Describe how they work together.

7. What are your issues? What do you want to say? How can you say it through making art? In a group, discuss issues that need to be addressed in your school, peer group, or community.

8. What is the qualitative method of teaching art? What do you think of it?

9. What does the text say is the major reason for the fear of making art, and how do the authors suggest it can be overcome? What do you fear when you make art? How do you overcome your own fear?

10. Children go through two stages—presymbolic and symbolic—in relation to making art. Beyond that, what are the primary symbolic stages of artistic development in children? How do you think an art teacher could successfully deal with the lessening of confidence and artistic production that comes at around age nine or ten?

11. In your mind, how is teaching studio art for life different from or the same as teaching art as design? Discuss this in your group.

FURTHER READING

Anderson, T. (1992). Art of the eye, the brain, and the heart. *Art Education, 45*(5), 45–50.

Berensohn, P. (1969). *Finding one's way with clay.* New York: Simon & Schuster.

Brown, M., & Korzenik, D. (1993). *Art making and education.* Urbana: University of Illinois.

Ecker, D. (1966). The artistic process as qualitative problem solving. In E. Eisner & D. Ecker (Eds.), *Readings in art education* (pp. 57–68). New York: Blaisdell.

Edwards, B. (1999). *Drawing on the right side of the brain.* New York: Jeremy P. Tarcher/Putnam.

Franck, F. (1993). *Zen seeing, zen drawing.* New York: Bantam/Doubleday.

Gardner, H. (1994). *Art education and human development.* Santa Monica, CA: Getty Center for Education in the Arts.

Kindler, A. (Ed.). (1997). *Child development in art.* Reston, VA: National Art Education Association.

Nicolaides, K. (1969). *The natural way to draw.* Boston: Houghton Mifflin.

Shahn, B. (1957). *The shape of content.* New York: Vintage.

Smith, R., Wright, M., & Horton, J. (1999). *An introduction to art techniques.* London: Dorling Kindersley.

Truitt, A. (1984). *Daybook: The journal of an artist.* New York: Penguin.

Wachowiak, F., & Clements, R. (2001). *Emphasis art: A qualitative art program for elementary and middle schools* (7th ed.). New York: Longman.

Walker, S. (2001). *Teaching meaning in art making.* Worcester, MA: Davis.

New Technologies and Art Education

Separation of Church and State, Justin Fetterman, Northview High School, Fulton County Schools, Atlanta, GA. Jessica Booth, Art Teacher. *In response to a beginning-level computer graphics assignment, a student raises issues related to the separation of church and state in his collage of images.*

TECHNOLOGY AND CULTURE

Technologies, Old and New

In the broadest and most basic sense, technology simply extends the physical functions of our hands (as with a shovel or a clamp), our eyes (as with binoculars), our ears (as with radar), and so on. In art education, technology encompasses everything from a crude chunk of charcoal used to make a mark on coarse brown paper to a digital camera and PowerPoint. But when we refer to technology now, we usually mean advanced electronics such as video and digital imaging, and especially computer-generated ephemera and their transmission over the Internet: in short, computer-driven digital technology that seems to extend not just our physical but our mental functions.

René Descartes said, "I think, therefore I am." According to Bailey (1996), Descartes was referring particularly to understanding and memory. Interestingly, both functions are becoming dominated by computers; in other words, mental tasks are being assigned to electronic circuits. Moreover, computers are now evolving and designing the next computers. Today's children may reach adulthood in a world where computers are more numerous and in some ways smarter than they are, a world where human thought no longer holds the exclusive franchise. Bailey suggests that one of our most important tasks will thus be to remain involved, to take part in the digital evolution conceptually, morally, and philosophically as well as technically.

Our culture is usually quite clear about what technology is and how to develop it but perhaps less clear about *why*. Postman (1992) notes that in Plato's *Phaedrus*, King Thamus chastises the god Theuth for inventing writing. Theuth considers writing the be-all and end-all, but Thamus fears that writing, as an external device for recollection, will destroy people's capacity to remember oral narratives. People who rely on written repositories of information might seem wise but would really be ignorant if they could not decipher the information or discern what was important in it. There is perhaps some truth in Thamus's prediction. In our own digital era, we hear many people express the same fear about a possible next step in thinking: digitally formed cybercommunication. But for the purposes of this book we will take neither Thamus's side nor Theuth's: we will simply explore the *why* of contemporary technologies and then address the what and how with regard to art education.

Computer Technology: Advocates and Critics

Digital technology has both advocates and detractors as a cultural tool and in particular as an educational tool. Its advocates welcome computer technology and the

Internet as the wave of the future. Most universities and school systems are wired for cyberspace or are planning to be. Most universities and even many school districts have put a huge effort into developing "distance learning," facilities and instruction where students learn in classrooms separated from the instructor or even at home. The most enthusiastic advocates see such technology as limited only by hardware, software, and cost. Cyberspace culture, they maintain, emancipates the individual, providing infinite information and possibilities for action. Some advocates have argued that the Internet is also a tool for democracy. Shiva suggests that equality of opportunity can be achieved if we understand a few simple concepts about the Internet. First, the Internet is not an end but a means—a process or strategy. Second, in cyberspace we create our own sense of space and time. Third, although the Internet is under no one's control, it has organically developed community standards. Fourth, the Internet is based on people, not government. So the Internet is blind to color, caste, and ethnicity. Fifth, it is its own culture, and its possibilities are limitless.

On the other hand, the detractors of digital technology argue that it is no panacea. Bowers (2000) suggests that it may actually be an instrument of social injustice, putting more distance between the haves and the have-nots. He notes that in the United States the 20 percent of the total workforce who are professionally engaged in computer technologies earn as much as all the rest of the workforce combined. Many critics insist that we need to assess the social and political impact of information technology. Some argue that cyberculture is a continuation of a patriarchal, individualist tendency in western culture, a tendency to put "man" above the environment and to consider nature as simply a soulless resource. They believe that this tendency began with the Industrial Revolution and is now spinning out of control. In their view, the computer culture is removing human beings even farther from the earth as the source of life. In this respect, too, they say, computer culture contributes to social injustice because it ignores or actually destroys indigenous communities, which are often poor and nonliterate. Bowers argues that the most important issue in education today is recognizing the connections between computer-mediated technologies—with their supporting software, assumptions about learning, and surrounding culture—and ecologically destructive patterns.

Somewhere between the advocates and the detractors is a place where we can probably be comfortable. Certainly, computers connect us with people around the world, creating networks of support and research; but computers can also disconnect us from our relatives or friends in the same room. Sustainable computer technology may depend on our awareness of both effects. Individuals particularly need to be aware of what they are connecting to, what values they are supporting, and who and what they may be disconnecting from. This kind of understanding entails the cultural examination and self-reflection that many contemporary artists (some of whom we discuss here) engage in. It also entails education—not just technical training, but education about the values and mores of the computer culture.

New Technologies: Artists, Issues, and Ideas

Almost seventy years ago, Walter Benjamin, writing about photography and the mechanical reproduction of images, recognized that technological changes also bring about changes in consciousness and in culture. Benjamin said that photography and mechanical reproduction had supplanted original, individualized, and singularly produced images. He thus anticipated the issues of ethics and ownership that have arisen in the digital era, when anyone with rudimentary computer skills can manipulate any image to alter its content, meaning, and authorship simply by wielding a mouse or clicking a button. Who's to say this can't be done? Who's to say it shouldn't be done? An image by Ansel Adams or Pablo Picasso is available for everyone to own, to alter, and to use in any way he or she sees fit. There's virtually no constraint—moral, physical, or other.

The artist Sherrie Levine (see Chapter 5) argues that it is a good thing to disenfranchise the "aura" of the singular work and to confiscate the originality or creative genius of dead white men such as Edward Weston and Georges Braque. And the ability to claim and manipulate images and text as the artist Barbara Kruger does may be a factor in democratization: the twenty-first century counterpart of the printing press. Whether digital technology is considered a leveler or a menace to morality and the environment, it has brought as much change as the Renaissance or the Industrial Revolution. Today, we can all construct our own reality, or at least our own virtual reality, in cyberspace.

In art for life, all three perspectives—the sense of self, place, and community—are affected by digital technology, particularly by the immense amount of information that now comes from cyberspace as well as from traditional electronic media. Most if not all of the information received as ephemera from a TV screen or a computer monitor exists nowhere in our immediate physical reality and yet exists everywhere. Data were once a luxury and the lack of data was an impediment to developing meaning, but now meaning is threatened by a flood of data. That makes the problem not getting information but sorting it. How can we organize this information, deciding what is worthy of our attention? How can we decide what is truthful? Relevant? Ethical? Useful? How can we relate to it? Many artists who are exploring issues of media, ephemera, authorship, authority, source, truth, and meaning ask these same questions.

High Tech: The Early Days

Early on, video artists took up these topics. Video was often used to comment on or mimic television. In the mid-1960s, video was regarded as a more populist or democratic medium than the traditional high arts of painting and sculpture, since videos were relatively inexpensive to make and represented popular culture. The best-known early video artist, Nam June Paik, built television monitor "performance sculptures" with multiple screens that were manipulated to create multi-textured, distorted, often dizzying effects, mimicking and mocking the popular media. Since then, video technology has permeated our culture: it is used in surveillance cameras, computer-generated imagery, virtual environments, home movies, multimedia installations, interactive websites, and so on.

Issues of Authorship, Truth, and Power

http://www.mhhe.com/artforlife1
Visit our website to learn more about these and other artists who use contemporary technologies for art for life.

Two artists who use newer media to explore authorship, truth, and power from a feminist perspective are Barbara Kruger and Sherrie Levine. They borrow images from high art and from mass culture and turn an image back upon itself to create meanings never intended by the original artist. Kruger and Levine claim images of others, putting these images into new contexts to make feminist statements about power, position, and privilege in the world of art and in society. In *We Don't Need another Hero*, Kruger, a former commercial artist for Condé Nast, used text and appropriated imagery of a girl (who looks like someone from the 1950s) feeling a boy's arm muscle to comment on dominance, submission, and social consequences.

Levine for many years simply repainted, exactly, the work of artists such as Georges Braque; later she appropriated the work of famous photographers such as Brett Weston, rephotographing it without change. In both instances she was trying to make the point that originality can't be owned by anyone, especially by dead white men. More recently, Levine has taken to making "copies" for which there are no originals, as a response to the commodification of contemporary culture. Her inspiration is Warhol, who, in the 1960s, wanted his Brillo boxes and other images to be mechanical, authorless, and machine-like, implying that culture itself had these characteristics.

Another artist, Laurie Simmons, has explored the way the media shape the imagination and self-concept of girls. She creates installations, such as *Red Library,* in which dolls—Barbie, in particular—mimic adults' behavior.

FIGURE 9.1   Jenny Holzer, *Truisms,* electronic sign installation, 1977–79. Dupont Circle, Washington, D.C. *This image combines four signs expressing Holzer's view of the world in short messages intentionally placed in public places to surprise and confront viewers and disrupt their typical experience with the visual environment.*

Cindy Sherman also explores the world of dressing-up as an assumed identity perpetuated through the media. In her black-and-white self-portrait *Film Stills,* she examines cinematic fetishism by dressing up as a fallen woman, a wide-eyed innocent, a movie star, and so on, moving from one fiction to another without ever revealing herself, becoming woman-as-construct of the media, as a reflection of the gaze of the "other."

Jenny Holzer also explores media and marketing, moving beyond traditional aesthetics into conceptual art. Holzer makes authoritative pronouncements—"Abuse of power comes as no surprise," "Money creates taste," "Your actions are pointless if no one notices"—on posters, T-shirts, digital display boards, and, recently, the Internet. Her statements have the ring of truth, but are they true? What makes them authoritative? Who says so? How do we know?

Krzysztof Wodiczko and Hans Haacke consider who controls power, and how, in the information age. Haacke creates mock advertising campaigns as slick as those of Madison Avenue but designed to subvert corporate meanings and values. Wodiczko, a refugee from Poland during the communist era, explores authoritarian messages of the government and corporations by projecting slides of contradictory images on monuments and buildings that symbolize power. (We devote a chapter to Wodiczko's socially activist work in Part Three.)

Bill Viola

Bill Viola uses video and digital media to address social and personal issues. Attracted to nonwestern traditional cultures, Viola focuses on life as a continuum related to nature. He was born in 1951 in New York and began experimenting with video art in the 1970s as an undergraduate in the College of Visual and Performing Arts at Syracuse University. Early in his career he met and worked with Nam June Paik, Peter Campus, and the musician David Tudor, all of whom he credits with shaping his career. Viola created numerous installations incorporating video during the 1980s and 1990s. He keeps abreast of technological advances. His photo shoots are often technically complex, but his work typically has to do with human, personal themes: contemplation, spirituality, the passage of time, identity, and archetypal contrasts of humans and animals in contexts of decay, overcrowding, and industrial pollution.

Recent Installations by Bill Viola

A recent installation at the Detroit Institute of Art, called *Science of the Heart,* is described as follows:

> An empty brass bed sits in a dark room. Floating a few feet about the headboard is a color video projection of a living, beating human heart. The sound of the beating fills the room. The videotape has been manipulated in time so that the heart gradually speeds up to a high-pitched intensity and then slows down to extremely slow, single beats until finally coming to rest in silence as a still image. After a pause, the heart begins beating again. (http://www.dia.org/exhibitions/BillViola/pages/main.html)

Critics suggest that the bed in the room is a symbol for significant human events: birth, sex and reproduction, death. The heart symbolizes the rhythm of life as it goes from stillness to motion and then returns to stillness; this also suggests the cycle of birth, death, and rebirth. In some cultures the heart, rather than the brain, is believed to be the center of the intellect. In our culture we associate the heart with emotion. In this installation the heart's accelerating beat reflects our own passion, pain, panic, and calm, as though Viola is suggesting that emotion and spirit are linked to the physical function of the heart. (For a still image of this installation, see Color Plate 14.)

Starting with his earliest video installations, Viola has maintained two primary themes: mortality and consciousness. Both appear in *The Tree of Knowledge,* his first computer-generated work. In this installation, Viola explains, there is a 50-foot corridor, about 3 feet wide, which opens into a black void. It is empty except for a small tree. As you move down the corridor toward the image, the movement triggers a sensor, beginning an image sequence of the growth of a tree from sapling to maturity and decay:

> The sequence goes through a blossoming period, fruit grows and falls, the leaves turn color, until finally when you have reached the end of the corridor, the leaves fade and only the plain white branches of a lifeless form remain. The piece is called the *Tree of Knowledge* because human knowledge, the human condition, arises out of our awareness and understanding of the consequences of our temporal existence. (Rutledge, 1998, p. 75)

In this piece the tree is realistic but is clearly computer-generated. Viola has explained that he didn't want the tree to be a specific type, and he made the tree gnarled as it aged, more rapidly than this would happen in nature. He also wanted the viewer to experience the tree as only a visual image, so no sound was included in this installation. Although the tree is an animation, it retains a natural connection to reality, and the aging process as an image gives structure to time, like a genealogy.

For Viola, sensory perception is almost a spiritual activity that leads the viewer to a heightened awareness of both culture and nature. Ross describes Viola as a new kind of realist artist involved with the actual processes of life. Viola himself says that he is drawn to the latent web of connections in our inner lives and that he develops themes based on human experience and cycles in the physical world.

Viola's work has been described by Lovejoy (1997) as the visual equivalent of song. Viola is considered radically expressive and technically daring; he uses slow motion, rapid editing, deep zooms, and panoramic scans that seem to be a natural perceptual process. But the technology is just the means, not the end. The point is to communicate something personal in an authentic cultural context. Viola is very critical of music videos, for example, because of their tendency to appropriate images and styles from Africa or the Amazon simply as decoration or exoticism, removing them from their authentic contexts for the purpose of making money.

Before beginning a film Viola writes or sketches in a notebook the sequence of events and images he plans to include. He tries to select images that will be visually compelling and meaningful for the viewer. He also writes down quotations from theologians and philosophers, past and present, and his own creative ideas. Next, he finds an appropriate format for his ideas. The viewpoint of the camera and how the video images will be presented to the viewer are all a part of the message.

Viola considers the perceptual experience of the viewer as he plans the architectural space necessary for the multisensory experience. Because it needs so much space, Viola's work has almost always been shown in museums rather than galleries. In the past few years Viola has been involved in a number of retrospective exhibits, and he says that until he put there retrospectives together, he himself did not fully realize how certain themes had guided his work. However, although he has returned to the same themes or ideas from time to time, he feels that each piece is valid as a marker in time and as technology, and that his views have evolved. His *Slowly Turning Narrative* of 1992 is a meditation on the self and on potentially infinitely changing states of being (Lovejoy, 1997); Viola suggests that "the work is just the container for the idea, and the design of the container can change" (Rutledge, 1998, p. 76).

Digital Interactivity

With the exception of Viola and Jenny Holzer, most of the artists just discussed have worked to this point more in traditional electronic media, which were more accessible than digital media. Generally, until the 1980s newer media artists used nondigital photography, film, and video. Digital (computer) imaging became prevalent when powerful personal computers and the World Wide Web were developed in the late 1980s. Now, it is so easy to obtain images from the Web, and so much software is available for manipulating images, that a primary issue for computer artists is virtual interactivity—the involvement of the viewer as a co-artist. For example, in Otto Piene's light installations and Joy Wulke's laser shows, the viewer initiates and controls the effects.

In addition to site-specific work, the web is also used for interactivity. Jenny Holzer now puts her truisms online and asks participants to response. Live performances may take place all over the world at the same time, not separated by geography or time. For example, the interactive Oudeis Project featured artists from four continents and Hawaii participating all at once. In another interactive piece, *White Devil*, Paul Garrin explores surveillance and authority. The viewer "walks" through a neighborhood under the watchful eyes of surveillance cameras and dogs, becoming aware of issues of privacy, trespass, and authority.

With regard to obtaining and disseminating images and text, the web is becoming essential for digital artists. In 1996, the Guggenheim Museum sponsored web-based exhibits—possibly the first major museum to do so. Nearly every major art museum in the world now has virtual tours of its collection on its homepage.

Given our concern with visual culture, we'd be remiss if we didn't note what is arguably the most sophisticated use of digital technology for artistic purposes today: the artistry in Hollywood movies and other commercial productions. *Monsters Inc.*, the *Lord of the Rings* trilogy, *Dinotopia*, and older films such as *Jurassic Park* and *Toy Story* run technical rings around the most advanced efforts of independent artists. This is a topic for serious consideration in art education.

FIGURE 9.2 *How do advanced technologies work? Most of us really don't know. Technology is in constant flux, and teachers and student must be ready to adapt to and integrate change.* NON SEQUITUR © 2002, Wiley Miller. Dist. by UNIVERSAL PRESS SYNDICATE. Reprinted with permission. All rights reserved.

NEW TECHNOLOGIES: ISSUES, CONTENT, AND STRATEGIES FOR ART EDUCATION

Whatever you may think of new technologies, they will certainly be part of your teaching and learning environment. Especially, digital (computer-generated) technologies will become a larger part of art education as well as general education. Issues related

FIGURE 9.3 *Dinosaur,* 2000, film still from movie. Animation by computer. Walt Disney Studios. *This animation frame of Aldar bonding with the lemurs is typical of the fantastic worlds created through animation and computer graphics. Film animation relies on the viewer's brain to process a rapid series of images as though he or she is seeing continuous action. In some cases computer-generated effects are so lifelike that we view these animations as reality.*

to computers in art, culture, and education will arise in your future, so it's a good idea to take a look at these issues now and consider where you stand.

Practically Speaking: Technology in the Classroom

New technology has always been a factor in art education. At the beginning of the twentieth century, new methods of printing and new colored papers revolutionized educators' practices. In the 1960s, educators debated whether television and advanced teaching machines would replace teachers. As we entered the twenty-first century, computers were changing what we do. We do not expect computers to replace teachers, but the educational purposes and objectives of computer-based learning continue to evolve.

Describing the numerous ways in which technology has affected art education is a complex task. Computers have made many art teachers less isolated by providing e-mail, listserves, and websites specifically designed for and by teachers in the field. Access to the Internet has significantly expanded art educators' resources for lesson plans, information about museums and galleries, and images. For students, the computer may serve as a source of information, an interactive learning tool, and an efficient means of storing and documenting their visual and written work. At base, of course, technology in the art classroom, like all other vehicles and tools for learning, depends on the teacher's interest, expertise, and resources and on the students' needs and interests.

Some Functions of Computer Technology in Art Education

Computer technology serves at least three functions in art education, which will be discussed next. One is research, a second is communication, and the third is creative imaging.

Research and Communication   It is useful to consider computer-based research and communication together because they both rely heavily on the World Wide Web. The web was first developed in 1989 as a user-friendly overlay and access system for the Internet. Now, websites for art educators include nonprofit informational sites, such as the Getty's Artsednet; professional societies' sites, explaining, for example, aesthetics or environmental art; university and school systems' sites;

http://www.mhhe.com/artforlife1
Visit our website to find links to find useful art education websites.

commercial sites, such as Binney and Smith's or Davis Publications; any number of sites of museums and other public institutions; formal educational sites such as Blackboard.Com; and library-based search engines. At these sites you will find philosophical treatises, how-to instructions, chat rooms, lesson plans, and so on. The web may be students' most accessible source of information and their most accessible vehicle for certain types of communication.

The network of images and interactions on the web is often referred to, mistakenly, as virtual reality. Cyberspace is not virtual reality in the sense that a user wears a helmet and becomes involved in certain physical activities and sensations, nor is it virtual reality in the sense that a user physically becomes part of it, as in the movie *The Matrix.* However, our experiences on the web are self-contained, removed from (though in certain ways analogous to) normal three-dimensional reality. We enter and leave the web feeling that we are entering and leaving another universe.

In any case, the web has become immensely attractive. Art education students once had to be forced to go onto the web to do research; now, if they aren't assigned to seek out hard copy, preservice students' first instinct is to go to the web. And if what they seek isn't there, contemporary students tend more and more to think that it doesn't exist at all. As in the movie mentioned above, if it isn't on the matrix, it simply isn't. The postmodern condition is no longer just theoretical; we now live in the web-based self-referential reality that Jacques Derrida predicted. The web, however, is not language itself, as he supposed, but computerized knowledge. Such knowledge and the structures and habits that pertain to it are now almost indispensable for success in life. Future art teachers and their students must be familiar with the language and structure of computing and the World Wide Web for the purposes of research, communication, and imaging.

Accordingly, most of us are required to invest in technical apparatus, always upgrading hardware and software and learning new systems to keep up with changes that presumably represent improvements and progress. There is no end to this process. Lyotard (1984) described computer literacy of this sort as an efficiency model; that is, values such as goodness, truth, and beauty apply only in the context of procedural efficiency. For example, most of us have colleagues and friends who start out talking about imaging on the computer but end up talking simply about the machine itself and how to make it work most efficiently. This is qualitatively different from talking about how to use a brush.

Computer literacy, and the type of communication it entails, requires a shift of consciousness: from ends to means and from truth to performance. This is reflected in policy in art education and general education. Our cultural capital now is efficiency and functional skills rather than conceptual ends or ideals. The knowledge we value is technical, not conceptual. Our most pressing question is "Can we?"—not "Should we?" If you doubt this, count the number of philosophers employed in your institution (or count the policy planners, poets, or painters) compared with the number of technical support workers. Count the number of arts programs and assess their funding compared with distance-learning programs and computer training. Assess the amount of money spent on traditional art supplies or even textbooks compared with the amount spent on technical support. Art educators and their students must have technical skills—particularly computer skills—and must develop an attitude at least conducive to maintaining and continuously upgrading those skills.

Creative Imaging   The third function of digital technology, creative imaging, also relies on the web because it involves downloading software, information, and images. But most creative imaging is done on-site, on the user's own computer, with imaging software such as Adobe Photoshop and Claris Works. Whatever software is used, **digital imaging** is very unlike traditional imaging or even traditional electronic imaging because, rather than presenting an optical trace like a photograph or a drawing, it creates imagery from a nonperceptual source: a sequence of numbers in the computer. Unlike traditional media, which start with human perception and

Online Research as Constructivist Learning

One of the most promising aspects of technology is its promise for constructivist teaching and learning. Computer-based research in particular can be an effective strategy for art for life because it allows students to pursue their own directions and meanings, independently and in their own time (Freedman, 1997). As Gregory (1996) notes, "Technology can be a useful vehicle in helping students gain control over their own learning, their own life, and ultimately can help them find the answers to their questions" (p. 54). Many art teachers have challenged students to seek answers on the Internet and through interactive hypermedia resources. This authentic learning encourages students to think creatively and critically so as to make connections between multiple links that provide information. Often, they can collaborate to discover new links and sources of information. Students may follow Internet links from virtual galleries to artists' websites to online newspaper interviews to critics' articles. As Prater (2001) suggests, "Moving from link to link, students connect ideas and develop their own interpretation of the social, cultural, and artistic contexts of narrative art" (p. 46).

Online research involves contemporary, postmodern, nonhierarchical, nonlinear thinking and the use of weblike strategies such as linking, interactivity, interconnectedness, openness, and collaboration (Julian, 1997). Groups of students, teachers, or both may be collaboratively linked with others to produce a learning network or exchange, in which the dialogue may become as important as the artwork being investigated or produced. To begin the inquiry, the teacher may pose questions, or students may initiate their own research and generate their own questions. This approach to authentic learning allows for peer support not only in the local classroom, but also in a virtual global classroom that may include students with widely diverse backgrounds and viewpoints.

Attaining information from the Internet or anywhere, however, is not useful in and of itself; without a context or meaningful focus, it will not always lead to wisdom or even to understanding. Thoreau saw most American inventions as improved means to unimproved ends (Shepard, 1961). With that warning in mind, teachers should become guides and facilitators as students explore the Internet, helping them to reach an understanding of the real world. Inquiry, dialogue, and exchange on the Internet, as anywhere else, may generate more questions than answers. Yet if it establishes patterns of learning and relationship to others in a local classroom and a global community, then it has contributed to art for life.

---

attempt to represent it through some trace, the computer starts with and translates algorithms, logical procedures (not vision), into visual form. Don't be fooled by the windows and icons on your computer. They may look like drawings or photographs, but they aren't, at least not in the traditional sense. They're pixels (picture elements), or rather pixel structures. The image that you perceive, the picture on your computer screen, is a simulation based on a mathematical model.

The basic tool of digital imaging is the computer. The essence of digital imaging is that the computer enhances the artist's ability and freedom to appropriate, alter, extend, and manipulate images with a freedom unparalled in history. Computer art is predominantly an act of reproduction rather than original production. But this reproduction does result in something original in (and representing) a new **virtual reality,** separate from the real world. The computer can scan, paste, replicate multiple images, and erase. Therefore, a constructed or imported image is not static or finished—it becomes information, subject to further manipulation in the artist's or someone else's computer. The image is simply part of a process. This implies that reality is fluid and always in flux. It also implies that information is outdated almost immediately and that, at best, only the strategies for dealing with information can achieve some constancy.

The logical conclusion is that, as Lovejoy puts it, seeing is no longer believing. Even if you start with a straightforward digital photograph, the computer's capacity to seamlessly alter, manipulate, add to, and recontextualize it makes it endlessly malleable—yet it will retain an aura of truth. For example, Bert from *Sesame Street* ended up on posters of Osama bin Laden, suggesting a relationship that was in fact totally manufactured.

FIGURE 9.4   *Pulse Field,* 2003, experimental exhibition at Georgia State University, Atlanta, GA. Craig Dongoski and Robert Thompson, coordinators. *A French sound collective, Quïe Dire, produced a sound snapshot of Atlanta that explored the relationship between sound and image. In this installation, images were heard rather than seen. Other aspects of the exhibit documented contemporary and historic forms of sound art.*

Teachers and students in art education therefore need to address issues in the ethics of representation as never before. Power, authority, authorship, identity, and even environmental degradation are all factors. Art educators are beginning to address these issues. Mercedes (1998), for example, agrees that the web and its culture are now patriarchal but suggests that new technologies, especially computers, can be applied to challenge dominant western patriarchal aesthetics from a feminist perspective. Garoian and Gaudelius (2001) argue that identity is not neutral but is associated with body consciousness and with technology and culture, and that critical consciousness is essential to understanding and balance. They cite the performance art of Stelarc, Orland, Goméz-Peña, and others who explore a potential posthuman cyborg existence.

Creative Expression and Aesthetic Experience through Virtual Reality   Virtual reality or virtual environment (VE)—in the typical sense, in which a user is immersed in a digitally generated "space" of sound and images—can become an interactive aesthetic experience, which is likely to become more and more prevalent in art and art education. In a VE experience, a new creative process occurs each time the viewer encounters the artwork, depending on the viewer's interaction with and immersion in the work. Consequently, VE and other digital technology may change our definitions of artist and viewer. As art becomes more interactive, the artist's role will depend increasingly on the receiver, who will become a coproducer of the work. Although setting up a VE requires considerable time, it is not impossible in the art classroom, and it might be undertaken in collaboration with other disciplines or a computer lab. Some VE products are already commercially available, and although these do not offer total immersion, they do offer interaction with the real world.

Social Content and New Technologies

Sleeter and Grant (1987) suggest that the Internet can be used to explore global diversity and global connectivity. Using the web, students can critically examine issues in their own communities, the nation, and the world through cooperative thinking and learning activities. Keifer-Boyd (2001) developed a hypermedia strategy for the web; she argues that it changes art criticism from a linear, singular, formalist process into a weblike, nonhierarchical activity that allows for multiple interpretations. Keifer-Boyd suggests that with the increasing use of hypermedia, the teacher is changing from a giver of knowledge to a facilitator of students' own critical and reflective aesthetic discourse.

Cason (1998) found that once students became familiar with the technology, their ability to make connections in research was better with interactive multimedia than with traditional means, and their understanding of content went deeper. This result requires seeing beneath the virtual surface and connecting one link to another thematically rather than being confined by the artificial boundaries of any single discipline. Tomaskiewicz (1997) supports our belief that these themes should be related to students' real-life concerns. Certainly that is the way themes are used by computer artists in the world beyond school, such as Bill Viola.

STUDYING BILL VIOLA: AN EXAMPLE OF TECHNOLOGICALLY BASED TEACHING AND LEARNING

As content, use one of Bill Viola's videos, *The Crossing*, in which two figures are gradually and simultaneously engulfed with fire and water and then disappear. As the video loops continuously, the figures continuously reappear and are engulfed again, symbolizing transformation and change throughout life. (Note that the figures were mannequins filmed in a studio.)

http://www.mhhe.com/artforlife1
Visit our website to find out more about Bill Viola and other artists using digital media.

Key Concepts

1. Important human themes are being communicated. (Students will critique the video and engage in dialogue and research in an effort to determine what these themes are.)

2. It's not the medium but how the medium is used that determines whether something is art. (Video and computer-generated technology are part of the popular culture and may be used for many purposes, including art. To explore this concept, students will compare and contrast commercial video and computer-generated images with Bill Viola's installation pieces.)

3. In addition to the traditional elements of art, light, motion, time, and sound are important elements used in video, film, and computer-assisted technology.

Procedure

The teacher may ask the students to consider and discuss the ways video or film presentations are used in popular culture. Their responses may include special events recorded in news videos, surveillance in banks and stores, family videos, TV commercials, music videos, virtual Internet tours (for example, in real estate), and academic documentation (Lachapelle, 1999). Examples should be made available or brought in by the students (or both); these can be on videocassette, on CD-ROM, or obtained through the Internet. In examining these examples, the group should be made aware of the interactions of light, motion, time, and sound. Overlays and relationships of images and sound are significant in video design. Looking for the unexpected and the incongruous is a useful strategy in the search for meaning. Sound bites and inlaid visuals are important in relation to the larger context of the video. Sometimes video is digitized so that it may be manipulated or enhanced on the computer or used more easily with other computer technology. Can you find examples of images that belie your knowledge of how things are in the real world? How and why does that happen in advertising? What's the point of altering reality?

In *Science of the Heart* on the website of the Detroit Institute of Art, Bill Viola uses video to make an artistic statement. The teacher might ask students to discuss how an artist's use of technology might or might not be different from other uses of video in popular culture. What does the fact that the work is in a museum say to us? As a notebook assignment (see Chapter 10), the students might be asked to compare the use of time in Viola's work and in videos they see in popular culture.

http://www.mhhe.com/artforlife1
Visit our website to link to the Detroit Institute of Art.

In order to consider the speed and number of images they see in the mass media daily, students might record all the visual images they see during one day and at the end of the day write a short sentence describing the message each image conveyed to them. What is the overall impact of seeing so many attention-demanding images? Students might also notice the use of lighting in portraits or commercial advertising. What mood is conveyed through light, shadow, or darkness? The use of time, light, and space as metaphors is a new element for students to consider as they investigate Viola's work. Through a critique and discussion of the work—including its formal qualities, symbolism, meaning, purpose, and larger social context and implications—students will be in a position to understand video art in a social and personal context, both for its own sake and for understanding why and how to engage video art.

At the conclusion of the critique and discussion, the teacher could follow up by asking students to visit the rest of the installation and video pieces on the museum website in order to find ideas, pieces, and themes that inspire them or that they would like to investigate further. Viola's notebooks are also included in one of his retrospectives. They might be interesting for students to explore, especially if the research is preparation for making their own videos. The notebooks show how Viola develops his ideas both conceptually and visually and may provide clues for students' own planning.

Viola's work deals with life issues that will probably merit more than one discussion through the web or in class. Students could compare their interpretations of his work, and of other work they find, not only with their classmates' interpretations but also with art critics' interpretations. The teacher may provide the critics' reviews, or students may find them online or in print journals. As always in art for life, the point is to relate the topic to students' own issues, concerns, and ways of seeing their larger cultural milieu.

After their critique, dialogue, and research, students may or may not create art; if they do, they can apply their heightened awareness of video (both digital and traditional), its potential, and its impact on and significance for individuals and the culture. One of the first things they'll note is that making a video is not a one-person operation. It takes a team of people who understand their own roles and the need to cooperate. As a team, the students can plan and execute a studio project. Depending on the technology available in the school, the students could first choose a theme; then develop storyboards; then use a video recorder (most media centers now have such a recorder for classroom use), still photos, computer graphics, or a combination of any of these technologies to create their own series of images, video, or animation. If the students' piece is more than a one-screen video, they will need to plan an

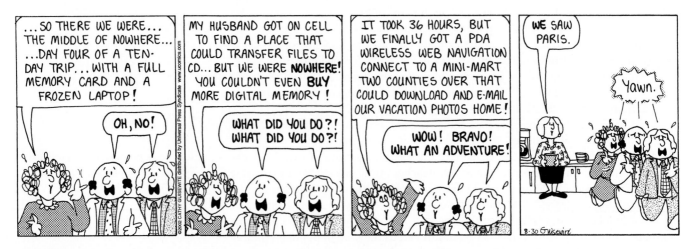

FIGURE 9.5   *What does this cartoon say about what we think is interesting and important? Do you agree? Is it a good thing?* CATHY, © 2002 Cathy Guisewite. Reprinted with permission of UNIVERSAL PRESS SYNDICATE. All rights reserved.

appropriate space for their installation. They may also want to develop a class web-site where they can post their creation, and probably they'll want to store the product on a disk or CD to be included in their portfolios.

CONCLUSION

Computer-based instruction raises complex ethical, moral, and philosophical concerns. Since the Internet has become one of the mass media and a part of popular visual culture, many artists have addressed these issues.

The average person sees 3,500 commercial images a day. How can we help students become more critical consumers of visual images? Just as they consider the message, meaning, structure, and implications of commercial print ads, students should consider the messages they see in film, on television, and on the Internet. They need to also consider how much these messages have become part of their cultural narrative. How do visual images affect our individual and collective identity? Does the barrage of images we all receive impair our ability to absorb and synthesize their meanings? How does this affect our collective cultural or national narrative?

We cannot yet measure the full impact of the mass media on young people who have grown up in the era of electronic and digital media, but it is important to ask questions about this. Does computer technology blur the lines between physical reality and cyberspace, between the ethical and the unethical, and between individual and collective responsibility? Can this technology disconnect us from immediate local reality? Gregory observes that when students navigate cyberspace in silence, their minds may be active but their bodies simply sit still. Do we see such behavior in most other human interaction? Is it healthy? Students may have access to pornography, racist chat rooms, and violent computer games in their excursions on the information superhighway. What is the impact of this on their understanding and actions? If the impact seems harmful, what should be done? What can be done? Heightening students' awareness of such issues may help them to think critically about cyberspace not only as a source of learning and entertainment but also as a culture with a value structure.

There are also legal and ethical issues related to the appropriation and manipulation of images. Is it right for Sherrie Levine to appropriate images? If so, is it also right for students to do? Digital appropriation and manipulation of photography is a serious ethical issue. In our society, the photograph has generally been interpreted as a truthful representation of the world. Even though appropriation of images has become common in postmodern culture and is a widespread strategy in contemporary commercial art, many questions remain about the artistic integrity, morality, and legality of such practices. "The digital medium is one of instant replication and perfect fidelity; therefore, the notion of the original, the aura of uniqueness, and the attraction of ownership will have to undergo reinterpretation and change" (Nadaner, 1985, p. 46). Who owns images and for what purpose are questions that students should consider as they work with computer images and explore the capabilities and processes of the medium.

Digital reality may come to dominate our concept of intelligence itself. Artificial intelligence is no longer just an idea. We are in a new era, a qualitatively different world "authored by a partnership of sequential human minds and autonomous parallel electronic circuits" (Bailey, 1996, p. 221). So we must look at computer imaging, communication, and research as processes that are not intended to function in the same way as traditional art materials and must learn, as Johnson (1996) suggests, to "extend our manual capacities into virtual, cooperative spaces" (p. 43). That relationship is what we seek in art for life. The challenge is not to lose our relationship to the here and now as we extend our relationship with cyberspace.

QUESTIONS FOR STUDY AND DISCUSSION

1. Do you agree that technology is just an extension of the body and mind? Why or why not?

2. Are you an advocate or a critic of digital (computer) technology? Why?

3. How is a virtual community the same as and different from an actual (physical) community? Are people equally accountable to each other in both? What are the advantages or disadvantages of each for making connections through art?

4. Do you find communicating easier and more pleasant in person or on the web? Do you discuss different kinds of things on the web from in person?

5. Do you think the Internet gives easier access to art and artists than, for example, the library or art

magazines? To decide, go online to find out more about Sherrie Levine, Barbara Kruger, Laurie Simmons, Cindy Sherman, Jenny Holzer, Krzysztof Wodiczko, Hans Haacke, Bill Viola, or another artist who uses digital technology extensively. Share what you've found with the group. Start a hard-copy or website-based resource center based on what you found. If you found that the web gives artists prominence, do you think this increases their persuasiveness? Does it increase the value of their work?

6. Find a museum website other than the ones we've provided in the McGraw-Hill link. Describe how easy it is to access, how valuable the work is that you found, and how valuable the experience was to you.

7. According to the text, computer technology serves at least three functions in art education. What are they?

Which of the three do you think will be most valuable to you in your teaching?

8. As a practical matter, what hardware and software do think you'll need for web-based research with your students? What will you need for creative imaging? If, because of budget constraints, you had to choose between traditional supplies and new technology, what would be your choice? Why?

9. Explain digital imaging in terms of numbers and pixels.

10. Are you more creative on or off the computer? Why? Discuss this question with your group and devise strategies to facilitate creative digital imaging for students at various grade levels.

Further Reading

Art Education, 55(4). (2002). (Thematic issue on technology and assessment.)

ArtsEdNet at http://www.getty.edu/artsednet/

Ashford, J. (2002). *The arts and crafts computer: Using your computer as an artist's tool.* Berkeley, CA: Peachpit.

Bailey, J. (1996). *After thought: The computer challenge to human intelligence.* New York: HarperCollins.

Blackboard.com at http://www.blackboard.com/

Bowers, C. (2000). *Let them eat data: How computers affect education, cultural diversity, and the prospects of ecological sustainability.* Athens: University of Georgia Press.

Detroit Institute of Art website for Bill Viola: Relating to Science of the Heart is: http://www.dia.org/exhibitions/Bill Viola/pages/main.html.

Keifer-Boyd, K., Centofanti, J., Lan, L., Lin, P., MacKenzie, N., Peréz, A., & Hill, G. (2001). Cyberfeminist House at http://www.ken-\art.ttu.edu/kkb/house.html

Lovejoy, M. (1997). *Postmodern currents: Art and artists in the age of electronic media.* Upper Saddle River, NJ: Prentice Hall.

Lyotard, J. F. (1984). *The postmodern condition: A report on knowledge* (trans. G. Bennington & B. Massumi). Minneapolis: University of Minnesota Press.

Postman, N. (1992). *Technolopoly: The surrender of culture to technology.* New York: Knopf.

MODELS FOR INSTRUCTION
INTRODUCTION TO
PART THREE

Thematic Inquiry

As we described in Chapter 1, the *aim* of art for life is to help students prepare for success in school as well as in life, through teaching and learning centered on art. The *goals* that follow from this aim are that the students will

1. Understand that art and visual culture are communication about things that count;

2. Understand that art has both intrinsic and extrinsic value and meaning, and that its forms, meanings, uses, and values are both aesthetic and functional.

3. Make art and study art and visual culture, both individually and cooperatively, to express themselves as well as find out about the world.

To achieve the aim and goals of art for life, teaching and learning must focus on making art for meaning, and understanding the meanings in the art and visual culture of others. To make and receive meaning, students must be able to make connections, to understand relationships between one thing and another and between one person and another. The central strategy is therefore to structure teaching and learning around **themes** rather than around the traditional elements and principles of design, media, historical periods, or art disciplines.

In developing and exploring themes, students should be encouraged to address real issues and solve real problems that are significant beyond the classroom. Themes should be taken first from personal experience and contemporary art and culture, which are accessible and immediately compelling to students. Each theme should be allowed to expand naturally or organically to include artifacts and performances from many times and cultures that reflect the students' interests and concerns. In this way students learn about themselves and about others in relation to themselves, and can develop tolerance and a sense of global community. This is so because the rituals that support cosmology and beliefs in all cultures—including our own—have many artistic elements and in fact are frequently inseparable from the arts. When students realize that art reflects and perpetuates cultural values, they can examine the art and visual culture of many societies to see how others have examined life issues. Students can also try out other people's ideas and forms, and then adopt as their own the ones that fit.

In an increasingly multicultural world, art education should focus on ideas and works of nonwestern cultures, indigenous cultures, ethnic and cultural minorities, as well as on traditional western art and ideas. Students who move beyond the confines of their own culture may come to see others not as foreign and different but as people who, although they may express themselves differently, have familiar drives, emotions, and sensibilities. An excellent example of this approach is the International Guernica Children's Peace Mural Project (see Chapter 15).

Thematic inquiry can lead to personal transformation and social reconstruction; thus the themes should be chosen from real life. They should be focused on who we are, where we think we belong, and our sense of community. The artwork or visual artifact is the medium—the tool for exploring these themes. It is not an end in itself.

As demonstrated in Chapters 10 through 15, art for life should begin with visual culture and artistic processes, products, and performances as the means of exploring specific themes. A thematic approach will most likely take students across disciplines: they will frequently take up concerns associated with social studies, history, psychology, even mathematics and science. But art for life is essentially inquiry through artistic means, so the themes should lend themselves to inquiry and expression through art.

Central Themes in Art for Life

The three overarching themes in art for life are (1) a sense of self, (2) a sense of place, and (3) a sense of community. These themes encompass most personal and social concerns. But they are broad rather than precise, so they are only a starting point for developing more specific themes that can guide teaching and learning. Following is a discussion of more particular themes arising from each overarching theme. These specific themes are only examples to get you started. Many more themes are possible, and some of them appear or are implicit in the examples that make up Part Three.

A Sense of Self

Themes involve relationships. A theme cannot simply be love or fear, for example; it must be love *of* something or fear *of* something. Examples: My love for my family, my partner, my friends, babies, my car, my computer, my clothes, my garden, my books, my colored pencils, fishing, the beach, the mountains, myself. My fear of failure, death, illness, poverty, war, violence, rejection, chaos, disorder, change, darkness, the spotlight, wolves, snakes, spiders, conversations in which I reveal myself. Love and fear are sometimes considered the two primary emotions, but of course there are many other emotions that can lead to themes. Examples: The joy I feel in being loved, the thrill of roller blading, my nervousness in public speaking, my shame at betrayal, my pride in my children or my girlfriend or boyfriend, my satisfaction in finding a good pair of shoes.

A Sense of Place

The sense of place has to do not only with what we personally feel and think about the environment but also with how we suppose others may think and feel about it. Examples: The comfort I take in my own room, my home, my special place. An environment that soothes me—the beach, the mountains, the desert, the city, a bubbling stream, a coral reef. Someplace exciting—a roller coaster, a nightclub, a fire, the top of a tall building or the summit of a mountain, a speeding car. Someplace illicit, dangerous, or challenging; a lonely place; a sacred place; a place that feels alien; a place that feels like home; a place we should protect. All these themes are about your relationship or someone else's relationship to a place or the idea of a place; they are not just about a place itself.

http://www.mhhe.com/artforlife1
Visit our website to learn more about art and the environment.

A Sense of Community

The sense of community is based both on the sense of self and on the sense of place. It's an extension of yourself, a sense of your place in the group, and thus a sense of how others might feel, what they might need at particular times and places and in general. Many of the relationships of emotion to self and emotion to place also apply to community. Examples: The excitement (or alienation, loneliness, fear, or comfort) of being in a crowd. The rightness or wrongness of people in a place—for example, in villages, cities, a pristine forest, the Antarctic, outer space. Our sense of fear or conquest in the face of wilderness; the satisfaction of fitting in. Trust, betrayal, loyalty, group mores. All these relationships begin with the individual and extend to place and to community.

Themes Steer, but Art Drives

The artistic performance or visual artifact should be a starting place and a touchstone for inquiry (see Chapter 5). The central discipline is art, not social studies, history, geography, or science. Themes are addressed not through history or social studies but through art. (For instance, a mural may focus on the theme of peace, or heroic sculpture on military domination, or Jackson Pollock's paintings on self-expression.) The idea is to look at art, not historical records or mathematical formulas, to discover what insights it provides about life. Other disciplines provide context; they shed light on the theme being examined, in which art is central.

Exploring a topic through art lets students become intimately acquainted with art as form, performance, product, personal expression, and social instrument. Themes are the conceptual center. Making and studying art are the means of addressing the concepts involved. Themes steer. Art drives.

The Instructional Units That Follow

In Part Three you will find practical thematic units of instruction focused on fundamental human concerns. Because we believe that students are best reached with content that is meaningful in their lives, the content here is primarily contemporary art and ideas. But because we also believe that no one culture or time has acquired all the significant knowledge, we extended the content as appropriate to include artifacts and performances from many times and cultures that reflect concerns of contemporary life. The themes and artworks here have been selected with an eye to social and environmental issues. The units of instruction have been structured to encourage your students to participate actively in developing meanings and assessing their own processes, content, techniques, strategies, and values.

In these units of instruction, we adhere to the principle that meaningful assessment follows from learning objectives and desired outcomes as well as implemented procedures. The assessment strategies we have devised for each unit follow from the core concepts and skills to be attained, which in turn follow from our central tenet—that teaching and learning in art should be for the sake of life. In most of the units, we begin with the visual arts and visual culture but then move to cross-disciplinary strategies and concerns and ultimately to real life.

The units also reflect our belief that good art curricula have both closed-ended objectives, designed to teach skills and concepts, and open-ended objectives, designed to allow students to express themselves using the concepts and skills they've developed. In the best of all worlds, skills and concepts are developed as a result of students' exploring their own meaningful relationships with the real world. Even students' self-expression can be assessed on that basis. In the best lessons, assessment is integrated with learning.

To repeat: these units of instruction are just examples. We hope you will use them; but you are welcome to modify them to fit your own purposes, and we invite you to share modifications, and your own newly constructed units, with us and other readers on our website. When it is your turn to develop a curriculum, we hope you will incorporate real-world themes, use strategies that promote understanding of those themes, provide open and closed learning, and establish outcomes and assessments that follow from the content of a lesson and contribute to social justice in the world.

http://www.mhhe.com/artforlife1
Visit our website to see or share your own art for life units of instruction and lesson plans.

What Drives You?
Research Notebooks and
a Sense of Self

Pages from research notebook, Debbie Zhuang, Atlantic Community High School, Delray Beach, FL., Genia Howard, art teacher. *Student research notebooks allow students a place to express a range of ideas and feelings. Here, Debbie Zhuang reflects on how she feels about the World Trade Center bombings both visually and verbally, connecting her own feelings to the expressions of other artists, and to the meaning of events in the world.*

OVERVIEW

This is an extended thematic examination by students of something they care about, in which art is not an end but a means of exploring the students' own values, meanings, mores, and understandings. Students will develop a research sketchbook or notebook in order to consider one or more issues, forms, or ideas through critical, historical, and aesthetic inquiry; visual examination and note taking; personal reflection; and creative visual expression. By doing this, students will find out not only something about their topic but also something about themselves both as individuals and in their social context.

KEY CONCEPTS

Students will examine who they are, as individuals and as members of their society, through examining something that they care about, and will also develop artistic, critical, synthetic, creative, and reflective abilities through that process. They will explore deeply personal aspects of self-expression in the arts and will find that personal reflection is a respected and important activity, strongly influenced by social as well as individual factors.

CONTENT BASE

For the purposes of authentic instruction and assessment, research notebooks are a type of "process portfolio." They relate to real-life concerns and involve the development of practical strategies and skills in and through art. They reflect authentic instructional goals and strategies by addressing students' real-life concerns. The tasks are structured to accommodate students' individual learning styles, aptitudes, and interests. (For a visual example of a student process portfolio, look at the Chapter 10 opening image and Color Plate 15. Eric Barkin, *Creative Research Portfolio* (1999).)

Research notebooks produced by International Baccalaureate students in public high schools in Florida illustrate an effective approach.* In the first example, a student of Hispanic background begins her research workbook with the stated intention of exploring pre-Columbian petroglyphs in the Rio Loa Valley in Chile—a site she says she has visited with her father, an archaeologist. It is apparent from her writing that her heart is in this investigation. She describes the rocks, the environment, the Atacoma Desert, the local culture, and her experiences there in a

---

*The following passage describing students' notebooks is adapted from T. Anderson. The International Baccalaureate model of content-based art education. *Art Education, 47*(2), 19–24.

careful, detailed, earnest way. She draws maps and draws and photographs the petroglyphs. She describes, critically analyzes, and evaluates them, using historical references and anthropological sources to enrich and support her personal research.

Then she begins to experiment, spray-painting hand prints into her journal in the way of indigenous artists and forming her own personal hieroglyphs and symbols. She begins to learn about other artists who have motivations similar to her own. She goes to art fairs where she talks to artists, takes pictures of their work, and records what they tell her. She begins to develop an interest and do research on contemporary environmental art and artists. One of these artists is Robert Smithson, who works with archetypal forms such as the spiral. She develops spiral imagery, first imitating Smithson's *Broken Circle* and then generating her own ideas. We leave the book with an examination of Christo and his *Surrounded Islands*, but this is not an ending. The student's personal involvement and critical appreciation will continue.

A second example is a young man whose goal is to be an engineer and who is interested in comic books, mechanical drawing, world affairs, and fashion. He ties all these interests together, very impressively, by planning and beginning to develop two comic books, which evolve through two extended workbooks. One comic book, called *Bogotá,* is about upheaval and intrigue in South America and a war that results in there being only three South American countries, with another, Panamerica (a new political entity consisting of the former United States, Mexico, and Canada), intervening in South American affairs.

The young artist draws his own friends, as clothing models, in action poses, and as characters in his story. He also researches comic book masters, particularly from Japanese culture. He invents cars and motorcycles for his characters after making drawings and doing research in automobile magazines and journals. He also incorporates computer images and designs computer environments for his characters. These come from his research on computers, which has included not only journals but discussions and interactions at trade fairs, computer stores, and so on. His personal desires and interests give life and unity to the work as a whole.

A third example is a young man who explores computer graphics. He considers hardware and software, and he traces computer graphics back to graphic imagery that was not generated by computers. He discovers M. Escher and begins to explore the connections between art and mathematics, particularly geometry. This leads him to experimental work of his own: he makes pencil renderings of interrelated fish forms and computer graphics of animal subjects, modeled on Escher's work. This student's experiments become more sophisticated when he visits galleries that display computer-generated art and talks to the artists. He then buys a new mouse, and new possibilities emerge. He does research on computer-generated imagery in *Star Trek III* and the Indiana Jones movies, which give him new ideas. His interest in pixels leads to an interest in Seurat's and Signac's pointillism, which he then brings to bear on computer imagery. He learns how computer imagery enhances X rays and how it has increased the understanding of oil spills in the Arabian Gulf. He begins to explore programming and also commercial designing with the computer. This notebook begins with the student's announcement that he will be a computer major in college because he admires the logic of computers, but it ends with his claim that he will someday be the world's greatest computer artist.

These three research notebooks have a great deal in common: they are personally motivated, critically analytical, based on content and themes, and related to the writers' culture; moreover, each writer takes multiple approaches to exploration. The goal is not dry, factual analysis but personal development. Inquiry begins with and returns to the student's own interests; also, it begins with art and then expands to include other disciplines as appropriate.

The process is open-ended so that a student can follow changing paths toward new horizons. Exploration, expression, and communication involve not simply existing forms or ideas but the discovery of something new: the values, constructs, and sensibilities inherent in aesthetic and other forms. The teacher's job is to help

FIGURE 10.1   *Bin's Used Cars,* Eric Barkin, Atlantic Community High School, Delray Beach, FL. Genia Howard, Art Teacher. *This page is part of a complicated exploration of current world events and the media's portrayal of them. Student notebook portfolios are process folios recording student progress as they investigate topics of interest and develop concepts and themes visually and verbally.*

students develop skills and refine their sensitivity so that they can remain focused on the problems they set for themselves. Thus although the process is open-ended, research notebooks entail closed-ended objectives that address skills and concepts as well as the open-ended instructional outcomes in which students use skills and concepts attained for personally meaningful ends.

In effect, students construct reality as well as discover it. A great deal of human behavior is learned, and learning is often transmitted through communicative institutions such as reading and writing, the arts, music, mathematics, and now electronic imagery. Humans, unlike animals, have cultural resources to draw on and need not relearn rudimentary lessons generation after generation: we stand on the shoulders, walk in the tracks, and swim in the wake of those who have come before us. Still, we receive and use our cultural inheritance in individual ways. One purpose of research notebooks is to help students integrate, synthesize, and utilize inherited knowledge in a way that is uniquely their own.

In guiding this activity, the teacher needs to provide basic skills and concepts and sensitive feedback to individual students at frequent intervals. Teachers can approach the activity in various ways, but certain skills and concepts must be taught so that students can do their own exploration. For some guidance on this feedback, refer to the chart on page 10. And feedback often accounts for the difference between really strong work by students and less impressive work. There is creativity in instruction as well as in learning. In this activity, creativity includes the teacher's sensitive application of accrued knowledge at the point when it will benefit the learner most.

With regard to art for life, research notebooks contribute to the development of fully functioning, sensitive, broadly educated young people. These notebooks require students to develop skills in historical methodology; the descriptive, analytical, and interpretive skills of art criticism; the evaluative skills of aesthetics; and the skills of decision making, construction, and evaluation involved in studio art. The notebooks may also require the skills of anthropology, psychology, and other disciplines. Perhaps most important, students develop the ability to evaluate, synthesize, and make meaning.

Notebooks also arouse an impulse to learn and provide strategies for learning. A notebook involves discovery rather than inculcation. It fosters critical thinking, decision making, flexibility, and ultimately, in some students, creativity and critical appreciation. These are worthy goals not only for art education but for education in general.

OBJECTIVE

Over the course of a semester (or more), students will develop a conceptually connected research notebook focused on a theme, form, or concept of their own choosing, incorporating art history, art criticism, aesthetic inquiry, visual studies, personal reflection, and creative visual artwork, of a length to be agreed upon beforehand.

SPECIAL LOGISTICS

Research notebooks should generally be hardcover, perhaps 8 by 10 inches or 10 by 14 inches. They should have at least 100 pages. The context for the development of the notebooks can be almost anything: personal introspection, student field trips to museums, the ball park and art fairs, family trips to Bali or Europe or the grocery store.

RESOURCES

The primary physical item is an unlined hardcover sketchbook with at least 100 pages for each student. Examples of research notebooks are also useful, as are examples of artists' journals such as Leonardo's or Anne Truitt's. Other resources will depend on the students' needs and topics.

http://www.mhhe.com/artforlife1
Visit our website to engage in dialogue with others about research notebooks.

PROCEDURE

Students should be introduced to the idea that art is an act of (exploratory) intelligence and should be introduced to artists' research notebooks as examples. They should be introduced to the idea that artists search for inspiration and that inspiration can come from many kinds of sources and strategies. Students should be told that they will be asked to focus on something they care about, and they should be introduced to the strategies of criticism, aesthetic inquiry, historical and contextual research, visual studies, and creative visualization as the means to find out about it. They should be introduced to the sample research notebooks (see the Content Base on page 173 and the web link).

To start, students may use various strategies, depending on their propensities. One strategy is to write a story about themselves; another is to make a list of, say, twelve things they really care about; another is to begin drawing—either drawing from life or doodling—perhaps while making accompanying notes about why they're attracted to what they're drawing. This should be homework. Students should come to class with ideas in their books about what they would like to look into and how they might start going about that. There should be a general discussion, with each student presenting his or her idea to the class and receiving feedback, cautions, encouragement, and additional ideas from the group. Usually, it is at this point that students get excited about the project.

Initially, students can work on their research notebooks in class, but as they get used to this project, it should be thought of primarily as homework. If the teacher expects 100 pages to be completed during a semester, the rate of completion might be about ten pages every two weeks. Every two weeks, then, the notebooks should be given to the teacher for feedback. This consistent feedback—a dialogue between the teacher and student—is very important to the success of the notebooks (see Evaluation on page 177).

At the outset and in feedback, the teacher should emphasize connective, thematic thinking. Critiques of artworks, historical research, and visual studies should all be related and should support the topic, form, or concept chosen. To repeat, though, the process should be open-ended, and the students should be flexible. Students should not feel that they are locked into the topic which first interested them or into the route that first occurred to them. Being confined to the initial subject or approach would indicate that the project had failed, because students would not have discovered anything new.

Since the teacher's role in this is to help students get to where they want to go, one common form of feedback will be to suggest directions, artists, and resources. These suggestions will be based on what is already presented in the notebooks. The teacher should write comments on "stickies" or in the books themselves about issues of concern, insights, and so on. As we mentioned above, the notebooks and the teacher's feedback should be considered a dialogue. The teacher can suggest books, images, art movements, and so on for students to follow up on. Another important task for the teacher is to encourage visual exploration, in balance with verbal exploration; otherwise, the notebooks can become overly verbal and overly academic. The teacher should emphasize that the visual feeds the verbal, which in turn feeds the visual. The notebooks should not be illustrated reports. They should be personal explorations using both verbal and visual means.

EVALUATION

Assessment is focused not only on the product but also on the process of learning, as reflected in each student's record of his or her strategies. One criterion is that students should explore a theme, idea, or form in a connected way and in a cultural context. A second criterion is that they should balance critical analysis, historical and contextual research, aesthetic inquiry, visual studies, personal reflection (both visual and written), and creative personal expression in some visual art form. A third criterion is that the chosen theme, topic, or form chosen by the students be open-ended: that is, open to development and change as information and insights are gained. A premise of this activity is that how knowledge is gained is part of the knowledge itself—that how we find out is inseparable from what we find out. This premise implies that the content of art is not art itself. To understand art, students should think of it as an expressive medium and a process within a context.

Thus students should also see the research book as a process—an inner dialogue. Rather than preparing a formal report on an artist, followed by a critique of his or her work, followed by some formal visual studies, and so on, students should be encouraged to think on paper, both visually and verbally, with all the turns and dead ends that such thinking may imply. Doodling, crossing out, and personal reflection are as important as doing research and recording information. The only way students can fail is not to explore, not to connect what they are exploring with other material, and not to use the disciplinary strategies described above. It is impossible to make "mistakes" about content. Therefore, the workbooks are markers of a process rather than reports designed primarily for the teacher. In other words, students should not feel that what they record in these notebooks will be seen by the teacher as "wrong."

Other formal criteria for evaluation (suggested by Gardner (1989) for process portfolios):

1. Ability to conceptualize and carry out a project.

2. Inclusion of historical and critical materials that are related to or help explain the student's own work.

3. Regularity, relevance, and precision of entries.

4. Ability to think directly in an artistic medium.

5. Signs of development and connection from one work or set of works to another.

6. The student's sensitivity to his or her own development.

7. Ability to express personal meanings and to give them some kind of universal form.

In addition, a quantitative criterion is probably necessary. It's not unreasonable to expect 100 pages over the course of the year, and indeed many teachers (for example, in International Baccalaureate programs) expect 200.

The research notebooks should be an ongoing project during the entire semester or school year. Cooperative formative evaluation should be continuous during that time. That is, both the teacher and the student should assess the quality, quantity, and direction of the research notebooks as well as the strategies being used, their effectiveness, and their balance in relation to what is being sought or discovered.

As noted earlier, an effective strategy is to have students turn in their research workbooks about every two weeks with a given number of pages completed. This may be something like a page a day. Although this may not seem flexible enough for a creative process, our experience has been that such guidelines are necessary to keep the students involved. As Dashiell Hammett reportedly said to his wife, Lillian Hellman, when she complained about not getting any writing done: "Damn it, Lilly, you just have to put your butt in the chair and write." In the notebooks, students make progress simply by keeping at it.

However, grading on an A–F scale when the notebooks come in every two weeks may be detrimental to the students' motivation and sense of personal responsibility. Rather, the instructor should read, critique, and give feedback each time the books come in. The teacher should function as a guide, suggesting directions, strategies, and content for research. A word of encouragement, or a warning about insufficient work or about misdirection is also in order. The instructor may want to use a check mark to indicate a satisfactory performance, a check-minus for less than satisfactory performance, or some such system.

Students, of course, must be aware of the criteria for satisfactory performance. Appropriate summative criteria might include these:

1. A clear, meaningful theme addressed in a connected way (although the theme may change during the course of the project).

2. Use of (at least) the disciplinary strategies of art criticism, art history, aesthetic inquiry, and visual (studio) examination, as well as personal reflection and individual creative artistic production.

3. Balance of critical, historical, and visual research and creative visual output (see the examples in Content Base beginning on page 174). The student and instructor should agree on what balance makes sense, given the student's overall idea.

4. Appropriate length (say, 100 or 200 pages).

5. Meaningful, sensitive, in-depth content appropriate in form and approach.

Criterion 5 is the most important but the most difficult to apply. However, the student's success in attaining this goal will be obvious at least by the end of the project—and probably much sooner, if the teacher has provided ongoing formative assessment and the student has engaged in self-reflection. The instructor and the student should cooperate in making the final determination of significance (meaning) and the "rightness" of form. The student's contribution might be a final reflection, or the student and the instructor might engage in a final dialogue or negotiation to decide whether the criteria were met.

FURTHER READING

Bender, S. (2001). *Keeping a journal you love.* Cincinnati, OH: Walking Stick.

Burton, J. (2000). The configuration of meaning: Learner centered art education revisited. *Studies in Art Education, 41*(4), 330–335.

Congdon, K., Stewart, M., & Howell White, J. (2002). Mapping identity for curriculum work. In Y. Gaudelius & P. Speirs (Eds.), *Contemporary issues in art education* (pp. 108–116). Upper Saddle River, NJ: Prentice Hall.

Fox, S., & Ganim, B. (1999). *Visual journaling: Going deeper than words.* Theosophical Publishing House.

Gardner, H. (1989). Zero-based arts education: An introduction to Arts Propel. *Studies in Art Education, 30*(2), 71–83.

James, P. (2000). Working toward meaning: The evolution of an assignment. *Studies in Art Education, 41*(2), 146–163.

James, P. (2000). I am the dark forest: Personal analogy as a way to understand metaphor. *Art Education, 53*(5), 6–11.

Lamott, A. (1994). *Bird by bird: Some instructions on writing and life.* New York: Pantheon.

Stout, C. J. (1999). Artists as writers: Enriching perspectives in art appreciation. *Studies in Art Education, 40*(3), 226–241.

Thompson, J. (2000). *Making journals by hand.* Gloucester, MA: Rockport.

11

A Sense of Community: Krzysztof Wodiczko and the Social Responsibility of Art

Guitarist, Russell Berger, Druid Hills High School, DeKalb County Schools, Decatur, GA. Betsy Epps, Art Teacher. *When students are challenged to find personally meaningful subjects for their artwork, the spirit of the artist, as well as the dignity of the subject and community, is often revealed.*

OVERVIEW

In this unit students will address social issues in and through art. In the process they will gain some sense of the potential for cooperation between artists and the community regarding those issues. Specifically, they will examine and discuss the work of Krzysztof Wodiczko, which reflects social and ecological concerns, and they will generate their own list of concerns and create art based on an ecological or social issue that matters to them.

KEY CONCEPTS

The driving ideas in this unit are that art can induce people to focus on things that count, socially; that art can be interactive, rising from and reflecting community concerns; and that through this interactive, communal focus on social issues people can come to see art as a vital, integral part of daily life. Students will recognize that some social problems can be addressed through activism in art and that they can initiate similar activism.

CONTENT BASE: KRZYSZTOF WODICZKO AND THE SOCIAL RESPONSIBILITY OF ART

The Polish-born designer and artist Krzysztof Wodiczko uses his art to engender debate about social problems, hoping to make people think about solutions. Some of Wodiczko's most famous works are images projected on well-known buildings. Using large projectors mounted on trucks, Wodiczko thrusts his art into public view and into the public's consciousness (Haus, 1993). The projections are temporary (even fleeting), but they persist in the mind's eye, and at least some have been documented. Some of his photographic images on monuments make points about the political nature of the institutions involved. For example, immense pictures of missiles projected on the Civil War Memorial in Brooklyn's Grand Army Plaza commented on the arms race between the United States and the former Soviet Union; pictures of homeless people projected on statues of Washington and Lafayette in New York City contrast the lofty ideals embodied in the statues with the reality of homelessness in America; and images of colonialism and slavery projected on the Museum of Man in San Diego point to the dark side of the city's early history.

In 1999, Krzysztof Wodiczko was awarded the Hiroshima Art Prize for his contribution to world peace. Wodiczko had interviewed numerous Japanese people who were traumatized by the atomic bombing of Hiroshima. He photographed their hands and projected those images around the base of a concrete building that survived the bombing and eventually became a monument to peace. The series of controversial projections was seen by thousands of people in Hiroshima and was televised throughout Japan. Wodiczko initiated this project in Hiroshima because it

FIGURE 11.1 *Homeless Vehicle,* Krzysztof Wodiczko, 1988. *Wodiczko insists that implicit in the impermanence of the* Homeless Vehicle *design was an expectation that its function become obsolete.* *ROM*

is a city where peace education is compulsory, and the peace monument there was in danger of being taken for granted by a young generation with different problems to solve. Opening discussion and debate about the role of the peace monument in contemporary Hiroshima broke the silence among several generations of Japanese about how peace is defined both historically and in contemporary society.

Wodiczko's work is pointedly political. In fact, one of his projections, in Poland in 1975, made government officials nervous enough to censor his work. After this experience, Wodiczko moved to Canada; he became a permanent resident in 1980. He then became head of the Interrogative Design Group at the Massachusetts Institute of Technology and taught art and photography courses in the visual arts program of the department of architecture there. Wodiczko's work was included in the Whitney Biennial 2000 and the Venice Architectural Biennale 2000.

Today, Wodiczko lives in New York City and continues to apply his skill in industrial design to produce many works. One of the most notable is the *Homeless Vehicle* project. Wodiczko had countless discussions with homeless people to discover their needs and concerns and then designed a vehicle for them. The prototype is a rocket-shaped metal compartment large enough to crawl into and lie down or sit up in. It also has room for storing personal belongings and collecting up to 500 bottles and cans scavenged for cash. As well as providing shelter and protection, the *Homeless Vehicle* gave homeless people a sense of respect. Instead of removing them from sight, the vehicle made them more prominent and legitimized their status as members of the urban community.

For Wodiczko, the vehicle is a metaphor, meant to awaken the public to the plight of the homeless. Yet he noted that it was often seen as a threat:

> People envision practically hundreds of thousands of vehicles taking over the city . . ., which is horrifying. . . . There should be no need for the vehicle. . . . What I design now is for a world that shouldn't be. . . . It's horrifying from any design point of view. This is a design that should not exist because the situation should not exist (1993, p. 157).

Wodiczko attributes his passion for art as public service to his parents. In Poland under the communist regime, his mother produced music for television theater and his father was the conductor of the Polish Philharmonic Orchestra. Both parents gave him an early understanding of the social responsibility of the arts.

OBJECTIVES

1. Students will discuss social activism in art by examining and interpreting the artworks of Krzysztof Wodiczko.

2. Students will brainstorm to develop ideas for a work of interactive community art based on their perceptions of community needs and their research regarding quality-of-life issues in the community.

3. Students will collectively select a topic of social concern and an artistic approach and create an interactive artwork in which the community participates.

4. Students will present their work of art to the community for feedback, acting as interpreters of and guides to the work as necessary.

5. Utilizing feedback from the community and the instructor, a "portfolio reflection sheet," discussion, and self-evaluation in relation to social issues in art, students will assess the instrumental and aesthetic success of the project and brainstorm to suggest future related activities.

RESOURCES

Resources include images of the work of Wodiczko and the information supplied in the Content Base, as well as images of works of other socially concerned artists, as appropriate. Materials for making art may include research sketchbooks, mural paper or board, paint, camera and film, pencils, water and containers, color slides and projectors or digital cameras and an LCD projector, and installation materials, as appropriate.

http://www.mhhe.com/artforlife1
Visit our website to find out more about Krzysztof Wodiczko and other socially concerned artists.

PROCEDURE

Discussion and Reflection on Social Issues and Art

The instructor may begin by showing images of the *Homeless Vehicle* by Krzysztof Wodiczko and asking students for their reactions. Discussion about the possible purposes of the vehicle should be encouraged before students are made aware of its intended purpose. After they are told about its function, further discussion should be encouraged, especially in relation to its form and function; this should lead naturally to the problems associated with homelessness.

Sample questions for discussion might include these: What features of the *Homeless Vehicle* do you think are most useful to the occupant? Are there features that you think are not very useful? Does this vehicle look comfortable? Why or why not? Is the *Homeless Vehicle* aesthetically pleasing? Why or why not? Is aesthetics the point? Does this work or any work have to be aesthetic to be art? Is this art? Does the shape of the *Homeless Vehicle* remind you of anything else? Does its shape communicate any other message or meaning? Do you think Wodiczko used this shape on purpose? Wodiczko never intended to market these vehicles widely, so why do you think he made these few? Can you think of another solution or design for housing homeless people?

The instructor can provide contextual information (see Content Base), explaining that Wodiczko was educated in Poland as an industrial designer, noting how he arrived at the idea of this portable home, and emphasizing that he sought input from street people in New York City in order to design something that would meet their needs—that the work is therefore community-based and interactive.

Some residents of New York feared that these vehicles were going to be mass-produced and would overrun the metropolitan area. As we mentioned, Wodiczko never intended this—but should he have intended it? Should he have made more

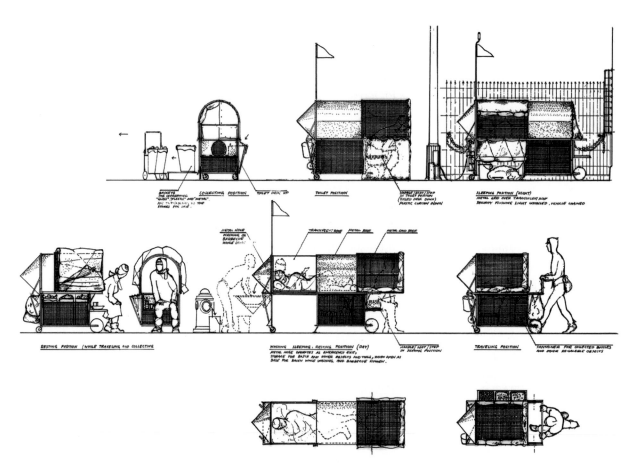

FIGURE 11.2 *Plans for the Homeless Vehicle, 1988. Wodiczko collaborated with people living on the streets in New York City to design a vehicle that would support their needs and strategies for survival.*

vehicles? Is the point simply to draw attention to homelessness? Is the point to make homeless people more conspicuous so that their fellow citizens will deal with the issue of homelessness? Or is the point to provide a solution? If hundreds or thousands of homeless vehicles were produced and given to the homeless, would the vehicle still be art? Does it matter? Is the vehicle a good solution?

Discussion of the invisibility of street people to the average passerby is a pithy tactic for discussion. Do students have any personal experiences to relate? Why do we choose to ignore the homeless? Why do we walk on by and not make contact, for example? At the end of the session, students could be given the task of thinking about other social issues they think are significant and/or tracking down/researching anyone—especially artists—who are dealing with social issues in their work.

Research Notebook

This activity can be done in class or as homework. Students should consider some of the features Wodiczko included in his *Homeless Vehicle* and then, after brainstorming as a group, work in their notebooks, reflecting on, researching, and sketching additional features they think might be helpful, or even constructing totally different solutions. They may also write a paragraph that describes their personal reactions to the problem of homelessness in this country and potential solutions. Research on the web or in books and journals could also be useful. Students might visit a shelter and ask homeless people about their needs and concerns. Like Wodiczko, they should consider all plausible and even some implausible solutions. Writing out or sketching criteria or a list of the needs of street people may help students to develop alternative solutions. Students may also create diagrams, as Wodiczko did, to explain design features or solutions. Individual work should be augmented and supported by substantive, directed discussion in class, with students thinking about how they will ultimately make socially activist art.

Making Art

Following the discussion and research, the teacher can ask students to bring back to the group as many social issues—homelessness, violence, drugs, starvation, inequality, war, political repression, and so on—as they can think of. Students who found additional information about activists in general and activist artists should be encouraged to share their findings. They should then brainstorm to develop ideas about using art to address these issues. Students should be reminded that in brainstorming a lot of ideas are sought and that negativity discourages creativity. They should withhold judgment and use their imagination. The teacher might remind students that these are complex issues, and it will take everyone working together to make a difference.

The first task is to discuss, negotiate, and agree on a theme or topic. This should be a concern—perhaps a local issue—that is socially important. Real-life experience can be invaluable in this planning process. For example, if the students decide to consider homelessness, they could visit a shelter or work in a soup kitchen so as to really see the plight of homeless men, women, and children. This would give valuable insights for designing a living space, a vehicle, or something else to meet their needs.

The second task is to figure out how to present the issue in an artwork that is community-friendly and in fact encourages the community to participate. One strategy might be small-group discussion, with the small groups reporting to and negotiating with the large group. Certainly, the individual doodling, research, analysis, and reflection in the students' notebooks should be brought to bear in these discussions and negotiations. The class might decide on a mural, an installation, a projection, or something else, but the form should not be predetermined.

In consultation with the instructor, the group should choose what artwork to make. For example, a solution might be a prototype homeless vehicle. Or teams of students could develop alternative vehicles. They could then ask community members to test the vehicles for a period of time. (Or an installation could be developed; see the discussion of Ciel Bergman and Nancy Merrill in Chapter 12.)

To understand some critical procedures, let's assume the students have decided to make an antiwar mural. First and foremost, input from the community is a critical factor in activist art, and such input should be sought during planning and completion of the project. Students could interview citizens in the community about their primary concerns regarding war and peace and incorporate those themes in the mural. The students could leave the mural incomplete, inviting community members to finish it.

Cooperation is critical as the artistic team develops the theme and content and then constructs the mural. If cooperation can't be achieved for one large mural, the students could form smaller groups of four or five members to develop smaller murals, each based on different issues but with a related theme. Factual, current information obtained from research is important to keep the students involved and willing to take responsibility for the project.

Thumbnail sketches are a good way to start visualizing the project and also to solidify the theme and subthemes. The teacher also might want to show students different approaches to murals. Some murals are very painterly and highly realistic; others resemble a collage style, employing a more graphic or symbolic approach. As the class looks at everyone's sketches, themes and styles will begin to coalesce. As far as possible, everyone's concerns should be addressed. In developing the cartoon, students should consider the shape of the space to be painted. Once a cartoon of the mural has been done and agreed on, it can be projected onto the wall (if the cartoon is done to scale). Everyone should be involved in painting all parts of the mural so that no one seems to "own" a particular section or figure.

This is only an example, and the specifics are only suggestions. If no space is available for a mural or an installation, students can consider alternative means of presenting their message. Keith Haring's work became popular on greeting cards and T-shirts. Billboard companies often donate space for educational purposes. Shopping centers may have space for temporary exhibits. Or the students may develop a functional sculpture or a media projection, as Wodiczko did.

Beyond the actual making of art, a major objective of this unit is to enable students to decide how they can best present their ideas outside the classroom. For example, working through appropriate channels, students may secure a place to display the work. This teaches them communication skills necessary for understanding the social nature of art and its potential for addressing social and ecological issues in the community. Any number of approaches can be taken, but local issues will probably be most effective in inspiring students and community members, and the research will be easier for such themes. Examples include crime or racial problems in your own city, or a new dam that will flood farmland, or the demolition of a revered landmark. Remember that the project requires some participation by the community. Community might consist of the school as a whole, including students' peers and other teachers and administrators. But reaching out to the larger community (if possible) makes for a more authentic situation and a more powerful impact on learning.

EVALUATION

Each student can be asked to respond to content-centered, interpretive, and evaluative questions in the review of his or her research journal, in the class discussions and planning process, and in the final studio activity. Sample questions follow: Describe the *Homeless Vehicle* and its purpose. Whom did Wodiczko ask to help him design it? Why? What's an installation? What's the purpose of Wodiczko's media installations? What is art for art's sake? What is art for life's sake? When if ever does art leave the realm of art and become merely a social project? Why? What do you think is the biggest social problem right now? Why? Do you think it can be addressed effectively through art? Does something have to be aesthetic (beautiful) to be a work of art? Does it have to be well crafted? What are the advantages of art for art's sake and art for life's sake? What are the disadvantages of each? Which do you think is better, for what purposes? If you were to do this sort of project again, what would you do differently? Why? Use criteria and evidence from your journal, from your other research, from the community's feedback, and from the aesthetic and technical qualities of the final project and other visual work to support your arguments:

1. What was the final project intended to do? Did it do that? How do you know?

2. What did you learn about social or environmental problems?

3. What did you learn about art?

4. What did you learn about yourself in the course of doing this unit?

Grades for this unit can be based on the thoroughness, quality of thinking, visualization, and depth of research notebooks; students' participation in group discussions; and students' participation and cooperation in the development of the final project. Teachers may wish to weight specific individual aspects of students' performance according to the impact of these components on the overall learning process and on the quality or level of achievement. Remember that summative evaluation has both criteria (what will be accomplished) and benchmarks (expected levels of accomplishment) within some system (a certain number of points, for example, for each component or criterion).

FURTHER READING

Borja-Villel, M. (1992). *Krzysztof Wodiczko: Instruments, projections, vehicles.* Barcelona: Fundacio Antoni Tapies.

Felshin, N. (Ed.). (1995). *But is it art? The spirit of art as activism.* Seattle, WA: Bay.

Frances Loeb Library: Krzysztof Wodiczko. Minneapolis: Walker Art Center. *http://www.gsd.harvard.edu/library/ services/references/bibliographies/wodiczko.html*

Freshman, P. (1992). *Public address.* Minneapolis: Walker Art Center.

Gablik, S. (1991). *The re-enchantment of art.* New York: Thames and Hudson.

Haus, M. 1993). The bombs on the building walls. *Art News,* 92(8), 154–157.

Krzysztof Wodiczko: Projections. http://www.rolandcollection. com/rolandcollection/section/36/666.htm

Spleen—An Interview with Krzysztof Wodiczko. *http://www. thespleen.com/subersions/pshychopathology/index. php?artID=69*

Yale DMCE: Lecture99: Krzysztof Wodiczko, Critical Vehicles. *http://www.yale.edu/dmca/lectures99/wodiczko.html*

A Sense of Place and of Community: Sea Full of Clouds—Ciel Bergman, Nancy Merrill, and Ecological Consciousness

Environmental Puzzle Mural, Parker Mathis Elementary, Lowndes County, GA. Melody Milbrandt, Art Teacher. *This collaborative puzzle mural was created by fifth-grade students in response to social and environmental concerns investigated during a study of activist artwork.*

OVERVIEW

In this unit students will address social and environmental issues in and through art. In the process they will gain some sense of the potential for interactive cooperation between artists and the community in addressing those issues. Specifically, they will examine and discuss Ciel Bergman and Nancy Merrill, whose art reflects ecological and social concerns, and will generate their own list of concerns and create their own art, based on an ecological or social issue that concerns them.

KEY CONCEPTS

The essential ideas in this unit are that art can draw attention to matters that count, socially and environmentally; that art can be interactive, rising from and reflecting community concerns; and that through communal interaction on social and environmental issues people can come to see art as a vital, integral part of daily life. Students will see that some artists address social or ecological problems through activism.

CONTENT BASE

In 1987 Ciel Bergman collaborated with Nancy Merrill to create an installation at the Contemporary Arts Forum, a museum in Santa Barbara, California. Bergman and Merrill spent several hours a day for five weeks picking up all the non-biodegradable material they found along the beaches of Santa Barbara. They hung this material from the ceiling, creating the focus for the work, *Sea Full of Clouds, What Can I Do* (See Color Plate 16, Bergman and Merrill, *Sea Full of Clouds, What Can I Do.*) The ceiling was hung with trash, dark to light, like rain clouds. At the entrance was an Ionic column made of Styrofoam coolers, suggesting that the root of the surrounding malaise was western culture. Additional trash was scattered about the floor, which was covered with flour.

Entering the installation was like entering a temple. Since the room was dimly lit, it took people awhile to realize that they were viewing trash. Surrounding the cloud of trash hanging from the ceiling Bergman painted a black wall mural, approximately 14 by 17 feet, symbolic of grief, with seven windows opening to a sunset and the sea. In the center of the room was a fire pit of ashes, reminiscent of a Native American prayer altar. There were disturbing photographs of sea animals, such as seals, with plastic wrapped around their necks. But the installation was serene and quiet. Gentle sounds of the ocean and animals filled the air as the viewer was confronted with the havoc humans have brought to the environment.

The active participation of the audience was an important part of the experience. Visitors were invited to write a prayer and wrap a prayer stick using natural materials provided around the altar. After the exhibit, 380 of these prayer sticks were cast into the sea as an offering of hope. The artists offered two walls of the gallery as surfaces for people to write on. In the Lakota tradition, south is the

FIGURE 12.1 Ciel Bergman (aka Cheryl Bowers) and Nancy Merrill, detail of the prayer sticks and fire ring within *Sea Full of Clouds*, 1987, museum installation. *The fire ring, constructed in the Lakota native tradition, served as a place for meditation, reflection, and prayer. Today, Ciel Bergman lives in New Mexico; she continues to use environmental themes in her paintings. Nancy Merrill lives in Seattle; she creates works that she places in the natural environment and calls them "works without audience."*

direction of childhood fear, so people wrote their fears for the earth on the south wall. East is the traditional direction of hope, inspiration, and the future, so people wrote their dreams of a gentler, kinder, cleaner world on the east wall. In the room's dim light and serene atmosphere people felt free to be honest, and much of the writing was quite profound. Many thoughts and prayers were written for other species, as well as for a human awakening. Eventually, comments from viewers covered both walls. In addition, the artists sat at the ash altar each day for one hour and invited viewers to sit with them in silence or engage in a conversation about the environment. In this way, the artists created a plea for conservation and recycling in a poetic, almost sacred way.

Bergman believed that the basic issue was of personal choice and empowerment versus helplessness in relation to the environment. Merrill observed that even though the installation was about global healing, some personal healing also took place in it.

Instead of the usual opening, a closing of the exhibit was held in a public forum to discuss what should be done with the trash. This forum, as well as the exhibit itself, brought to the museum many people who did not usually attend gallery exhibitions. People from all walks of life and professions became involved in the project. The impact on the citizens of Santa Barbara was so great that the city instituted a program for recycling plastic. As Bergman (Gablik, 1991) stated:

> Art may not change anything, but the ideas we have about ourselves we project into the world. Negative images have a way of coming alive just as positive images have. If we project images of beauty, hope, healing, courage, survival, cooperation, inter-relatedness, serenity, imagination, and harmony, this will have a positive effect. Imagine what artists could do if they became committed to the long-term good of the planet? If all artists would ever pull together for the survival of humankind, it would be a power such as the world has never known. (p. 155)

Nancy Merrill was interviewed by the artist Tom Kennedy in Seattle, Washington, in August 1995. She talked about her philosophy of art as well as how *Sea Full of Clouds* evolved.

TK: How did you become involved with Ciel?

NM: Ciel (pronounced C. L.) Bergman (aka Cheryl Bowers) was a professor at the University of California at Santa Barbara whose work I really admired. She's a wonderful painter and always saw her painting as meditation. She felt that the ocean is sacred, so she painted it, but not like the waves crashing things you see at over people's sofas or in motels.

TK: Not a pretty seascape?

NM: (Laughter.) Her paintings are pretty, but they are also big and compelling. One day I went on an artists' studio tour. I met her there and she explained she was going to be doing a show at the Santa Barbara Forum. I volunteered to help, not really as a peer, but more as an assistant. I was an emerging artist, while she was a professional with an established reputation. However, as the show went along it became a collaboration, and so we shared the concept, because she had the space. She had the commitment to do an exhibit and we both started, I guess, our attempt toward relevancy. We were both really tired of seeing the same artists, at the same art receptions, talking about the same things. We thought, wouldn't it be great if lawyers, doctors, scientists, children, or any other people would be involved in the art arena?

    The installation became as much a comment on greater audience involvement with art as anything else. *Sea Full of Clouds* was a very community-oriented, topical piece. Our dream came true and all kinds of people came to this show. They wrote on the walls, wrote us letters, and had conversations. I felt energized. It was also quite beautiful. You may not be able to tell from the photographs, but what you are looking at is trash.

TK: What kinds of materials did you use? How did you find it? Where did it come from?

NM: Well, Santa Barbara is on the coast of California, and a kind of a resort. It's a beautiful town, a place where people don't litter, yet the litter is brought to them by the ocean. This is ten years ago when they were just discovering that floating trash and plastic [were] choking sea life and destroying the ocean. We began collecting trash that had washed up on the beach. We wore rubber gloves and were really careful not to touch stuff that might be dangerous. It didn't stink or anything, because it had been washed by the ocean, even the Pampers and stuff. (Laughter.) We started making clouds out of this trash. It involved walking on the beach for several hours a day. We spent several weeks collecting all sorts of debris: plastic, Styrofoam, anything that floats.

TK: This really isn't what some people might think of as typical art material, and a finished permanent art object was not the result. What do you think makes this art?

NM: Well, I'm not sure that it is. I mean defining art is hard. I can tell you I would say that both Ciel and I are regarded by some criteria as artists. We make art, we have degrees in art, we call ourselves artists, or other people refer to us as artists, so I guess we are. I mean it's a free country. You can call yourself whatever you want.

TK: It does make a strong statement, I think.

NM: If one calls it that.

TK: If that's a criterion for art.

NM: Right! With regard to a definition of art, I think installations are tricky. I think it had moments of art and I think it was a terrific way to bring some new life into an art space. This was a nonprofit gallery that had all different kinds of things going on. I think it was quite beautiful. What happened in there was beautiful, but that's not to say that all art is beautiful.

TK: That's true. What actually went on during the exhibit?

NM: We installed all the trash and painted the walls. It was a meditative kind of space. The floor was covered with flour. It gave it a sort of eerie look. It either looked like heaven or the aftermath of a nuclear bomb. It was very, very serene and quiet. There were pictures on the wall that showed seals with plastic wrapped around their necks. There was space for people to write and all kinds of literature that people could read, but it was very passive. You could either participate with that or not. Nobody lectured anybody.

TK: You said it was quiet. Was there a recording of the ocean?

NM: Yes, ocean music in the background. There was a wall that said " Hopes," and a wall that said "Fears," and some people came in and wrote really goofy stuff on there, but other people wrote real heartfelt things. It was pretty interesting. I guess it was about maybe global healing, but it was also very much about personal healing. I would say that some personal healing went on in this space during this time. Plus it brought people into the gallery who didn't ordinarily attend. Ciel or I spent a lot of time in the installation, answering questions and just conversing with people. We often sat on the floor for these discussions. It was very interesting.

TK: Was there an opening or a closing ceremony?

NM: Yes, there was a closing, which was a bit unusual. Someone performed a beautiful Native American flute piece and it was quite moving. People from all walks of life attended and talked about how to dispose of the exhibit. Since we had picked up all this trash we had to decide how to dispose of it. There were a lot of good ideas. This was before recycling of even paper was going in a big way, so it initiated a lot of discussion about recycling in that area. Ultimately, the trash did go to the Dumpster. At that time there was no better solution. People did take a lot of the beautiful natural items home.

TK: What did you hope to accomplish by this exhibit? Do you feel you were successful?

NM: I can't speak for both of us, but for me I was very tired of art museums and art exhibits. I felt like a lot of what I saw were people's little jokes. The art scene at that point seemed to be art for art's sake. I was more interested in making something and giving it away, or decorating an envelope and mailing it. On a personal level I was working in an archive, for the widow of an artist. I spent most of my time cataloging, insuring, touching, moving, dealing with this leftover art from this person's career and I think that this was a bit of a catharsis for me to do something . . .

TK: Relevant?

NM: Well, and also something unplanned. We went into it with the title. We had no idea we were going to pick up plastic out of the ocean. We had no idea. It just happened. It kept evolving because of the people that became involved.

TK: So the installation invited audience participation?

NM: Hugely. And that's something very important that I thought the exhibit accomplished. I believe in access. For example, I told you about when I was a kid I thought only one person in the class could be an artist. That was the first obstacle. The second one was nobody in my family valued artists. I don't think they knew any either. While they could be happy that I could draw or I could make stuff, that's where it stayed. People need to see art as a vital, integral part of daily life.

TK: Do you think artists should become involved in issues, like the environment, in their work?

NM: I think they're already involved. See, I think that most people are involved in something either literally or emotionally. For example, I plant trees. I'm a tree planter. I've planted trees for the city. I've planted trees for the victims of AIDS. I've planted trees just because the city had extras. The fact that I plant trees has nothing to do with the fact that I'm an artist, although I plant them artfully, I'm sure. (Soft laughter.) So in this installation I brought a lot of what I already believe, value, or practice into a visual arena. Maybe that's where art comes in. Since artists are more visual, using that forum is our job. Beyond making beautiful pictures or talking, blah, blah, blah, about art, art, art, I think we can be visual eye-openers, which leads to greater awareness, understanding, and conceptual problem solving.

TK: Well, it certainly makes people think.

NM: Yes, and feel.

TK: Well, Nancy, it's been nice talking with you. Do you have anything else you want to say or add?

NM: This has been a lot of fun. I care a lot that people understand that art can be a part of their life in any amount they want. I just think there are some people who just think that they can't do it. There are lots of definitions of art. Anybody can make this metal ring with seaweed hanging from it, but whether or not we all call it art is a different story. I think that just like music or any other creative pursuit, it's a very nice thing to have in your life. It's a fun thing to casually notice and study over a long period of time. It gives me a lot of joy that way.

OBJECTIVES

1. Students will discuss social and ecological activism in art, examining and interpreting the artworks of Ciel Bergman and Nancy Merrill and other activist artists.

2. Students will brainstorm about and do research on a variety of community concerns, then collectively choose a topic. They will include community input and participation in the process.

3. Students will create a work of art and present it to a community audience, encouraging participation and feedback.

4. Using feedback from the community and the instructor, a "portfolio reflection sheet," discussion, and self-evaluation, students will assess the instrumental and aesthetic success of the project and brainstorm future related activities.

RESOURCES

Resources include images of the work of Bergman and Merrill from this text and from the weblink as well as the information supplied in the Content Base (page 189) and other images and research on artists concerned with the environment and social issues, as appropriate (see also "Further Reading"). Art materials may include research sketchbooks, mural paper or board, paint, camera and film, pencils, water and containers, trash, natural materials, and installation materials, as appropriate.

http://www.mhhe.com/artforlife1
Visit our website to find more information about environmental art and artists, as well as pictures of *Sea Full of Clouds*.

PROCEDURE

Research and Reflection on Environmental Issues and Art

The instructor can show images of the installation *Sea Full of Clouds*. As students look at the images, the instructor can read the Content Base (including the interview with Nancy Merrill). The instructor should reemphasize that the installation was focused on environmental concerns and that it was an interactive work. Also, input from the community was sought, and there was a reception at the end of the exhibit period (rather than an opening reception). The closing reception included a forum for exchanging ideas on cleaning the beaches and recycling. Students should be made aware that this project was very successful and actually led to recycling in the city. It should be emphasized that Bergman and Merrill's work is activist. It tries to get people to do something, to address issues beyond the aesthetic, beyond the work of art itself.

To promote discussion, the teacher might begin by asking: What is art? In this case even one of the artists is unsure, so do you think this project is art? Why or why not? Are functional objects works of art? Is something art if no art object is actually made, as with the projections in Chapter 11? What about installations? What about art made with junk? Is everything thing called art truly art? Who decides, and what criteria apply? What's the difference between activism in art and activism that really can't be called art? Does putting trash into a museum setting make it art? If trash can be art, can anything be art? What makes objects change from non-art to art? Bergman and Merrill picked up a lot of the trash for the installation from the beach. Was this act part of the artwork? Why or why not? Other questions: In creating an installation, artists often juxtapose objects in unexpected ways within a specific space, hoping that the audience will interact with the work in that space. Which senses were engaged as the audience viewed this installation? Do you think this installation would have been as effective if it had been created as two-dimensional artwork or sculpture? Why or why not? Can you think of other instances when space is manipulated to communicate an idea, mood, or feeling? What kind of mood was created in the installation? How do you think that mood influenced the audience's interaction with the work?

Another set of questions: Some areas in this installation replicated Native American rituals, such as the fire ring and prayer sticks. Why do you think these were included? Do you think it was all right to take sacred rituals out of their original setting and put them in another? How does that affect their authenticity and meaning? How did it affect the power of this installation, in your mind?

The instructor might also ask: Do you think there is merit in having a closing rather than an opening reception? Does it matter when a reception is held? Does hearing an artist talk about his or her work change your perception of a work? Is that good or bad? Should you automatically believe what an artist tells you about his or her work, or rely more on your own interpretation? Why?

Research Notebook

This activity can be done in class or as homework. In their research notebooks, students can be asked to reflect on and articulate some major ecological themes and problems, do some research, and work out solutions based on art for bringing attention to those problems. The instructor could present some examples of artists who address environmental themes, in addition to Bergman and Merrill, to start the students' thinking processes. Artists who might be useful in this regard include Andy Goldsworthy, Nancy Holt, Ana Mendieta, Dennis Oppenhiem, Carl Andre, and Robert Smithson. Another avenue to explore would be traditional Australian Aboriginal or Navajo art (see Chapter 15), which was intended to keep the natural world in balance.

Making Art

Following discussion and individual exploration and research in the notebooks, the teacher can ask students to bring back to the group and brainstorm as many ecological problems—endangered species, recycling, destruction of the rain forests, global warming, and so on—as they can think of. Students who have additional information about activists in general and activist artists, and other ideas, should be encouraged to share their findings at this point. The teacher might remind students that these are complex issues and it will take everyone working together to make a difference.

The first task is to discuss, then negotiate and agree on, a theme or topic. This should be a concern that is ecologically important, if possible a local issue. The second task is to figure out how to present the issue in an art that is "community-friendly" and encourages community participation. These two steps might be accomplished through small-group discussion, followed by reports to the large group and negotiation. The doodling, research, analysis, and reflection in the students' research notebooks should be brought to bear in group discussion and negotiation. The artistic approach the class decides on might be selected from a variety of traditional and nontraditional possibilities: for example, students might work individually or collaboratively to create an installation, a live performance, a videotaped public service announcement, a commercial, a skit, a computer graphic, or an animation sequence.

If students do choose an installation, they will need to consider the meaning they wish to communicate by the arrangement of objects within the space. They may want to take a multisensory approach by including music or a recording of prose or poetry, objects that may be picked up and held as well as seen, movement of objects or around objects that helps create meaning, and an activity that calls for a response from the viewer. In developing their ideas, the students need to be sensitive to local environmental issues. They can learn about such issues from interviews, newspapers, local TV, and discussion. The more input from the community, the better.

Thumbnail sketches are a good way to start visualizing the project and also to solidify the theme and subthemes. The group may also want find and share different approaches to environmentally concerned art: for example, the work of Nancy Holt and Andy Goldsworthy. The teacher might assign specific environmental artists to specific students, who will do research on the Internet and report back to the class. As the class hears about the work of artists and looks at everyone's sketches and themes and styles, larger ideas will begin to emerge and coalesce. As far as possible, everyone's concerns should be addressed.

Enabling students to decide how best to present their ideas beyond school is, again, a major objective of this unit. The importance of local issues should be emphasized, such as the destruction of the natural environment through over-development and urban sprawl, traffic pollution, waste treatment facilities, and groundwater contamination. The project should reflect a connection to the local community and input from that community.

Community Interaction

As in Chapter 11, the work produced is to be interactive; thus there must be participation by and feedback from the community. Activist artworks and performances, in fact, never exist just for themselves; they are always produced to achieve some extrinsic purpose. The artists want to move people to think, feel, and then act. The exact nature of the action desired will be clear from the work that is developed.

Definitions of community may also vary, depending on the age and maturity of the students and the flexibility of the school or class. In some cases, students may construct and present their art off-campus, or parents and community leaders may be invited to the school to view and interact with the students and the art. The use of technology may be another way for students to interact with or receive feedback from others—in the school, in the local community, or across the world.

EVALUATION

Each student can be asked to respond to a content-centered review in his or her research journal. Sample questions follow: What did Ciel Bergman and Nancy Merrill try to accomplish in their installation? What did they use as material? Why did they have a closing rather than an opening reception? Do you think what they did was art? Why or why not? Describe how an installation is different from traditional art forms. What do you think is the worst environmental problem right now? Why? Do you think it can be addressed effectively through art? Is activist art the same as or different from advertising, which is also trying to get you to buy into something? Which of the artists we've discussed is most effective, in your mind, as an artist? Why? Which is most effective as an activist? Who has taken up the most important issues? If you were to do this sort of project again, what would you do differently? Why? Use criteria and evidence from your journal, from your other research, from the community's feedback, and from the aesthetic and technical qualities of the final product (and other visual work—for example, work in your notebook) to support your arguments:

1. What was the final project intended to do? Did it succeed? How do you know?

2. What did you learn about social and environmental problems?

3. What did you learn about art?

4. What did you learn about yourself in the course of doing this unit?

If it's necessary to give students a grade for this unit, the grade can be based on the thoroughness, quality of thinking, visualization, and depth of their research notebooks, their participation in group discussion, and their participation and cooperation in the development of the final product. Some grading or weighting system can be used, in relation to the criteria, as the instructor sees fit.

FURTHER READING

Anderson, H. (2000). A river runs through it: Art education and a river environment. *Art Education, 53*(6), 13–17.

Art Education, 50(6). (1997). (Thematic issue: art and the environment.)

Ciel Bergman. *http://www.emal.com/art/Bergman_info.htm*

Blandy, D., Congdon, K., & Krug, D. (1998). Art, ecological restoration, and art education. *Studies in Art Education, 39*(3), 230–243.

Earthworks.org, a site for contemporary earthworks. *http://www.earthworks.org/links.html*

Gablik, S. (1991). *The re-enchantment of art.* New York: Thames and Hudson.

Garoian, C. (1998). Art education and the aesthetics of land use in the age of ecology. *Studies in Art Education, 39*(3), 244–261.

Goldsworthy, A., & Goldsworthy, A. (1990) *Andy Goldsworthy: A Collaboration with Nature.* New York: Abrams.

Hicks, L. (1992–1993). Designing nature: A process of cultural interpretation. *Journal of Multicultural and Cross-Cultural Research in Art Education, 10–11,* 73–88.

Holt, Nancy. Image and critique of Sky Mound. *http://www.getty.edu/artsednet/images/Ecology/sky.html*

Hull, Lynne. Ecology Art Website. *EcoartHull@cs.com*

Krug, D. (1999). Ecological restoration: Mierle Ukeles, *Flow City.* In *Art and Ecology: Ecological Art Perspectives and Issues. http://www.getty.edu/artsednet/resources/Ecology/Issues/ukeles.html*

Lippard, L. (1998). *Lure of the local: Senses of place in a multi-centered society.* New York: New Press.

Mendieta, Ana. Website: A comprehensive guide to her work. *http://www.hungryflower.com/leorem/mendieta.html*

Papanek, V. (1995). *The green imperative: Natural design for the real world.* New York: Thames and Hudson

Smithson, Robert. *http://www.robertsmithson.com/films/films.htm*

13

A Sense of Self, of Place, and of Community—Fred Wilson's Installation Art and Reconstruction of the Historical Narrative

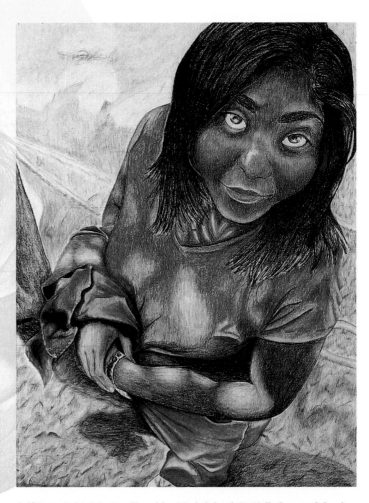

Self-Portrait, Iris Martin, Chamblee High School, DeKalb County Schools, Atlanta, GA. Kymberly Landers, Art Teacher. *This self-portrait, drawn from an unusual viewpoint, exemplifies complex artistic problem solving resulting in a more interesting composition than a traditional frontal view. Viewer interest and speculation are heightened about this moment in Iris's life by her use of dramatic bird's-eye perspective and foreshortening.*

OVERVIEW

Students will take up the work of the installation artist Fred Wilson. Wilson recontextualizes objects in museum collections to question stereotypes, generalizations, and social reification, especially in regard to power and privileges one group may have over another. He rearranges objects to redirect the viewer's attention so that ideas, themes, and generalizations are seen in a new way. On the basis of their examination of his work, students will consider the role of the museum in defining, developing, and preserving a cultural heritage. They will consider whether the museum's portrayal of the past is the "truth" or a construction based on certain human sensibilities. They will also consider what art is, what it does, and whether history may be reconstructed as our perceptions of truth are altered. If possible, students will visit a local museum and discover "buried" themes by noting how objects are displayed. Finally, students may create an art installation of their own, after discussing a theme or themes they want to address.

KEY CONCEPT

The key concept in this unit is that objects and their presentation can be "mined"— dug up, brought to light, and examined—for the values, mores, and assumptions embedded in them. The purpose of this activity is to explore the value constructions we often misconstrue as the given truth, with the goal of including all people equally in society. The obvious benefit for students of cultural and ethnic minorities is that they can move inward from the margins and recognize their own stake in American culture. The benefit for students of the white majority is that they can better understand themselves and others by seeing themselves with new eyes. As Banks and Banks (2001) put it, for America to be successful as a society, we *all* have to be successful. That means getting out of our encapsulated ethnic and social worlds and recognizing that we have a shared past and a shared future.

ISSUES AND ASSUMPTIONS

1. History is constructed by people and usually reflects the point of view of those who are dominant in a society.

2. Art is a social artifact and a social performance. It is executed in a social context and reflects that context.

3. Museums, as social institutions, collect and maintain objects of value, usually reflecting the values and traditions of the dominant culture. In this way they have constructed a history that has been perceived as truth. By failing to include objects and alternative interpretations from entire segments of society,

or including such material but displaying it in stereotypical ways, museums in fact present only one of many possible truths.

4. Art may be presented and viewed from various philosophical perspectives, such as formalism or contextualism.

5. Art need not be the construction or fabrication of an object; it may consist of an act, a demonstration, a presentation, or a process. For example, **installation art** may create meaning simply by selecting certain objects or arranging objects in a certain way.

CONTENT BASE

Fred Wilson's installations send a message about how museums represent, misrepresent, or omit work by racial and ethnic minorities. The art critic Judith Stein (1993) says that Wilson has "formidable narrative skills and a talent for fashioning installations that pack a punch more powerful than their individual components" (p. 113). Wilson, the child of African American and Native American parents, has taken social injustice as his subject and the museum and its practices as his medium.

In his compelling exhibition *Mining the Museum,* Wilson used only the artifacts available from the Maryland Historical Society to create a chilling portrayal of slavery and a callous, inhumane social structure. In a standard exhibition case labeled *Metalwork, 1793–1880,* he showed a set of repoussé silver goblets, as well as silver urns and decanters, next to a crude pair of rusty slave shackles. The point was to contrast the life of the powerful with the life of the powerless, to get viewers to consider the lives of all the people of that time, to make those who were previously ignored or peripheral noteworthy and significant.

Another dramatic installation in this exhibition is *Cabinet-Making, 1820–1910,* a tableau composed of a whipping post surrounded by a variety of ornate Victorian chairs. The post symbolizes the horrors of slavery; the chairs symbolize the opulence and complacency of the dominant white culture of the period. An ironic touch is that among the chairs is one with the logo of the Baltimore Equitable Society.

Through such juxtapositions of artifacts and creative revisions of labels, Wilson began to uncover other aspects of a diverse and sorrowful history, long ignored.

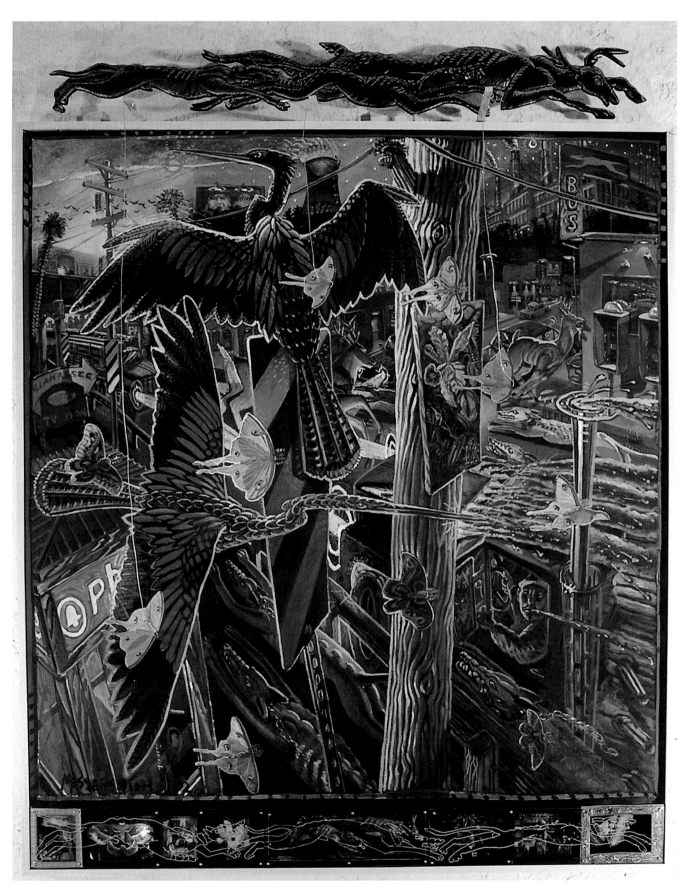

COLOR PLATE 10   Mark Messersmith, *Afternoon of the Faun,* 2002. *Messersmith's environmental message is clearly communicated in his detailed and sensuous paintings. This combination of strong message and effective composition provide a balanced example of artistic blending of contextual and formal concerns.*

COLOR PLATE 11 Roger Shimomura, *Untitled*, 1985. *Pop art and ukiyo-e prints are combined in this work to present an image of bicultural identity. During WWII, as a child, Shimomura was held with members of his family in an Idaho internment camp, while his uncle served in combat with the 442nd division of Japanese-Americans.*

COLOR PLATE 12 *Bayeux Tapestry, 1066. Embroidery of wool and linen, 230 ft. long and 20 in. wide. This section of the tapestry declares in Latin that "Here the English and the French died together in the battle." The Bayeux Tapestry was designed to convey a prudent moral lesson about personal and social loyalty as well as document the brutality and horror of war and the ultimate victory of William the Conqueror.*

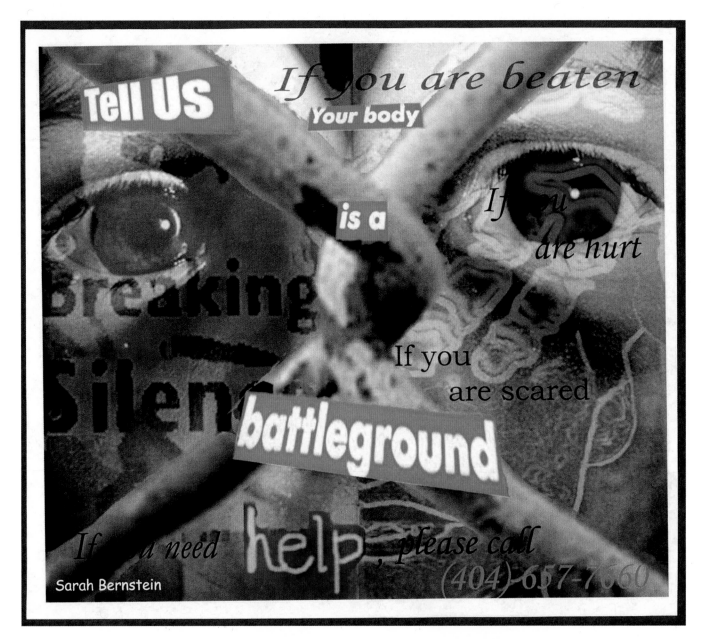

COLOR PLATE 13 Sarah Bernstein, *Child Abuse,* 2003. Northview High School, Fulton County, GA. Jessica Booth, Art Teacher. *After discussing the art of Betye Saar students responded to the question, "If you could change the world where would you start?" This sensitive multi-layered computer graphic communicates the student's concern for the problem of child abuse.*

COLOR PLATE 16 Ciel Bergman (aka Cheryl Bowers) and Nancy Merrill, *Sea Full of Clouds, What Can I Do,* 1987. Museum Installation at the Contemporary Arts Forum, Santa Barbara, CA. Photo courtesy of William B. Dewey. *Bergman and Merrill spent several hours a day for five weeks collecting biodegradable material found along the Santa Barbara beaches and hung it from the museum's ceiling as a focus of the installation.*

COLOR PLATE 17 Charnelle Holloway, *Altar to Abused Women.* Gallery Installation, Spelman College, Atlanta, GA. *Holloway created this installation in response to cases of domestic violence in her community. The knife with a gilded handle of gold, encased in Plexiglass represents a ceremonial knife of justice upon the altar.*

COLOR PLATE 18 *Guernica Project Children's Peace Mural.* Tokushima, Japan. Toshifumi and Yasuda Tadashi, directors. *In executing this mural, the children's input was integrated with adult decision making in a very formalized process. Children had considerable input in the content and design of the mural in this beautiful collaborative work.*

COLOR PLATE 19 Tibetan Monks, *The Kalachakra (Wheel of Time).* Tibetan Monks labor many days to make this delicate mandala with colored sand, which represents the universe. The mandala healing process may not be completely understood through Western sensibilities, but the goal is universally comprehensible; to renew and give energy to our life force, to bring order from chaos, to understand and accept that we should be true to ideals of balance and beauty in our every day lives.

FIGURE 13.2   Fred Wilson, *Globe or Truth Trophy and Pedestals*, from *Mining the Museum*, 1992. *In* Mining the Museum *Wilson challenges the nature of historical truth: who construes it, how, and how it is sustained and passed on. Wilson's goal in reconstructing history is to obtain respect for everyone in our pluralistic society.*

For example, although 80 percent of the population of Baltimore is African American, there is typically little to represent them in the Historical Society Museum. This gap was pointed out in Wilson's arrangement of low wooden pedestals supporting busts of Henry Clay, Napoleon Bonaparte, and Andrew Jackson. None of these famous men had ever lived in Maryland, but the museum had deemed their busts worthy of acquisition and display. Wilson placed to the left of these busts three empty pedestals bearing the names of celebrated African Americans who were Marylanders: Harriet Tubman, Frederick Douglass, and Benjamin Bannaker. The museum's collection did not include their portraits. In one of the most disturbing pieces, a Ku Klux Klan hood, found in an attic of a home in Baltimore, was placed in a baby carriage. This was part of a grouping called *Modes of Transport 1770–1910*. It suggests that racial attitudes and prejudice begin in childhood.

Wilson is asking: Where am I, as an African American, in this institution? Each piece in the exhibit reminds visitors that historical truth is subjective and dependent on the authority of those who develop and dispense the information. According to Lisa Corin (1994), curator of the Contemporary Museum, Wilson's exhibit calls attention to the fact that "history is itself an interpretation that is always carried on in the context of contemporary events. . . . The contingency of historical "truth" is who makes it, who learns it, and who passes it on" (p. 73). Almost every evaluation of *Mining the Museum* has mentioned its emotional impact and its effect on how the audience perceived African American history. Not only visitors but members of the museum's staff had to confront their beliefs about history and about the role of the museum.

In his earlier work, too, Wilson raised questions about art and its environment in the museum setting. *The Struggle between Culture, Content, and Context* demonstrated the significance of the presentation of art objects, and thus the power the museum wields by choosing how to exhibit its holdings. This complex relationship was further explored in Wilson's work *The Colonial Collection*, in which African masks, made for commercial purposes, were wrapped in French and British flags. Wilson reminded viewers that many artworks in museum collections

http://www.mhhe.com/artforlife1
Visit our website to learn more about Fred Wilson's work.

are spoils of war, forcibly acquired during punitive expeditions by imperial and colonial powers.

All along, Fred Wilson has confronted museums and the public by questioning their assumptions about history and perspectives on history. Wilson continues to be involved in reconstructing history by shifting our attention; instead of looking at the artifacts of the dominant culture in isolation, we see them in a larger sociopolitical context—particularly, we see them in terms of oppression of African Americans. The point is to help us all redefine our relationships with each other, our view of justice and power, and the role museums play in presenting and preserving a cultural heritage. The larger goal is respect for everyone in our pluralistic culture.

OBJECTIVES

1. Students will examine the work of Fred Wilson and consider the role of the museum in defining, developing, and preserving cultural heritage. They will also consider the relationship of institutions like museums to the construction of history, and how history may be reconstructed as our perceptions of truth are altered.

2. (Optional) Students will visit a local museum, which they will "mine." That is, they will attempt to uncover themes that are "buried" in the way exhibits are displayed.

3. As a team, students will create an installation that reconstructs our understanding of an issue or theme they have developed and agree on as a group.

SPECIAL LOGISTICS

If possible, arrangements should be made to visit a local art or history museum.

RESOURCES

Resources include a still camera, film, and processing; or a digital camera and computer and printer. Fred Wilson's installations and information and resources from individual and collective research can be accessed from the weblink.

PROCEDURE

First, the instructor may ask students what they think the purpose of an art museum is. All ideas should be considered. Then the instructor might present Fred Wilson and the exhibition *Mining the Museum*, using the Content Base (page 200), accompanying photographs, and weblink images and resources. Discussion should follow. To guide discussion, the instructor might use the following questions.

1. Now what do you think is the purpose of a museum?

2. Who decides what is on display in a museum? (This would be a good opportunity to address or readdress the institutional theory of art. See Chapter 5.)

3. What criteria do you think should be used to select work for an art museum? Remember that the museum in question is a historical museum. Should its criteria be different from those for an art museum? (Again, this would be a good opportunity to use information from Chapter 5, especially to direct the conversation toward essentialism, which relies the criteria of skill, elaboration, and formal beauty for their own sake, versus contextualism, which sees function and social context as crucial to artistic merit.)

4. Why do you think Fred Wilson called his exhibit *Mining the Museum?*

5. Wilson combined objects such as slave shackles and silverware to direct our attention away from the affluent white upper class and toward the unnamed African American slaves and even well-known African Americans who are part of history but are often excluded from traditional museum exhibits. Wilson has shown us an alternative view of American history. Is it valid? Is it true? Is it as true as the history constructed by the museum staff? Could there be more than one honest view of history? How so? Is history "the truth" or is it constructed? By whom is it constructed? Can it change over time?

6. In *Mining the Museum,* Wilson seemed to be claiming that, for the most part, African Americans' history has not been treated equally with that of the dominant white culture in our cultural institutions or has been left out altogether. Almost everyone has at some time been left out of a game or some other event. If that has ever happened to you, how did it make you feel? How do you think Fred Wilson responded to feeling left out?

7. Instead of creating an art object, Wilson creates installations. Given the information in the Content Base, what do you think an installation is? Installations (unlike painting or sculpture) are only temporary. Do you think installations are works of art, even if no art object is created? Why or why not? If an installation is art, where does the art lie: in the piece, in the picture that represents it, or in the idea?

Following the discussion, which may last several days, a trip to a local art or history museum is desirable, if it is feasible. Students should be aware that they are looking for subliminal themes, that is, assumptions that are "buried" in the way objects are displayed. At the museum, it may be productive to ask students to notice exactly what things are displayed (what kinds of things, and by extension what's missing), how they are grouped, and how they are labeled. For example, the Field Museum (a natural history museum) in Chicago has a spectacular collection of Native American totem poles, masks, and so on from northwest coast cultures. Why aren't they in the Art Institute of Chicago, a nearby art museum? Why is Horatio Greenough's sculpture of George Washington in the history section of the Smithsonian complex in Washington, D.C., rather than in the art section? No doubt there are similar examples of categorization in your local museum that can be used to start the discussions.

As students look at artifacts from the past, they can speculate about how people living in the year 2500 will view the artifacts of our culture. Will they be able to understand what was valued in our western society? What behaviors will they consider characteristic of our dominant culture? How might objects be classified? Might classification be by function, material, the social class of the owner, or other criteria? How might future anthropologists categorize our mass-produced objects? How might the form or function of an Evian water bottle be analyzed (assuming that the bottle is discovered intact)? Which objects from our culture will be considered historical artifacts, and which will be considered art?

Students should continually think of alternative ways to categorize objects and artworks. It may be fruitful to divide students into small groups, then bring them together as a large group to share ideas, then reconvene in smaller groups.

Back at school, the students and the instructor might have a brainstorming session about possible themes for an installation of their own, to reconstruct historical or cultural ideas. The key to meaning, as students will have discovered by now, is in the placement, grouping, and labeling of the exhibition, all of which should be other than what is expected. One possibility is to have students bring objects from home that somehow represent their identities: objects that have personal, familial, ethnic, cultural, or social significance; objects that the students see as indicating membership in a group. The objects, when they are placed together and discussed, will suggest groupings and maybe even give a new direction to themes already discussed.

To start the discussion of grouping, students might decide cooperatively which of the objects would be traditionally placed in an art museum and which would go into a history museum. To achieve the goal of inclusion and democratic ideals, how would the items be grouped? How would they be grouped to achieve *exclusion?*

When students have agreed on a theme, and on the consequent content and grouping, they should start working on the installation. Aesthetics should be addressed at this point. For the installation to be art, must the items be arranged aesthetically? If so, what's the best arrangement? Why? Do we want to enhance the effect by using colored backing cloth or paper, or a display case, or the like? This aspect of the installation should be addressed as students move and arrange the items.

The final stage is documenting the exhibition by taking photographs. The photographs and an accompanying description of the process and the (social) point of the exhibit, as well as the nature of installation art in general, should be displayed with the installation.

EVALUATION

Formative evaluation is built into this unit. Students' work will have been assessed by the instructor—and students will assess their own and one another's work—throughout the process of understanding Wilson's work and his challenge to stereotyping, analyzing the categorization done by museums and other institutions, discussing these topics, mining a museum, and developing an installation.

For a summative evaluation, following completion of the installation, students could be asked to write individual critical essays, which might be structured as follows:

1. Who is Fred Wilson, and what does he do?

2. Describe the installation you have made. What is its point? How did you go about making this point? What were your aesthetic considerations? Is it a good piece? Why or why not?

3. Describe history as you understand it—the way it comes into being and is preserved, as well as the role of social institutions such as museums in this process.

EXTENSION OR ALTERNATIVE

Fred Wilson creates studio work as well as installations. Another artist who challenges stereotypes of African Americans, usually in a humorous way, is the painter Robert Colescott. In his work of the 1970s and 1980s Colescott invited the viewer to take a new perspective on race relations and racial stereotypes. To accomplish this, Colescott presented his own versions of famous paintings—for example, he showed George Washington (as George Washington Carver) crossing the Delaware in a boat full of mammies, banjo players, and other stereotypes. (see Figure 7.2 on page 118, Colescott's *Washington Crossing the Delaware.)* In another work, called *Eat Dem Taters,* he showed Van Gogh's potato eaters as antebellum slaves.

Colescott studied with Fernand Léger in the late 1940s, began to focus his drawings on African American stereotypes in the 1970s, and continues to present stereotypes in a broader sense today. He uses images from popular culture in addition to making racial parodies of masterpieces of art, and his work is both funny and shocking. It appeals to viewers with humor, then shakes their comfortable social foundations.

After examining the studio work of both Fred Wilson and Robert Colescott, students could make paintings, drawings, or sculptures that expose social stereotypes.

FURTHER READING

Banks, J., & Banks, C. (2001). *Multicultural education: Issues and perspectives.* New York: Wiley.

Barrett, T. (1994). *Criticizing art: Understanding the contemporary.* Mountain View, CA: Mayfield.

Colescott (Robert). *http://www.artcyclopedia.com/artists/colescott_robert.html*

Colescott (Robert). Video and overview of work. *http://imageexchange.com/videos/lsvideo/4113.shtml*

Corin, L. (Ed.). (1994). *Mining the museum: Installation by Fred Wilson.* New York: New Press.

UCSF Diversity Project Homesite. http://www.ucsf.edu/daybreak/1999/06/24_wilson.html (good overview of Fred Wilson's recent work).

Wilson, F. (1993). *Mining the museum 2, Discipline-based art education and cultural diversity.* Seminar proceedings, August 6–9, 1992, Austin, TX. Santa Monica, CA: J. Paul Getty Trust.

14

A Sense of Self and of Community—Exploring Issues of Identity through the Artwork of Charnelle Holloway

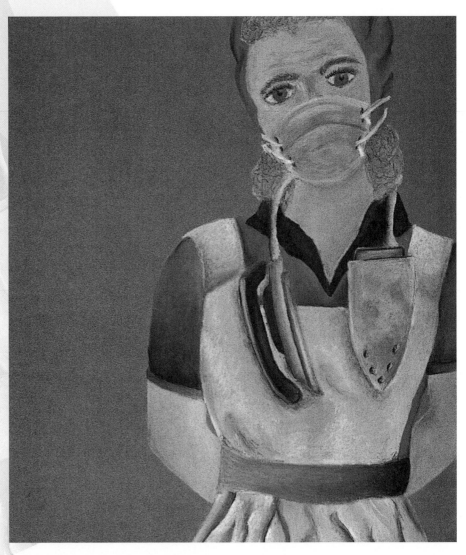

Changing Roles, Yasmin Zaki, Druid Hills High School, DeKalb County Schools, Decatur, GA. Betsy Epps, Art Teacher. *Yasmin researched the changing roles of women during World War II and used the image of the nurse to represent the new challenges and accomplishments of women during this period. The unplugged irons around the nurse's neck symbolize women's replacement of domestic tasks with careers.*

OVERVIEW

In this lesson students will discuss how meaning and identity are constructed through symbol and metaphor, the relationship of function to design, and the impact of design on popular culture. Students will first explore the artist's role in the design of objects, such as jewelry, used in daily life. They will discuss the cultural and historical associations of the terms *art* and *craft* and how those terms may be associated with objects in the market and in art museums. Next, students will look at metalwork by Charnelle Holloway and consider the artist's technical skills as well as her use of cultural symbols and metaphor to create feminist messages. Holloway's work reflects concern for everyone in the community. Traditional gender roles and stereotypical images of women and men will be discussed.

KEY CONCEPTS

The key ideas for this unit are

1. Artists may choose to emphasize their technical skills as well as a message in their work.

2. Identity involves issues of gender and biological and social roles.

3. Building a functional community requires all its members to take personal responsibility.

4. As discussed in other lessons, artists do not live in a vacuum; they often create art in response to daily events or social concerns.

5. Function, craft, innovation, and meaning influence the design of objects used every day.

CONTENT BASE

Charnelle Holloway was born in Atlanta, Georgia, in 1957 to a family that encouraged participation in the arts.* Her mother, Jenelsie Holloway, was a painter and taught art at Spelman College; she encouraged Holloway's efforts in music and the visual arts. As a child, Holloway spent many hours playing and attending artistic events on the Spelman College campus, so when she accepted a teaching position there in 1987 she felt very much at home.

As an artist Holloway was attracted by three-dimensional media and enjoyed the ongoing debate about whether jewelry is an art or a craft. Initially, she preferred

http://www.mhhe.com/artforlife1
Visit our website to learn more about Charnelle Holloway and other feminist artists and ideas.

---

*Information here is based on a presentation by Charnelle Holloway at Spelman College and on personal communication, June 2002, Atlanta, Georgia.

simple, elegant geometric shapes in her work, which was influenced by Art Deco. Today her work is still elegant but now it has characteristics of traditional African art, the black community, relationships, and spirituality.

Holloway has said:

> I have never really considered myself a feminist artist, though today I am often called that. I guess I just began to use my artwork to respond to issues I encountered in life that need to be addressed. It just happened that particular events occurred that moved me to respond from a feminist perspective. In the early 1990s I was tremendously affected by the AIDS epidemic. In the African American community I felt women were shouldering an unnecessary burden for that health issue, so I responded by creating a chastity belt for men, constructed from brass. Although this is sometimes viewed as a humorous solution, it was my way of stating that AIDS is everyone's problem. I wanted to increase awareness that everyone has to take responsibility for his or her own actions.

Holloway considers her three-dimensional artwork as a concrete, tangible way to participate in the world. Her aim is to combine her technical expertise in metalwork with a personal and creative statement as a visual artist. *Heirloom Box (Forget Me Not)*, for instance, is a very personal silver box, containing a San-cofa symbol from Ghana that means "Go back and fetch it." Holloway suggests that we go back to our past in order to go to our future. In this box she has included special objects from her family, such as a comb, photographs, and lima beans. The viewer sees these objects through a Plexiglas lid.

Holloway's personal experience and her heritage as an African American woman merge in *Fertility Belt for the Career Woman*. In this mixed-media belt, Holloway combines traditional African symbols as a tribute to women who postpone childbearing to pursue other commitments. The traditional fertility figure used by the Ashanti of Ghana, *akua ba,* was constructed from repoussé sterling silver, combined with bronze and other metals. African symbols such as *adinkra* (symbols stamped on African cloth) are also incorporated. Two adinkra are included in the belt: one symbol is *nkyinkymiie* (twistings), which represents toughness, adaptability, devotion to service, and the ability to withstand hardship; the second is *nyame biribi wo soro,* standing for hope and aspiration. The belt also has cowry shells, symbols of fertility that were once used as currency in Africa.

In *Altar for Abused Women*, Holloway responds to cases of domestic violence that resulted in the deaths of two coworkers. A knife with a gilded handle, encased in Plexiglas, represents a ceremonial knife of justice. The candles on each side of the altar represent a vigil for victims of abuse. Holloway has remarked that in one case, she had no idea that the woman was being abused. The installation expressed her own indignation at social attitudes that prevent women from speaking out and saving themselves. In the other case, an abused woman resorted to violence in self-defense. Along with the altar, the installation includes three wooden boxes bearing statements related to abuse. For example, on the largest box is printed, "For the hand or foot that hit or kicked me." On another box, which appears to have money sticking out of each side, there are the words, "For the hit man to avenge my death." (See Color Plate 17, Charnelle Holloway, *Altar for Abused Women.*)

Holloway expresses concern for spiritual and intellectual choices that can enhance or destroy life in an entire community. One example is *Trinity,* a series of small sculptures created from repoussé metalwork. The sculptures have slightly different but closely related features, forming the trinity: *One Who Measures, One Who Spins, One Who Cuts.* These three female spirits appear in the mythology of various cultures, sometimes as witches but more often as three fates. According to Holloway, "The three fates traditionally represent three female spirits which appear at the beginning of each individual's life. They represent different aspects of faith and have different personalities and duties. One spirit spins and weaves the thread of life, another measures the threads, determining the way you will go

http://www.mhhe.com/artforlife1
Visit our website for links to information about Akan cultural symbols, including textiles and jewelry from Ghana.

in your life, and the third cuts the threads of life when you leave." Each figure is freestanding. Metallic fabric is used for the clothing, curled wire for the hair, repoussé for the faces, and casting for the hands and feet. Such figures have been found in many cultures for thousands of years and are often used in ceremonies, rituals, worship, or play. (Dolls in our own culture, by contrast, are typically considered only toys.)

Holloway has created symbolic jewelry for celebrities such as Maya Angelou and Oprah Winfrey. A gold brooch made for Maya Angelou incorporates a symbolic bird flying from a cage, in reference to Angelou's well-known work *I Know Why the Caged Bird Sings*. A brooch made for Oprah Winfrey uses the adinkra symbol *bi inka bi,* "bite not each other."

Holloway is highly skilled and attentive to detail, but the outstanding characteristic of her work is perhaps her identity as an African American woman. She believes in women's collective ability to change conditions in the world. She sees women today as often providing a type of underground support for one another in a western society that is still primarily patriarchal. She continues to respond to events around her, express her heritage, and remind others of their own. The work of Charnelle Holloway challenges us to give something back to the community and make the world better for others.

Objectives

1. Students will examine metalwork by Charnelle Holloway and discuss its functions and the messages it expresses through symbols and metaphors.

2. Students will discuss the differences between the conventional terms *art* and *craft.* They will evaluate mass-produced commercial products by applying criteria such as function, message, and craft. They will also compare the role of the commercial product designer with that of Charnelle Holloway. In what ways are their goals alike and different?

3. Students will design a work that has a specific traditional function but also conveys meaning through symbols or a particular form. They will consider what attributes contribute to successful functioning in the design of their work. They will also do research on symbols from a specific culture and use metaphor to create meaning. They will evaluate their work on the basis of craft, functional design, and message.

4. Students will create a mask that depicts their identity as they think the external world sees them and as they view themselves.

Resources

A variety of mass-produced functional objects that carry a message in form and content should be provided. Materials are needed for constructing a functional piece of jewelry in some chosen medium or media. (Or provide students with found materials for a lesson on recycling, or a choice of materials and processes.) Provide reference sources for metalwork and jewelry from other cultures and for symbols, legends, and myths (or fairy tales) from our culture or others. Also provide reference sources for information on social issues such as domestic abuse, equal opportunities in employment, child care, women's health, and aging.

Procedure

As an introduction to this unit, the instructor will ask students to explain the difference between art and craft. Since *art* and *craft* are terms used in popular culture, the teacher may wish to list attributes of both on the board. Looking at work from

FIGURE 14.1 *Charnelle Holloway,* gold brooch created for Maya Angelou. *Holloway constructed a symbolic reference to Angelou's well-known book,* I Know Why the Caged Bird Sings, *in this exquisite personalized jewelry.*

http://www.mhhe.com/artforlife1
Link to more information about Maya Angelou at our website.

traditional cultures may make students aware that much of what has been considered craft in western culture is considered art in many other cultures. In Navajo culture, as in many other traditional societies, the word *art* does not exist, yet objects produced for daily or ceremonial use are aesthetically pleasing and may fit within the western concept of art. At the same time, these objects meet the functional criteria that usually define craft. Since the modernist period, self-expression and conceptual originality have often been used in the West as criteria of artistic merit, but art and craft are not mutually exclusive. Some artists concentrate on technique and skill; others do not. Similarly, some craftspeople design utilitarian objects that communicate conceptual meaning beyond function. Today the boundary between art and craft is blurred, but owing to the use of both terms in popular culture, and the specific creative behaviors associated with each term, misconceptions persist.

After looking at metalwork from ancient peoples such as the Egyptians, Etruscans, and Syrians, students may consider artifacts that have decorative, ceremonial, and functional attributes. The identity of artisans of ancient cultures is rarely known. Modern western sculptors such as Auguste Rodin and David Smith have been recognized for their artistic use of metal, but modern jewelers such as Robert Ebendorf, Arline Fisch, Albert Paley, Eleanor Moty, J. Fred Woell, and Olaf Skoogfors are rarely mentioned in traditional art history texts. This omission suggests that the importance of small-scale metalwork remains, as in the past, unrecognized in the world of art.

Jewelry, perhaps even more than most visual objects, reflects the time and place in which it is created, because jewelry is often designed for function and for purposes of identity. Symbols used in jewelry often reveal the gender, age, and interests of the wearer. In both traditional and contemporary societies jewelry denotes wealth and social status. A comparison of the decorative adornments worn in Kuba, Navajo, many Asian, and western cultures suggests that bodily adornment, including jewelry, is a universal practice. The teacher will display images from other cultures along with images of western movie actors and rock stars, politicians, royal families, and classmates all wearing jewelry. As students consider the images, the following questions can be asked: Do these examples of jewelry differ? What image does each person convey? Is jewelry, along with clothing, hairstyle, and makeup, part of a person's projected image? Is image the same thing as identity? The teacher will ask students to discuss these concepts.

Looking at Art and Visual Artifacts

The jewelry of Charnelle Holloway offers students an opportunity to examine individual pieces custom-made for specific people. Most students know about Oprah Winfrey's career, and her influence as a highly successful African American woman. As they look at the brooch created for Winfrey by Holloway, the instructor will explain that the adinkra (symbol) incorporated into it represents an old saying, "Bite not each other." The instructor will ask: Why do you think Holloway chose this symbol to use in the piece? Do you think this is an appropriate symbol for Winfrey? Why or why not? Consider any other symbols that students might know. Does everyone understand these symbols? Why or why not? Students will discuss the use of symbols and how membership in a particular group may be necessary to identify certain symbols: national symbols, symbols for roads and maps, school mascots, religious symbols, and symbols of clubs. Sometimes jewelry identifies its wearer as a member of a particular group (examples are the Christian cross and school or national emblems). The teacher will then ask students to discuss whether such symbolic jewelry is important and why.

The second piece of jewelry by Holloway was created for Maya Angelou. It incorporates a stylized bird flying from a cage, a symbolic reference to Angelou's *I Know Why the Caged Bird Sings.* Discuss whether or not the jewelry represents this literary work well. Students might also discuss the role images play in learning and memory. At this point students might be asked to find a poem or story that they would like to represent symbolically in a jewelry design.

Depending on the nature of the class, students may simply complete a sketch or design as the studio component of this lesson or use the design to actually construct a piece of jewelry from metal, clay, or laminated paper. In designing jewelry, the functional aspects of each piece should be considered, such as its weight, edges that might poke or scratch the wearer, and the size and type of pins or bindings required for comfort, safety, and durability. The type of material used in construction is also an important consideration. Sometimes designs are very difficult to execute in the materials available. Students will discuss the process of designing a functional object and the factors they think are important. Once students have sketched or created their jewelry, they might consider how they would develop this piece of jewelry into a collection or body of work for distribution. For whom would they design jewelry? How would the jewelry be marketed? Would they choose mass distribution or would they prefer to create individual pieces for specific buyers? How is the work of a designer of objects for mass distribution different from that of an artist like Charnelle Holloway?

A look through a department store, an automobile magazine, and ads for real estate will help students consider the vast number of objects and structures in our society that are continually changed and updated by designers. The teacher will ask students to consider reasons that many designs, such as those for automobiles, continually evolve. (Consider new technology, consumers' demands, economics, planned obsolescence, and style.) Such items suggest a design-conscious consumer. Students will discuss how they determine if an object is well designed or just well promoted in advertisements. They will consider the relationship between form and function. Is it important to understand the function of an object to appreciate its design? What factors do we associate with "good design"? Where do most of our ideas regarding design come from? Think of designers who have signature lines in department stores (for example Gucci, Calvin Klein, Michael Graves, and Martha Stewart). Beyond the designers' names, are their products unique? Ask again: Is there a difference in the design or appearance of their products, or is the difference in their advertising strategies? To get at an answer, the teacher might wish to have students do research in local stores. In their research notebooks, students verbally compare and contrast the products from a designer's line with products not from that line. Students also might sketch two or three items to depict the differences in styles among different lines of products. After the trip to the store, students should discuss their conclusions. (If students do not have convenient access to shopping areas, the instructor may provide catalogs and magazines.)

Students might then return to their own jewelry design and develop an advertising campaign for it as a style or line. Along with considering a market for their product, students will need to consider the materials they would use in mass production and the approximate cost of producing a single piece of jewelry. As students explore the process of transforming an artist's work into a mass-produced item, the teacher may point out the importance of careers related to art in the design of products, packaging, advertising, and marketing. An extension of this lesson could be research on careers in the arts, including visits to job sites.

Constructing Identity through Art

Charnelle Holloway does metalwork other than jewelry. In many of her works she constructs objects from metal and combines them with other materials to create installations with personal as well as social messages. The teacher will present background information about Holloway and show the following works: *Chastity Belt for Men, Heirloom Box, Fertility Belt for the Career Woman, Altar for Abused Women,* and *Women Trio* (or *Trinity*).

http://www.mhhe.com/artforlife1
Find pictures of these works on our website.

Students will examine Holloway's metalwork and discuss

1. The variety of intentions, materials, and themes in her work.

2. The use of symbols and metaphor to express identity.

3. The social issues Holloway addresses.

Questions and Topics for Research and Discussion

After showing the images, the teacher will remind students that Charnelle Holloway did not feel she was presenting a particularly feminist viewpoint. The teacher will lead a discussion based on the following questions: Does this body of work represent a feminist point of view? Why or why not? Could (would) a man create these or similar works? Do the metal figures in *Trinity* remind you of doll-like figures in other cultures? Remind students of examples of small sculptural figures found in different cultures (African, Native American, American). Students will discuss the variety of uses of such figures and consider the importance of play in western culture. For example, how are dolls regarded in western culture? Why are dolls a popular toy for girls? What roles do different dolls suggest for girls? Some dolls are called "action toys" and are promoted as toys for boys. How do advertising and marketing in our culture affect gender roles? How are gender roles perpetuated? Some adults in our culture collect dolls. What role do collections like this play in our culture? Can you think of any other mythical characters represented by feminine sculpture? Who are some of the mythical women depicted in painting? Have these images influenced our cultural view of women? In what ways? Where did our ideals about gender roles originate? Do different cultures have different gender roles or expectations? What are some of the differences?

What are some of the traditional stereotypical images women confront in the media and marketplace? (Examples include Snow White, the wicked witch, the sex goddess, the princess, Mother Earth, Supermom, and the dumb blonde.) How are girls affected by these female stereotypes? What about images of men? In American culture, do we perpetuate stereotypical images of men? (Examples include the white knight, prince, iron man, bad boy, superman, patriarch, and villain.) How are boys affected by stereotypical images of men? How can stereotypical images be avoided or dispelled? Are stereotypes harmful? Do stereotypes serve any useful purpose in our culture? Is an association with a gender role a positive or negative aspect of identity? Explain.

Making Art

After looking at and discussing Holloway's work, students will create an "identity mask." They will first look in newspapers and magazines to find images and articles that depict their gender in stereotypical ways. Students will discuss how such images and articles reinforce cultural expectations and roles. If students find images or articles that depict a gender-related social issue, they may want to discuss with the class how this issue relates to identity and if any stereotyping is involved. For example, is there evidence to support the contention that more women are victims of physical abuse than men? If so, why does that occur? Charnelle Holloway's work suggests that women sometimes strike back. How does the cycle of domestic abuse affect our society? Another issue addressed by Holloway is AIDS. We typically associate this disease with homosexual men, yet if we look at pictures of the AIDS quilt we see that this disease has taken the lives of many women and children (see Figure 2.1 on page 24). Why is Holloway's message of individual responsibility so important?

On one side of a plastic mask (coated with lubricant) students will first create a casting of the mask with papier-mâché, newspaper, or plaster gauze. After removing the cast mask from the mold, students will make a collage of images and words that they would like to project to the public, or the expectations that the external world conveys about their gender, on the outside of the mask. As in Holloway's artwork, race, class, and ethnicity may also affect expectations about gender roles. On the inside of the mask students will make a collage of words and images that represent some of their personal emotions, thoughts, hopes, or fears. Certain words and images related to identity may appear on both the inside and outside of the mask, but some students may want to emphasize the differences between social expectations and personal feelings. Students may add more paint—or found materials, such as wood, feathers, shells, or stones—to their masks on the inside and outside to elaborate on the image or mood created. The masks will be hung without names so that only the outside shows. Students will discuss differences and similarities among their masks from the external view. Later, the teacher will move and rehang the masks, when students are not present, so that only the back of each mask is displayed in a new location. Students will compare and contrast the backs of the masks. If students feel comfortable, they may remove their masks from the display and hold each mask so that both sides can be displayed and discussed. This discussion should lead to an examination of individual differences, both external and internal, important to dispelling stereotypical notions about identity. How do internal and external worlds define individual identity? Discuss what it means to construct identity.

EVALUATION

The instructor may develop studio criteria for the students' masks: for example, communication of a message or mood, craft, and elaboration of materials. Students may express their ideas about inner and outer worlds in discussions and by writing in their research notebooks. Topics for research introduced in this lesson include the following: images of women in art and advertising, cultural use of small sculptured figures, marketing of dolls in the West, gender roles, feminist art, and stereotyping. These and related themes may be explored in other artworks and research. Much has been written in feminist literature about the traditional portrayal of women in art from a masculine viewpoint. Doing research on the historical role of women in the arts will help students understand feminist issues and concerns. Discussing work by other well-known artists concerned with issues of identity (including Barbara Kruger, Cindy Sherman, Judy Chicago, Miriam Schapiro, Jenny Holzer, Elizabeth Murray, Lorna Simpson, Adrian Piper, Mary Kelly, Sherrie Levine, Betye Saar, and Emma Amos) will also broaden students' understanding of feminism.

FURTHER READING

Art: 21—Barbara Kruger. *http://www.pbs.org/art21/artists/kruger* (Biography and clips from the PBS show).

ArtsNet Minnesota: Inner Worlds—Betye Saar. *http://www.artsconnected.org/artsnetmn/inner/saar.html*

Betye Saar. *http:www.netropolitan.org/saar/saarmin.html*

Chadwick, W. (2002). *Women, art, and society* (3rd ed.). New York: Thames and Hudson.

Charnelle Holloway Biography. *www.wcenter.spelman.ed*

English, H. W., and Dormer, P. (1995). *Jewelry of our time: Art, ornament and obsession.* New York: Rizzoli International.

Internet Resources for Jewelry/Metalsmithing. *http://www.library.unisa.edu/au/internet/pathfind/jewellery.htm*

Raven, A., Langer, C., & Frueh, J. (Eds.). (1988). *Feminist art Criticism: An anthology.* New York: HarperCollins.

Robinson, J. T. (1999). *Bearing witness: Contemporary works by African American women artists.* New York: Spelman College and Rizzoli International.

15

A Sense of Self, of Place, and of Community— Art for Peace

Panama City, Florida, peace mural detail. *This mural, executed within two months after the 9/11 tragedy, is one of more than 70 in the* Guernica Children's Peace Mural Project. *The child whose poem is used here lives in the inner city and knows the effects of violence firsthand. Project directors: Michelle Creel and Jerry Pilcher.*

OVERVIEW

The focus of this unit is art for peace through community-centered, collectively developed works of art, specifically **community murals** and **mandalas.** The goal is to give students, through collective problem solving, a sense of themselves and by extension a sense of others as members of a group, working for world peace. In working with others toward a common aesthetic goal, students may come to understand and respect one another's similar and different values, mores, and sensibilities.

KEY CONCEPTS

The primary concepts are collective identity and group problem solving through aesthetic means; the goal of balance, security, and well-being for individuals and the group; and making art as a pattern for living and understanding life.

CONTENT BASE*

On August 6, 1945, at 8:15 A.M., the United States dropped an atomic bomb from a plane on Hiroshima, Japan, instantly incinerating about 70,000 people; another 100,000 or so would die of the effects by the end of 1945. Three days later, another bomb was dropped on Nagasaki, killing another 40,000 people. Shortly thereafter, on August 14, Japan surrendered, ending World War II.

To commemorate the fiftieth anniversary of the bombing of Hiroshima and the end of World War II, Abe Toshifumi, a professor of art education in Osaka, with Art Japan, developed the idea of building a bridge of peace between the United States and Japan by helping children in these countries know each other not as foreigners or aliens but as fellow human beings with shared feelings, concerns, hopes, and fears. The children were to achieve this understanding by making murals and participating in workshops on human values. The larger goal was international peace. The first mural was painted in Tallahassee, Florida, and taken to Tokushima, Japan, where another mural was made in response. With support from the Art Japan Cultural Network, we decided to expand the project to every country of the world that we could involve.

This was the birth of the Guernica Children's Peace Mural Project (GCPMP), an idea that is still alive. In fact, in November 2001, two months after terrorists had destroyed the World Trade Center in New York, a display of sixty-seven peace murals opened on Kronplatz, a mountain in the Italian Alps. This exhibition included a mural painted in the United States after 9/11 and one made collectively, on-site, by

---

*Earlier versions of this section were published as T. Anderson (2002), Mandala: Constructing peace through art. *Art Education*, *55*(3), 33–39, and T. Anderson (1997), Art, education, and the bomb: Reflections on an international children's peace mural project. *Journal of Social Theory and Art Education*, *17*, 71–97.

Palestinian and Israeli children. The premise of the GCPMP project was and is that peace depends on intercultural understanding and that one way to approach this understanding is through art.

Concurrently with the Guernica Peace Mural Project, another initiative for peace through art gained momentum, especially in the United States, as exemplified by an event at Florida State University in the spring of 2001. Ten Tibetan Buddhist monks from the Drepung Gomang Monastery conducted chants and performances and created and ritually dismantled a sand mandala. This project seeks local balance and world peace through making art and through ritual. Accordingly, Tibetan monks from a number of monasteries toured the United States and elsewhere to make people aware of the Chinese invasion of Tibet and to promote world peace in general. This is the Mandala Peace Project.

To understand how these projects promote peace and how the concepts involved can be used in teaching and learning for life, it is useful to consider the processes and products.

http://www.mhhe.com/artforlife1
Visit our website to link to GCPMP and Mandala Peace Project sites.

The Guernica Peace Mural Project

We'll start with the Guernica Children's Peace Mural Project. To achieve peace, GCPMP is developing and exchanging children's peace murals. Each mural is on a canvas the size of Picasso's famous antiwar painting *Guernica* (about 25½ by 12 feet). These children's murals are developed in workshops during which the concept of peace is explored, not only in abstract terms but also in concrete, specific terms. Children are asked to envision how they can promote peace as citizens of their own country and the world, in a locally and culturally specific manner. When a mural is completed, it joins the group and is sent to the next site, where it is seen by children who execute a mural in response.

Goals and Processes   The children and sponsors of this project are of different cultural backgrounds, but the organizing committee believes that certain human concerns are universal and that one such concern is to live safely in peace. Since art is an instrument of culture, the children of different countries express these univer-

FIGURE 15.1   Pablo Picasso, *Guernica*, 1937, approximately 25 feet 6 inches by 12 feet. *The Guernica Children's Peace Mural Project takes inspiration from Picasso's 1937 antiwar masterpiece.*

FIGURE 15.2   Peace mural opening, Tallahassee, Florida. *The premise of
this project is that peace rests on intercultural understanding and that aesthetic expression through art can be a vehicle for this
understanding.*

sal concerns differently; the power of the project lies in this unity of purpose and
diversity in approaches. If children examine the paths they take to reach common
goals, it is our hope that their understanding, tolerance, and respect for one another
will grow.

Making murals seemed a natural activity for this project, particularly because
community murals emphasize group identity and cooperative problem solving.
Usually, there is an adult team consisting of an artistic director, an organizer of fi-
nances and logistics, and others, as well as the children's team, which varies in age
and makeup from site to site.

Workshops often begin with a presentation of a core concept related to peace,
or with brainstorming about what peace means and how it can be attained. At some
point, preferably through cooperative interaction between the children and the
adults, the theme of the mural begins to crystallize. Usually, everyone comes to
realize that peace can be achieved only if we first understand each other. For example, in making the mural in Tallahassee we asked ourselves what we could do to
help the children of Japan understand who we are and what we like. We decided
that we could send symbolic gifts to the children in Japan, and we decided to paint
portraits of ourselves holding the things we care about most. These would be our
gifts of peace. *A Gift of Peace* became our theme and title.

In another discussion we generated a list of possible gifts that would suggest
the American character, particularly through objects and activities valued by the
children. Further discussion centered on how we would get these gifts to Japan.
One adult proposed that the children show themselves flying, as in the book *Tar
Beach* by Faith Ringgold. Many of the children knew this story and agreed enthusi-
astically. They then depicted themselves taking off and flying, carrying gifts that included peace signs, fried chicken and french fries, a chocolate milk shake,
skateboards, a rap CD, kittens, American flags, sports equipment, Nike tennis
shoes, and a novel about the Sweet Valley twins.

We executed the mural over the course of about a week. During this time children with special needs visited the gallery workspace, engaging in making the
mural and in other activities. Again inspired by Faith Ringgold, the adults decided
to use her quilting device to give everyone equal access to the mural while still
maintaining the high aesthetic quality of the whole. Thus each special arts student
was given a square of his or her own to paint as a border to the mural. Many

special arts students were not able to grasp or execute the concept of the mural but nevertheless painted freely in their designated squares, with help from adults or other children.

The Tokushima workshop, in Japan, differed from the Tallahassee workshop in interesting ways. The team in Tallahassee started with only a minimal concept and made many decisions about content, form, and strategy spontaneously during the course of the week. As a result, the final form and content were not completely known until the mural was done. In Tokushima, the process was more formal and deliberate. The adult team there met frequently, and at some length, every day before the children came and after they left, allowing everyone to speak and reaching consensus on all significant aspects of the project before any action was taken. The children were also integrated into the process of reaching a consensus and making decisions in a much more formal way than in Tallahassee. In the workshop at Tokushima, unlike the workshop in Tallahassee, formal sessions began and ended each studio experience, and in these sessions the children were asked to express their opinions about what the content of the mural should be and how that content should be expressed. In short, there was a formal attempt to reach a consensus at each stage of the process. (See Color Plate 18, the Tokushima Peace Mural).

In Japan, the structural components were also formulated in advance. Very little, if anything, was left to chance. Spontaneous decisions about major issues during the process seem to have been considered undesirable, even unacceptable. The mural team did not welcome surprises regarding form or process. Innovation evidently required group consensus. The adults and children in Tokushima seemed more conscious than the Tallahassee team of how one change affects the whole.

Seeing the Process as Culture   At the risk of resorting to stereotypes, we might say that the most obvious difference between these two murals is the Japanese collectivist sensibility versus the American individualist sensibility. In the mural made in Tallahassee, each representation was chosen and executed by an individual and represents that person's style and level of skill or talent. In fact, the theme itself is also individualistic. The idea of depicting our own favorite items in order to help someone else understand us may even seem egotistical to cultures outside North America. The individual portraits dominate the image and are all separate and distinct, standing out starkly against an almost empty background. Yet collectively the portraits define a group sensibility because each contributes to the overall theme and composition. This mural has the spirit of individuals cooperating within a loose structure.

The Japanese mural reflects the idea of convention as a highly desirable quality, the result of doing something correctly, according to form. The ultimate social authority for the Japanese is not the individual but the group. One of the most important concepts in Japanese culture is *shikata*, or *kata* for short: literally, "way of doing things." It refers to proper form and order, with an emphasis on people serving and supporting one another, particularly within ancient hierarchical social structures. Over the centuries, doing things the right way, following various *kata* as guides, has been sanctified, ritualized, and equated with morality. Being "out of *kata*" is a moral offense against society. Form thus becomes ethics, and policies (ways of doing things) become principles. This beautifying of the body and the heart through correct action also signifies mutual dependence *(amae)* in Japanese society and education, as opposed to the western ideal of independence. The most highly prized qualities for students to develop are compliance and harmonious behavior.

The Japanese children's mural reflects these values. It might be overstating the case to say that there is greater uniformity in the Japanese mural; still, the whole does appear more homogeneous, more of an expression of one collective mind, than the American mural. (See if you agree by comparing Color Plate 18 and Figure 15.2 on page 217.) The theme and the treatment of it are collective rather than individual. The imagery and composition conform to *shikata*. There are no sloppy passages; there is a uniformly high level of skill in composition and rendering; there are multiple, mutually reinforcing centers of interest, none of which dominates the others; and there is appropriately conventional imagery that will not call attention to itself above other elements. There is little or no individual portraiture; each figure is generic, proportionally small, and in a sense stereotypical—that is, conventional and standardized.

To repeat: the point of the Guernica Peace Mural Project is human understanding through art. The process is at least as important as the product, because the participants learn to cooperate with their own local team and with the international team, serving a larger goal in individual, local ways. From this they learn that we are all the same and all different, and that our differences must be respected and even embraced.

We are not all alike, but we are all people, and we do have some universal impulses, although these impulses take different forms in different circumstances and different cultures. Form is significant because it gives us access to the inner life of others, or shuts us out. Understanding another culture through making and examining art may thus be a bridge to world peace.

The Mandala Peace Project

The idea that the world we inhabit may be actually constructed by what we know is also central to the Mandala Peace Project. Richard Anderson (1990) asks, "What if other people . . . live in different realities, traverse different worlds, and believe that the universe around them (and within them) is fundamentally different from the world I inhabit?" (p. 95). This idea of a constructed—not a given—world is central to the purposes and forms of healing mandalas.

Healing mandalas are created by a number of cultures, perhaps most notably by Tibetan Buddhists and by the Navajo people in North America. These mandalas are believed to restore or protect individuals or the environment. They are temporary works, composed of sand, grain, pollen, flower dust, and other natural, usually granular materials. Chanting, prayers, and blessings accompany both the Tibetan and the Navajo mandalas during the process of composition, the healing ceremony itself, and the dismantling. The Navajo ceremony, in fact, is called a "sing."

The Navajo sings are designed to help someone who is ill or unfortunate, or to maintain health or balance. A sing lasts nine days and consists of all-night singing, daytime prayers, chants that reiterate creation stories, and ritual cleansing. During sings the Navajo make sand paintings appropriate to the healing that is sought. The goal of a sing is to restore balance and beauty, or *hozho*, to the universe so as to put things right for the afflicted person. In Navajo cosmology, thought and speech brought the world into being; thus thought and speech—through the sings, for example—actually affect the material as well as the spiritual world, bringing it back to order and balance. Sings in a sense re-create the world and restore it to its natural condition through ceremony and the production of art. The goal is to walk in beauty. It's this process, not the art product, that counts. Artful living is said to keep people healthy and keep the world harmonious.

Rituals of Peace: Practicing Correct Thought and Action   Tibetan Buddhism has similar ideas about balance and harmony through correct thought and speech and ceremony or ritual. Although outsiders cannot understand rituals at an emic or intrinsic level, certain aspects of the process and forms can be understood and used by outsiders in their own practices—in this case, in art for life.

The first aspect is the idea of ritual as a way to understand, value, keep, and pass on our culture and our humanity. The development of mandalas by the Navajo and the Tibetan Buddhists involves ritual as a sort of social glue that holds people together. Outsiders may not understand the intricate connections among forms, beliefs, and processes; but we can, with some effort, understand the world-making function of art in the Navajo and Tibetan cultures.

One of the most important ways we learn is by going through the processes others go through, imitating or copying them. A fundamental premise of the Japanese *shikata* is that inner order (the individual heart) and outer order (the cosmos) are connected through appropriate form or actions on the part of the individual. This idea is central to many Asian and some North American cultures and to the construction of mandalas. The mandala and the ceremony are inseparable.

The Way of the Tibetan Mandala Ceremony   The "way" of the Tibetan Buddhist mandala consists of eight steps (Arguelles & Arguelles, 1985). Step 1 is purification, which usually consists of cleansing and purging the body of toxic elements, as through fasting, so that consciousness is not bogged down by bodily demands. Fasting is also conducive to stimulating and heightening the senses and to facilitating visions, as Jesus, Buddha, and many Native Americans all believed.

Step 2 is meditation. The idea is that outward-flowing energies are turned inward to achieve a quiet center. Anyone who has successfully thrown a pot on a potter's wheel will understand this principle. The hardest part, especially for the beginner, is getting it centered, which involves understanding that the pot's center comes from your own.

Step 3 is the creation of an inner organized field pattern called orientation. Only through orientation—for example, orienting oneself to the rising sun—can one understand the larger field, or the cardinal points. Orientation takes different forms in different cultures; two examples are the censer in Catholic churches and praying toward Mecca in Muslim mosques. In Native American cultures, the six cardinal directions—east, west, north, south, above, and below—are each significant. Each has its own powers, represented by its own colors and imagery within the circle of the sand painting. In the mandala process of both the Native Americans and the Tibetan Buddhists, orientation is usually connected with chanting, prayer, singing, dancing, burning incense, and sometimes ritually eating and drinking, in which the person or earthly phenomenon to be healed is somehow represented in the center. The orientation ceremony is usually presided over or conducted by a priest or healer. The purpose is to bring all who participate and all their energies into psychic harmony.

Step 4 is the actual construction of the mandala. There are two basic types of mandalas: one is meant to transmute demonic forces; the other is a cosmic fortress. The issue of balance addressed in the fortress mandala in Tallahassee was world peace and blessings for the community. It began with an opening ceremony in which ten monks, dressed in ceremonial orange robes and feather headdresses, consecrated the site and called forth the forces of goodness by chanting mantras, accompanied by brass horns, drums, and cymbals. Orienting themselves to the cardinal points on the compass, and using straightedges, strings, and tools for measuring circles, they drew an outline of the mandala. The monks then began to pour colored sand into place in the sections already drawn, using hollow brass tools that look like hand-rolled trumpets. They worked from the middle toward the edges, sitting on all four sides of the work. (An example of Tibetan monks working on a mandala may be seen in Color Plate 19, The Kalachakra.)

Subtleties began to appear in the process and the product. The mandala became three-dimensional in places, with mounds and ridges as high as an inch but only a small fraction of an inch wide. Subtle incising began to appear. The monks worked patiently and calmly, but with an intense focus and at a rapid pace. The process of developing the mandala took only four days because of time constraints.

The mandala was constructed grain by grain until it consisted of millions of grains of sand. The monks wore masks across their noses and mouths during the construction process so that a sudden sneeze or yawn would not destroy portions of the work. Yet people from the Tallahassee community came and went during this process, and although these spectators frequently stood very close, the monks never showed any concern for the fragile mandala. And they were right: the mandala wasn't disturbed in any way, even by a four-year-old who sidled up and sat practically in one monk's lap as he worked. Sometimes there were as many as a hundred people in the room while the monks worked, and yet nothing was ever hectic or loud. There was never a sense of "too much." The monks brought a calm center to the work and spread it through the gallery space. Even though some of the monks were more skilled than others, no monk was in charge of any given task or any area of the mandala. It was truly a collective, communal, nonhierarchical effort. And it felt like the construction of a world.

The construction was accompanied by rituals—the Tibetan equivalent of a sing—including a medicine Buddha *puja* seeking blessings for the local community, a *puja* for world peace, and a *milrepa* performance, all of which consisted of chanting accompanied by flutes, horns, and percussion instruments. The *milrepa* performance was also accompanied by food, drink, and blessings shared with all in attendance.

These ceremonies contributed to step 5 in the process: absorption. "Absorption involves the intense concentration and meditation upon the completion of the mandala so the contents of the work are transferred to and identified with the mind and body of the beholder" (Arguelles & Arguelles, 1985). Through absorption of the constructed consciousness represented in the structure of the mandala, consciousness can be achieved and balance and order attained.

After absorption comes step 6, ritual destruction. The point here is to achieve detachment from the work created. Since the essence of the work—its energy, its meaning—has already been absorbed by those who have engaged in it, and since the physical work has served its purpose of achieving inner balance and harmony, there is no further need for the physical work. Thus the mandala now must be symbolically deconstructed, a process that symbolizes detachment from the material world.

In Tallahassee, the head monk, wearing an elaborate feathered headdress and accompanied by ritual chanting, stood by the mandala. Then—eliciting an audible gasp from more than a hundred onlookers—he quickly but very deliberately pulled his thumb through the sand from the center to each of the four cardinal directions at the edge of the work. He then stood back and let the other monks take over. With small whisk brooms, they began to ritually sweep the colorful sands into piles on the mandala platform. As the sands were swept together, they turned gray.

After sweeping the sand and assorted flower petals into a ritual brass urn, the ten monks all arose and, still chanting and playing their horns and drums, carried the urn in procession out of the Florida State University gallery and into a waiting Chevy Suburban for a short trip to Wakulla Springs. It is considered auspicious to deposit material used in a mandala into running water, to disperse any negative energy it has collected. Many people followed to see the sand deposited in the huge springs, which are the source of a short, broad river flowing into the Gulf of Mexico. The monks seemed to feel that Wakulla Springs was a very auspicious place to deposit the remains of the mandala.

The ritual was over. But that wasn't the end of the mandala process. There are in fact two more steps. Unwittingly, a number of onlookers performed the next step simply by staying on at the diving tower to look into the water, watch the flower petals float downstream, and think about what had happened and what it meant to them. That was step 7: reintegration. It is an intuitive attempt to attain wholeness, to walk in beauty, as the Navajo would say, to become attuned to the greater rhythm and forces of the universe.

Finally, there is step 8: actualization. The whole mandala process is really just a prelude to actualization. The goal is to renew and give energy to our life force, to bring order from chaos, to understand and accept that both order and chaos are within us and are part of our being in the universe. The whole mandala process is simply to remind us of and give us a guide to the ongoing mandalic process in every living organism, so that we can attain truth, balance, and beauty in our everyday lives. This may sound exotic to westerners, but it really isn't very far from the classic western concept of the good, the true, and the beautiful as ideals for education.

OBJECTIVES

Following an examination of the Guernica Children's Peace Mural Project and the Mandala Peace Project, students will discuss what peace means to them and what practical artistic means they can take to foster peace. They will then collectively execute their idea in some medium. The key components are (1) research into war and peace and their causes and effects; (2) dialogue among students; (3) collective planning of a specific aesthetic process and product; and (4) presentation of the process, the product, or both to others, so as to contribute the goal of peace.

RESOURCES

http://www.mhhe.com/artforlife1
Visit our website to get resources on art and peace.

Resources for this unit depend on what the students decide to do. Sources for research can be found initially on the web link, which will lead to other sources. If you undertake the mural project, it is desirable to find muralists, critique their work, and if possible talk to them about issues, content, procedures, and problems. If you choose the mandala project, that sort of local resource may not be available.

The mandala can be executed on a square piece of Masonite or some other rigid material, using all sorts of (locally significant) materials: dirt, pennies, flower petals, colored sand. The materials for the mural depend on location to some extent, but they may include materials for cleaning the wall, primer, good-quality acrylic paint (exterior grade if you're painting outdoors), ladders, scaffolding, rags, brushes, composing materials for the model (such as pencils, watercolors, and white paper), and transfer tools for getting the model onto the wall. An opaque projector or overhead projector works well for this. If you construct a sculpture, prepare a performance, or select some other project, of course other materials will be required.

PROCEDURE

As noted under Objectives, after an examination of the Guernica Children's Peace Mural Project and the Mandala Peace Project, students can be asked to discuss what peace means to them and how they might want to address it collectively. Students are not limited to making mandalas or community murals and in fact may choose a performance, a sculpture, or some other form and process. However, to give a sense of the spirit of this project, a detailed description of the Mandala Peace Project procedure in one art education class follows.

The Mandala Approach

If students decide on the mandala, the procedures can follow from the eight steps described earlier. In our experience, it has been a bit of a stretch to get western students, especially older students, involved in some of the ideas and practices of the mandala project, such as the purification ritual. Still, they may rise to the occasion, so don't preclude that possibility. You may want to start simply by centering yourselves, sitting quietly in a circle to ponder what you are about to do.

Next, you will get a practical sense of what making a mandala is meant to achieve: something instrumental and concrete in the world, created by aesthetic means. With that in mind, brainstorming and deciding on an issue will follow.

Whatever the issue—environmental degradation or a social problem, for instance—it should be considered on a local level, and specifically rather than in the abstract. Consider the idea that everything is connected: the social and the environmental, the social and the psychological, the practical and the spiritual. You might ask how we can learn to trust each other to address the common good. How can we integrate our individual desires so as to address important issues?

The next stage, construction, could begin with students reflecting on their understanding of and commitment to the issue chosen and selecting material that reflects their concerns to contribute to the mandala. Again, the material should reflect the issue in a very specific, nonabstract way. For example, in the mandala project designed to bring social and ecological balance to the (red clay) hills of northern Florida, one student returned unneeded red clay pots to clay powder with a hammer and used the powder for the mandala. The group will not accept everyone's ideas uncritically, and the nature of the group process of negotiation and compromise will become clear to all. For example, another student in the same mandala project picked flowers from the grounds of the student union to add to the mix, but after group discussion decided that they'd be bad energy—learning something about herself and ecological and social responsibility in the process. In the discussions, a safe space should be made for everyone's ideas, and the comments should not become judgmental.

Cooperation and compromise are also important in designing and making the mandala itself, which should be designed to achieve communal ends. It is important to establish trust and common goals. As barriers between individuals break down, not only ideas but materials will be freely asked for and offered throughout the group, so that eventually the beans or pebbles or pennies brought by one will be used by nearly everyone.

Absorption (step 5) might consist of sitting in a circle, reflecting, and sharing. Then comes ritual destruction (step 6), which is critically important to the mandala process but surprisingly difficult psychologically. You'll find you've grown very attached to your creation, but letting go is necessary. Final reflection and integration will focus on letting go as well as on the connection of the process to the issue chosen. Among the insights that may be gained are that the process is as much about learning others' values and beliefs as about art. There may also be insights regarding the energy collected and released in the mandala and its power to change one's attitude from "I and mine" to "we and ours."

FIGURE 15.3 Pam Poucher works on the Students' Mandala at Florida State University. *An attitude of respect for the process and for local issues, concerns, and materials rose from developing this mandala centered on constructing* Balance in the Red Hills of North Florida.

The Community Mural Approach

The key factor in painting community murals is that they are communal and cooperative in content, in style, and as a process. Community murals in the school setting are an excellent way to express a common concern so as to facilitate cooperative learning and community spirit, which are both steps on the path to peace.

The mural project has many of the same components as the mandala project. A good way to start research is to critique some community murals, such as those of the Guernica Peace Project or other murals found on the web link. Ideally, you can look at local murals and perhaps talk to local muralists.

Next, there should be a discussion that reiterates the primary concerns of community murals—in particular, that they are collective expressions reflecting and conveying an issue or a sense of community. They are presenting a belief or advocating something like fairness, justice, or equality, or some other component of peace. Also, community murals are public—not private—art. This fact has implications for procedure, content, and style. The murals go beyond being merely decorative or pretty; they tackle social and community issues, and the style and content should be acceptable to all members of the community, or at least to the vast majority.

Then ask what are some local issues and concerns that might be expressed in a community mural, and how such expression might help us understand each other and so contribute to peace. The first phase, usually, is brainstorming. The task is to discover what people in the school or community consider significant and how to express it in a manner they can relate to. Sometimes this comes easily—for example, if a community is facing obvious social or environmental issues that are at the forefront of most people's minds. Frequently, however, no theme is immediately obvious. In that case, serious brainstorming and research may be required. A homework assignment (news clippings, family concerns, or both) will be useful to stimulate discussion. Possible themes or subjects can be written on the chalkboard as they are discussed. A vote can then be taken, or the group may arrive at some informal agreement. Everyone's opinion should be heard and respected. Everyone needs to feel like a stakeholder.

Students should take most or all of the responsibility for finding an interesting, vital, doable theme. The teacher needs to facilitate this process, staying in the background but remembering that he or she is the primary organizer and has the final responsibility for a suitable mural. Frequently there will be an impasse: the students will be unable to agree on a single subject or theme. In this case it's a good strategy to form smaller groups of students with similar interests to work on separate murals. Each teacher will also have to decide whether or not to shy away from controversial topics such as racism and environmental disputes—but controversial subjects can often make for the most interesting murals if they are approached sensitively and constructively.

Once a subject or theme has been determined, you must figure out how it will be approached. What attitude toward this topic will be expressed? The decision will determine the specific content of the mural and perhaps also the style. If the subject is somewhat controversial, the teacher as organizer should facilitate constructive ways to address it—for example, students could focus on ways to solve the problem rather than merely present it. Further discussion will ensue. It's important to remember in this discussion that, as public art, murals must conform to accepted public standards and taste.

Planning a community mural requires flexibility with regard to time and strategies. Depending on the students, the community, the school, and the nature of the mural, planning could take from a couple of days to weeks. Do not consider this time wasted if genuine interactive thinking and planning are taking place. Interaction is essential to this project. Students must be made aware that a community mural is a collective, cooperative activity. All students in the class should be made to feel that their input and participation are important in developing and painting the mural.

As the students discuss content, they should also be thinking about location and style. Sometimes the content will suggest a location; sometimes a location will suggest content. Murals can be painted off campus if special arrangements have been made (such as permission to use a site, and weekend or after-school sessions). Often, though, meaningful murals can be executed at the school, and these are logistically easiest. During or after the discussion of content and location, students should begin to do some visual planning and sketching in their groups. The question is, "How does our approach to this topic translate into visual form?"

The next step in planning is to execute a model. In the model, the paper format (relative dimensions and shape) should correspond exactly with the dimensions and shape of the wall to be painted. If the wall is 8 feet by 20 feet, for example, the paper should be 8 inches by 20 inches. The model can be executed in any number of ways, depending on the students' preferences, skills, and confidence. Usually models are collages, drawings or paintings from life, or some combination of these. Be sure to have a finished working model, in color, before beginning to work on the mural. It will prevent unpleasant surprises later on.

One strategy is for each student to develop a visual component of the theme, such as a particular ecological problem or a particular scene within the larger context of a local landscape. For example, in an underwater scene, a number of students might do individual fish, others reefs, some a sunken ship, and so on. Then the students can put their images together to make a rough model of where each component will be placed on the mural. This can be done in a very rudimentary, schematic way since if you work in this manner the individual images can be projected onto the wall with an opaque projector. At this point, the designers should be concerned only about placement. Again, the paper format should correspond exactly with the wall to be painted. The mural is now ready to be transferred to the wall.

Formative assessment should take place during this process. Have the students develop working models that meet the criteria of community-based murals. Do they deal appropriately with some subject or theme that is important in the local community? Are the style and the way the subject is approached both suitable? This assessment must be done before the teams go on to execute their murals.

Execution

Preparation of the wall is critical for adhesion and for the durability of the mural. The wall should be clean and dry. A painted flat latex wall is a good ready-made surface. Shiny or oil-base surfaces should be avoided. Walls that are unfinished need to be cleaned, prepared, and primed with the best primer you can afford before the students begin to paint the mural.

Once the wall is ready, there are at least three ways to transfer the model to the wall: using a grid, an opaque projector, or freehand. These methods can be combined. Our students have had success with each of the three. The easiest and most accurate device is the opaque projector, if you can get the room or space dark enough and can get back far enough from the wall to make it work. The second most accurate device, but by far the most tedious to use, is the grid. Corresponding grids are prepared for the model and the wall, and the wall drawing is done accordingly. The wall grid should be executed with a carpenter's snap line rather than a straightedge to save time. If some students are talented artists or if the style of the mural is sufficiently expressionistic to allow for minor compositional changes, the freehand method is the most efficient means. Crayon, chalk, and pencil are all good for drawing the mural cartoon on the wall because they are all somewhat malleable and erasable. Chalk is the most forgiving but also the least enduring; you may lose your line before you get the paint on.

The final step is the application of paint. Since each mural is different and each team is different, there are no magic formulas for painting the mural. We have found that it is best to let students work in a manner in which they feel comfortable. There are a few things that will make life easier, however. First, mix enough of a given color to do the whole job. Matching (wet) color after the fact to (dry) paint on the wall is next to impossible. Also, it's good to paint from the top down so that paint cannot drip onto a finished area. Another tip: as with any painting, it's good to go from background to foreground—so that, for example, a figure appears to be in front of the background. Otherwise, the brushwork in the sky, say, will look as though it has been painted up to the edge of a person or building and has suddenly stopped. Painting should also be done from general to specific, from large areas to detail, using the appropriate tools.

EVALUATION

The criteria for either the mural or the mandala project are as follows.

1. Was adequate research done on war and peace and their causes and effects?

2. Was there substantial, productive dialogue among students and between students and others about the meaning of peace and the ways it can be advanced through art?

3. Was there collective planning of a specific aesthetic process and a concrete aesthetic product?

4. Do the execution and the presentation of process and product to others contribute to the goal of peace?

Evidence that these four goals have been met includes (1) a theme based on a local community concern or problem, (2) incorporation of a positive solution, (3) the visual quality of the artwork, (4) the technical quality of the artwork, and (5) the quality of the experience of making the mural or mandala.

Students' self-assessment might stem from these questions: What did you learn about important social issues in this community? List the three that are most important in your mind and tell why you rank them so high. How would solving them contribute to peace in the community? How might that contribute to world peace? What did you learn about working cooperatively with others on a community project? What's good about it? What's hard about it? What technical and compositional problems did you encounter, and how did you solve them? How well did you do on this project as an individual? How well did your group perform? Were there any problems with cooperation or examples of excellent cooperation? What do you know now that you didn't know before about working (peacefully) with people ?

FURTHER READING

American Visionary Art Museum, 800 Key Highway, Baltimore, MD. Telephone 410-244-6500, online at *http://www. avam.org/exhibitions/warandpeace.html*.

Anderson, T. (1997). Art, education, and the bomb: Reflections on an international children's peace mural project, *Journal of Social Theory and Art Education, 17*, 71–97.

Anderson, T. (2002). Mandala: Constructing peace through art. *Art Education, 55*(3), 33–39.

Arguelles, J., & Arguelles, M. (1985). *Mandala.* Boston: Shambhala.

Children's Guernica Peace Project. Information can be accessed at *http://www.kids-guernica.org/* and also at *http://www.artjapan.com/GUERNICA-G/*

Dissanayake, E. (2000). *Art and intimacy: How the arts began.* Seattle: University of Washington Press.

Journal of Social Research in Art Education, 19–20. Special peace issue at *http://www.public.asu.edu/~ifmls/usseafolder/back. html*

Omega Institute. *http://www.eomega.org/popups/peacequotes. html.* (Homesite has excellent quotations about peace from Mohandas Gandhi, Martin Luther King, and others.)

Orr, P. (2002). Exploring the September 11, 2001, terrorist attack through an expressive mural project. *Art Education, 55*(2), 6–10.

Peace Mandala Project. *http://gomangtour.org*

Teaching Tolerance. (Biannual journal, mailed free to educators who request it. Can also be found on the web at *http://www.tolerance.org/teach/*)

Weale, A. (1995). *Eyewitness Hiroshima.* New York: Carroll & Graf.

Art Education for Life

Parrot in Sketchbook, Kristen Frenzel, Atlantic Community High School, Delray Beach, FL. Genia Howard, Art Teacher. *This page from a student's research notebook represents a part of her planning for her exhibition that is a component of her International Baccalaureate graduation examintion.*

Alfred North Whitehead said, "There is only one subject matter for education, and that is life in all its manifestations." That is the perspective we have taken in this book: that teaching and learning in art, in addition to helping students understand and appreciate art itself, should be for the sake of success in life beyond school. We are all one global community, and no one is outside the relationships that affect community for good or ill. Art education for life is about these relationships, about the way we understand ourselves and others at home and all around our small blue planet.

We consider the clinical, scientific approach to education (with its emphasis on efficiency rather than effectiveness) unsatisfactory, although it has traditionally been the norm. In such an approach the completion of a course of learning is viewed as the end of a process, and often the student retains little knowledge after leaving the classroom. Today, educators must help students come to view learning as not merely the acquisition of knowledge, but also the development of practices that provide them with a sense of identity, value, and worth. There must be a greater integration of process and product so that content is part of the process of learning and personally engages the students. These are characteristics of authentic art education: an organic, open-ended curriculum that connects product and process just as they are connected in the real world. In short, art education for life focuses real content and real connections in a real-world way.

Schools presumably exist to foster skills and concepts that will help children live useful and successful lives. Therefore, art should be taught at school in a way that shows it to be necessary, not just nice. It is necessary because it represents the values, mores, and beliefs of a group or society; serves as a social adhesive; and thus has survival value for human beings. Art in school should accordingly reflect the real-life meanings and skills of art and visual culture in society.

ART AS A QUEST FOR MEANING

The premise that art should be about something beyond itself is already well accepted outside western culture and western art education. In most cultures and through most of history, art has had functions beyond simply being decorative or beautiful. A primary function of art has been to tell human stories, to help us know who we are and how and what we believe. This function assumes that aesthetic forms can communicate. Thus artists use their skills in composition and technique to create artworks, artifacts, and performances that extend beyond themselves to tell us something about human experience.

THE PURPOSE OF ART EDUCATION FOR LIFE

The purpose of art education for life is to help students understand something about themselves and others through art and visual culture. The curriculum of art for life content and teaching and learning strategies are focused on personal and social expression of things that count in students' lives. Art for life is authentic, content-based education that recognizes works of art as both the windows and mirrors of our lives. Art for life is the story of individual human beings and the groups we live in, told through art.

CULTURE AS CONTENT FOR ART FOR LIFE

Where does artistic meaning come from? Someone once said that we have within us the DNA of the dinosaurs. Genetically and culturally, we are the product of our history. In this context, we have discusssed the nature, values, and strategies of traditional art and culture, modernism as a reaction to traditionalism, and then postmodernism as a response to modernism. We have also addressed our current visual culture. We then developed a conceptual outline of a comprehensive art for life curriculum and suggested strategies for its implementation.

MEANING THROUGH AUTHENTIC INSTRUCTION: THE EDUCATIONAL PHILOSOPHY OF ART FOR LIFE

The purpose of art education for life is to understand ourselves and others through making and studying art; its goal is social progress. Toward this end, students should have a comprehensive art education that enables them to construct deep meanings connected to the world beyond the classroom. This purpose is linked to an educational philosophy called authentic instruction. The central tenet of authentic instruction is education for life, the philosophical foundation of art for life.

The aim of art for life is to help students prepare for success both at school and in life through teaching and learning centered on art. The goals implied by this aim are that students will understand (1) that art and visual culture are visual communication about things that count; (2) that art has both intrinsic and extrinsic value and meaning; (3) that its forms, meanings, uses, and values are both aesthetic (psychological) and functional (social); and (4) that they will make art and study art and visual culture, both individually and cooperatively, in order to express themselves and to find out about meanings, values, and ways of life.

The educational strategies of art for life are teaching and learning that make real-world connections, involve the active construction of knowledge (as opposed to passive reception of knowledge from authorities), and foster the acquisition of a depth of intellectual, emotional, skills-based, and expressive knowledge, abilities, and sensibilities. The specific characteristics of teaching in art for life include (1) involving students in higher levels of cognition or thinking, (2) leading students in substantial conversations about the topics, (3) promoting social support for students' achievements, and (4) developing themes for teaching that support integrated learning beyond the art classroom.

Authentic instruction must be supported by authentic assessment. If something is worth teaching, worth including in the curriculum, then it deserves to be assessed. But standardized curricula and assessment frequently do little to help students find their way in life or find meaning and self-worth. Authentic instruction and assessment offer students educational experiences that do allow for the construction of meaning and can potentially transform students' lives. Such experiences empower students as well as teachers who seek a voice in the educational system. Throughout this text, we have suggested qualitative assessment strategies compatible with authentic instruction.

Authentic instruction relies on collaboration and cooperation rather than on so-called expert opinion or on authoritarian, top-down approaches. It de-emphasizes the egoistic artist as a model for art education and emphasizes collective, social, environmentally sound creativity. In seeking to make the world a better place, art for life is also concerned with the effects of our consumer culture and of the mass media and visual culture in general.

THE CURRICULUM AND EDUCATIONAL STRATEGIES OF ART FOR LIFE

Comprehensive art education has evolved from discipline-based art education, takes various forms, and is infused with the philosophy and qualities of authentic instruction. The curriculum of art for life is a socially responsible "whole-system" type of comprehensive art education. Using traditional as well as contemporary ideas, we have integrated aspects of several models of art education to serve the purposes of art for life. The art for life model has seven components. These are (1) an examination of contemporary visual culture, (2) a focus on individual creativity in a cultural context, (3) an examination of current technologies, (4) aesthetic inquiry, (5) art criticism, (6) art history (and other contextual examination of art and artistic processes), and (7) studio art production. We dedicated a chapter to each of these components in Part Two.

Toward the end of developing and understanding personal and social meanings, instruction and inquiry in art for life are based on themes rather than on elements and principles of design, media, time periods, artistic styles, and so on. Art is the means of understanding ourselves and others; it is not the end. The central themes, suggested in Chapter 1 and discussed in detail in the introduction to Part Three, are a sense of self, a sense of place, and a sense of community. These primary themes contain all the other themes used throughout the book as guides for specific instruction.

As they explore themes through art, students are encouraged to take up real issues and solve real problems that are significant beyond the classroom. The idea is to critically examine the ideas, feelings, and forms of others to find meaning and as a stimulus for students' own creative expression. Education must not only transmit culture but also provide alternative views of the world and strengthen the will to explore them.

Supporting (1) thematic instruction, the instructional strategies of art for life are (2) visual research and development of skills in making art, (3) dialogue and cooperative exploration, (4) critical analysis of art and its contexts, (5) historical and contextual research, (6) reflection on meanings and values of art in culture as well as self-reflection, and (7) self-expression in art. These strategies appear in the examples of instruction we give throughout the book. Fully developed examples of authentic instruction are provided in chapters 10–15.

THE CONTENT OF ART FOR LIFE

We live in an ever smaller, ever more interdependent world and in a culture of visual symbols. Cyberculture, television, movies, video games, advertising, and the visual environment constantly bombard us with their constructed meanings. The starting point of authentic art instruction is students' own drives, desires, and need to know about these aspects of the world they live in. Accordingly, the content of art for life begins with the pervasive visual culture, including the traditional fine arts but also popular culture, environmental design, commercial and advertising arts, and the arts of cultures other than one's own.

Art education for life has a particular interest in the commercial arts and in the critique of them by the fine arts, if only because they are so pervasive in our lives. The postmodern shift from primarily spoken and written communication to visual communication offers an opportunity for art education to counteract potentially manipulative media. Art education for life is also concerned with the art of non-western cultures. It recognizes that not all wisdom is held by the West—and that in an increasingly interdependent world, all of us need to learn what we can of and from one another. However, since most children in North America start with a stronger understanding of western culture than of others, we start with that. In short, the content for art for life begins with contemporary visual culture and with students' own interests, but it expands as appropriate to new understandings of both their own culture and the cultures of others, moving toward the goal of global community through art.

COMMUNITY AND SOCIAL GROWTH AS GOALS OF ART FOR LIFE

Dissanayake (1988) argues that art exists to foster the survival and flowering of the individual soul and spirit, and thus to promote the collective human soul. The keys to human survival and success, she says, are communal understandings and collective or cooperative efforts toward integrating those understandings for the common good. The roles of art are to help us understand ourselves and others and to engage with one another in the process of making, receiving, and embracing important meanings that are carried by the elegance of aesthetic form. The survival value of art has to do with its function of developing community.

Today, more so than ever before, the sense of community must be global rather than tribal. It must include all people rather than just people who look like us or live near us. In art for life, this enlarged concept of community includes the traditional sense of bonding through shared beliefs, the modernist idea of rising above our own immediate cultures, and the postmodern idea of embracing multiple narratives and multiple cultural perspectives, using visual means. This entails appreciating our own culture for its particular values and strengths, but also recognizing that it is not the only good or correct way of living in the world.

As a result of our advanced technologies (such as automobiles, synthesized chemicals, and nuclear weapons), the immense human population that strains the world's resources, and our increasing interdependence, we can no longer afford tribalism. We have come to a point where unmitigated tribal loyalty hinders rather than promotes survival. We have reached a point where all people either will or will not survive and prosper, together. Our ability to cooperate in groups must undergo a transformation from the immediate group to the group known as humankind.

How can we develop this sense of global community through instruction in art? From both postmodernism and tradition the recentering of art in the community, and thus in students' lives, is the basis of art for life. Art should be taught for the sake of what it can tell us, through aesthetic means, about life. From tradition it is valuable to retain the traditional emphasis on skill, craft, and elaboration of form. From modernism, it is valuable to retain the idea of the artist or art student as an independent, creative individual. And it is valuable, as well, to retain the poststructuralist idea of critique, especially critiques of art forms and their philosophical foundations, leading to the idea of competing philosophical systems or narratives.

The key to meaning making, though, lies in our ability to make connections—by understanding relationships between one thing and other and between one person and another. In teaching art for life, we must integrate art with students' human concerns. That is, teaching and learning should be centered on significant human *themes* that cross disciplines and media. Also, teaching and learning should go wherever ideas, spirit, and intuition may lead, rather than being confined by narrow disciplinary considerations such as media, composition, or other technical qualities of art.

Themes should be taken first from contemporary art and culture (which are most accessible to students) but then expanded, organically, to include artifacts and performances from many times and cultures as a reflection of the students' interests and concerns. Students should be encouraged to immerse themselves in real issues, to solve real problems that are significant beyond the classroom. This allows for a more open-ended system that can lead to personal transformation and social reconstruction. The themes should have to do with life and should describe our human stories. They should be focused on our sense of self, place, and community. The artwork is the medium, or the tool, for exploring these themes. It is not the end in itself.

Extending the narrative and communicative function of art from students' own culture to the cultures of others is a step toward global community. The rituals that support cosmology and other beliefs in all cultures are frequently inseparable from the arts. Students who are aware of this can consider visual culture and art cross-culturally to see how others have examined life issues, try their ideas and forms, then incorporate into their lives the ones that fit.

Through critically examining artworks within their own culture and cross-culturally, students may gain access to other attitudes, mores, and understandings and start to develop a sense of global community. Understanding others makes us see them as human. Through reaching out beyond their own culture, students may come to see others not as exotic or aliens but as people who, although they may express themselves differently, have human drives, emotions, and sensibilities much like their own. Integrated, theme-based content, then, is critical for developing a sense of global community.

CONCLUSION

Art education can help teachers and students develop relationships through which we come to understand ourselves and others: relationships that constitute not only the human community but the community of Gaia, the mother planet that gives us life. This is art education for life, art education that is not just nice but necessary, art education for the sake of survival. Is it too grand a claim that the world can be saved through instruction in art? Probably so. But we can still ask, if not through art, through what? Our ancestors understood that the most important values, traditions, and beliefs are carried on the elegant wings of aesthetic form. Are we not equal to that same wisdom today? The arts can provide a holistic, metaphoric understanding that is necessary for social and cultural health. Through the arts we de-

velop a unifying sensibility, a direction, and an ability to use our many other gifts and tools with elegance and wisdom. Let us repeat, if the world isn't to be saved through art, then how?

Mining existing artworks, performances, and visual culture—and creating new works—for aesthetic significance and meaning is the primary strategy in art education for life. The goal is to understand ourselves and others better, allowing more intelligent and meaningful action in the arena of life. Done well, it can lead to an enhanced quality of life for all of us. We invite you to join us in making community online at our McGraw-Hill web link. Share with us and others your own insights, lesson plans, and strategies for art for life.

http://www.mhhe.com/artforlife1
Visit our website to share ideas and lessons in art for life.

FURTHER READING

Dissanayake, E. (1988). *What is art for?* Seattle: University of Washington Press.

Dissanayake, E. (2000). *Art and intimacy: How the arts began.* Seattle: University of Washington Press.

Whitehead, A. (1929). *The aims of education and other essays.* New York: Macmillan.

KEY TERMS

A

Aesthetic Inquiry Systematically, aesthetics consists of asking questions, then developing arguments or theories in an attempt to answer these questions. Its content consists of these questions and answers, expressed as theories. For students of art and visual studies, aesthetic inquiry also consists of exploring their own and other's values through examining aesthetic artifacts and performances so as to understand themselves and others and ultimately make the world a better place (see also Reconstructionism and Social Reconstructionism).

Aesthetic Response A reaction to beauty or to visual artifacts. It is normally thought of as a heightened state of perception and emotion in which there is no interest in the functional aspects of the experience.

Aesthetics Most or all of the world's cultures have some philosophy of art and beauty, but aesthetics in the western philosophical tradition addresses the nature of art, beauty, and aesthetic experience, and talk about art and visual culture, from the West, and less authentically, from other cultures. Aesthetics is a highly sophisticated branch of philosophy.

Appropriation A postmodern strategy of taking something (style, form, content, or all three) from an existing work of art and using it *in toto* in a new work, frequently as a political act denying that the original artist or work "owns" the content or form. As a practical act, appropriation is different from copying a work in order to understand the technique or composition.

Art Criticism Talking about or writing about art. We undertake it because we want to know the meaning and significance of artworks (see also Critique).

Art History Through art, historic records of people and events include not only facts but also the spirit and emotion of the time. Art history is an attempt to understand this record, typically by focusing on artworks, artifacts, or artistic performances to find out how they were created, by whom, when, why, how, and in what context. Art historians look more for information *about* a work of art, whereas critics look for information *within* the work of art (see also Contextual Research).

Artistic Intelligence One's ability to make and understand meanings in aesthetic symbolic forms.

Artistic Style The way an artist or designer puts together the elements (media, composition, elements and principles of design, and so on) that carry the content of a work of art or a consciously designed visual artifact. Through artistic style, artists always tell us (deliberately or not) something about what they think and feel.

Artistic Symbols Aesthetic presentations that stand for something beyond themselves. Artistic symbols are not logical, linear, or discursive; they are subjective and affective.

Artwork A visual artifact, made by a person, that has as its purpose the presentation of human meaning in aesthetic form (see also Aesthetic Response).

Authentic Assessment Assessment directly connected to the process of teaching and learning. In authentic assessment, evaluation is intentionally intertwined with learning: students play a role in developing and applying the criteria. Evaluation is ongoing, nonstandardized, and based on performance.

Authentic Instruction Teaching and learning that have consequences in the real world, both as content that applies outside the classroom and as teaching and learning strategies that are useful in life. Authentic instruction promotes students' construction of learning in small collaborative groups, expects higher-level thinking, encourages substantive conversation about and responsibility for a topic, and takes a thematic approach to research and learning.

B

Biocultural and Biosocial Development The idea that children's development is affected by biological propensities and cultural influences. For example, we all seem to have a propensity to make some things beautiful and special. But because of cultural influences, in the Czech Republic that may take the form of a town of woodworkers whereas in the East Village in New York it may take the form of a neighborhood of postmodern installation artists. Also, because of family and peer influences, the woodcarvers may specialize in chairs, statues, or coffins. Beyond a certain point, individual development is primarily cultural.

Brainstorming Freewheeling discussion in which, ideally, everyone participates equally and contributes to an innovative or creative outcome.

Many alternatives to solving the problem at hand are encouraged. Negative criticism is not allowed, and judgment is deferred.

C

Cognition   In art for life, thinking which incorporates both the intellect and the emotions and which begins with sensory perception and kinesthetic sensations (muscle strain, butterflies in the stomach, and so on). Making and understanding visual images and art are cognitive activities.

Collaboration   Working together toward a common goal. Collaboration is socially conditioned and has cultural consequences. These consequences can include the development of tolerance for opinions other than one's own, leading to cross-cultural acceptance.

Community Murals   Large-scale, usually permanent two-dimensional works that are undertaken because of community desires and that reflect community values. Usually, the primary workers who construct such murals are members of the community. Community murals are typically activist and reconstructionist (see Reconstructionism).

Comprehensive Art Education (CAE)   An outgrowth and maturation of discipline-based art education (DBAE). DBAE focuses on making art, art criticism, aesthetics and aesthetic inquiry, and art history. CAE incorporates additional strategies and understandings. There are various forms of CAE, but all are discipline-centered, cognitive, thematic, interdisciplinary (as appropriate), and life-centered. Art for life is one model of CAE.

Conceptual Theory   Conceptualism, as an aesthetic theory, leaves the traditional realm of the aesthetic as a response to beauty, focusing instead on the idea embedded in an artistic act or artwork. Art is made and examined not for its aesthetic value but for the idea it contains.

Construction of Knowledge   A term implying that students actively develop knowledge rather than passively receiving it from teachers, textbooks, or other authorities. Constructing knowledge involves higher levels of thinking: analysis, synthesis, and evaluation. Such high-level

cognition engages not only the intellect but also the emotions and can take place through making and receiving art.

Constructivism   A theory of teaching and learning encompassing the idea that our understandings are constructed by us, not predetermined or given from on high. In constructivist learning theory, the emphasis is on active participation of the learner in the environment.

Contextual Research   Contextual research looks at the conditions surrounding an art form or a performance, rather than at the qualities of the form or performance, to understand the circumstances in which a work was created, used, and valued. Contextual information cannot be seen in the physical form, so contextual research has to do with art-in-context and visual culture rather than the object or performance itself. It consists of examining cultural and historical records and artifacts other than the one in question and interviewing people to determine the maker's motivations, how the artifact is or was used and valued, and so on (see also Art History).

Contextualism   The idea that the meaning and worth of art can be determined only in the context in which it is made and used. Contextualists think that art is or should be made and used for something beyond itself. This is a time-honored position in art education, in opposition to essentialism.

Contextualist Theory   Contextualists argue that the meaning of a work lies not so much in its form as in how it is viewed, valued, and used. Rather than applying internal or intrinsic criteria, contextualism values artworks in relation to their social significance.

Creative Self-Expression in Art   Making forms that carry human meaning. This is an intentional, purposeful act of making meaning through the use and manipulation of aesthetic tools such as composition, technique, and concepts. Creative self-expression may be judged by the appropriateness of the means in relation to the perceived expression in a social context (see also Creativity.)

Creativity   Conceiving, developing, or discovering unique connections be-

tween one thing and another. Creativity is both personal and social, because it involves making connections not only between form and meaning but also, especially for artists, between art and society. Creativity does not happen purely inside an individual's head, but in the interaction between a person's thoughts and a sociocultural context. It is in essence a social activity.

Critical Analysis   A strategy in art for life that involves thoughtfully talking and writing about art and visual culture. It systematically examines the forms of art and visual artifacts, their uses and meanings, and contextual information.

Critique   An oral or written description, analysis, and interpretation. With regard to art and visual culture, a critique involves digging (figuratively) below the surface of a work to find profound or hidden meanings in the work itself or in the way it is used or valued. Critiques may also take visual form. The point is to make visible what was hidden and invisible—that is, to understand how images and performances convey meanings and to understand the meanings conveyed.

D

Dialogue   In art for life, verbal and visual conversation between students, the teacher, and others about things that matter. The goal is mutual understanding and ultimately artistic and aesthetic actions and understandings that may have real-life consequences.

Digital Image   Any image achieved electronically without the use of film. Digital images may be recorded as still photos or moving (video) images or may be "drawn," using software such as Adobe Photoshop, directly on the computer.

Discipline-Based Art Education (DBAE)   In DBAE the focus is on understanding the artistic work or performance using four so-called disciplines of art—art production, art history, art criticism, and aesthetics—as strategies or approaches to that understanding (see also Comprehensive Art Education, CAE).

E

Essentialism   The belief that the value of art is intrinsic: that art is to be understood for its own sake, for its own qualities and their aesthetic and emotional effect. The artist who says, "The work should speak for itself" is taking an essentialist point of view. This is a time-honored position in art education, in opposition to contextualism (see also Formalist Theory).

Expressionist Theory   Expressionism finds excellence in the degree of a work's emotional power, which is usually achieved through exaggeration of form and color and animated, dynamic treatment of forms.

External Verity   In art history, external verity looks for confirmation to sources outside the account or art object for verification of its nature, status, and truth.

F

Feminist Theory   An important model for instrumentalist reconstruction. Feminist theorists deconstruct the patriarchal and hierarchical categorization of art of the modernist tradition and offer instead a more fluid understanding of art in relation to life. Feminist educators frequently extend their humanist concerns to all people and also advocate cross-cultural and multicultural critical strategies and content.

Formalist Theory   The idea that the excellence of a work has to do with its visual power, which is related to the unity, harmony, and power of interacting qualities within the work, unrelated to external criteria such as social or practical functions. In formalist theory art is seen as existing for its own sake, or at least primarily for the sake of our aesthetic response.

I

Installation Art   Art in which meaning is created simply by the way the artist selects and arranges objects in a display. Installation art may not actually involve the construction or fabrication of an art object; it relies instead on the meaning arising from relationships between preexisting objects in a particular context. Frequently, installation artists convey meaning by recontextualizing objects—that is, putting them in unexpected and previously unknown relationships. Usually the point of installation art is social criticism.

Institutional Theory   A form of contextualism. According to institutional theory, society decides collectively what is art and what is not art. This decision is based not only on physical qualities such as beauty, skill, and aesthetic (compositional) appeal, but more fundamentally on how these qualities are seen by the group as making the potential object or performance special and thus worthy of the status of art. Different groups make different decisions in different times and places; that is why classic Yoruban art has different forms and functions from classic Greek art. In institutional theory, there are no universal forms.

Instrumentalism   In art, the philosophy that artworks do or should do something in the world beyond simply being beautiful or decorative. Instrumentalists value artworks that, through their naturally aesthetic means, call us to action in the world.

Instrumentalist Theory   A form of contextualism. Instrumentalism finds excellence, not in the form itself, but in the degree to which an artwork or aesthetic performance can stimulate people to make some conceptual change or undertake some action that has a bearing on the social world. Propaganda art, religious art, and advertising are examples of instrumentalism.

Integrated Instruction   Instruction that utilizes more than one disciplinary domain or strategy to facilitate learning—for example, using art, social studies, and history to understand the themes of the American Civil War.

Interdisciplinary Instruction   When we seek and make meanings by asking a question or focusing on a theme, our aims and foci determine what we attend to and how. These purposes are very seldom restricted to a single discipline—say, art history or art criticism. Rather, they normally range across disciplines and reflect cross-disciplinary concerns. The protocol for examining meanings, then, is making connections between ideas and the forms in which ideas present themselves, rather than keeping these ideas separate within separate academic disciplines. Interdisciplinary instruction crosses the boundary between one discipline and another to pursue larger meanings.

Internal Verity   In art history, an artwork itself or an account of a work may be examined for flaws that suggest deception or misinterpretation. If there are no such flaws, the work may have internal verity.

M

Making Art   The act of creating aesthetic objects or engaging in aesthetic performances. We make art to make sense of things, to give meaning to our existence. To construct this meaning, we use a visual language consisting of compositional, technical, and conceptual tools and strategies. Artists connect ideas and emotions through the physical act of constructing aesthetic forms to represent their meanings. Kinesthesis and consciousness, body and head, coincide. The eye, the mind, the heart, and the hand interact and inform each other when we make art.

Mandalas   Temporary, usually symmetrical, often circular aesthetic forms that in some societies are believed to retore health and achieve social and ecological balance by restoring balance to people and their universe.

Metacriticism   In aesthetic terms, critical theory directed to examine systematically how we talk about art. It is not "art talk" but talk about how we talk about art.

Metaphor   A symbolic transformation that occurs when one thing (a visual image, a figure of speech, a musical configuration, or the like) in its entirety denotes another thing in its entirety: for example, the sun as life, a circle as wholeness, or Copland's musical composition as an Appalachian spring. Metaphor is not simply a cognitive nicety; it is central to our ability to think and to our creative activity.

Mimetic Theory   The idea that the best art accurately represents what is out there in the world. The aim is objective accuracy. Mimetic art is sometimes called naturalism or realism.

Modernism   A response to traditionalism. Modernism is a movement of the nineteenth and twentieth centuries that values individual rational independence and creativity over all else and considers individual creative self-expression the most important quality of art and artists. It is individually focused rather than socially focused like traditionalism.

N

Narrative   A story. Narrative reports—for example, in art history or art criticism or as the result of a critique—are "true" stories to the best of the critic's or historian's perceptual and analytic ability.

National Standards for Arts Education   Standards developed by a consortium of professionals in art, music, theater, and dance. These standards are not actually mandated by national legislation, though they are advocated by the National Art Education Association and almost every state has instituted some version of them. Most teachers have to show which state standards are met in their curriculum and lesson plans. The standards for visual arts are available through our web link.

http://www.mhhe.com/artforlife1
Visit our website to link to the National Standards.

New Technologies   In art for life, advanced, electronically generated technologies, such as video and digital imaging and especially computer-generated imagery and its transmission over the Internet.

P

Postmodernism   A response to modernism. Postmodernism is centered on critique more than on content. Postmodernism is not a philosophical system; rather, it is a critique of philosophy. Most types of postmodernism deconstruct the premises and values of older philosophical systems such as Romanticism, Marxism, and capitalism, turning them against themselves. Certain kinds of postmodernism such as feminism, environmentalism, and neo-Marxism reconstruct new premises, values, and ideas in place of the old ones they have deconstructed. In this way they attempt to move previous value systems to the periphery and bring new ones to the center.

Pragmatic Theory   A form of institutional theory, pragmatism sees functionality as truth. If something

works, socially and practically, then it is true. In art, pragmatism is grounded in a focus on the context in which a work is made, seen, or used.

Provenance   An important tool in art historical research, provenance is an examination of the history of the work through its ownership in an effort to establish its authenticity.

Q

Qualitative Instruction   Instruction in which the teacher's job is to enrich the curriculum and stimulate and challenge students to see more, sense more, remember more, and put their own visual imprint on ideas. Students are encouraged and helped to express themselves in the language, structure, and forms of art, visual artifacts, and design. Qualitative instruction entails consistent formative and ongoing evaluation in the form of feedback from instructor to student. It also entails continual reflection by students about their own work and the work of others.

R

Reconstructionism   An umbrella term referring to the idea or fact of changing society for the better, usually by applying a particular philosophy. In education, reconstructionists are usually thought of as liberal or radical political activists who believe that to make the world a better place, we need to start by reforming education with an eye to social justice and environmental balance.

Research Journals   In art for life, visual and verbal accounts of things that matter to students. Journals incorporate visual exploration, contextual research (including art history), critiques and other visual and verbal forms of art criticism, aesthetic inquiry, and above all personal reflection—which ties everything together.

S

Social Acculturation   The ways we are molded by and integrated into groups and society at large.

Social Construction of Meaning   Term referring to the idea that understanding of things in the world is constructed by groups of people—societies—rather than being given and predetermined.

Social Reconstructionism   In art for life, the critical examination of social reality, focused on art in its authentic contexts and on other forms of visual culture. The purpose is to suggest what is wrong in society and how it can and should be changed.

Studio Art   A common but outmoded term for artworks and the making of art, implying that all art work is made in a studio. The term thus has elitist implications (see Artwork and Making Art for more appropriate descriptions).

Substantial Conversation   In art for life, a critical component in high-level thinking and the construction of knowledge, involving both verbal and visual conversation. Observation, crucial to artistic expression, is immeasurably enhanced by shared experience and dialogue.

Symbolic Communication   Communication that makes connections between form and meaning—between a sign or symbol that is being constructed, with its nuances and particularities, and how it represents experience. Making and perceiving art and visual artifacts are forms of symbolic communication (see also Artistic Symbols).

Synectics   The joining together of different and apparently unrelated elements. Synectic methods are conscious approaches to constructing direct, personal, fantastic, or symbolic analogies in order to solve problems or generate ideas.

T

Thematic Instruction   In art education, teaching and learning centered on significant human themes rather than on the traditional elements and principles of design or units of instruction based on media, such as clay or pencil drawing. The three central themes for art for life are (1) a sense of self, (2) a sense of place, and (3) a sense of community. Themes are used to attain meaning. Ideas and emotions are elicited and taken to their natural conclusion. The guide is students' own logical and emotional connections.

Themes   Themes arise from our personal relationships to topics (for example, our love of horses, our fear of dogs or of meeting someone new, or the thrill of flying in an airplane).

When we make a topic human and personal through such connections, it becomes a theme.

Traditionalism   Art from traditional societies, supporting social values that are carried through aesthetic form from one generation to the next. Elaboration, beauty, and replication are the primary qualities valued in traditional art, and skill in achieving these ends is the primary quality valued in traditional artists.

V

Verity   A term used by historians to mean the truth.

Virtual Reality   An electronically generated image or more usually an entire electronically generated environment. It may appear real (three-dimensional) but in fact exists only electronically. The user is immersed in a digitally generated space of sound and images. Potentially, the aesthetic experience is totally interactive.

Visual Artifact or Performance   In art for life, something constructed by a person. It need not be constructed specifically for aesthetic expression, but it at least has an aesthetic component. Examples include shopping malls, clothes, television ads, footballs, paintings, and dance performances.

Visual Culture   Visual artifacts and performances of all kinds, as well as new and emerging technologies, inside and outside the art museum, and the beliefs, values, and attitudes imbued in those artifacts and performances by the people who make, present, and use them. The primary means of understanding visual culture in art for life is critique.

Visual Culture Art Education (VCAE)   The point of VCAE is to "read" and grasp the meanings of expressive visual artifacts and performances in order to succeed in life. VCAE includes all visual artifacts and performances: traditional high art, theme parks, shopping malls, the popular arts, and so on. It focuses on the artifact or performance within the culture where it is made and used. The object or performance is thought of as representing that culture.

W

Webbing   A form of verbal and visual brainstorming that encourages participants to construct thematic bridges between fragmentary bits of knowledge and find relationships between ideas. It is often used as a teacher-directed instructional strategy in group discussion, with the teacher or a student introducing a theme for exploration. After the theme is introduced students may brainstorm a list of questions about the topic, based on information they already have.

REFERENCES

Abbot, J., & Ryan, T. (1999). Constructing knowledge, reconstructing schooling. *Educational Leadership, 57*(3), 66–69.

Adams, M. (2002). Interdisciplinarity and community as tools for art education and social change. In Y. Gaudelius & P. Speirs (Eds.), *Mapping identity for curriculum work: Contemporary issues in art education* (pp. 358–369). Upper Saddle River, NJ: Prentice Hall.

Adbusters: http://www.adbusters.org/home/

Addiss, S., & Erickson, M. (1993). *Art history and education.* Urbana and Chicago: University of Illinois Press.

Aesthetics Online. *http://aesthetics online.org/ideas/sartwell.html*

Alwitt, L. F. & Mitchell, A. A. (Eds.). (1985). *Psychological processes and advertising effects.* Hillsdale, NJ: Laurence Erlbaum.

Amabile, T. M. (1996). *Creativity in context.* Boulder, CO: Westview Press.

American Visionary Art Museum, 800 Key Highway, Baltimore MD. Telephone 410-244-6500. ("War and Peace," available online at *http://www.avam.org/exhibitions/warand peace.html.)*

Anderson, H. (2000). A river runs through it: Art education and a river environment. *Art Education, 53*(6), 13–17.

Anderson, R. (1989). *Art in small-scale societies.* Englewood Cliffs, NJ: Prentice Hall.

Anderson, R. (1990). *Calliope's sisters: A comparative study of philosophies of art.* Englewood Cliffs, NJ: Prentice Hall.

Anderson, R. (2000). *American muse. Anthropological excursions into art and aesthetics.* Upper Saddle River, NJ: Prentice Hall. A look at value and meaning in the popular arts.

Anderson, T. (1981). The process of mural making, *School Arts 81*(1), 43–46.

Anderson, T. (1984). Contemporary American street murals: Their defining qualities and significance for art education. *Journal of Multicultural and Cross-Cultural Research in Art Education, 2,* 14–22.

Anderson, T. (1985). Toward a socially defined studio curriculum. *Art Education, 38*(5), 16–18.

Anderson, T. (1988). A structure for pedagogical criticism. *Studies in Art Education, 30*(1), 28–38.

Anderson, T. (1989). Interpreting works of art as social metaphors. *Visual Arts Research, 15*(2), 42–51.

Anderson, T. (1990). Attaining general critical appreciation through art. *Studies in Art Education, 31*(3), 132–140.

Anderson, T. (1991). The content of art criticism. *Art Education, 44*(1), 16–24.

Anderson, T. (1992). Art of the eye, the brain, and the heart. *Art Education, 45*(5), 45–50.

Anderson, T. (1993). Defining and structuring art criticism for education. *Studies in Art Education, 34*(4), 199–208.

Anderson, T. (1995). Toward a cross-cultural approach to art criticism. *Studies in Art Education, 36*(4), 198–209.

Anderson, T. (1995) Interpreting Snakebird: A critical strategy. In T. Barrett (Ed.), *Lessons for teaching art criticism.* ERIC:Art. (Available from Publications Manager, Social Studies Development, Indiana University, 2805 E. 10th St., Suite 120, Bloomington, IN 47405.)

Anderson, T. (1997). Talking with kids about art. *School Arts, 97* (1), 21–24.

Anderson, T. (1997). Toward a postmodern approach to art education. In J. Hutchens and M. Suggs (Eds.), *Art education: Content and practice in a postmodern era.* Reston, VA: National Art Education Association.

Anderson, T. (1997), Art, education, and the bomb: Reflections on an international children's peace mural project, *Journal of Social Theory and Art Education, 17,* 71–97

Anderson, T. (1998). Aesthetics as critical inquiry. *Art Education, 51*(5), 49–55.

Anderson, T. (2002). Mandala: Constructing peace through art. *Art Education, 55*(3), 33–39.

Anderson T. (2002). *Real lives: Art teachers and the cultures of school.* Portsmouth, NH: Heinemann.

Anderson, T., & McRorie, S. (1997). A role for aesthetics in centering the K–12 curriculum. *Art Education, 50*(23), 6–14.

Anderson, T., & Milbrandt, M. (1998). Authentic instruction in art: How and why to dump the school art style. *Visual Arts Research, 24*(1), 13–20.

Anderson, T. & Taylor, J. (1995). *A multicultural curriculum framework in the arts for the State of Florida.* Tallahassee: Florida Department of Education. (Available from ACE, College of Education, University of Central Florida, Orlando, FL 32816.)

Andrus, L. (2001). The culturally competent art educator. *Art Education, 54*(4), 14–19.

Anton, S. (2000). The virtual museum. *Flash Art, 33,* 39–42.

Arguelles, J., & Arguelles, M. (1985). *Mandala.* Boston: Shambhala.

Armstrong, C. (1990). *Development of an aesthetics resource: An aid for integrating aesthetics into art curricula and instruction.* Los Angeles, CA: Getty Center for Education in the Arts.

Arnheim, R. (1966). *Toward a psychology of art.* Berkeley: University of California Press.

Arnheim, R. (1969). *Visual thinking.* Berkeley: University of California Press.

Arnheim, R. (1986). *New essays on the psychology of art.* Berkeley: University of California.

Arnheim, R. (1989). *Thoughts on education.* Santa Monica, CA: Getty Center for Education in the Arts.

Arnowitz, S., & Giroux, H. (1991). *Postmodern education: politics, culture, and social criticism.* Minneapolis: University of Minnesota.

Art and Ecology Website, ArtsEdNet, at *http://www.getty.edu/ArtsEdNet/Resources/Ecology/Index.html*

Art Education, 50(6). (1997). (Special thematic issue edited by Don Krug. Has articles on art and the environment by Krug, Deborah Birt, and Mary Sheridan; Ronald Neperud; Cynthia Hollis, Elizabeth Reese, Frances Thurber, Doug Blandy, and David Cowan; and Louis Lankford.)

Art Education: Journal of the National Art Education Association, 51(3). (1998). (This thematic issue, edited by Mary Ann Stankiewicz, entitled "Community, Art, and Culture," has articles by Therese Marche; Christine Ballengee-Morris; John Howell White and Kristin Congdon; Catherine Coleman; Louis Rufer, Betty Lake, Ellen Robinson, and John Hicks; and Steve Elliott and Sue Bartley.)

Art Education: Journal of the National Art Education Association 52(4). (1999). Thematic issue edited by Paul Bolin, entitled Teaching Art as if the World Mattered, has articles by Peggy Albers, Lisa Lefler Brunick, Michelle Wiebe and Zederayko and Kelly Ward, and Elizabeth Manley Delacruz.

Art Education, 55(4). (2002).(Thematic issue entitled Technology and Assessment, edited by Pat Villenue. Has technology articles by Pamela Taylor and Stephen Carpenter, Douglas Marschalek, and Bonnie Halsey-Dutton.)

ArtsEdNet *http://www.getty.edu/artsednet/* (This ultimate online source for DBAE includes lesson plans, resources, and more.)

ArtsNet Minnesota: Inner Worlds—

Betye Saar. *http://www.artsconnected.org/artsnetmn/inner/saar.html*

Art 21—Barbara Kruger. *http://www.pbs.org/art21/artists/kruger* (Biography and clips from the PBS show.)

Ashford, J. (2002). *The arts and crafts computer: Using your computer as an artist's tool.* Berkeley, CA: Peachpit.

Atkins, R. (May–June, 2001). *http://www.artonpaper.com/archive.html*

Avery, P. G. (1999). Authentic assessment and instruction. *Social Education, 63*(6), 368–373.

Bacquart, J. B. (2002) *Tribal arts of Africa.* New York: Thames and Hudson.

Bailey, J. (1996). *After thought: The computer challenge to human intelligence.* New York: HarperCollins.

Baker, P. (1996). Authentic pedagogy boosts student achievement. *WCER Highlights, 8*(3). Madison, WI: Wisconsin Center for Education Research, University of Wisconsin-Madison.

Baker, S. (1961). *Visual persuasion: The effect of pictures on the subconscious.* New York: McGraw-Hill.

Ballengee-Morris, K. (1997). The mountain cultural curriculum: Telling our story. *Journal of Social Theory in Art Education, 17,* 98–116.

Ballengee-Morris, C., & Stuhr, P. (2001). Multicultural art and visual cultural education in a changing world. *Art Education, 54*(4), 6–13.

Banks, J., & Banks, C. (2001). *Multicultural education: Issues and perspectives.* New York: Wiley.

Barbosa, A. M. (1988). The underdevelopment of art education: The political intervention in Brazil. *Journal of Multi-Cultural and Cross-Cultural Research in Art Education, 5*(1), 27–38.

Barrett, T. (1988). A comparison of the goals of studio professors conducting critiques and art education goals for teaching art criticism. *Studies in Art Education, 30*(1), 22–27.

Barrett, T. (1994). *Criticizing art: Understanding the contemporary.* Mountain View, CA: Mayfield.

Barrett, T. (1997). *Talking about student art.* Worchester, MA: Davis.

Barrett, T. (2000). Studies invited lecture: About interpretation for art education. *Studies in Art Education, 42*(1), 5–19.

Barrett, T. (2002). Interpreting art: Building communal and individual understandings. In Y. Gaudelius & P. Speirs (Eds.), *Contemporary issues in art education* (pp. 291–301). Upper Saddle River, NJ: Prentice Hall.

Barrett, T. (2004). *Interpreting art: Reflecting, wondering, responding.* New York: McGraw-Hill.

Battin, M., Fisher, J., Moore, R., & Silvers, A. (1989). *Puzzles about art: An aesthetics casebook.* New York: St. Martin's.

Bayeux Tapestry. *http://www.sjolander.com/viking/museum*

Beane, J. A. (1998). Reclaiming a democratic purpose for education. *Educational Leadership, 56*(2), 8–11.

Beane, J. A. (2002). Beyond self-interest: A democratic core curriculum. *Educational Leadership, 59*(7), 25–28.

Bearing Witness. *www.tfaoi.com*

Bell, C. (1981/1914). *Art.* New York: Putnam.

Bender, S. (2001). *Keeping a journal you love.* Cincinnati, OH: Walking Stick.

Benjamin, W., (1978). *Illuminations.* New York: Schocken.

Bensur, B. (2002). Frustrated voices of assessment: History of assessment in the art room. *Art Education, 55*(6), 18–23.

Berensohn, P. (1969). *Finding one's way with clay.* New York: Simon & Schuster.

Berger, J. (1972). *Ways of seeing.* London: Penguin.

Berger, M. (1991). Interview with Fred Wilson. *Art in America, 79,* 131.

Berger, M. (1992). *How art becomes history.* New York: HarperCollins.

Bergman, Ciel. About Ciel Bergman: *http://www.emal.com/art/Bergman_info.htm*

Bergman, Ciel. *http://wayfinder.com/bergman/* Fine Art. Website of artist and work.

Beyond creating. (1985). Malibu, CA: Getty Center for Education in the Arts.

Bickley-Green, C., & Wolcott, A. (1995/1996). Some results of feminist collaboration in the visual arts: Changes in art history and art criticism. *Journal of Social Theory in Art Education, 15/16,* 160–190.

Binkley, T. (1987). Piece: Contra-aesthetics. In J. Margolis (Ed.), *Philosophy Looks at the Arts* (pp. 80–99). Philadelphia, PA: Temple University Press.

Black, J. Anderson. (1981). *A history of jewelry.* New York: Crown.

Blackboard.com. *http://www.blackboard.com/*

Blandy, D. & Congdon, K. (1991). *Pluralistic approaches to art criticism.* Bowling Green, OH: Bowling Green State University Popular Press. (An overview of alternative forms of art criticism.)

Blandy, D., Congdon, K., & Krug, D. (1998). Art, ecological restoration and art education. *Studies in Art Education, 39*(3), 230–243.

Bleiker, C. (1999). The development of self through art: A case for early art education. *Art Education, 52*(3). 48–53.

Bloom, B. S. (Ed.). (1956). *Taxonomy of education objectives: The classification of educational goals. Handbook I: Cognitive Domain.* New York: Longman.

Bolotin, P., Bravmann, S., Windschitl, M., Mikel, E., & Green, S. (2000). *Cultures of curriculum.* Mahwah, NJ: Lawrence Erlbaum.

Borja-Villel, M. (1992). *Krzysztof Wodiczko: Instruments, projections, vehicles.* Barcelona: Fundacio Antoni Tapies.

Boughton, D. (1986). How do we prepare art teachers for a multicultural society? *Journal of Multicultural and Cross-Cultural Research in Art Education, 4,* 94–99.

Boughton, D. (2002). *Art education and visual culture.* NAEA Advisory, Spring. National Art Education Association.

Bouvier, N. (1992). *The Japanese chronicles.* San Francisco: Mercury House.

Bowers, C. (1974). *Cultural literacy for freedom.* Eugene, OR: Elan.

Bowers, C. (1987). *Elements of a post-liberal theory of education.* New York: Columbia University Press.

Bowers, C. (2000). *Let them eat data: How computers affect education, cultural diversity, and the prospects of ecological sustainability.* Athens: University of Georgia Press.

Boyer, E. L. (1995). *The basic school: A community for learning.* Princeton, NJ: Foundation for the Advancement of Teaching.

Brodeur, D. R. (1998). Thematic teaching: Integrating cognitive and affective outcomes in elementary classrooms. *Educational Technology, 38*(6), 37–43.

Broude, N., and Garrard, M. D. (1994). *The power of feminist art: The story of the American movement of the 1970s, history, and impact.* New York: Abrams.

Broudy, H. (1987). Proper claims and expectations of an exemplary program. *FAEA Forum,* Fall 1987.

Brown, M., & Korzenik, D (1993). *Art making and education.* Urbana: University of Illinois.

Bruner, J. (1960). *The process of education.* Cambridge, MA: Harvard University Press.

Bruner, J. (1986). *Actual minds, possible worlds.* Cambridge, MA: Harvard University Press.

Bruner, J. (1996). *The culture of education.* Cambridge, MA: Harvard University Press.

Burton, J. (2000). The configuration of meaning: Learner centered art education revisited. *Studies in Art Education, 41*(4), 330–335.

Caine, R. N. (2000). Building the bridge from research to classroom. *Educational Leadership, 58*(3), 59–61.

Caine, R. N., and Caine, G. (1991). *Making connections: Teaching and the human brain.* Alexandria, VA: Association for Supervision and Curriculum Development.

Cameron, J. (2002). *The artist's way: A spiritual path to higher creativity.* J. P. Tarcher.

Carpenter, B. (2003). Never a dull moment: Pat's barbershop as educational environment, hypertext, and place. *Journal of Cultural Research in Art Education, 21,* 5–18.

Carpenter, E. (1974). *Oh! What a blow that phantom gave me.* New York: Bantam.

Cason, N. (1998). Interactive media: An alternative context for studying works of art. *Studies in Art Education, 39*(4), 336–349.

Casson, M., & Cubley, S. (1995). *Life, paint, and passion: Reclaiming the magic of spontaneous expression.* New York: J. P. Tarcher/Putnam.

Center for Global Environmental Education, *Journal of Everyday Earth. http://cgee.hamline.edu/see/journal/see_journ.html*

Chadwick, W. (2002). *Women, art, and society* (3rd ed.). New York: Thames and Hudson.

Chalmers, G. (1996). *Celebrating pluralism: Art, education and cultural diversity.* Los Angeles: Getty Education Institute for the Arts.

Chalmers, G. (2002). Celebrating pluralism six years later: Visual transculture/s, education, and critical multiculturalism. *Studies in Art Education, 43*(4), 293–306.

Chapman, L. (1978). *Approaches to art in education.* New York: Harcourt Brace Jovanovich.

Chapman, L. (1982). *Instant art, instant culture: The unspoken policy for American schools.* New York: Teachers College Press.

Charnelle Holloway Biography. *www.wcenter.spelman.ed*

Ciganko, R. (2000). Embedding life issues in cultural narratives for the third millennium. *Art Education, 53*(6), 33–39.

Clark, G., Day, M., & Greer, D. (1987). Discipline-based art education: Becoming students of art. *Journal of Aesthetic Education, 21*(2), 129–196.

Clark, G., & Zimmerman, E. (2000). Greater understanding of the local community: A community-based art education program for rural schools. *Art Education, 53*(2), 33–38.

Cobb, C. D., & Mayer, J. D. (2000). Emotional intelligence: What the research says. *Educational Leadership, 58*(3), 14–18.

Colescott, Robert. Resource directory. *http://www.artcyclopedia.com/artists/colescott_robert.html*

Colescott, Robert. *http://www.bampfa.berkeley.edu/exhibits/colescott/intro.html*

Colescot, Robert. Video and overview of work. *http://imageexchange.com/videos/lsvideo/4113.shtml*

Collingwood, R. (1983). *Principles of art.* Oxford: Clarendon.

Collins, G., & Sandell, R. (Eds.). (1996). *Art criticism from a feminist point of view: An approach for teachers.* Reston, VA: National Art Education Association.

Congdon, K. (1991). Feminist approaches to art criticism. In D. Blandy and K. Congdon (Eds.), *Pluralist Approaches to Art Criticism.* Bowling Green, OH: Bowling Green State University Popular Press.

Congdon, K. (2000). Beyond the egg carton alligator: To recycle is to recall and restore. *Art education, 53*(6), 6–12.

Congdon, K., & Blandy, D. (2001). Approaching the real and the fake: Living life in the fifth world. *Studies in Art Education, 42*(3), 266–278.

Congdon, K., Delgado-Trunk, C., and Lopez, M. (1999). Teaching about the Ofrenda and experiences on the border. *Studies in Art Education, 40*(4), 312–329.

Congdon, K., & Hallmark, K. (2002). *Artists from Latin American cultures.* Westport, CT: Greenwood.

Congdon, K., Stewart, M., & Howell White, J. (2002). Mapping identity for curriculum work. In Y. Gaudelius & P. Speirs (Eds.), *Contemporary issues in art education* (pp. 108–116). Upper Saddle River, NJ: Prentice Hall.

Constantino, T. (2002). Problem-based learning: A concrete approach to teaching aesthetics. *Studies in Art Education, 43*(3), 219–231.

Cook, L., & Wollen, P. (1995). *Visual display: Culture beyond appearances.* Seattle: Bay Press. (Visual culture examined from a museum studies perspective.)

Corin, L. (Ed.). (1994). *Mining the museum: Installation by Fred Wilson.* New York: New Press.

Costa, A. L. (Ed.). (1985). *Developing minds: A resource book for teaching and thinking.* Alexandria, VA: Association for Supervision and Curriculum Development.

Counts, G. S. (1932). *Dare the schools build a new social order?* New York: John Day.

Couple in the Cage: A Guatinaui Odyssey. *www.thing.net/~cocofusco/couple.html*

Csikszentmihalyi, M. (1990). *Flow: The psychology of optimal experience.* New York: HarperCollins.

Csikszentmihalyi, M. (1996). *Creativity.* New York: HarperCollins.

Csikszentmihalyi, M., & Robinson, R. (1990). *The art of seeing: An interpretation of the aesthetic encounter.* Malibu, CA: Getty.

Danto, A. (1987/1964). The artworld. In J. Margolis (Ed.), *Philosophy looks at the arts* (pp. 155–168). Philadelphia, PA: Temple University Press.

Darraby, J. L. (1995). Art, artifact, and architecture law. Deerfield, IL: Clark, Boardman, and Callagan.

Davenport, M. (2000). Culture and education: Polishing the lenses. *Studies in Art Education, 41*(4), 361–375.

Davies, G. A. (1999). *Creativity is forever.* Dubuque, IA: Kendall/Hunt.

DeBono, E. (1974). *Children solve problems.* New York: HarperCollins.

DeBono, E. (1990). *Lateral thinking.* New York: HarperCollins.

DeMente, B. L. (1993). *Behind the Japanese bow.* Lincolnwood, IL: Passport.

Derrida, J. (1978). *Writing and difference.* London: Routledge and Kegan Paul.

Desai, D. (2000). Imaging difference: The politics of representation in multicultural art education. *Studies in Art Education, 41*(2), 114–129.

Detroit Institute of Art, Bill Viola Website. *http://www.dia.org/exhibitions/BillViola/pages/main.html*

Dever, M. T., & Hobbs, D. (Spring 2000). Curriculum connections. The learn-ing spiral: Toward authentic instruction. *Kappa Delta Pi Record, 36*(3), 131–133.

Dewey, J. (1899). *The school and society.* Chicago, IL: University of Chicago Press.

Dewey, J. (1958/1934). *Art as experience.* New York: Capricorn.

Dewey, J. (1958). *Experience and nature.* New York: Dover.

Dewey, J. (1963/1938). *Experience and education.* New York: Collier.

Dickie, G. (1974). *Art and the aesthetic: An institutional analysis.* Ithaca, NY: Cornell.

Diket, R., & Mucha, L. (2002). Talking about violent images. *Art Education, 55*(2), 11–17.

Dissanayake, E. (1988). *What Is Art for?* Seattle: University of Washington Press.

Dissanayake, E. (1995). *Homo aestheticus: Where art comes from and why.* Seattle: University of Washington Press.

Dissanayake, E. (2000). *Art and intimacy: How the arts began.* Seattle: University of Washington Press.

Dobbs, S. (1998). *Learning in and through art.* Los Angeles: Getty Education Institute for the Arts.

Doll, W. E., Jr. (1993). *A post-modern perspective on curriculum.* New York and London: Teachers College Press.

Dorn, C. (1999). *Mind in art: Cognitive foundations in art education.* Mahwah, NJ: Lawrence Erlbaum.

Duncan, M. (1998, March). Bill Viola: Altered perceptions. *Art in America, 86,* March 1998, 62–70.

Duncum, P., & Bracey, T. (2001). *On Knowing.* Christchurch, New Zealand: University of Canterbury Press.

Duncum, P. (1999). A case for art education of everyday experiences. *Studies in Art Education, 40*(4), 295–311.

Duncum, P. (2001). Visual culture: Developments, definitions, and directions for art education. *Studies in Art Education, 42*(2), 101–112.

Duncum, P. (2001). Visual art education: My best view of our future. *http://216.239.51.100/search?q=cache:nWywJBujR90C:www.savaea.org.au/PaulDuncumPgmkr.pdf+visual+culture+education&hl=en*

Duncum, P. (2002). Clarifying visual culture art education. *Art Education, 55*(3), 6–11.

Duncum, P. (1995–96). Art education and technology: These are the days of miracle and wonder. *Journal of Social Theory in Art Education, 15/16,* 12–29.

Dundon, B. L. (1999–2000). My voice: An advocacy approach to service learning. *Educational Leadership 57*(4), 34–37.

Dunn, P. (1996). More power: Integrated, interactive technologies and art education. *Art Education, 49*(2), 6–11.

Earthworks.org, a site for contemporary earthworks. *http://www.earthworks.org/links.html*

Eaton, M. (1988). *Basic issues in aesthetics.* Belmont, CA: Wadsworth.

Eber, D. E. (1999). The aesthetic experience with a virtual environment work of art. *Journal of the Georgia Art Education Association, 2,* 1–3.

Eberle, R. (1977). *SCAMPER.* East Aurora, NY: DOK.

Ecker, D. (1966). The artistic process as qualitative problem solving. In E. Eisner & D. Ecker (Eds.), *Readings in art education* (pp. 57–68). New York: Blaisdell.

Ecker, D. (1991). The politics of aesthetic inquiry and multicultural art education. *Journal of Multicultural and Cross-cultural Research in Art Education, 9,* 7–10.

Ecker, D. (1997). Justifying aesthetic judgments. *Art Education, 50*(1), 21–25, 84.

Ecker, D. W. and Kaelin, E. F. (1972). The limits of aesthetic inquiry: A guide to educational research. *Philosophical redirection of educational research: Seventy-first yearbook of the National Society for the Study of Education.* Chicago: University of Chicago.

Eco, V. (1986). *Art and beauty in the middle ages.* (H. Bredin, Trans.). New Haven, CT: Yale University Press.

Edwards, B. (1999) *Drawing on the right side of the brain.* New York: J. P. Tarcher/Putnam.

Efland, A. (1976). The school art style: A functional analysis. *Studies in Art Education, 17*(2), 37–44.

Efland, A. (2002). *Art and cognition: Integrating the visual arts in the curriculum.* New York: Teachers College Press.

Efland, A., Freedman, K., & Stuhr, P. (1996). *Postmodern art education: An approach to curriculum.* Reston, VA: National Art Education Association.

Eisner, E. (1994). *The educational imagination: On the design and evaluation of school programs* (3rd ed.). New York: Macmillan.

Eisner, E. (1994). *Cognition and curriculum reconsidered*. New York: Teachers College Press.

Eisner, E. (2001). Should we create new aims for art education? *Art Education 54*(5), 6–10. (An argument for essentialism.)

Emerson, S. (Ed.). (1999). *Barbara Kruger*. Cambridge, MA: Museum of Contemporary Art Los Angeles and MIT Press.

English, H. W., & Dormer, P. (1995). *Jewelry of our time: Art, ornament and obsession*. New York: Rizzoli International.

Erickson, M. (1998). Effects of art history instruction on fourth and eighth grade students' abilities to interpret artworks contextually. *Studies in Art Education, 39*(4), 309–320.

Erickson, M. (2001). Images of me: Why broad themes? Why focus on inquiry? Why use the Internet? *Art Education, 54*(1), 33–39.

Erickson, M., & Katter, E. (1985). *Token response: An introductory aesthetics and criticism game*. Kutztown, PA: MELD.

Erickson, M., Katter, E., Evans, J., & Hall, S. (1999). *Visual culture: The reader*. London: Sage.

Evans, J., & Hall, S. (1999). *Visual culture: The reader*. London: Sage.

Evans, R. W., Avery, P., and Pederson, P. V. (1999). Taboo topics: Cultural restraint on teaching social issues. *Social Studies 90*(5), 218–222.

Ewen, S. (1988). *All consuming images: The politics of style in contemporary culture*. New York: Basic Books.

Farrar-Halls, G. (2000). *The illustrated encyclopedia of Buddhist wisdom*. Wheaton, IL: Quest.

Fatemi, E. (1999). Technology Counts '99: Building the digital curriculum. *http://www.edweek.org/sreports/tc99/articles/summary.htm*

Fahey, P. (1996). Magic eyes: Transforming teaching through first grade sketchbooks. *Visual Arts Research, 22*(1), 34–43.

Feinstein, H. (1982). Meaning and visual metaphor. *Studies in Art Education, 36*(4), 30–33.

Feinstein, H. (1996). *Reading images: Meaning and metaphor*. Reston, VA: National Art Education Association.

Feldman, D. (1980). *Beyond universals in cognitive development*. Norwood, NJ: Ablex.

Feldman, E. (1970). *Becoming human through art*. Englewood Cliffs, NJ: Prentice Hall.

Feldman, E. (1996). *Philosophy of Art Education*. Upper Saddle River, NJ: Prentice Hall.

Felshin, N. (Ed.). (1995). *But is it art? The spirit of art as activism*. Seattle, WA: Bay Press.

Field, J. (1957). *On not being able to paint*. Los Angeles: J. P. Tarcher.

Filby, N. N. (1991). *An action research approach to authentic curriculum and instruction*. CA: Office of Educational Research and Improvement. (ERIC Document Reproduction Service No. ED338615.)

Fogarty, R. (1999). Architects of the intellect. *Educational Leadership, 57*(3), 76–78.

Foster, H. (1983). *The anti-aesthetic: essays on postmodern culture*. Seattle: Bay Press.

Fox, S., & Ganim, B. (1999). *Visual journaling: Going deeper than words*. Theosophical Publishing House.

Frances Loeb Library: Krzysztof Wodiczko. Minneapolis: Walker Art Center. *http://www.gsd.harvard.edu/library/services/references/bibliographies/wodiczko.html*

Franck, F. (1993). *Zen seeing, Zen drawing*. New York: Bantam/Doubleday.

Freedman, K. (1991). Recent theoretical shifts in the field of art history and some classroom applications. *Art Education, 44*(6), 40–45.

Freedman, K. (1997). Visual art/virtual art: Teaching technology for meaning. *Art Education, 50,* (4), 6–12.

Freedman, K. (2000). Social perspectives on art education in the U.S.: Teaching visual culture in a democracy. *Studies in Art Education, 41*(4), 314–329.

Freedman, K., Stuhr, S., & Weinberg, S. (1989). The discourse of culture and art education. *Journal of Multicultural and Cross-Cultural Research in Art Education, 7,* 38–55.

Freedman, K., & Wood, J. (1999). Reconsidering critical response: Judgments of interpretation, purpose, and relationship in visual culture. *Studies in Art Education, 40*(2), 128–142.

Freire, P. (1970). *Pedagogy of the oppressed*. New York: Herder & Herder.

Freire, P. (1973). *Education for critical consciousness*. New York: Seabury.

Freshman, P. (1992). *Public address*. Minneapolis: Walker Art Center.

Frueh, J. (1991). Towards a feminist theory of art criticism. In H. Smagula (Ed.), *Re-visions: New perspectives of art criticism*. Englewood Cliffs, NJ:

Prentice Hall.

Frueh, J., Langer, C. L., Raven, A. (Eds.). (1994). *New feminist criticism: Art, identity, action*. New York: HarperCollins.

Fry, R. (1920). *Vision and design*. London: Chatto and Windus.

Fusco, C. (1995). *English is broken here*. New York: New Press.

Gablik, S. (1991). *The re-enchantment of art*. New York: Thames and Hudson.

Gablik, S. (1995). *Conversations before the end of time*. New York: Thames and Hudson.

Galbraith, L. (1997). Enhancing teacher education with new technologies. *Art Education, 50,* (5), 14–19.

Galvin, S. (1997). Scent memories: Crossing the curriculum with writing and painting. *Art Education, 50*(2), 6–12.

Garber, E. (1995). Teaching art in the context of culture: A study in the borderlands. *Studies in Art Education, 36*(4), 218–232.

Garber, E. (1996). Art criticism from a feminist point of view: An approach for teachers. In G. Collins & R. Sandell (Eds.), *Gender issues in art education: Content, contexts, and strategies* (pp. 21–38). Reston, VA: National Art Education Association.

Gardner, H. (1982). *Art, mind, and brain*. New York: Basic Books.

Gardner, H. (1989). Zero-based arts education: An introduction to Arts Propel. *Studies in Art Education, 30*(2), 71–83.

Gardner, H. (1991). *The unschooled mind: How children think and how schools should teach*. New York: Basic Books.

Gardner, H. (1994). *The arts and human development*. New York: HarperCollins.

Gardner, H. (1994). *Art education and human development*. Santa Monica, CA: Getty Center for Education in the Arts.

Gardner, H. (2000). *The disciplined mind*. New York: Penguin.

Garoian, C. (1998). Art education and the aesthetics of land use in the age of ecology. *Studies in Art Education, 39*(3), 244–261.

Garoian, C. (2002). Children performing the art of identity. In Y. Gaudelius & P. Speirs (Eds.), *Contemporary issues in art education* (pp. 119–127). Upper Saddle River, NJ: Prentice Hall.

Garoian, C., & Gaudelius, Y. (2001). Cyborg pedagogy: Performing resistance in the digital age. *Studies in Art Education, 42*(4), 333–347.

Geertz, C. (2000). Imbalancing act: Jerome Bruner's cultural psychology. In *Available light: Anthropological reflections on philosophical topics*. Princeton, NJ: Princeton University Press.

Geahigan, G. (1998). From procedures to principles and beyond: Implementing critical inquiry in the classroom. *Studies in Art Education, 39*(4), 293–308.

Geahigan, G. (1999). Description in art criticism and art education. *Studies in Art Education, 40*(3), 213–225.

Generali Foundation/Mary Kelly. *http://www.gfound.or.at/RUECK/altpro/kelly_e.htm* (Photographs and information about the Post-Partum Document 1973–1979 exhibition in 1998.)

Giroux, H. A. (1988). *Teachers as intellectuals: Toward a critical pedagogy of learning*. Boston, MA: Bergin and Garvey.

Giroux, H., & Simon, R. (1989). *Popular culture: Schooling and everyday life*. Westport, CT: Bergin and Garvey.

Goldberg, M. (2001) *Arts and Learning: An integrated approach to teaching and learning in multicultural and multilingual settings* (2nd ed.). New York: Longman.

Goldsworthy, A. (2001). *Midsummer snowballs*. New York: Abrams.

Goldsworthy, A., & Friedman, T. (Eds.). (1993) *Hand to earth: Andy Goldsworthy sculpture, 1976–1990*. New York: Abrams.

Goldsworthy, A., & Goldsworthy, A. (1990) *Andy Goldsworthy: A Collaboration with Nature*. New York: Abrams.

Goleman, G. (1996). *Emotional intelligence*. London: Bloomsbury.

Golfman, D., Kaufman, P., & Ray, M. (1992). *The creative spirit*. New York: Penguin.

Gooding-Brown, J. (2000). Conversations about art: A disruptive model of interpretation. *Studies in Art Education, 42*(1), 36–50.

Goodlad, J. (1984). *A place called school: Promise for the future*. New York: McGraw-Hill.

Goodman, N. (1968). *Languages of art*. New York: Bobbs Merrill.

Goodman, N. (1978). *Ways of worldmaking*. Indianapolis, IN: Hackett.

Gordon, C. (1999). Students as authentic researchers: A new prescription for the high school research assignment. *School Library Media Research, 2*.

Gordon, G. N. (1971). *Persuasion: The theory and practice of manipulative communication*. New York: Hastings.

Gordon, W. (1961). *Synectics*. New York: Harper & Row.

Gordon, W. (1973). *The metaphorical way of learning and knowing: Applying synectics to sensitivity and learning situations*. Cambridge, MA: Porpoise Books.

Gordon, W., & Poze, T. (1971). *Metaphorical way of learning and knowing*. Cambridge, MA: SES Associates.

Gordon, W., & Poze, T. (1972). *Strange and familiar*. Cambridge, MA: SES Associates.

Gowans, A. (1971). *The unchanging arts: New forms for the traditional functions of art in society*. Philadelphia, PA: Lippincott.

Grace, M. (1999). When students create curriculum. *Educational Leadership, 57*(3), 49–52.

Grant, C., & Sleeter, C. (1994). *Making choices for multicultural education: Five approaches to race, class, and gender* (2nd ed.). New York: Merrill.

Green, G. (1997). Televised gender roles in children's media: Covert messages. *Journal of Social Theory in Art Education, 17*, 23–39.

Green, M. (1995). *Releasing the imagination: Essays on education, the arts, and social change*. San Francisco, CA: Jossey-Bass.

Greenberg, C. (1939). *The collected essays and criticism*. Chicago: University of Chicago Press.

Greenberg, C. (1961). *Art and culture: Critical essays*. Boston: Beacon.

Greer, W. (1984). A discipline-based view of art education. *Studies in Art Education, 25*(4), 212–218.

Gregory, D. (1996). Art education reform: Technology as savior. *Art Education, 49*(6), 49–54.

Guay, D. (2002). The dynamic project, theme based issues, and integrative learning. In Y. Gaudelius & P. Speirs (Eds.), *Contemporary issues in art education* (pp 302–316). Upper Saddle River, NJ: Prentice Hall. 302-316.

Guilfoil, J. (2000). From the ground up: Art in American built environment education. *Art Education, 53*(4), 6–12.

Guilfoil, J. (2002). Teaching art with historic places and civic memorials. In Y. Gaudelius & P. Speirs (Eds.), *Contemporary issues in art education* (pp. 250–263). Upper Saddle River, NJ: Prentice Hall.

Guilford, J. P. (1967). *The nature of human intelligence*. New York: McGraw-Hill.

Hagaman, S. (1990). The community of inquiry: An approach to collaborative learning. *Studies in Art Education, 31*(3), 149–157.

Hagaman, S. (1990). Philosophical aesthetics in art education: A further look at implementation. *Art Education, 43*(4), 22–24 & 33–37.

Hall, E. T. (1969). *The hidden dimension*. Garden City, NJ: Doubleday.

Halsy-Dutton, B. (2002). A model of implementing technology into art history education: Artifacts in cyberspace. *Art Education, 55*(4), 19–24.

Hamblen, K. (1984). An art criticism questioning strategy within the framework of Bloom's taxonomy. *Studies in Art Education, 26*(1), 41–50.

Hamblen, K. (1985). Developing aesthetic literacy through contested concepts. *Art Education, 38*(5), 10–24.

Hamblen, K. (1988). Cultural literacy through multiple DBAE repertoires. *Journal of Multicultural and Cross-Cultural Research in Art Education, 6*, 88–98.

Hamblen, K., & Galanes, C. (1997). Instructional options for aesthetics: Exploring the possibilities. *Art Education, 50*(1), 75–83.

Hanes, J., & Weisman, E. (2000). Observing a child use drawing to find meaning. *Art Education, 53*(1), 6–11.

Hart, L. (1992/93). The role of cultural context in multicultural aesthetics. *Journal of Multicultural and Cross-Cultural Research in Art Education, 10/11*, 5–19.

Hart, L. (1995). Taking the next step: Terminology, meaning, and cultural context in multicultural education. *Journal of Multicultural and Cross-Cultural Research in Art Education, 13*, 78–84.

Harvard Project Zero. Educational Research Group: *http://www.pz.harvard.edu/whatsnew/Whatsnew.html*

Haus, M. (1993). The bombs on the building walls. *Art News, 92*(8), 154–157.

Heartney, E. (2001). *Postmodernism*. Cambridge, UK: Cambridge University Press.

Heller, N. G. (1997). *Women artists: An illustrated history* (3rd ed.). New York: Abbeville.

Hendry, J. (1986). *Becoming Japanese: The world of the preschool child*. Honolulu: University of Hawaii.

Henry, J. (1963). *Culture against man.* New York: Random House.

Hershey, J. (1946/1983). *Hiroshima.* New York: Random House.

Hicks, L. (1991). The politics of difference in feminism and multicultural art education. *Journal of Multicultural and Cross-Cultural Research in Art Education, 9,* 11–26.

Hicks, L. (1992–1993). Designing nature: A process of cultural interpretation. *Journal of Multicultural and Cross-Cultural Research in Art Education, 10–11,* 73–88.

Hockstaeder, L. (2000). An Israeli museum wallows in trash. *Washington Post,* March 18, 2000. *http://www. washingtonpost.com/wp-srv/WPlate/2000-03/18/059l 031800-idx.html* (Report on a project by Mierle Ukeles.)

Holt, Nancy. Image and critique of Sky Mound. *http://www.getty.edu/artsednet/images/Ecology/sky.html*

Hull, Lynne. Ecology Art Website. *EcoartHull@cs.com*

Hume, H, (1998). *The art teacher's book of lists.* Englewood Cliffs, NJ: Prentice Hall.

Hutchens, J., & Suggs, M. (Eds.) (1997). *Art education: Content and practice in a postmodern era.* Reston, VA: National Art Education Association.

Interstate New Teacher Assessment and Support Consortium. *http://www.ccsso.org/intaspub.html#Arts*

Internet Resources for Jewelry/Metalsmithing. *http://www.library.unisa.edu/au/internet/pathfind/jewellery.htm* (Good reference from the University of South Australia Library, links to variety of resources.)

Irwin, R., Rogers, T., & Wan, Y. (1999). Making connections through cultural memory, cultural performance and cultural translation. *Studies in Art Education, 40*(3), 198–212.

Ittleson, W. H., Pronshansky, H. M., Rivlin, L. G., & Winkel, G. H. (1974). *An introduction to environmental psychology.* New York: Holt, Rinehart, and Winston.

Jagodzinski, J. (1983). Historical criticism. Paper presented at the 1983 National Art Education Association Conference, Detroit, MI.

James, P. (1999). The blocks and bridges: Learning artistic creativity. *Arts and Learning Research, 16*(1), 110–133.

James, P. (2000). Working toward meaning: The evolution of an assignment. *Studies in Art Education, 2000, 41*(2), 146–163.

James, P. (2000). I am the dark forest: Personal analogy as a way to understand metaphor. *Art Education, 53*(5), 6–11. (Good at getting at the potential for reflective thinking about meaning and aesthetic form.)

Jeffers, C. (2000). Drawing on semiotics: Inscribing a place between formalism and contextualism. *Art Education, 53*(6), 40–45.

Jeffers, C. (2002). Tools for exploring social issues and visual culture. In Y. Gaudelius & P. Speirs (Eds.), *Contemporary issues in art education* (pp. 157–169). Upper Saddle River, NJ: Prentice Hall.

Johnson, M. (1995–1996). Portrait of the computer artist: Between worlds. *Journal of Social Theory in Art Education, 15/16,* 30–45

Johnson, M. (1996). Made by hand. *Art Education, 49*(6), 37–43.

Jones, L. S. (1999). *Art information on the Internet: How to find it, how to use it.* Phoenix, AZ: Oryx Press.

Joselit, D., Simon, J., & Saleci, R. (1998). *Jenny Holzer.* New York: Phaidon.

Josephson, S. (1996). *From idolatry to advertising: Visual art and contemporary culture.* Armonk, NY: M. E. Sharp.

Journal of Aesthetic Education 21(2). (1987). (The definitive, Getty-sponsored articulation of discipline-based art education. Articles by Ralph Smith (Ed.); Evan Kern; Arthur Efland; Maurice Sevigny; Gilbert Clark, Dwayne Greer, and Michael Day; Frederick Spratt; Eugene Kleinbauer; Howard Risatti; Donald Crawford; and David Henry Feldman.

Journal of Aesthetic Education, 35(4). (2002). (This thematic issue, a symposium on nonwestern aesthetics, includes articles by Blocker (on nonwestern aesthetics as a colonial invention), Abiodun (on African aesthetics), Meyer (on Native American aesthetics), and Man (on a suggested return to aesthetic experience in socialist China).

Journal of Aesthetics and Art Criticism. (All issues; published by the American Society for Aesthetics.)

Journal of Multicultural and Cross-Cultural Research in Art Education, 18. (2000). (Thematic issue devoted to visual culture art education, with articles by Kevin Tavin, Brent Wilson, Paul Duncum, and Kerry Freedman.)

Journal of Social Research in Art Education, 19–20. Available from United States Society for Education through Art. *http://www.public.asu.edu/~ifmls/usseafolder/back.html* (This double issue, in response to 9-11-01, is a peace theme issue.)

Journal of Social Theory and Art Education, 18. (1998). (This thematic issue, edited by Jan Jagodzinski, focuses on community and art education and includes articles by Deborah Smith-Shank, Rita Irwin, Christine Ballengee Morris, Seymour Simmons III, and Gay Leigh Green.)

Jowett, G. S., & O'Donnell, V. O. (1986). *Propaganda and persuasion.* Newbury Park, CA: Sage.

Julian, J. (1997). In a postmodern backpack: Basics for the art teacher online. *Art Education, 50*(3), 23–42.

Jung, C. (1964). *Man and his symbols.* Garden City, NJ: Doubleday.

Kaelin, E. (1989). *An aesthetics for art educators.* New York: Teachers College Press.

Kaelin, E. (1994). Social problems in contemporary art. In Charles M. Dorn (Ed.), *Proceedings of the conference the ethics of change in cultural organizations.* (Available from the Center for Arts Administration, 123 MCH, B-171, Florida State University, Tallahassee, FL 32306.)

Kant, E. (1914/1790). *Critique of judgment.* (Trans. J. Bernard). London.

Karge, B. (1998). Knowing what to teach: Using authentic assessment to improve classroom instruction. *Reading and Writing Quarterly: Overcoming Learning Difficulties, 14*(3), 319–331.

Katter, E. (1987). Within culture: The place for art in America's schools. *Journal of Multicultural and Cross-Cultural Research in Art Education, 5,* 73–82.

Keifer-Boyd, K. (1996). Interfacing hypermedia and the Internet with critical inquiry in the arts: Preservice training. *Art Education, 49*(6), 33–41.

Keifer-Boyd, K. (1997). Interactive hyperdocuments: Implications for art criticism in the postmodern era. In T. Hutchens and M. Suggs (Eds.), *Art education: Content and practice in a postmodern era.* Reston, VA: National Art Education Association.

Keifer-Boyd, K., Centofanti, J., Lan, L., Lin, P., MacKenzie, N., Peréz, A., & Hill, G. (2001). Cyberfeminist House. *http://www.ken-\art.ttu.edu/kkb/house.html*

Keifer-Boyd, K. (2002). Open spaces, open minds: Art in partnership with the earth. In Y. Gaudelius & P. Speirs (Eds.), *Mapping identity for curriculum work: Contemporary issues in art education* (pp. 327–344). Upper Saddle River, NJ: Prentice Hall.

Kellman, J. (1999). Drawing with Peter: Autobiography, narrative and the art of a child with autism. *Studies in Art Education, 40*(3), 258–274.

Key, W. (1972). *Subliminal seduction: Ad media's manipulation of not innocent America.* Englewood Cliffs, NJ: Prentice Hall.

Kids Guernica Peace Project. (Information can be accessed at *http://www.kids-guernica.org/* and also at *http://www.artjapan.com/GUERNICA-G/*)

Kindler, A. (Ed.). (1997). *Child development in art.* Reston, VA: National Art Education Association.

Kindler, A. (1998). Culture and development of pictorial repertoires. *Studies in Art Education, 39*(2), 147–167.

Kindler, A. (1999). From endpoints to repertoires: A challenge to art education. *Studies in Art Education, 40*(4), 330–349.

Kindler, A. (2000). From the u-curve to dragons: Culture and understanding of artistic development. *Visual Arts Research, 26*(2), 15–28.

Kindler, A., & Darras, B. (1998). Culture and development of pictorial repertoires. *Studies in Art Education, 39*(2), 147–167.

Kindler, A., & Darras, B. (1998). Social understanding of the purposes of art. *INSEA News, 4*(3), 6–7.

Koberg, D., & Bagnall, J. (1974). *The universal traveler.* Los Altos, CA: William Kaufman.

Koestler, A. (1964). *The act of creation.* New York: Macmillan.

Koos, M., & Smith-Shank, D. (1996). The World Wide Web: Alice meets cyberspace. *Art Education, 49*(6), 19–24.

Kovalik, S., with Olsen, K. (1997). *ITI: The model: Integrated thematic instruction* (3rd ed.). Kent, WA: Books for Educators. (How to pursue thematic inquiry across disciplines.)

Krug, D. (1999). Ecological restoration: Mierle Ukeles, *Flow City.* In *Art & Ecology: Ecological art perspectives and issues. http://www.getty.edu/artsednet/resources/Ecology/Issues/ukeles.html*

Krug, D. (2002). Teaching art in the contexts of everyday life. In Y. Gaudelius & P. Speirs (Eds.), *Contemporary issues in art education* (pp. 181–197). Upper Saddle River, NJ: Prentice Hall.

Krug, D., & Cohen-Evron, N. (2000). Curriculum integration positions and practices in art education. *Studies in Art Education, 41*(3), 258–275.

Kruger, Barbara. *Barbara Kruger: Signs of Postmodernity.* Barbara Kruger remakes signs. *http://www.wdog.com/rider/writings/real_kruger.htm*

Kruger, Barbara. *http://krypton.mnsu.edu/~schatc/gallery2.html http://www.wdog.com/rider/writings/real_kruger.htm*

Krynock, K., & Robb, L. (1999). Problem solved: How to coach cognition. *Educational Leadership 57*(3), 29–32.

Krzysztof Wodiczko, Alien Staff. http://www.mit.edu:8001/afs/athena.mit.edu/course/4/4.395/www/krystof.html

Krzysztof Wodiczko: Projections. http://www.rolandcollection.com/roland collection/section/36/666.htm

Krzysztof Wodiczko Wins Hiroshima Art Prize. http://web.mit.edu/arts/visual/wodiczko.hiroshima.html

Lachapelle, R. (1999). Informant-made videos: A research and educational tool. *Studies in Art education, 40*(3), 242–257.

Lai, A. (2002). From classrooms to chatrooms: Virtualizing art education. *Art Education, 55*(4), 33–39.

Lai, A., & Ball, E. (2002). Home is where the art is: Exploring the places people live through art education. *Studies in Art Education, 44*(1), 47–66.

Lamott, A. (1994). *Bird by bird: Some instructions on writing and life.* New York: Pantheon.

Langer, S. (1957). *Problems of art.* New York: Scribner.

Langer, S. (1980). *Philosophy in a new key: A study in the symbolism of reason, rite, and art.* Cambridge, MA: Harvard University Press.

Lanier, V. (1982). *The arts we see: A simplified introduction to the visual arts.* New York: Teachers College Press.

Lankford, L. (1992). *Aesthetics: Issues and inquiry.* Reston, VA: National Art Education Association.

Lauter, R. (1999). *Bill Viola.* New York: Prestel.

Leavitt, T. (1960). Are advertising and marketing corrupting society? It's not your worry. In C. H. Sandage and V. Fryburger (Eds.), *The role of advertising.* Homewood, IL: Irwin.

Leland, N., & Williams, V. (1994). *Creative collage techniques.* Cincinnati: North Light.

Linker, K. (1991). From imitation to the copy to just effect: On reading Jean Baudrillard. In H. Smagula (Ed.), *Re-visions: New perspectives of art criticism.* Englewood Cliffs, NJ: Prentice Hall.

Lipman, M. (1988). *Philosophy goes to school.* Philadelphia, PA: Temple University Press.

Lippard, L. (1983). *Overlay: Contemporary art and the art of prehistory.* New York: New Press.

Lippard, L. (1990). *Mixed blessings: New art in a multicultural America.* New York: Pantheon.

Lippard, L. (1995). *Overlay: New art and the art of prehistory.* New York: New Press.

Lippard, L. (1998). *Lure of the local: Senses of place in a multi-centered society.* New York: New Press.

Lipsey, R. (1988). Mark Rothko: They are not pictures. *Parabola, 13*(1), 52–61.

London, P. (1989). *No more second-hand art: Awakening the artist within.* Boston: Shambhala.

Lovejoy, M. (1997). *Postmodern currents: Art and artists in the age of electronic media.* Upper Saddle River, NJ: Prentice Hall.

Lowenfeld, V. (1947). *Creative and mental growth.* New York: Macmillan.

Lyotard, J. F. (1984). *The postmodern condition: A report on knowledge.* G. Bennington & B. Massumi, Trans.). Minneapolis: University of Minnesota Press.

MacCurdy, E. (Trans. and Ed.). (1958). *The notebooks of Leonardo da Vinci, volumes I and II.* New York: Reynal and Hitchcock.

Manheim, A. R. (1998). The relationship between the artistic process and self-actualization. *Art Therapy, 15*(2), 99–106.

Manning, M., Manning, G., & Long, R. (1994). *Theme immersion: Inquiry-based curriculum in elementary and middle schools.* Portsmouth, NH: Heinemann.

Maquet, J. (1986). *The aesthetic experience: An anthropologist looks at the visual arts.* New Haven, CT: Yale University.

Marche, T. (2000). Toward a community model of art education history. *Studies in Art Education, 42*(1), 52–66.

Marschalek, D. G. (2002). Building better web-based learning environments: Thinking in "3s." *Art Education, 55*(4), 13–18.

Marshall, J. (2002). Exploring culture

and identity through artifacts: Three art lessons derived from contemporary art practice. In Y. Gaudelius & P. Speirs (Eds.), *Mapping identity for curriculum work: Contemporary issues in art education* (pp. 279–290). Upper Saddle River, NJ: Prentice Hall.

Mattil, E. (Ed.). (1966). *A seminar in art education for research and curriculum development.* University Park, PA: Pennsylvania State University.

McFee, J. (1961). *Preparation for art.* San Francisco: Wadsworth.

McFee, J. (1986). Cross-cultural inquiry into the social meaning of art: Implications for art education. *Journal of Multicultural and Cross-Cultural Research in Art Education, 4,* 6–16.

McFee, J. (1996). Interdisciplinary and international trends in multicultural art education. *Journal of Multicultural and Cross-Cultural Research in Art Education, 14,* 6–18.

McFee, J. (1998). *Cultural diversity and the structure and practice of art education.* Reston, VA: National Art Education Association.

McFee, J. K., & Degge, R. (1980). *Art, culture, and environment: A catalyst for teaching.* Dubuque, IA: Kendall/Hunt.

McLuhan, M. (1964). *Understanding media: The extensions of man.* New York: McGraw-Hill.

McRorie, S. (1996). On teaching and learning aesthetics: Gender and related issues. In G. Collins & R. Sandell, (Eds.), *Gender issues in art education: Content, contexts, and strategies.* Reston, VA: National Art Education Association (pp. 30–39).

McRorie, S. (1996). Pentimento: Philosophical inquiry as research in art education. *Australian Journal of Art Education, 19*(3), 6–13.

Mednick, S. A. (1962). The associative basis of the creative process. *Psychological Review, 69,* 220–232.

Mendieta, Ana. *http://www.hungryflower.com/leorem/mendieta.html*

Mercedes, J. (1998). The application of feminist aesthetic theory to computer-mediated art. *Studies in Art Education, 40,* 1, 66–79.

Metalsmithing Related Articles. *http://jewelrymaking.about.com/library/blmetop.htm.*

Metropolitan Museum of Art. *http://www.metmuseum.org/home.asp* (Gives access to the collection, resources,

and contact information.)

Meyers, W. (1984). *The image makers: Power and persuasion onMadison Avenue.* New York: Times Books.

Mikel, E. R. (2000). Deliberating democracy. In P. B. Joseph, S. L. Bravmann, M. A. Windschitl, E. R. Mikel, & N. S. Green (Eds.), *Cultures of curriculum* (pp. 94–114). Mahwah, NJ: Lawrence Erlbaum. Center for Education Research, WCER Highlights. *http://www.scer.wisc.edu.*

Milbrandt, M. (1998). Postmodernism in art education: Content for life. *Journal of Art Education 51*(6), 47–53.

Milbrandt, M. (2002). Elementary instruction through postmodern art. In Y. Gaudelius & P. Speirs (Eds.). *Contemporary issues in art education* (pp. 317–326). Upper Saddle River, NJ: Prentice Hall.

Milbrandt, M. (2002). Addressing contemporary social issues in art education: A survey of public school art educators in Georgia. *Studies in Art Education, 43*(2), 141–157.

Mirzoeff, N. (1999). *An introduction to visual culture.* London: Routledge.

MIT Architecture. Krystof Wodiczko Profile. *http://architecture.mit.edu/people/profiles/prwodicz.htl*

Moore, P., & Reynolds, J. (1999). Growing up southern: An interdisciplinary project exploring family stories based on selected works of art by Benny Andrews. *Art Education, 52*(1), 26–31.

Moore, R. (Ed.). (1994). *Aesthetics for young people.* Reston, VA: National Art Education Association.

Nadaner, D. (1985). Responding to the image world: A proposal for art curricula. *Art Education, 37*(1), 9–12.

Nadin, M. (1989). Emergent aesthetics–aesthetic issues in computer arts. *Leonardo: Computer Art in Context Supplemental Issue, 22,* 43–48.

National Assessment Governing Board. (1994). *Arts education assessment and exercise specifications.* Washington, DC: Council of Chief State School Officers.

Neperud, R. (Ed.). (1995). *Context, content, and community in art education.* New York: Teachers College Press.

Newmann, F., & Wehlage, C. (1995). *Successful school restructuring: A report to the public and educators.* Center on Organization and Restructuring of Schools. (Distributed by American Federation of Teachers, Association for Supervision and Curriculum De-

velopment, National Association of Elementary Schools Principals, National Association of Secondary School Principals.)

Newmann, F. M., Secada, W. G., & Wehlage, G. G. (1995). *A guide to authentic instruction and assessment: Vision, standards, and scoring.* Madison: Wisconsin Center for Education Research.

Newmann, F. M., & Wehlage, G. G. (1993). Five standards of authentic instruction. *Educational Leadership, 50* (7), 8–12.

Nicaise, M., & Barnes, D. (1996). The union of technology and teacher education. *Journal of Teacher Education, 54*(6), 43–48.

Nicolaides, K. (1969). *The natural way to draw.* Boston: Houghton Mifflin.

Nicosia, F. M. (1983). Advertising management and its search for useful images of consumers. In L. Percy and A. G. Woodside (Eds.), *Advertising and consumer psychology.* Lexington, MA: Lexington Heath.

Nochlin, L. (1988). *Women, art, and power and other essays.* New York: Harper & Row.

Noddings, N. (1992). *The challenge to care in schools: An alternative approach to education.* New York: Teachers College Press.

O'Barr, W. (1994). *Culture and the ad: Exploring otherness in the world of advertising.* Boulder, CO: Westview.

Olsen, J. C., & Reynolds, T. J. (1983). Understanding consumers' cognitive structures. In L. Percy and A. G. Woodside (Eds.), *Advertising and consumer psychology.* Lexington, MA: Lexington Heath.

Omega Institute. *http://www.eomega.org/popups/peaceQuotes.html.* (Homesite has quotations about peace from Gandhi, Martin Luther King, and others.)

Orr, P. (2002). Exploring the September 11, 2001, terrorist attack through an expressive mural project. *Art Education, 55*(2), 6–10.

Osborn, A. (1963). *Applied imagination.* New York: Scribner.

Packard, V. (1957). *The hidden persuaders.* New York: David McKay.

Papanek, V. (1971). *Design for the real world.* New York: Pantheon.

Papanek, V. (1995). *The green imperative: Natural design for the real world.* New York: Thames and Hudson.

Parnes, S. (1981). *The magic of your mind.*

Buffalo, NY: Creative Education Foundation.

Parsons, J., & Blocker, H. (1993). *Aesthetics and education.* Urbana: University of Illinois.

Parsons, M. (1987). *How we understand art: A cognitive developmental account of aesthetic experience.* Cambridge, UK: Cambridge University Press.

Parsons, M. (1998). Integrated curriculum and our paradigm of cognition in the arts. *Studies in Art Education, 39*(2), 103–116.

Patton, S. F. (1998). *African-American art.* New York: Oxford University Press.

Peace Mandala Project. *http://gomang tour.org*

Pearson, P. (2001). Towards a theory of children's drawing as social practice. *Studies in Art Education, 42*(4), 348–365.

Pelfrey, R., & Hall-Pelfrey, M. (1985). *Art and mass media.* New York: Harper & Row.

Perkins, D. (1999). The many faces of constructivism. *Educational Leadership, 57*(3), 6–11.

Piaget, J. (1963). *The origins of intelligence in children.* New York: Norton.

Piaget, J. (1976). *The child and reality.* New York: Penguin.

Pirsig, R. (1999/1974). *Zen and the art of motorcycle maintenance: An inquiry into values.* New York: Morrow.

Pitt, S. P., Updike, C. B., & Guthrie, M. E. (2002). Integrating digital images into the art and art history curriculum. *Educause Quarterly, 25*(2), 38–44.

Postman, N. (1992). *Technolopoly: The surrender of culture to technology.* New York: Knopf.

Prater, M. (2001). Constructivism and technology in art education. *Art Education, 54*(6), 43–48.

Prater, M. (2002). Art criticism: Modifying the formalist approach. *Art Education, 55*(5), 12–17.

Project Zero. *http://www.pzweb.harvard. edu/Default.htm*

Purpel, D. E. (1989). *The moral and spiritual crisis in education: A curriculum for justice and compassion in education.* Granby, MA: Bergin and Garvey.

Raths, L. E., Harmin, M. & Simon, S. B. (1978). *Values and teaching: Working with values in the classroom* (2nd. Ed.). Columbus, OH: Charles Merrill.

Raven, A., Langer, C., & Frueh, J. (Eds.). (1988). *Feminist art criticism: An anthology.* New York: Harper-Collins.

Ravens, A. (1993). *Art in the public interest.* New York: DaCapo.

Redfern, H. (1986). *Questions in aesthetic education.* London: Unwin and Allen.

Rees, A. L., & Borzello, F. (Eds.). (1991). *Rethinking art history.* London: Camden.

Ringold, F. (1991). *Tar Beach.* New York: Crown.

Risatti, H. (1990). *Postmodern perspectives: Issues in contemporary art.* Upper Saddle River, NJ: Prentice Hall.

Risatti, H. (1993, February). Formal education. *New Art Examiner,* 12–15.

Roberts, H. E. (2001). A picture is worth a thousand words: Art indexing in electronic databases. *Journal of the American Society for Information Science and Technology, 52*(11), 911–916.

Robins, C. (1984). *The pluralist era: American art, 1968–1981.* New York: Harper & Row.

Robinson, J. T. (1999). *Bearing witness: Contemporary works by African American women artists.* New York: Spelman College and Rizzoli International.

Robinson, K. (2001). *Out of our minds: Learning to be creative.* Oxford: Capstone.

Rogers, C. (1969). *Freedom to learn.* New York: Merrill.

Root, D. (1996). *Cannibal culture: Art, appropriation, and the commodification of difference.* Boulder, CO: Westview.

Ross, D.A., & Sellars, P. (1997). *Bill Viola.* New York: Whitney Museum of Art in association with Flammarion, Paris.

Ross, K. R. (1998). Blending authentic work projects and instructional assignments: An adaptive process. *Educational Technology Research and Development, 46*(3), 67–79.

Roth, R., & Roth, S. K. (1998). *Beauty is nowhere: Ethical issues in art and design.* Amsterdam: B. V. Overseas Publishers Association.

Rostan, S. M. (1998). A study of the development of young artists: The emergence of an artistic and creative identity. *Journal of Creative Behavior, 32*(4),278–301.

Roukes, N. (1982). *Art synectics.* Calgary, Alberta, Canada: Juniro Arts.

Rush, J. (1987). Interlocking images: The conceptual core of a discipline-based art lesson. *Studies in Art Education, 28*(4), 206–220.

Rush, M. (1999). *New media in late twentieth century art.* New York: Thames and Hudson.

Rutledge, V. (1998). At the end of the optical age. *Art in America, 86,* 70–76.

Saar, Betye—Main Page. *http://www. netropolitan.org/saar/saarmin.html.*

San Francisco Museum of Modern Art, Bill Viola Website. *http://www.sfmoma. org/espace/viola/dhtml/content/frvideo tapes1.html*

Sartwell, C. (2000). Teaching non-Western aesthetics: Teaching popular art. *http://aesthetics-online.org/ideas/ sartwell.html*

Sarup, M. (1995). *An introductory guide to post-structuralism and postmodernism.* Athens: University of Georgia.

Saunders, R. (Ed.). (1998). *Beyond the traditional in art: Facing a pluralistic society.* Reston, VA: National Art Education Association.

Saussure, F. (1966). *A course in general linguistics* (W. Baskin, Trans.). New York: McGraw-Hill.

Sava, I. (2000). The little mermaid: The construction of self through narrative and the visual arts. *Journal of Multicultural and Cross-Cultural Research, 18,* 86–105.

Savedoff, B. (1992). Transforming images: Photographs of representations. *Journal of Aesthetics and Art Criticism, 50*(2), 93–106.

Schere, M. (1999). The understanding pathway: A conversation with Howard Gardner. *Educational Leadership, 57*(3), 12–16.

Schumacher, P. (1990). Art for existence's sake: A Heideggerian revision. *Journal of Aesthetic Education, 24*(2), 83–89.

Shahn, B. (1957). *The shape of content.* New York: Vintage.

Shepard, O. (Ed.). (1961). *The heart of Thoreau's journals.* New York: Dover.

Shin, S. (2003). *The effects of a metacognitive art criticism teaching strategy that incorporates computer technology on critical thinking skill and art critiquing ability.* Dissertation completed at Florida State University.

Shiva, V. (1996). *Arts and the Internet: A guide to the revolution.* New York: Allworth.

Siegesmund, R. (1998). Why do we teach art today? Conceptions of art education and their justification. *Studies in Art Education, 39*(3), 197–214.

Siegle, D. (2002). Creating a living portfolio: Documenting student growth with electronic portfolios. *Gifted Child Today, 25*(3), 60–65.

Simpson, J. (1996). Constructivism and connections making in art education. *Art Education, 49*(1), 53–59.

Sims, L. (1986). *Robert Colescott: A retrospective, 1975–1986.* New York: The Museum. (Available used from Amazon.com.)

Slan, J. (1999). *Scrapbook story telling.* St. Louis, MO: EGF. (Catching your life story in words and pictures.)

Slatkin, W. (2001). *Women artists in history: From antiquity to the present.* Upper Saddle River, NJ: Prentice Hall.

Slattery, P. (1995). *Curriculum development in the postmodern era.* New York: Garland.

Slavko, M. (2000). Designing digital environments for art education/exploration. *Journal of American Society for Information Science, 51*(1), 49–56.

Sleeter, C., & Grant, C. (1987). An analysis of multicultural education in the United States. *Harvard Educational Review, 57*(40), 421–444.

Smith, N. (1983). *Teaching children to paint.* New York: Teachers College Press.

Smith, R. (1986). *Excellence in art education.* Reston, VA: National Art Education Association. The essentialist perspective.

Smith, R., Wright, M., & Horton, J. (1999). *An introduction to art techniques.* London: Dorling Kindersley.

Smith-Shank, D., & Schwiebert, V. (2000). Old wives' tales: Questing to understand visual memories. *Studies in Art Education, 41*(2), 178–190.

Smithson, Robert. *http://www.robertsmithson.com/films/films.htm*

Society of American Silversmiths. *http://www.silversmithing.com* (Professional organization solely devoted to the preservation and promotion of contemporary silversmithing.)

Soep, E., & Kotner, T. (1999). Speaking the mind and minding the speech: Novices interpreting art. *Studies in Art Education, 40*(4), 350–372.

Sontag, S. (1980). *Under the sign of Saturn.* New York: Farrar, Straus, & Giroux.

Sousa, D. A. (1998). The ramifications of brain research. *School Administrator, 55*(1), 22–25.

Spleen—An Interview with Krzysztof Wodiczko. http://www.thespleen.com/subersions/pshychopathology/index.php?artID=69

Stankiewicz, M. (2000). Discipline and the future of art education. *Studies in Art Education, 41*(4).

Staniszewski, M. A. (1995). *Believing is seeing: Creating the culture of art.* New York: Penguin.

Starko, A. (1995). *Creativity in the classroom: Schools of curious delight.* White Plains, NY: Longman.

Stein, J. (1993). Sins of omission. *Art in America, 81,* 110–115.

Stephenson, C. C., & McClung, P. A. (Eds.). (1998). *Images Online: Perspectives on the Museum Education Site Licensing Project.* Los Angeles, CA: Getty Information Institute.

Sternberg, R. J. (1999). *The handbook of creativity.* Cambridge, MA: Cambridge University Press.

Stokrocki, M. (1988). Understanding popular culture: The uses and abuses of fashion advertising. *Bulletin of the Caucus on Social Theory and Art Education, 8,* 69–77.

Stokrocki, M. (2001). Go to the mall and get it all. *Art Education, 54*(2), 18–23.

Stokrocki, M., & Buckpitt, M. (2002). Computer animation at an Apache middle school: Apache children's use of computer animation technology. In Y. Gaudelius & P. Speirs (Eds.), *Contemporary issues in art education.* Upper Saddle River, NJ: Prentice Hall.

Stokrocki, M., & Kirisoglu, O. (1999). Art criticism in Turkey: Prospects and problems of exploring a tapestry. *Art Education, 52*(1), 33–39.

Stone, R. (2002). *Best practices for high school classrooms: What award-winning secondary teachers do.* Thousand Oaks, CA: Corwin Press.

Stout, C. (1999). The art of empathy: Teaching students to care. *Art Education, 52*(2), 21–24, 33–34.

Stout, C. J. (1999). Artists as writers: Enriching perspectives in art appreciation. *Studies in Art Education, 40*(3), 226–241.

Stout, J. (1995). Critical conversation about art: A description of higher order thinking generated through the study of art criticism. *Studies in Art Education, 36*(30), 170–188.

Stout, J. (2000). In the spirit of art criticism: Reading the writings of women artists. *Studies in Art Education, 41*(4), 346–360.

Szekely, G. (1988). *Encouraging creativity in art lessons.* New York: Teachers College Press.

Szkudlarek, T. (1993). *The problem of freedom in postmodern education.* Westport, CT: Bergin and Garvey.

Tarnas, R. (1991). *The passion of the Western mind.* New York: Harmony.

Taylor, Maggie. *http://www.maggietaylor.com/indexframe.html*

Taylor, P. (1997). It all started with trash. *Art Education, 50*(2), 13–18.

Taylor, P. (2002). Service learning as postmodern art and pedagogy. *Studies in Art Education, 43*(2), 124–140.

Taylor, P. (2002). Singing for someone else's supper: Service learning and empty bowls. *Art Education, 55*(5), 46–52.

Taylor, P. G., & Carpenter, S. (2002). Inventively linking: Teaching and learning with computer hypertext. *Art Education, 55*(4), 6–12.

Teaching Tolerance. (Biannual journal, mailed free to educators who request it, can also be found on the Web at *http://www.tolerance.org/teach/.*

Tell, C. (1999/2000). Generation what? Connecting with today's youth. *Educational Leadership, 57*(4), 34–37.

Thompson, J. (1990). *Twentieth century theories of art.* Ottawa, Canada: Carleton.

Thompson, J. (2000). *Making journals by hand.* Gloucester, MA: Rockport.

Thompson, W. (1991). *The American replacement of nature.* New York: Doubleday.

Thoreau, H. D. (1951). *Walden.* New York: Norton.

Tileston, D. W. (2000). *Ten best teaching practices: How brain research, learning styles, and standards define teaching.* Thousand Oaks, CA: Corwin Press.

Tomaskiewicz, F. (1997). A ten-year perspective on visual art technology. *Art Education, 50*(4), 13–16.

Toward civilization: A report on arts education. (1988). Washington, DC: National Endowment for the Arts.

Trend, D. (1992). *Cultural pedagogy: Art/education/politics.* New York: Bergin and Garvey.

Truitt, A. (1984). *Daybook: The journal of an artist.* New York: Penguin.

UCSF Diversity Project. *http://www.ucsf.edu/artucsf/port/slide1.html* (Site showing slides of Fred Wilson's (non-installation) studio pieces.)

UCSF Diversity Project Homesite. *http://www.ucsf.edu/daybreak/1999/06/24_wilson.html.*

Uelsmann, J. *http://www.uelsmann.net/indexframe.html*

Ukeles, Mierle Laderman. The Rotten Truth about Garbage. *http://www.astc.org/exhibitions/rotten/ukeles.htm*

(Will also take you to The Rotten Truth about Garbage website, *http://www.astc.org/exhibitions/rotten/rthome.htm.*

Viola, Bill (September 15–December 31, 2000). Detroit Art Institute, Knight Gallery and N230. *http://www.dia.org/exhibitions/BillViola/pages/main.html*

Viola, Bill, exhibition (September 15–December 31, 2000) 25-Year Survey Exhibition, San Francisco Museum of Modern Art. *http://www.sfmoma.org/espace/viola/dhtml/content/fr video tapes1.html*

Von Neuman, R. (1982). *The design and creation of jewelry.* Radnor, PA: Chilton.

Von Oech, R. (1986). *A kick in the seat of the pants.* New York: Warner.

Wachowiak, F., & Clements, R. (2001). *Emphasis art: A qualitative art program for elementary and middle schools* (7th ed.). New York: Longman.

Walker, H. (2001). Interviewing local artists: A curriculum resource in art teaching. *Studies in Art Education, 42*(3), 249–265.

Walker, S. (2001). *Teaching meaning in art making.* Worcester, MA: Davis.

Wasson, R., Stuhr, P. L., & Petrovich-Mwaniki, L. (1990). Teaching art in the multicultural classroom: Six position statements. *Studies in Art Education, 31*(4), 234-246.

Weale, A. (1995). *Eyewitness Hiroshima.* New York: Carroll & Graf.

Weinstein, S., Drozdenko, R., & Weinstein, C. (1986). Effects of subliminal cues in print advertising upon brain response, purchase intentions, and simulated purchase. In J. Olson and K. Sentis (Eds.), *Advertising and consumer psychology* (3rd ed.). New York: Praeger.

Weir, R. (1998). *Leonardo's ink bottle: The artist's way of seeing.* Berkeley, CA: Celestial Arts.

Weisman, E., & Hanes, J. (2002). Thematic curriculum and social reconstruction. In Y. Gaudelius & P. Speirs (Eds.), *Contemporary issues in art education* (pp. 170–179). Upper Saddle River, NJ: Prentice Hall.

Weitz, M. (1979). The role of theory in esthetics. In M. Radar (Ed.), *A modern book of esthetics* (5th ed.). New York: Holt, Rinehart, and Winston.

Wertsch, J. V., & Tulviste, P. L. S. Vygotsky and contemporary developmental psychology. In H. Daniels (Ed.) (1996). *An introduction to Vygotsky.* (53–74). New York: Routledge.

White, B. (1998). Aesthetigrams: Mapping aesthetic experiences. *Studies in Art Education, 39*(4), 321–335.

White, J. (1998). Pragmatism and art: Tools for change. *Studies in Art Education, 39*(3), 215–229.

Whitehead, A. (1929). *The aims of education and other essays.* New York: Macmillan.

Whitney Museum of American Art: Barbara Kruger. *http://www.tfaoi.com/aa/1aa/1aa667.htm*

Wiggins, G. (1987). Teaching to the (authentic) test. *Educational Leadership,* 41–47.

Wiggins, G. (1989). The futility of trying to teach everything important. *Educational Leadership, 47*(3), 44–58.

Wigginton, E. (1989). Foxfires grows up. *Harvard Educational Review, 59*(1), 24–50.

Williamson, J. (1978). *Decoding advertisements.* London/New York: Marion Boyars.

Wilson, B. (1997). *The quiet evolution: Changing the face of arts education.* Los Angeles: Getty Center for Education in the Arts.

Wilson, B., Hurwitz, A., & Wilson, M. (1987). *Teaching drawing from art.* Worcester, MA: Davis.

Wilson, F. (1993). *Mining the museum 2: Disciplined-based art education and cultural diversity.* Seminar proceedings, August 6–9, 1992, Austin, TX. Santa Monica, CA: J. Paul Getty Trust.

Wilson, Fred. *http://www.bampfa.berkeley.edu/bca/arc.html*

Wilson, T., & Clark, G. (2000). Looking at and talking about art: Strategies of an experienced teacher. *Visual Arts Research, 25*(2), 40–50.

Wilson-McKay, S., & Monteverde, S. (2003). Dialogic looking: Beyond the mediated experience. *Art Education, 56*(1).

Windschitl, M. A. (2000). Constructing understanding. In P. B. Joseph, S. L. Bravmann, M. A. Windschitl, E. R. Mikel, N.S. Green (Eds.), *Cultures of curriculum* (115–136). Mahway, NJ: Lawrence Erlbaum Associates.

Witmer, S., & Borst, J. (1999). Getting teens to talk about art. *Art Education, 52*(5), 33–38.

Wittgenstein, L. (1960) Games and definitions. In M. Radar (Ed.). *A modern book of esthetics* (3rd ed.). New York: Holt, Rinehart, and Winston.

Wong, W. (2001). Visual medium in the service and disservice of education. *Journal of Aesthetic Education, 35*(2), 25–37.

Woodman, M., and Mellick, J. (1998). *Coming home to myself: Reflections for nurturing a woman's body and soul.* Boston, MA: Red Wheel/Weiser.

Woods, L. (2000). Showcase the work of your students and your art program. *Arts and Activities, 128*(1), 38–39.

Works of Barbara Kruger. *http://www.eng.fju.edu.tw/LiteraryCriticism/feminism/kruger/krugertm* (Pieces juxtaposing words and images.)

Wyrick, M. (2002). Art for issues' sake: A framework for the selection of art content for the elementary classroom. In Y. Gaudelius & P. Speirs (Eds.), *Contemporary issues in art education* (pp. 212–225). Upper Saddle River, NJ: Prentice Hall.

*Yale DMCE:*Lecture99:Krzysztof Wodiczko, Critical Vehicles. *http://www.yale.edu/dmca/lectures99/wodiczko.html*

Yokley, S. (1999). Embracing a critical pedagogy in art education. *Art Education, 52*(5), 18-24.

Yokley, S. (2002). If an artwork could speak, what would it say? Focusing on issues for elementary art education. In Y. Gaudelius & P. Speirs (Eds.), *Contemporary issues in art education* (pp. 198–211). Upper Saddle River, NJ: Prentice Hall.

Zimmerman, E. (1990). Issues related to teaching art from a feminist point of view. *Visual Arts Research, 16*(2), 1–9.

Zurmeuhlen, M. (1990). *Studio art: Praxis, symbol, and presence.* Reston, VA: The National Art Education Association.

PHOTO CREDITS

Chapter 1

p. 4: The Metropolitan Museum of Art, New York. The Photograph Study Collection. The Arts of Africa, Oceania and the Americas. Gift of Lester Wundermann, 1996. 1996.458.62; p. 5: Collection of Whitney Museum of American Art. Purchase, with funds from the Friends of the Whitney Museum of American Art. 68.12. Courtesy of the artist; p. 6: © 2003 AP Wide World Photos/Jay Sailors.

Chapter 2

p. 24: © 2003 AP Wide World Photos/Ron Edmonds; p. 29: Courtesy of Trayce Marino, Program Coordinator, Youth Art Connection, Atlanta Boys and Girls Club of Atlanta and Cathy Byrd, Georgia State University Gallery Director.

Chapter 3

p. 44: Margaret Bourke-White/Time Life Pictures/Getty Images; p. 47: Courtesy of Tom Anderson; p. 48: Courtesy of the artist and Metro Pictures; p. 49: Courtesy of Melody Milbrandt and Mira Owens; p. 52: Los Angeles County Museum of Art. Purchased with funds provided by the Mr. and Mrs. William Preston Harrison Collection. Photograph © 2004 Museum Associates/LACMA. © 2004 C. Herscovici, Brussels/ Artists Rights Society (ARS), New York; p. 53: Courtesy of the artists and Franklin Furnace Archive; p. 54: Courtesy of the artists Coco Fusco and Guillermo Gomez-Pena. Photo: Cristina Taccone; p. 55: Marlon Heard and Kristine Amdur, Georgia State University Art Education students, Atlanta, Georgia; p. 57: © Jeff Koons; p. 58: Courtesy: Mary Boone Gallery, New York

Chapter 4

p. 69: Museum Folkwang, Essen/© 2004 Artists Rights Society (ARS), New York/VG Bild-Kunst, Bonn; p. 75: © Jerry N. Uelsmann; p. 76: Courtesy of Ronald Feldman Fine Arts, New York. © 2004 Artists Rights Society (ARS), New York / VG Bild-Kunst, Bonn

Chapter 5

p. 83: Florida State University, Special Collections, R. M. Strozier Library, Tallahassee, Fl.; p. 86: Courtesy of Tom Anderson; p. 87: © Betye Saar; Courtesy of Michael Rosenfeld Gallery, LLC, New York, NY, Courtesy University of California, Berkeley Art Museum. Photo Benjamin Blackwell.; p. 90: Collection Center for Creative Photography, University of Arizona ©1981 Arizona Board of Regents.

Chapter 6

p. 101: Courtesy of the artist © David Hammons; p. 102: Scala/Art Resource, NY/© 2004 The Munch Museum/The Munch-Ellingsen Group/Artists Rights Society (ARS), New York; p. 107: © Sally Mann; Courtesy of Edwynn Houk Gallery, New York; p. 108: © Miriam Schapiro; p. 109: © Jerry D. Jacka Photography; p. 110: The Metropolitan Museum of Art, New York. The James F. Ballard Collection. Gift of James F. Ballard, 1922 (22.100.51)

Chapter 7

p. 118 (top): © Paul Seheult; Eye Ubiquitous/CORBIS; p. 118 (bottom): Courtesy of the artist and Phyllis Kind Gallery, New York; p. 124: Face-Time Continuum (2002), Jacques Bordeleau, Sun Valley, Idaho. Viteous glass enameling; fused glass; cement and grout; wooden doors. Total length 30'; height 8'; p. 125: Courtesy of the Public Art Fund/ Photo: Peter Bellamy; p. 126: Detail from the Bayeux Tapestry—11th Century. By special permission of the City of Bayeux. p. 129 (top): Courtesy of Brent Sikkema NYC; p. 129 (bottom): © Gordon Parks; p. 136: Courtesy of Mary Boone Gallery, New York

Chapter 8

p. 140: Liu Nan, Tallehassee, Florida.

Chapter 9

p. 158: © Jenny Holzer. © 2004 Jenny Holzer/Artists Rights Society (ARS), New York; p. 161: Everett Collection, Inc.; p. 164: Courtesy of Craig Dongoski, Georgia State University and Robert Thompson. Photo courtesy of Melody Milbrandt.

Chapter 11

p. 182: Courtesy of the artist and Galerie Lelong, New York; p. 184: Courtesy of the artist and Galerie Lelong, New York.

Chapter 12

p. 190: Photo courtesy of Ciel Bergman (aka Cheryl Bowers), Coyote, New Mexico and Nancy Merrill, Seattle, Washington.

Chapter 13

p. 200: Courtesy of the artist and Metro Pictures; p. 201: Courtesy of the artist and Metro Pictures

Chapter 14

p. 209; Charnelle Holloway, Spelman College, Atlanta, Georgia

Chapter 15

p. 216: Museo Nacional Centro de Arte

Reina Sofia, Madrid. © 2004 Estate of Pablo Picasso/Artists Rights Society (ARS), New York; p. 217: Courtesy of Tom Anderson; p. 223: Courtesy of Pamela Poucher, Florida State University, Art Education student.

Color Plates

Plate 1: © 2004 greenmuseum.org; plate 2: Courtesy Nam June Paik and Smithsonian American Art Museum; plate 3: Courtesy of Alexander and Bonin, New York, Photo: Martha Cooper; plate 5: © Michael T. Sedam/CORBIS; plate 7: Courtesy of Ray Burggraf, Florida State University, Tallahassee Florida; plate 8: Walker Art Center, Minneapolis. Gift of the T. B. Walker Foundation, Gilbert Walker Fund, 1942; plate 9: © Judith F. Baca, Division of the Barrios and Chavez Ravine from the Great Wall of Los Angeles, 1983. www.sparcmurals.org; plate 10: Courtesy of Mark Messersmith, Florida State University, Tallahassee Florida. Oil on canvas, 71" x 87".; plate 11: Courtesy Bernice Steinbaum Gallery, Miami, Florida; plate 12: Scala/Art Resource, NY; plate 14: © Bill Viola. Photo: Kira Perov; plate 15: Michelle Creil and Jerry Pilcher directors. Photo courtesy of Tom Anderson; plate 16: Ciel Bergman (aka Cheryl Bowers), Coyote, New Mexico and Nancy Merrill, Seattle, Washington. Photo courtesy of William B. Dewey.; plate 17: Charnelle Holloway, Spelman College, Atlanta, Georgia AP; plate 18: Courtesy of Toshifumi and Yasuda Tadashi; plate 19: © Brecelj Bojan/CORBIS SYGMA

ILLUSTRATION INDEX

INDEX

Page numbers in **bold** refer to captions.